I0069851

Waymaker Principles of Management

Lumen Learning

Your Waymaker Principles of Management textbook is a compilation of articles written by instructors for universities around the country. The entire compilation is provided free of charge online at https://courses.lumenlearning.com/suny-mcc-supervision/ under a Creative Commons Attribution license.

You can access or even copy all the material here, for your own reference, even after the semester ends.

There are many different authors; look to the "Licenses and Attributions" section at the end of each chapter to identify contributors.

by State University of New York Press

ISBN: 978-1-64176-010-2

CONTENTS

MODULE 1: INTRODUCTION TO MANAGEMENT

WHY IT MATTERS: INTRODUCTION TO MANAGEMENT

Why learn about management?

Most people today know Nokia as a mobile phone maker, but the company began its commercial life as a paper manufacturer.

Before the heyday of Apple iPhones, Nokia dominated the mobile phone market. Would it surprise you to know that Nokia began in 1871 in Finland as a paper mill company? Later, it diversified into making rubber tires and boots, laid cables, and eventually moved into making emergency radiophones and commercial car phones. Over the course of its evolution, Nokia's top managers stayed focused on the external business environment and were willing to make the hard decisions—regardless of how risky or uncertain they seemed at the time—to stay competitive, even if it meant the organization had to change industries and retrain its workforce. (Note: Satpathy, S. (2014, April 26). A brief history of Nokia: From a paper mill, to the world's biggest mobile company to being acquired by Microsoft | Latest Tech News, Video & Photo Reviews at BGR India. Retrieved July 28, 2017, from http://www.bgr.in/news/a-brief-history-of-nokia-from-a-paper-mill-to-the-worlds-biggest-mobile-company-to-being-acquired-by-microsoft/)

That management focus is even more essential today. ThyssenKrupp AG, a major steel manufacturer in Germany, is responding to competitive market challenges created by cheap Chinese steel by reducing its steel production. Instead, it is fast becoming the leader in manufacturing next-generation elevators—once a sideline and now the company's profit-driver. (Note: Andresen, Tino. "Germany's Biggest Steelmaker Set to Unveil a Future Beyond Steel." Bloomberg.com. June 19, 2017. Accessed July 28, 2017. https://www.bloomberg.com/news/articles/2017-06-19/germany-s-biggest-steelmaker-set-to-unveil-a-future-beyond-steel.) ThyssenKrupp is facing issues similar to those addressed by Nokia a century earlier.

How do organizations survive in a world where conditions are constantly changing? Who makes the difficult decisions that result in the success or failure of the organization? Is making good business choices an art or a science? The study of management answers these kinds of questions. To think of managers as people hunkered down in offices handling routine decisions is to miss the most important and dynamic aspect of management. Managers enable businesses to adapt and thrive in today's competitive global markets.

As you read, keep these two companies in mind. We will revisit Nokia and ThyssenKrupp at the end of this module.

INTRODUCTION TO MANAGEMENT

What you'll learn to do: describe what management is

People have different ideas of what management is based on their experiences in the working world, but most experts agree that management is a combination of both people and processes.

WHAT IS MANAGEMENT?

Learning Outcome

- Describe what management is.

Introduction

Management is everywhere. Any time people work to achieve a goal, they are engaging in management. At least as far back as the building of pyramids in ancient Egypt or Mesoamerica, people have used principles of management to achieve goals. Today, organizations of all types—social, political, and economic—use management techniques to plan and organize their activities.

Constructing a pyramid was one of history's earliest management goals.

Two Aspects of Management

When people talk about **management**, they may be referring to very different aspects. They may be talking about the people who are the managers, especially those people in **strategic** positions who make important decisions for the organization, such as the executive officers, president, or general manager. Or, they may be referring to the activities and **functions** of an organization to achieve organizational goals.

Management As People

The people with the responsibility and authority to determine the overall direction of the organization are often referred to as the management of the organization. Management has the authority to decide what the goals of the organization should be and how those goals will be achieved. Individuals in **upper management** must be aware of conditions in the organization's environment and have knowledge of the total resources of the organization. They put these two together to determine the most promising path for the organization to pursue.

Let's look at a small-scale illustration. Imagine a family considering their vacation plans. They have a goal: to get away from home and work to spend an enjoyable week or two together. To achieve their goal they must first make a number of related decisions such as these: Where will we go? How will we get there? Where will we stay? What will we do while we are there?

These decisions cannot be made without considering the resources they have available for the trip. Perhaps they have saved money for the trip or they decide to take out a small loan. Maybe they will rent an RV and camping equipment or buy into a timeshare. They might be experienced backpackers or they might enjoy just chilling at the beach. The family's decision makers must plan on how to use their resources—both **material resources**, such as money and equipment, and **intellectual resources**, such as knowledge and experience—to create a successful vacation. But deciding what they are going to do is not enough; they need to actually do things to get ready for their trip. They may need to make reservations, schedule time off work, get their car serviced, or buy a new camera and appropriate clothing and gear. Finally, if they have made all the right decisions and all the necessary arrangements, they can go on their trip and have a great time.

Management As Process

As we saw in the earlier example, decision making and planning are required before actions are taken. Defining the goals of the organization, planning the actions to meet the goals, and organizing the resources needed to carry out the actions are all vital functions of management. Planning and organizing ensure that everyone in the organization is working together toward meeting goals.

Organizations, like families, also have goals. In large organizations, the goals are usually formally defined. A corporate goal may be to increase market share by 12 percent in two years or to provide 250 free meals per week to a local shelter. In small organizations or family businesses, the goals may be more general and informal, such as to provide a unique dining experience to patrons or to be able to retire comfortably in five years.

All organizations—businesses, the military, government departments, nonprofit service providers, or public school systems—require management because they all are trying to achieve goals. And although it may seem straightforward, the management process is complex. In most cases, management functions include:

- applying and distributing organizational resources effectively
- acquiring new resources when necessary
- analyzing and adapting to the ever-changing environment in which the organization operates
- complying with legal, ethical, and social responsibilities of the community
- developing relationships with and among people to execute the strategies and plans

Management Defined

Perhaps the most critical of all the management processes listed earlier is creating the systems and processes that allow people to work effectively toward organizational goals. In fact, many people define management as the art of getting things done through people. Although technology and data are increasingly important in modern organizations, people continue to be a primary focus of management. Putting this all together, we can propose a definition of management: management is the process of planning, organizing, leading, and controlling people in the organization to effectively use resources to meet organizational goals.

INTRODUCTION TO PRIMARY FUNCTIONS OF MANAGEMENT

What you'll learn to do: explain the primary functions of management

The activities of successful businesses can be analyzed by looking at four key roles or tasks: planning, organizing, leading, and controlling. These primary functions are the foundation of effective management.

PRIMARY FUNCTIONS OF MANAGEMENT

Learning Outcomes

- Explain the primary functions of management.
- Differentiate between the planning, organizing, leading, and controlling functions of management.

We have defined management as a process to achieve organizational goals. A **process** is a set of activities that are ongoing and interrelated. **Ongoing** means that the activities are not done in a linear, step-by-step fashion where responsibility is passed from one activity to the next. Instead, the activities are continued as new activities are started. **Interrelated** means that the results of each activity influence the other activities and tasks. It is the responsibility of management to see that essential activities are done efficiently (in the best possible way) and effectively (doing the right thing).

The **management process** consists of four primary functions that managers must perform: planning, organizing, leading, and controlling. It is important to realize that the management process is not always linear. It does not always start with planning and continue through each step until organizational goals are achieved because it is not possible to plan for every problem the organization will face. As the management process proceeds, changes and modifications are made when unforeseen events arise. Managers make sure the necessary changes are implemented and that the unity and integrity of the entire process is maintained.

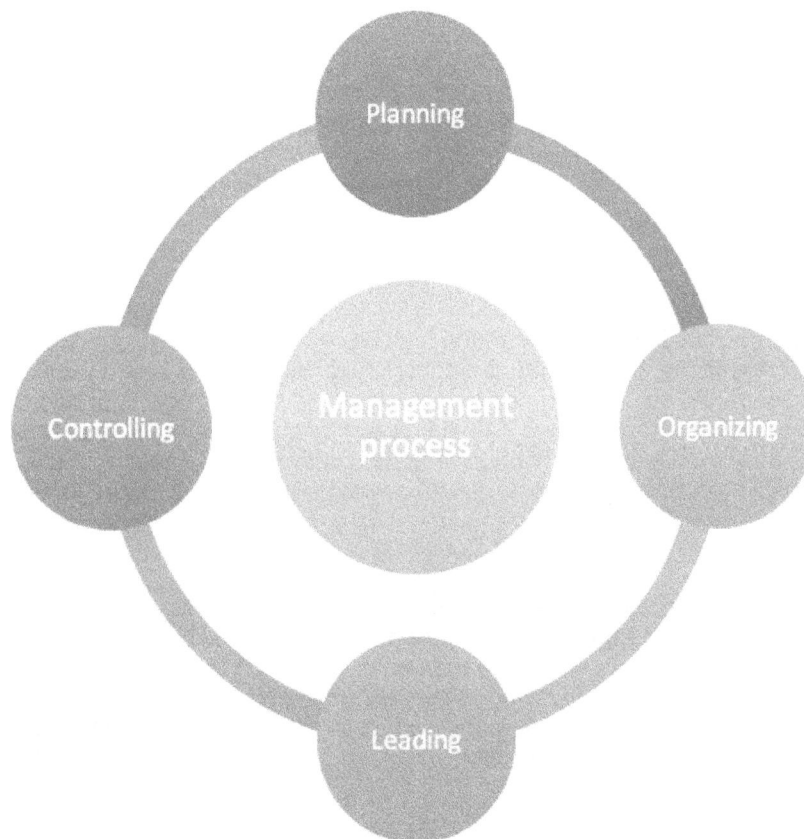

The key functions in the management process are connected, but not always linear.

Planning

Planning means defining performance goals for the organization and determining what actions and resources are needed to achieve the goals. Through planning, management defines what the future of the organization should be and how to get there. **Strategic plans** are long-term and affect the entire organization. A strategic plan bridges the gap between what an organization is and what it will become. **Tactical plans** translate strategic plans into specific actions that need to be implemented by departments throughout the organization. The tactical plan defines what has to be done, who will do it, and the resources needed to do it.

For instance, recall the example used at the beginning of this module. It described how ThyssenKrupp AG decided to become an elevator manufacturing and servicing company because of increased competition from Chinese steel. The management of the company set a goal of deriving the majority of its revenue from elevator related activities. To do this, the management team made plans to create partnerships or take over existing elevator companies. The team devised plans to develop new human resources and to acquire other material resources. The company also had to divest existing steel-related resources to raise capital for the new initiative. This example is a long-term strategic plan that will take years to complete and require many changes along the way. But it starts by defining a goal and a preliminary path to achieve it.

Organizing

Once plans are made, decisions must be made about how to best **implement** the plans. The **organizing** function involves deciding how the organization will be structured (by departments, matrix teams, job responsibilities, etc.). Organizing involves assigning authority and responsibility to various departments, allocating resources across the organization, and defining how the activities of groups and individuals will be coordinated.

In the case of ThyssenKrupp AG, the management had to determine how to support two very different sets of activities if it were to achieve its long-term goal. Management needed to continue steel production activities to provide continuity of funds as the emphasis gradually shifted to elevator production. It also had to develop new skills and resources to build the company's elevator capabilities. A new organizational structure was needed that could support both business activities as one was downsized and the other built up.

Leading

Nearly everything that is accomplished in an organization is done by people. The best planning and organizing will not be effective if the people in the organization are not willing to support the plan. **Leaders** use knowledge, character, and charisma to generate enthusiasm and inspire effort to achieve goals. Managers must also lead by communicating goals throughout the organization, by building commitment to a common vision, by creating shared values and culture, and by encouraging high performance. Managers can use the power of reward and punishment to make people support plans and goals. Leaders inspire people to support plans, creating belief and commitment. Leadership and management skills are not the same, but they can and do appear in the most effective people.

It is very difficult to motivate people when plans involve radical change, particularly if they include downsizing and layoffs. Many people are naturally resistant to change. When the change means loss of jobs or status, people will be very resistant. At ThyssenKrupp, the labor unions vehemently opposed the shift from steel production to elevator manufacturing. Although the people involved in the new business functions were excited by the plans, people involved with steel production felt abandoned and demotivated. Management would have been wise to get union support for its vision of the company's new future.

Controlling

There is a well-known military saying that says no battle plan survives contact with the enemy. This implies that planning is necessary for making preparations, but when it's time to implement the plan, everything will not go as planned. Unexpected things will happen. Observing and responding to what actually happens is called controlling. **Controlling** is the process of monitoring activities, measuring performance, comparing results to objectives, and making modifications and corrections when needed. This is often described as a **feedback loop**, as shown in the illustration of a product design feedback loop.

Fix it, improve it, make changes

Sell the improved product

Assess progress (is it selling?)

Ask customers if they like the new product

Product design feedback loop

Controlling may be the most important of the four management functions. It provides the information that keeps the corporate goal on track. By controlling their organizations, managers keep informed of what is happening; what is working and what isn't; and what needs to be continued, improved, or changed. ThyssenKrupp had little experience in elevator manufacturing when it was making plans. It was developing new products and processes and entering new markets. The management knew it could not anticipate all the difficulties it would encounter. Close monitoring as the plan progressed allowed the company to make changes and state-of-the-art innovations that have resulted in a very successful transition.

Watch the following video for an overview of the management process and a simple example of how the management functions work together.

https://www.youtube.com/watch?v=9Ir70kcHf-w

Who Directs Each Function?

Although these functions have been introduced in a particular order, it should be apparent that the different activities happen at the same time in any one organization. The control function ensures that new plans must be created. Leaders often step up as needed when a crisis or unexpected bump demands immediate action. All managers perform all of these functions at different times, although a manager's position or level in the organization will affect how much of his or her time is spent planning as opposed to leading or to controlling. We will look more closely at different types of managers in the next section.

INTRODUCTION TO TYPES OF MANAGERS AND THEIR ROLES

What you'll learn to do: describe the primary types of managers and the roles they play

Managers function in a number of roles including leading, sharing information, and making decisions. How often they play a particular role depends on the level they occupy and the type of organization. We'll talk about the differences between top managers, middle managers, first-line managers, and team leaders.

TYPES OF MANAGERS

Learning Outcome

- Differentiate between the functions of top managers, middle managers, first-line managers, and team leaders.

Vertical Management

Vertical management, also called top-down management, refers to the various levels of management within an organization. Managers at different levels are free to focus on different aspects of the business, from strategic thinking to communicating information to operational efficiency. During the nineteenth century and much of the twentieth century, vertical management was highly structured with many layers of management (as depicted by a pyramid). In industries where processes and conditions are stable and where ongoing innovation is less critical, the vertical structure of management can still be very efficient. Workers in labor-intensive industries such as manufacturing, transportation, and construction need to follow established procedures and meet specific goals. Everyone knows who is in charge and assumes the job they do today will be the same next year or in five years.

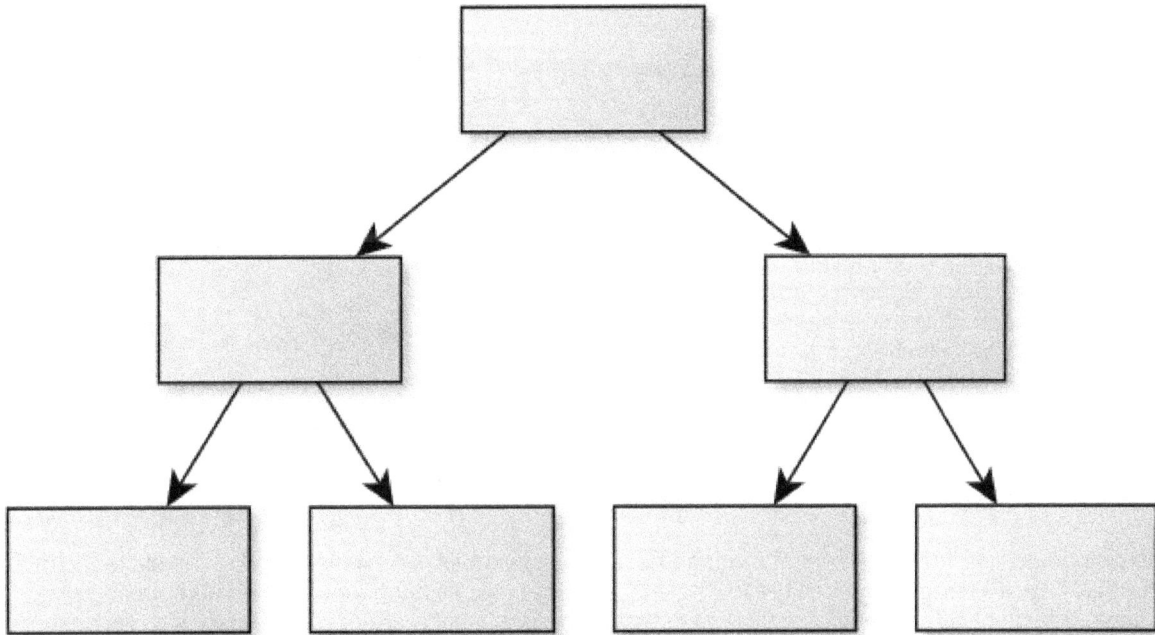

Vertical management in a traditional organizational structure

A main disadvantage of vertical management is that it limits information flow from the lower levels of the organization to the upper levels (like water, information flows downhill easily). Without easy two-way communication, top management can become isolated and out of touch with how its plans affect core processes in the organization. It also fosters vertical thinking. Vertical thinking refers to using traditional and recognized methods to solve particular problems. It is the opposite of "thinking outside of the box." The digital age exposed the shortcomings of management that addressed problems in formal or bureaucratic approaches at the expense of creativity and innovation. Today, many organizations use "flatter" structures, with fewer levels between the company's chief executives and the employee base. Most organizations, however, still have four basic levels of management: top, middle, first line, and team leaders.

Top-Level Managers

As you would expect, top-level managers (or top managers) are the "bosses" of the organization. They have titles such as chief executive officer (CEO), chief operations officer (COO), chief marketing officer (CMO), chief technology officer (CTO), and chief financial officer (CFO). A new executive position known as the chief compliance officer (CCO) is showing up on many organizational charts in response to the demands of the government to comply with complex rules and regulations. Depending on the size and type of organization, executive vice presidents and division heads would also be part of the top management team. The relative importance of these positions varies according to the type of organization they head. For example, in a pharmaceutical firm, the CCO may report directly to the CEO or to the board of directors.

Top managers are ultimately responsible for the long-term success of the organization. They set long-term goals and define strategies to achieve them. They pay careful attention to the external environment of the organization: the economy, proposals for laws that would affect profits, stakeholder demands, and consumer and public relations. They will make the decisions that affect the whole company such as financial investments, mergers and acquisitions, partnerships and strategic alliances, and changes to the brand or product line of the organization.

Middle Managers

Middle managers have titles like department head, director, and chief supervisor. They are links between the top managers and the first-line managers and have one or two levels below them. Middle managers receive broad strategic plans from top managers and turn them into operational blueprints with specific objectives and programs for first-line managers. They also encourage, support, and foster talented employees within the organization. An important function of middle managers is providing leadership, both in implementing top manager directives and in enabling first-line managers to support teams and effectively report both positive performances and obstacles to meeting objectives.

Middle managers must be good communicators because they link line managers and top-level management.

First-Line Managers

First-line managers are the entry level of management, the individuals "on the line" and in the closest contact with the workers. They are directly responsible for making sure that organizational objectives and plans are implemented effectively. They may be called assistant managers, shift managers, foremen, section chiefs, or office managers. First-line managers are focused almost exclusively on the internal issues of the organization and are the first to see problems with the operation of the business, such as untrained labor, poor quality materials, machinery breakdowns, or new procedures that slow down production. It is essential that they communicate regularly with middle management.

Team Leaders

A team leader is a special kind of manager who may be appointed to manage a particular task or activity. The team leader reports to a first-line or middle manager. Responsibilities of the team leader include developing timelines, making specific work assignments, providing needed training to team members, communicating clear instructions, and generally ensuring that the team is operating at peak efficiency. Once the task is complete, the team leader position may be eliminated and a new team may be formed to complete a different task.

MANAGEMENT ROLES

Learning Outcome

- Differentiate between leadership, informational, and decision-making roles.

Management Roles

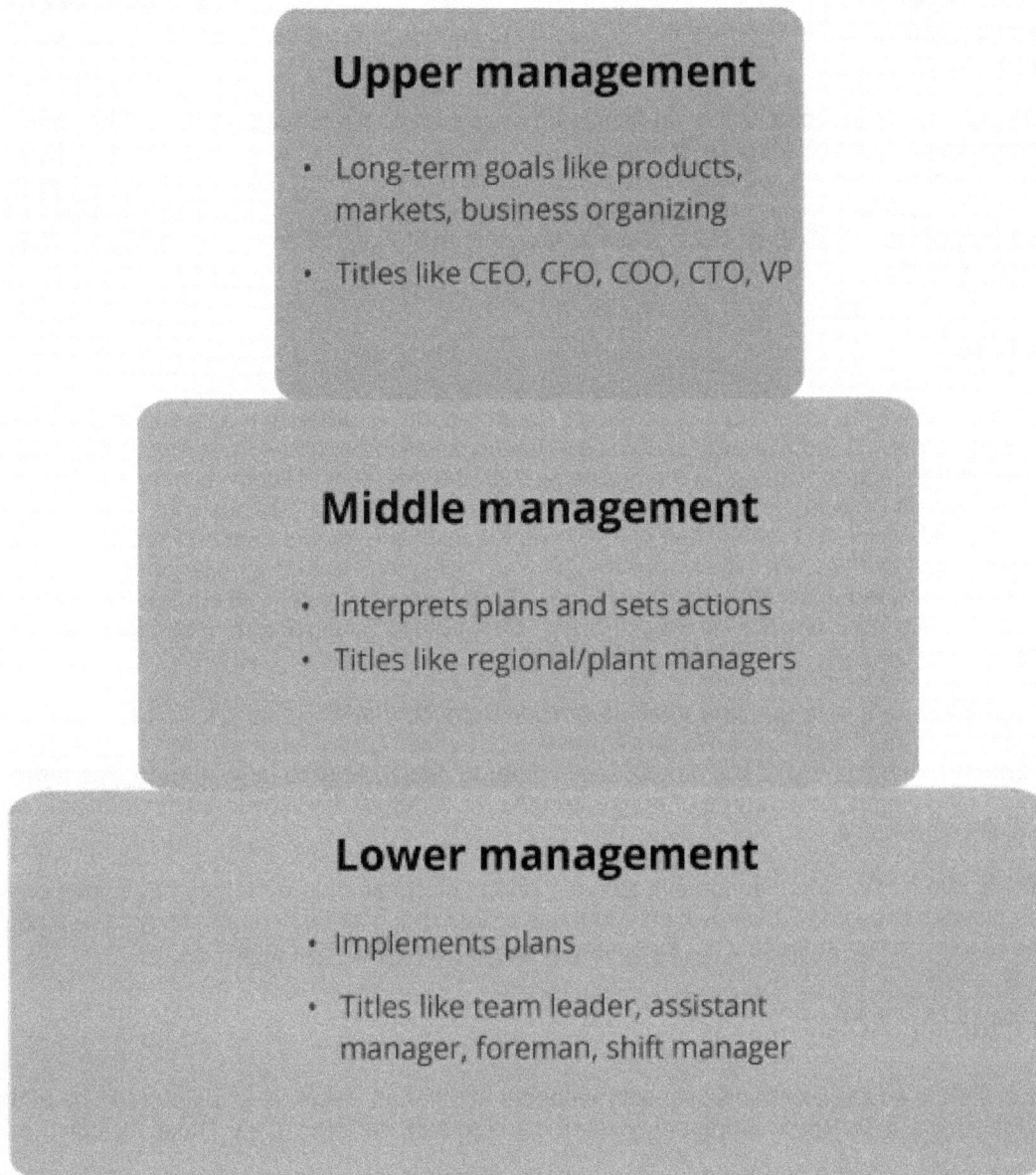

Upper management

- Long-term goals like products, markets, business organizing
- Titles like CEO, CFO, COO, CTO, VP

Middle management

- Interprets plans and sets actions
- Titles like regional/plant managers

Lower management

- Implements plans
- Titles like team leader, assistant manager, foreman, shift manager

Roles and functions of managers in a top-down organizational structure

We have discussed the types (levels) of managers and some of their responsibilities but not their specific activities. All managers must be comfortable with three main types of activities or roles. To do their jobs, managers assume these different roles. No manager stays in any one role all of the time, but shifts back and forth. These roles are leadership (or interpersonal), informational, and decision making. They were written about in detail in the 1970s by Henry Mintzberg, a professor at McGill University in Canada. His classifications are still one of the most studied descriptors of management roles today. (Note: B. (2016, September 20). Mintzberg's Management Roles - Boundless Open Textbook. Retrieved July 28, 2017, from https://www.boundless.com/management/textbooks/boundless-management-textbook/introduction-to-management-1/additional-roles-and-skills-of-managers-20/mintzberg-s-management-roles-127-605/)

Leadership and Interpersonal Roles

Which type of manager spends more time in leadership activities? The short answer is all effective managers display leadership characteristics. Leadership is the ability to communicate a vision and inspire people to embrace that vision.

Top managers are often required to fulfill what Mintzberg described as **figurehead** activities. They are the public face of the management team and represent the business in legal, economic, and social forums. (Note: Ibid.) Middle managers are also leaders, although their focus may be more on **interpersonal** skills, such as motivating employees, negotiating salaries, and encouraging innovation and creativity. First-line managers lead both by example when they actively participate in the tasks assigned to their workers and by modeling the policies and work ethics of the organization.

Informational Roles

Informational roles involve the receiving and sending of information—whether as a spokesperson, a mentor, a trainer, or an administrator. A top manager is a voice of the organization and has to be aware that even personal opinions will reflect (for better or worse) on the business. With the free flow of information on the Internet, it is very difficult for top managers to separate their personal identities from their corporate positions. For example, there was a consumer backlash in 2017 when Uber CEO Travis Kalanick accepted a seat on President Trump's economic advisory council. Kalanick initially said that he was "going to use [his] position on the council to stand up for what's right." He resigned a few days later in response to the protest. (Note: Pittsburghers Protest Uber As CEO Reacts To Public Outcry. (n.d.). Retrieved July 28, 2017, from http://pittsburgh.cbslocal.com/2017/02/04/ pittsburgh-uber-protest/)

Middle managers must skillfully determine what information from top management should be shared with others, how it should be interpreted, and how it should be presented. Similarly, they must weigh the value of information they receive from first-line managers and employees in order to decide what to forward to top management. If transmitted information tends to be untrue or trivial, then the manager will be viewed as a nonreliable source and his or her opinions discounted.

The informational role for first-line managers is primarily one of disseminating what they have been given and helping the employees to see how their own contributions further organizational goals. They have a responsibility to see that the employees understand what they need to be successful in their jobs.

Decision Making Roles

All managers are required to make decisions, but managers at different levels make different kinds of decisions. According to Mintzberg, there are four primary types of management decision roles. These include the following:

- **Entrepreneur.** The entrepreneurs in a firm are usually top-level managers. They identify economic opportunities, lead the initiative for change, and make product decisions.
- **Disturbance handler.** Top and middle managers will react to disturbances (unexpected events) in the organization—whether internal or external. They will decide what corrective actions should be taken to resolve the problems.
- **Resource allocator.** All levels of management will make resource allocation decisions, depending upon whether the decision affects the entire organization, a single department, or a particular task or activity.
- **Negotiator.** Depending on the effect on the organization, most negotiation is done by top and middle-level managers. Top managers will handle negotiations that affect the entire organization, such as union contracts or trade agreements. Middle-level managers negotiate most salary and hiring decisions. (Note: Mintzberg's Management Roles - Boundless Open Textbook.)

To summarize, managers must play many roles. Some are better than others in particular roles and will tend to be called on for those jobs. Putting a diverse management team in place will ensure that the organization has enough managers to meet most challenges.

INTRODUCTION TO THE ADVANTAGES OF MANAGING PEOPLE WELL

What you'll learn to do: explain the advantages that arise from managing people well

An organization—especially a for-profit business—needs something that drives customers to buy its products or services over a competitor's. How do managers ensure that employees embrace that advantage so that the company not only survives but thrives?

THE ADVANTAGES OF MANAGING PEOPLE WELL

Learning Outcome

• Explain the advantages that arise from managing people well.

What Makes a Good Manager?

We have discussed details about managers and what they do, but we haven't considered what makes a good manager. Briefly, a good manager helps an organization succeed. Success means the following:

• An organization is **effective**: it is accomplishing things that support the vision and mission.
• An organization is **efficient**: it is doing things in the best possible manner.
• An organization is **sustainable**: it is generating revenue to support its continued operation.

In the definition of management, we recognized that managers achieve results by working with people to meet organizational goals. This implies that a good manager achieves effectiveness, efficiency, and sustainability through the people in the organization. In this section, we will look more at how managing people well contributes to organizational success.

Southwest Airlines is known for their fun-loving flight attendants who make customers feel welcome and comfortable.

Why People Are Important

People are considered resources because well-trained and experienced employees are the main source of effectiveness, efficiency, and sustainability. They provide effectiveness when they understand the goals of the organization and focus their energy on tasks that support the goals. Second, people provide efficiency by being very good at doing the tasks that support the goals. They provide sustainability because the people in an organization are both unique and lasting. Most of the resources an organization has are not unique and can be copied by competitors. Equipment, technology, and methods can all be copied by competitors. It may take time, but eventually competitors can duplicate most of the things an organization has or does. But competitors cannot copy people. The skills and experience of people and the way they are managed to achieve high performance is very difficult for competitors to reproduce.

For example, Southwest Airlines is famous for operating at low cost. It achieves low costs because the company is very selective in the people it hires, and it creates a friendly and supportive environment. In return, the people in the organization are willing to work hard to support the company. According to Gary Kelly, the CEO of Southwest, "Our people are our single greatest strength and most enduring long-term competitive advantage." (Note: About Southwest. (n.d.). Retrieved July 28, 2017, from https://www.southwest.com/html/about-southwest/index.html?clk=GFOOTER-ABOUT-ABOUT) **Competitive advantage** means that the business outperforms its rivals in the market because customers prefer its products or services. Other airlines have attempted to copy Southwest by operating low-cost subsidiaries. United, Continental, Delta, and Alitalia all started low-cost subsidiaries, but they all failed. The failures were due in large part to their inability to copy Southwest's low-cost, high-performance workforce. (Note: I. (2015, June 10). How Is Southwest Different From Other Airlines? Retrieved July 28, 2017, from http://www.investopedia.com/articles/investing/061015/how-southwest-different-other-airlines.asp)

People are a cost because they must be paid. All of the benefits listed earlier increase the longer people stay in the organizations. They understand and become better at their jobs over time. And the organization contributes to their learning by providing training and development opportunities. The organization gets the greatest benefit by retaining its employees to gain from their experience. One of the main reasons employees, particularly highly skilled employees, quit is because they can get higher wages somewhere else. Companies that depend on a stable and reliable workforce must provide excellent wages and benefits.

The software firm SAS is an example of a company that is committed to retaining its workforce. Outstanding benefits and perks are a big part of the compensation package that SAS offers its employees. SAS employees and their families have free access to a health club with tennis and basketball courts, a fitness room, and pool. There's a free on-site health care clinic, free "work-life" counseling, and low-cost child care. Because of its commitment to its employees, SAS is consistently listed as one of the top ten best places to work. And because of the contributions of its employees, as of 2012 SAS has had thirty-seven consecutive years of record earnings. (Note: Crowley, M. C. (2013, January 22). How SAS Became The World's Best Place To Work. Retrieved July 28, 2017, from https://www.fastcompany.com/3004953/how-sas-became-worlds-best-place-work)

Watch the video below to find out more about what makes SAS a great company to work for. While you watch it, think about how the perks SAS offers to its employees help create a competitive advantage through people.

Watch this video online: https://youtu.be/RtANL3MMjPs

PUTTING IT TOGETHER: INTRODUCTION TO MANAGEMENT

At the beginning of this module, we presented examples of how two management teams reimagined their organizations in order to survive in a changing and competitive global environment. After its beginning as a paper mill in 1871, Nokia grew and combined with other firms to incorporate in 1967 as a diversified corporation producing paper, electronics, rubber, and cable. At every opportunity, Nokia took advantage of merging and entering new markets until, by 2000, it was a leader in the telecommunications industry. (Note: The rise, dominance, and epic fall - a brief look at Nokia's history. (n.d.). Retrieved July 28, 2017, from http://www.gsmarena.com/the_rise_dominance_and_epic_fall__a_brief_look_at_nokias_history-blog-13460.php)

A slowdown in the mobile phone market plus a disastrous recall to correct faulty cell phone batteries contributed to a downturn in profit that eventually led to Microsoft's partnering with and then acquiring Nokia in 2014. (Note: Ibid.) In some ways, Nokia's very success led to its demise. Its top managers failed to recognize the impact the smartphone would have on the mobile phone market. They failed to anticipate their customers' needs.

Meanwhile, the top management at ThyssenKrupp AG has recognized that to save its organization, the time to change is now. From a major German steel manufacturer, the company leadership is transforming it into an "industrial goods company with a stake in a steel joint venture." (Note: Andresen, T. (2017, June 19). Germany's Biggest Steelmaker Set to Unveil a Future Beyond Steel. Retrieved July 28, 2017, from https://www.bloomberg.com/news/articles/2017-06-19/germany-s-biggest-steelmaker-set-to-unveil-a-future-beyond-steel) If it succeeds (and the indications are good), then will management continue to adapt as market conditions change?

ThyssenKrupp AG was once known for steel production. Now, due to its management's ability to adapt to the changing environment, it can count manufacturing wheelchair lifts and other goods as part of its repertoire.

This module covered the primary management functions needed in all organizations: planning, leading, organizing, and controlling. We looked at four common levels of managers: top, middle, first line, and team leaders. Finally, we discussed how the managers in an organization or business create a competitive advantage by managing people well.

MODULE 2: HISTORY OF MANAGEMENT

WHY IT MATTERS: HISTORY OF MANAGEMENT

Why learn about the history of management?

https://vimeo.com/80777503

If you were asked to list the most innovative companies in the world today, it is likely that you'd put Amazon near the top of that list. Do you remember the buzz generated when Amazon announced that it would be applying for the necessary permits to deliver packages by drone? Likewise, it is an amazing sight to enter an Amazon distribution center and see the carefully choreographed dance as humans and robots work together to fill customer orders. Amazon is at the cutting edge of modern business.

Now ask yourself, could there possibly be any similarities between managing a modern technology company like Amazon and managing the large industrial steel companies that dominated U.S. industry in the late 1800s and into the turn of the twentieth century?

What might surprise you is the answer: yes! What you will learn during this module as you study the history of management is that many principles developed during the Industrial Revolution are still in practice in today's Information Revolution. So pay close attention as you study these historical concepts of management and relate them to your experiences and studies of successful businesses today. The similarities may astonish you.

INTRODUCTION TO SCIENTIFIC MANAGEMENT

What you'll learn to do: describe the contributions of Frederick W. Taylor, Frank and Lillian Gilbreth, and Henry Gantt to the field of scientific management

Scientific management is the term used to describe the works produced by the earliest theorists and researchers in management. This section will examine some of the key contributions of pioneers in this field.

SCIENTIFIC MANAGEMENT

Learning Outcomes

- Explain the concept of scientific management.
- Summarize the work of Frederick W. Taylor.
- Summarize the work of Frank and Lillian Gilbreth.
- Summarize the work of Henry Gantt.

Prior to the early 1900s, there was no management theory as we think of it today. Work happened as it always had—those with the skills did the work in the way they thought best (usually the way it had always been done). The concept that work could be studied and the work process improved did not formally exist before the ideas of Frederick Winslow Taylor.

The **scientific management** movement produced revolutionary ideas for the time—ideas such as employee training and implementing standardized best practices to improve productivity. Taylor's theory was called scientific because to develop it, he employed techniques borrowed from botanists and chemists, such as analysis, observation, synthesis, rationality, and logic. You may decide as you read more about Taylor that by today's criteria he was not the worker's "friend." However, Taylor must be given credit for creating the concept of an organization being run "as a business" or in a "businesslike manner," meaning efficiently and productively.

Frederick W. Taylor

Before the Industrial Revolution, most businesses were small operations, averaging three or four people. Owners frequently labored next to employees, knew what they were capable of, and closely directed their work. The dynamics of the workplace changed dramatically in the United States with the Industrial Revolution. Factory owners and managers did not possess close relationships with their employees. The workers "on the floor" controlled the work process and generally worked only hard enough to make sure they would not be fired. There was little or no incentive to work harder than the next man (or woman).

Taylor was a mechanical engineer who was primarily interested in the type of work done in factories and mechanical shops. He observed that the owners and managers of the factories knew little about what actually took place in the workshops. Taylor believed that the system could be improved, and he looked around for an incentive. He settled on money. He believed a worker should get "a fair day's pay for a fair day's work"—no more, no less. If the worker couldn't work to the target, then the person shouldn't be working at all. Taylor also believed that management and labor should cooperate and work together to meet goals. He was the first to suggest that the primary functions of managers should be planning and training.

In 1909, Taylor published *The Principles of Scientific Management*. In this book, he suggested that productivity would increase if jobs were optimized and simplified. He also proposed matching a worker to a particular job that suited the person's skill level and then training the worker to do that job in a specific way. Taylor first developed the idea of breaking down each job into component parts and

Frederick Taylor (1856–1915) is called the Father of Scientific Management.

timing each part to determine the most efficient method of working. Soon afterward, two management theorists, Frank and Lillian Gilbreth, came up with the idea of filming workers to analyze their motions. Their ideas have since been combined into one process (called time and motion studies) for analyzing the most productive way to complete a task.

Scientific management has at its heart four core principles that also apply to organizations today. They include the following:

- Look at each job or task scientifically to determine the "one best way" to perform the job. This is a change from the previous "rule of thumb" method where workers devised their own ways to do the job.
- Hire the right workers for each job, and train them to work at maximum efficiency.
- Monitor worker performance, and provide instruction and training when needed.
- Divide the work between management and labor so that management can plan and train, and workers can execute the task efficiently.

Taylor designed his approach for use in places where the work could be quantified, systemized, and standardized, such as in factories. In scientific management, there is one right way to do a task; workers were not encouraged (in fact, they were forbidden) to make decisions or evaluate actions that might produce a better result. Taylor was concerned about the output more than worker satisfaction or motivation. Taylor's work introduced for the first time the idea of systematic training and selection, and it encouraged business owners to work with employees to increase productivity and efficiency. And he introduced a "first-class worker" concept to set the standard for what a worker should be able to produce in a set period of time. Scientific management grew in popularity among big businesses because productivity rose, proving that it worked.

Today, an updated version of his original theory is used by such companies as FedEx and Amazon. **Digital Taylorism** is based on maximizing efficiency by standardizing the tools and techniques for completing each task involved with a given job. Every task is broken down to the smallest motion and translated into an exact procedure that must be followed to complete that task. Because everyone is operating in the same mechanistic way, it increases predictability and consistency while reducing errors. It is relatively easy for managers to replace workers and retain the same productivity. The criticism of this type of management approach is similar to that of Taylor's original theory: It reduces worker creativity; it requires management to monitor all aspects of employee behavior; and it is unforgiving to workers who don't meet the standard.

Frank and Lillian Gilbreth

Two more pioneers in the field of management theory were Frank and Lillian Gilbreth, who conducted research about the same time as Taylor. Like Taylor, the Gilbreths were interested in worker productivity, specifically how movement and motion affected efficiency.

As stated above, the Gilbreths used films to analyze worker activity. They would break the tasks into discrete elements and movements and record the time it took to complete one element. In this way, they were able to predict the most efficient workflow for a particular job. The films the Gilbreths made were also useful for creating training videos to instruct employees in how to work productively.

Taylor and the Gilbreths belonged to the **classical school of management**, which emphasized increasing worker productivity by scientific analysis. They differed, however, on the importance of the worker. Taylor's emphasis was on profitability and productivity; the Gilbreths were also focused on worker welfare and motivation. They believed that by reducing the amount of motions associated with a particular task, they could also increase the worker's well-being. Their research, along with Taylor's, provided many important principles later incorporated into quality assurance and quality control programs begun in the 1920s and 1930s. Eventually, their work led to the science of ergonomics and industrial psychology. (**Ergonomics** is the scientific discipline concerned with understanding the interactions of humans with other elements of a system.)

You can watch some of the Gilbreths' films below to get an idea of how they documented their time and motion studies in an effort to increase efficiency and safety.

Lillian Gilbreth. The book and film Cheaper By the Dozen were based on her and Frank's experiences raising twelve children according to their theories of time and motion studies.

https://s3-us-west-2.amazonaws.com/courses-images/wp-content/uploads/sites/1972/2017/07/21224314/Original_Films_Of_Frank_B_Gilbreth_Part_II.ogv.240p.webm

Henry Gantt

Henry Gantt (1861–1919) was also an associate of Taylor. He is probably best known for two key contributions to classical management theory: the Gantt chart and the task and bonus system.

The **Gantt chart** is a tool that provides a visual (graphic) representation of what occurs over the course of a project. The focus of the chart is the **sequential performance of tasks** that make up a project. It identifies key tasks, assigns an estimated time to complete the task, and determines a starting date for each element of a task. Gantt differentiated between a **terminal element** that must be completed as part of a larger task. The related terminal elements together created what he called the **summary element**.

ID	Task Name	Predecessors	Duration
1	Start		0 days
2	a	1	4 days
3	b	1	5.33 days
4	c	2	5.17 days
5	d	2	6.33 days
6	e	3,4	5.17 days
7	f	5	4.5 days
8	g	6	5.17 days
9	Finish	7,8	0 days

An example of a simple Gantt chart

The Gantt chart has multiple benefits for project management:

- It aids in the breakdown of tasks into specific elements.
- It allows for the monitoring of projected timelines.
- It identifies which tasks are dependent upon a prior task or element and which are independent and can be completed at any time.

Let's apply the Gantt chart principles to a simple project. Imagine that you want to paint a room. The summary element is the finished, painted room. The individual terminal tasks might include calculating the square footage of the room, preparing the walls, choosing the paint, purchasing the paint, putting down the drop cloth, taping the windows, applying the paint, and final cleanup. Some of these elements are independent, and some elements are dependent upon others. Purchasing the paint is dependent upon knowing the square footage and choosing the paint color. Before painting can start, the walls must be prepared and the paint must be purchased. But purchasing the paint is not dependent upon preparing the walls—these tasks could be started at the same time.

Gantt also promoted the task and bonus plan that modified Taylor's "a fair day's pay for a fair day's work" premise. Gantt wanted to establish a standard (average) time for a piece of work or task. Then, if a worker took more that the standard time, his pay was docked. But if he took less time, he was paid for the additional pieces of work and a bonus of up to 20 percent more. Also known as the progressive rate system, this plan was preferred by workers who were willing to work harder for additional wages.

Although Gantt is not the best known of the classic management theorists, many of his ideas are still being used in project management.

There are several distinct tasks involved in painting a room.

Key Points

Scientific management was the first widespread promotion of rational processes to improve efficiency. The goal was to develop a standard against which work performance could be measured. Training became an important part of the management process. By the 1930s, however, many unions and workers were suspicious of the intentions of scientific management.

INTRODUCTION TO BUREAUCRATIC MANAGEMENT

What you'll learn to do: describe the contributions of Max Weber and Henri Fayol to the field of bureaucratic management

Bureaucratic management looks at how large organizations with layers of management can operate in an efficient, rational manner. Weber and Fayol, the original proponents of this style of management, were fighting favoritism and incompetence, common in large organizations at the time. Unfortunately, when taken to extremes, the same concepts became associated with red tape and obstructionism.

BUREAUCRATIC MANAGEMENT

Learning Outcomes

- Explain the concept of bureaucratic management.
- Summarize the work of Max Weber.
- Summarize the work of Henri Fayol.

Scientific management was concerned with individual tasks and how workers could do those tasks most efficiently. Around the same time that Frederick Taylor was developing his theory of scientific management, other theorists were considering entire systems, such as government departments and large businesses, and trying to figure out how to manage them more effectively. The most influential of these theorists were Max Weber (pronounced *Vay'- ber*), and Henri Fayol. Between them, they defined the characteristics of organizations and the functions of managers that we still accept today.

Max Weber and Bureaucratic Theory

Weber was born in Germany in 1864 and grew up during the time when industrialization was transforming government, business, and society. Weber was interested in industrial capitalism, an economic system where industry is privately controlled and operated for profit. Weber wanted to know why industrial capitalism was successful in some countries and not in others. He believed that large-scale organizations such as factories and government departments were a characteristic of capitalist economies.

Weber visited the United States in 1904 to study the U.S. economy. It was here that he observed the spirit of capitalism. He noted that capitalism in the United States encouraged competition and innovation. He also realized that businesses were run by professional managers and that they were linked through economic relationships. He contrasted this with capitalistic practices in Germany where a small group of powerful people controlled the economy. In Germany, tradition dictated behaviors. People were given positions of authority based on their social standing and connections, and businesses were linked by family and social relationships.

Max Weber proposed bureaucracy as the optimum form of organization.

Weber was concerned that authority was not a function of experience and ability, but won by social status. Because of this, managers were not loyal to the organization. Organizational resources were used for the benefit of owners and managers rather than to meet organizational goals. Weber was convinced that organizations based on rational authority, where authority was given to the most competent and qualified people, would be more efficient than those based on who you knew. Weber called this type of rational organization a bureaucracy.

Weber identified six characteristics or rules of a bureaucracy. They are summarized in the following table.

Characteristic of the Bureaucracy	Description
Hierarchical Management Structure	Each level controls the levels below and is controlled by the level above. Authority and responsibilities are clearly defined for each position.
Division of Labor	Tasks are clearly defined and employees become skilled by specializing in doing one thing. There is clear definition of authority and responsibility.
Formal Selection Process	Employee selection and promotion are based on experience, competence, and technical qualification demonstrated by examinations, education, or training. There is no nepotism.
Career Orientation	Management is separate from ownership, and managers are career employees. Protection from arbitrary dismissal is guaranteed.
Formal Rules and Regulations	Rules and regulations are documented to ensure reliable and predictable behavior. Managers must depend on formal organizational rules in employee relations.
Impersonality	Rules are applied uniformly to everyone. There is no preferential treatment or favoritism.

Weber thought bureaucracy would result in the highest level of efficiency, rationality, and worker satisfaction. In fact, he felt that bureaucracy was so logical that it would transform all of society. Unfortunately, Weber did not anticipate that each of the bureaucratic characteristics could also have a negative result. For example, division of labor leads to specialized and highly skilled workers, but it also can lead to tedium and boredom. Formal rules and regulations lead to uniformity and predictability, but they also can lead to excessive procedures and "red tape." In spite of its potential problems, some form of bureaucracy is the dominant form of most large organizations today. The "pyramid" organizational structure, with responsibility split into divisions, departments, and teams, is based on principles of bureaucracy. It is used by nearly all large corporations. Weber's idea that hiring and promotion should be based on qualifications, not social standing, is built into U.S. labor laws.

Today, the term "bureaucracy" has taken on negative connotations. It is associated with excessive paperwork, apathy, unresponsiveness, and inflexibility. This is unfortunate, as Weber's ideas have spread throughout the industrial world and transformed the way organizations are run and structured. Your school is probably structured as a bureaucracy. If you have shopped at a department store, it is a bureaucracy, and your city government is also a bureaucracy.

Henri Fayol and Administrative Theory

Henri Fayol was born in France in 1841. Although older than Weber, he witnessed many of the same organizational developments in Europe that interested Weber. Fayol was a mining engineer who became the head of a large mining company. He wanted managers to be responsible for more than just increasing production. The story goes that he came to this insight when a mine was shut down after a horse broke a leg and no one at the mine had authority to purchase another. Fayol saw this as a direct failure of management to plan and organize the work. Following this, Fayol began experimenting with different management structures.

He condensed his ideas and experiences into a set of management duties and principles, which he published in 1916 in the book *General and Industrial Management*. Fayol incorporated some of Weber's ideas in his theories. However, unlike Weber, Fayol was concerned with how workers were managed and how they contributed to the organization. He felt that successful organizations, and therefore successful management, were linked to satisfied and motivated employees.

Henri Fayol founded the school of administrative management.

Fayol's five duties of management were as follows:

- **Foresight:** Create a plan of action for the future.
- **Organization:** Provide resources to implement the plan.
- **Command:** Select and lead the best workers through clear instructions and orders.
- **Coordinate:** Make sure the diverse efforts fit together through clear communication.
- **Control:** Verify whether things are going according to plan and make corrections where needed.

These duties evolved into the four functions of management: planning (foresight), organizing (organization), leading (command and coordinate), and controlling (control).

Fayol also proposed a set of fourteen principles that he felt could guide management behavior, but he did not think the principles were rigid or exhaustive. He thought management principles needed to be flexible and adaptable and that they would be expanded through experience and experimentation. Some of Fayol's principles are still included in management theory and practice, including the following:

- **Scalar chain:** An unbroken chain of command extends from the top to the bottom of the organization.

- **Unity of command:** Employees receive orders from only one superior.
- **Unity of direction:** Activities that are similar should be the responsibility of one person.
- **Division of work:** Workers specialize in a few tasks to become more proficient.

Key Points

The work of Weber and Fayol forms the basis of management theory and practice still in use today. Weber's rules for bureaucracy govern most large organizations, from multinational organizations to armies, hospitals, and universities. Fayol's duties of management help us understand the functions of managers in any type of organization.

INTRODUCTION TO HUMANISTIC MANAGEMENT

What you'll learn to do: describe the contributions of Mary Parker Follett and Elton Mayo (Hawthorne studies) to the field of humanistic management

Scientific management has both its proponents and its detractors. The most dynamic of these critics initiated a new movement called humanistic management, which shifted management emphasis from things (pay, breaks, schedules, and quotas) to people and work relationships.

HUMANISTIC MANAGEMENT

Learning Outcomes

- Explain the concept of humanistic management.
- Summarize the work of Mary Parker Follett.
- Explain the significance of Elton Mayo's work (Hawthorne studies).

As you've probably deduced from the name, **humanistic management** theory places a great emphasis on interpersonal relationships. An earlier section discussed scientific management and how it focused on productivity and reducing costs by developing efficiency standards based on time and motion studies. Its critics took issue with scientific management's emphasis on quotas and standards that were the same for all workers.

Very little evidence exists that the new quotas set for workers were unreasonable or that laborers who could not meet that quota were routinely fired. But concern was expressed by workers who complained about lower standards of workmanship and lower wages under what was called the set-piece system. Labor unions began addressing the growing fear of the workers that all but an elite few would soon be out of work. Even the U.S. government got involved in the conflict between managers and workers, calling on Frederick Taylor to testify before Congress about the aims of his proposals. It was out of this context that a new management theory evolved that examined social rather than economic factors. The humanistic approach looked to the individual worker and group dynamics rather than to authoritative managers for effective control.

Mary Parker Follett

Mary Parker Follett's teachings, many of which were published as articles in well-known women's magazines, were popular with businesspeople during her lifetime. But she was virtually ignored by the male-dominated academic establishment, even though she attended Radcliffe University and Yale and was asked to address the London School of Economics. In recent years her writings have been "rediscovered" by American management academics, and she is now considered the "Mother of Modern Management."

Follett developed many concepts that she applied to business and management, including the following:

Mary Parker Follett is now considered the "Mother of Modern Management."

- A better understanding of lateral processes within organizational hierarchies. These concepts were applied by DuPont Chemical Company in the 1920s in the first matrix-style organization. A matrix organizational structure uses a grid rather than a pyramidal system to illustrate reporting paths. An individual may report both to a functional manager (such as sales or finance) and to a product manager.
- The importance of informal processes within organizations. This is related to the idea of authority deriving from expertise rather than position or status. For example, an informal group may form in an organization (during or outside of official work hours) to socialize, form a union, or discuss work processes without management overhearing.
- Noncoercive power sharing, which she called **integration**, to describe how power operates in an effective organization. She wrote about the **"group principle"** that characterized the whole of the organization, describing how workers and managers have equal importance and make equal contributions.
- Coining the term "win-win" to describe cooperation between managers and workers. She also talked about **empowerment** and **facilitation** rather than control.
- Promoting conflict resolution in a group based on constructive consultation of equals rather than compromise, submission, or struggle. This is known as the **constructive conflict** concept.

Follett devoted her life's work to the idea that social cooperation is better than individual competition. In her 1924 book *Creative Experience*, Follett wrote "Labor and [management] can never be reconciled as long as labor persists in thinking that there is a [management] point of view and [management] thinks there is a labor point of view. These are imaginary wholes which must be broken up before [management] and labor can cooperate."

Elton Mayo and the Hawthorne Experiments

The Hawthorne experiments were a series of studies that took place in a Western Electric plant near Chicago during the late 1920s and early 1930s—the heyday of scientific management. The original experiment was designed to isolate factors in the workplace that affected productivity. The researchers alternatively offered and then took away benefits such as better lighting, breaks, shortened work schedules, meals, and savings and stock plans. But regardless of whether the change was positive or negative, the productivity of the test subjects increased. For example, when lighting was increased, productivity increased—as expected. What was not expected was that as lighting was diminished, productivity still increased. It was not until the lighting levels were near candlelight luminosity and the women could not see their work that productivity decreased. At this point, an Australian-born sociologist named Elton Mayo became involved.

Mayo visited the Hawthorne facility and advised the researchers to adjust how they interacted with the workers (subjects). A new trial was started with a smaller group of subjects. Again, benefits were both added and subtracted. Previous experiments had gathered data from the subjects by asking simple "yes or no" questions to more easily quantify their responses. But instead of "yes or no" questions, Mayo advised the researchers to employ the **nondirective interview method**. This allowed the researchers to be more informal and social and to develop relationships with the workers. Mayo discovered that there were several reasons why productivity increased despite the withdrawal of benefits, including the following:

- A feeling of group cohesion
- The friendlier attitude of the researchers (supervisors)
- The attention that being part of the study brought to the individuals

In interviews with the test subjects, it was discovered that the reason productivity increased was because the subjects were simply "having more fun." Mayo theorized that workers were motivated more by social dynamics than by economic or environmental factors.

Mayo published his findings in 1933 in "The Human Problems of an Industrialized Civilization." In this treatise, Mayo predicted that a group with negative behaviors and few social bonds would have very little chance of succeeding at the task. A group with a high sense of mission and close team awareness would be the most likely to achieve its goals. The remaining teams would have mixed degrees of success. The implication for organizations, of course, is to foster groups with a sense of mission and strong interpersonal relationships.

Key Points

The humanistic approach developed to balance the super-rationality and mechanics of scientific management theories. It recognized the importance of the social needs of the individual workers and the effects of group dynamics on efficiency and productivity. It expanded the traditional list of workforce motivation beyond tangible and economic factors. But it was not the end of management theory. Many more interpretations and theories followed.

INTRODUCTION TO CURRENT DEVELOPMENTS IN MANAGEMENT PRACTICES

What you'll learn to do: describe current developments in management practices

Although many of the principles described by twentieth century management researchers are still in use, they are being applied in widely different ways. Building on the advances in technology and social psychology, management theory has become more specialized to meet the continually arising challenges organizations face by operating in a global economy.

CURRENT DEVELOPMENTS IN MANAGEMENT PRACTICES

Learning Outcomes

- Explain the concept of operations management.
- Explain the concept of systems management.
- Explain the concept of information management.
- Explain the concept of contingency management.

In the twenty-first century, organizations face many new challenges. Some people would argue that society and the economy have changed so radically that the last century's management practices and theories are no longer relevant. The truth is management has become more important than ever. Almost everything we do today as individuals or organizations requires us to interact with large-scale institutions, such as government agencies, banks, health-care providers, insurance companies, school systems, universities, online retailers, and technology service providers. How has management theory and practice evolved to manage this new organizational and business environment? Interestingly, it has become both more specific and more general.

Forces Shaping Management

Several forces are significantly shaping management practices today, including the pace of change, technology, globalization, diversity, and social expectations. Let's look at each of these in more detail.

The Pace of Change

Managers must understand that society, politics, the economy, and technology are changing at an unprecedented rate. In 2001, Ray Kurzweil proposed that in the twenty-first century our rate of progress would double every decade. (Note: Kurzweil, R. (2001, March 7).

Organizations are changing faster than ever thanks to social and technological forces.

The Law of Accelerating Returns. Retrieved August 01, 2017, from http://www.kurzweilai.net/the-law-of-accelerating-returns) This means that over the next one hundred years, we will experience changes that would have taken twenty thousand years in the past. This presents a vexing problem for management. On one hand, managers need predictability and stability to develop and implement plans effectively. On the other hand, they need adaptability and flexibility to respond to opportunities. *How does management provide both stability and flexibility?*

Technology

The primary factor driving change is the development of computer and information technology. Fifty years ago, almost no one knew about computers except from science fiction books and movies. Today nearly everyone uses a smartphone with more power than the computers that guided rockets to the moon in 1969. Many of the routine jobs analyzed by Frederick Taylor and the Gilbreths are now automated, done by computers and robots. It has been estimated that robots will perform 50 percent of current jobs within twenty years. *What is the role of management when machines instead of people are doing work?*

Globalization

Globalization refers to the increasing ease of flow between countries. It includes economic, political, social, and cultural interactions. In particular, **economic globalization** is creating one global marketplace, making it easier to conduct business across borders. Globalization has allowed companies to perform many manufacturing jobs in low labor-cost countries. As a result, the United States has shifted from a manufacturing economy to a service and information economy. Consider the following comparison:

YEAR	MOST VALUED COMPANY IN THE U.S.	MARKET VALUE	NUMBER OF EMPLOYEES
1964	American Telegraph and Telephone (AT&T)	$267 billion	759,000
2015	Google	$370 billion	55,000

This table shows that technology workers today produce nearly twenty times more value for a company than manufacturing workers did in the past. *How does management lead and control this new knowledge worker?*

Diversity

Since the turn of the century, the U.S. workforce has become more diverse in almost all dimensions, including race, gender, ethnicity, and age. In 1950, women made up about 30 percent of the workforce; in 2015 women made up about 47 percent of the workforce. By 2024, ethnic and racial minorities are expected to comprise 40 percent of the workforce. And for the first time, there are now five generations of workers in the workforce, from veterans born between 1928 and 1946 to iGens born after 1994. This diversity provides a tremendous resource to organizations. People from different backgrounds have unique perceptions, experiences, and strengths. This can promote creativity and innovation that stimulates unique problem solving. But it also brings different expectations and norms about behavior and attitudes. *How can management capitalize on the advantages of diversity while accommodating differences?*

Social Expectations

From the start of the Industrial Revolution until the middle of the twentieth century, management could look inward to determine how to best use resources to meet organizational goals. Although government passed laws to address the worst abuses, organizations primarily interacted with the external environment through the marketplace. The expectation of public, private, and civic organizations was that they would provide the goods and services society required. This attitude also began to change around the middle of the twentieth century as organizations, especially businesses, were viewed as social, as well as economic, actors. The positive and negative impacts of organizations on the wider environment—alongside the products and services they provided—were also considered outputs of production. Now managers have to satisfy not only their customers but also a wider set of stakeholders, from government agencies to community groups. *How does managing stakeholders get incorporated into management theory and practice?*

Current Developments in Management

We don't yet have the answers to most of these questions. No "grand theories" like those we have discussed previously in this module have emerged to address these new challenges. That is not to say that management has not responded; it has, in two ways:

- Management has become more specific with the formation of different disciplines. Managers now focus on specific aspects of organizational management: operations management, financial management, marketing management, human resource management, etc. By limiting the number of factors and issues they must deal with, managers can develop practices that address the specific issues they face in their discipline.

- Management has also become more general. Managers are not provided with an instructional manual that tells them how to manage. Instead, they are given a **toolbox** of different theories and practices. Effective managers need to know what tool to use and how to use it in different circumstances.

Let us consider some current developments in management.

Operations Management

Operations management is concerned with all of the physical processes involved in producing and delivering goods and services to customers. Operations management is the "guts" of a manufacturing or service company. It is concerned with all aspects of converting materials and labor into goods and services as efficiently as possible. Operations managers must work closely with every department in the business to ensure that products are manufactured as efficiently as possible. The same forces that are transforming organizations and management are transforming all aspects of operations management, from design to production.

Operations managers are involved with the initial product design to incorporate features that facilitate production. Sometimes small changes that don't affect function, such as the number of different types of screws used in an assembly, can have a significant impact on production costs. Today, many manufacturing firms are using computer-aided design that will translate design plans directly into instructions for computer-controlled machinery and robotics. Operations managers also manage the **supply chain** to find the best sources for high-quality materials and supplies at the lowest cost. Operations managers have become international operations managers, as supplies come from anywhere in the world and manufacturing can be done anywhere in the world.

Operations managers are also responsible for materials **inventory**. This consists of materials that will be used in production or for performing services. Some amount of inventory is needed to prevent delays in production or servicing. The worst thing that can happen to an auto manufacturer is to have an assembly line stop because of a shortage of a basic part, such as spark plugs or tires. On the other hand, maintaining inventories is a significant cost for companies, so they want to minimize the amount of inventory on hand. Operations managers must balance the need for maintaining sufficient inventory with the need for reducing costs. They now schedule deliveries and manage inventory using techniques such as just-in-time to optimize the amount of inventory on hand. This frequently involves developing long-term, cooperative partnerships with suppliers. Inventory management is a huge concern for Amazon, for instance, which maintains an inventory of millions of products. It has developed specialized techniques to maintain enough inventory to avoid lost sales without holding costly excess inventory.

All of these activities support operation management's main function: the manufacturing of products or the delivery of services. Operations managers must be concerned not only with cost and quantities but also be responsible for delivering quality. They design and supervise production processes and service delivery using modern methods such as lean manufacturing and Six Sigma. Six Sigma is a systematic set of practices used to reduce defects or complaints. The goal of Six Sigma is fewer than 3.4 defects per one million parts produced, transactions performed, or services delivered.

Finally, operations management works with marketing and sales to make sure goods and services are delivered where and when they are needed. They use sophisticated technology, such as point-of-sale data collections and **integrated ordering** systems, to forecast demand for products and services. This information is feedback through the entire system, from ordering materials and supplies to scheduling production. Operations management is responsible for making sure everything and everyone is working together to deliver what the customer expects.

Information Management

If operations management is the guts of a business, information management is the nervous system. Organizations today depend on the availability and accuracy of information to make decisions at every level. Information management is concerned with the collection, preservation, storage, processing, and delivery of information. The purpose of information management is to make sure information is available to the right people at the right time in a form that they can apply.

Data security has become a critical element of systems management.

Information management is not a new concept. Businesses and organizations of all sorts have always required information about their internal and external conditions to manage effectively. Although the need for information is not new, the volume of information available, the means of gathering information, and the methods of processing information into useful knowledge have all been transformed.

A recent development in information management is the use of big data. **Big data** refers to incredibly large amounts of data available to organizations today and how that data can be analyzed for useful information. Big data comes from a variety of sources, including social media, business transactions, government interactions, and education and health experiences, to name a few. It also comes in a variety of formats from structured, numeric data to unstructured text data, social media, and telephone calls.

Methods are being developed to mine this data to extract useful information about individual behaviors. An example of using big data that went viral a few years ago was how Morton's Steak House delivered a steak dinner to a man getting off a plane at Newark airport. The man had tweeted: "Hey @Mortons – can you meet me at newark airport with a porterhouse when I land in two hours?" Morton's continually mines social media for use of its name. Its data analytics captured the tweet, identified the man's name, determined that he was a frequent customer (and a frequent tweeter), and determined what his favorite meal was. Within two hours, Morton's had a tuxedo-clad waiter deliver the meal as the man got off the plane. (Note: McMillan, Graeme. (2011, August 23). Man Uses Twitter to Get Free Morton's Steak Dinner Delivered to Airport. Retrieved August 01, 2017, from http://techland.time.com/2011/08/23/man-uses-twitter-to-get-free-mortons-steak-dinner-delivered-to-airport/) Think of the amount of data that had to be analyzed to make this happen—the amount of information on social media, the number of customers Morton's has served, and the number of meals that have been ordered. This is more than finding a needle in a haystack. It is more like finding a specific pebble in a mountain of gravel.

Systems Approach to Management

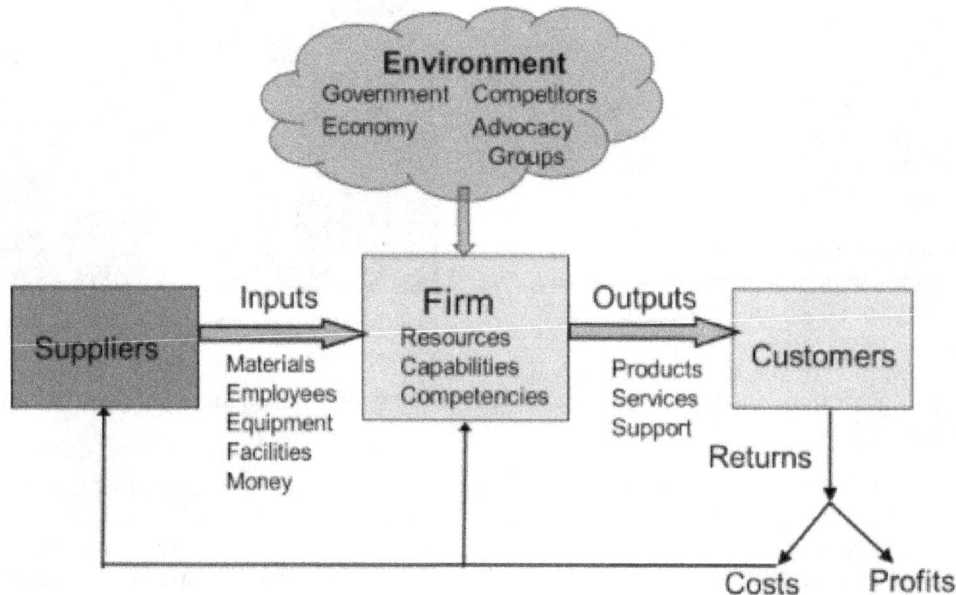

Organizations operate as open systems

A **systems approach** to management recognizes that organizations are open systems that interact with and are dependent on their environment. In a continual process, they obtain necessary inputs, transform the inputs into finished goods and services, and deliver their outputs to the market. The organization gets feedback from the market in two forms. First, it receives revenue. The revenue provides finances to support the organization and to acquire additional inputs needed for production. Revenue can also finance organizational improvements, such as upgraded equipment, development of new or improved products and services, or expansion of facilities. Any revenue that is not reinvested in supporting or improving the organization can be disbursed to owners as dividends.

The second form of feedback is information on how well the organization is doing. Organizations get direct information from customer surveys, customer service complaints, and social media. Starbucks, for example, started a customer blog to get feedback on the customer's experience. Based on the results, it made changes to speed up service even though that increased cost.

The systems approach to management focuses on performance of the whole production process, including the customers' process. The process is usually split by specialties within the company, and each specialist tries to optimize his contribution. But more efficiency for one function may cause delays or bottlenecks elsewhere in the process, hurting overall production. The systems approach analyzes these interactions and makes decisions to improve overall production.

The system model also shows that companies are open to environmental influence. Factors such as political instability, economic conditions, consumer tastes, demographics, legal requirements, and the physical environment all can affect an organization. Successful organizations must be able to detect, understand, and respond effectively to changes in the external environment. These factors are discussed in more detail in the following module.

Contingency Management

Unlike the topics discussed earlier, **contingency management** is not a specific function. It is a general approach to management practice that basically says there is no one best way to manage.

The management theories we discussed earlier had implicit assumptions that management concepts were universal. That is, what worked in one organization would work in others. Certainly some modifications would be made for specific circumstances, but the principles of scientific management and bureaucracy were assumed to apply in any organization. The contingency view rejects this assumption. In contingency management, every situation is considered unique. Managers must adapt theory and practice to match the situation by identifying the key contingencies, or factors, in the situation.

Contingencies might include the industry in which the company operates. For example, an effective organizational structure for an Internet company such as Google would not be the same as a manufacturing company such as General Motors. Another contingency factor is the country in which the company operates. U.S. management methods do not work well in France. The type of employee is also a contingency factor—incentive systems that work for manual laborers do not work for **knowledge workers**. Effective managers need to be able to interpret the contingencies of a situation to determine which approach would be more effective.

Key Points

Conditions are much different now than they were a hundred years ago when many management theories were developed. However, many of the ideas that originated then are still relevant. Rather than abandon years of management experience, managers today need to adapt and modify theory and practice to meet today's conditions. Understanding the historical concepts in management provides a foundation for developing new practices and methods

PUTTING IT TOGETHER: HISTORY OF MANAGEMENT

At the outset of this module, we contrasted Amazon with the great businesses of the past and asked if the management principles developed a century ago are still relevant today. Let's consider that question again in more detail given what you have now learned.

It is estimated that Amazon processes more than six hundred million shipments every year. How important do you think efficiency is to the company's leadership? Consider the time and motion studies developed in the school of scientific management and their applicability to quickly processing orders in one of Amazon's distribution centers. If you are a manager at an Amazon warehouse, it is vital that you measure all aspects of productivity.

The key principles of management are timeless.

Now consider for a moment the scope of Amazon's empire. When most people think of Amazon, they think about the marketplace and the ability to buy almost anything on the company's website. CEO Jeff Bezos, however, often refers to the three pillars of Amazon's business: marketplace, Amazon Web Services (AWS), and the company's Prime membership service. Each of these units is massive in its own right. Additionally, Amazon has more than forty subsidiaries such as Zappos.com, Diapers.com, and Goodreads. (Note: Mac, R. (2016, April 06). Jeff Bezos Calls Amazon 'Best Place

In The World To Fail' In Shareholder Letter. Retrieved August 01, 2017, from https://www.forbes.com/sites/ryanmac/2016/04/05/jeff-bezos-calls-amazon-best-place-in-the-world-to-fail-in-shareholder letter/#509750be7bc5)

With a business that large and diverse, how can leadership possibly maintain control? Think back to what you learned about the bureaucratic school of management and how that might apply to a company like Amazon. In that section, you learned that the four functions of management are planning, organizing, leading, and controlling. These skills are vital to maintaining focus across such a massive organization.

The competition for talent is intense in the global marketplace. With the emergence of social feedback sites such as Glassdoor, no employer can ignore the needs of its employees and remain competitive in the human resource space. Managers at Amazon are not immune to this reality. Your knowledge of the history of humanistic management and its focus on employee conditions has provided you with key insights into effectively managing human capital.

Think of your study of the history of management principles in this module like tools in a toolbox. Every management challenge you face will require a different set of tools to resolve. By understanding the broad spectrum of management theories, you are adding more tools to the box. This will, in turn, make you better equipped to manage the modern business organization.

MODULE 3: PLANNING AND MISSION

WHY IT MATTERS: PLANNING AND MISSION

Why does a business need to define its mission and engage in planning?

Dan Smith is a management consultant with the firm Business Advisors. He's sitting in his office one day when the telephone rings. He picks it up and hears the voice of Tom Wilson, an old high school friend. "Hi Dan. This is Tom Wilson from Southside High. Remember me?" They discuss old times for a few minutes, and then Tom gets down to business.

"Dan, I need your help. I started a business several years ago, and we're in trouble."

Dan quickly searches his memory and recalls that Tom started a business called Sun City Boards several years ago selling high-end surfboards on the West Coast. Last Dan had heard, the business was doing well. "Yeah Tom. I remember when you started your shop, but I thought the business was growing successfully."

Defining the organization's mission and creating a plan to achieve it is the roadmap to success.

Tom replies, "We did well the first couple of years, but things haven't been good for a while now. We're losing money, and I'm not sure how much longer I can keep the doors open."

Dan assures Tom that he is happy to help and asks him to send a few items over to prepare for a trip to visit his operations. "Just send me a copy of your current business plan, financial forecasts, and annual operating budget."

There's a pause on the other end of the line, and then Tom says, "Well, I can send you our bank statements and invoices. We don't have any of the other documents you're asking about."

Based on that response, Dan already has a good idea of the organization's problem: an obvious lack of planning that never bodes well for a business.

In this module, you're going to learn about the importance of an organization establishing a clear vision and mission and how they guide the business planning cycle. The business plan is the roadmap that guides the organization to success.

INTRODUCTION TO MISSION, VISION, AND VALUES

What you'll learn to do: distinguish between mission, vision, and values

You learned earlier that the four main functions of management are planning, organizing, leading, and controlling. Planning is the initial step that guides and informs all the others. It starts with clarity of purpose and goals formalized in the organization's vision, mission, and values statements. These statements are the foundation for all activities in an organization and direct the behaviors of all the people in the organization.

MISSION, VISION, AND VALUES

Learning Outcomes

- Distinguish between mission and vision in business.
- Explain how a values statement can support the goals of an organization.

In September 2007, Countrywide Financial sent a message to all of its employees. The message contained the following statement of its mission:

> Countrywide remains steadfastly committed to our mission of delivering and preserving homeownership.
>
> ~Angelo R. Mozilo, chairman and CEO
>
> ~Dave Sambol, president and COO

However, it seemed that Countrywide was mostly interested in delivering commissions and profits to the company by financing high-risk mortgages to unqualified borrowers. When the housing market collapsed, borrowers defaulted on their high-interest loans and the company fell apart. Countrywide faced a flood of lawsuits charging it had used deceptive practices to entice people into loans they could not afford. Mozilo, the CEO, was charged with insider trading and is now banned from serving as an officer or director of a public company. The company was sold to Bank of America in 2008.

The vision, mission, and values statements guide the behaviors of people in the organization. But when the statements are not supported, people have no guidance. Do you think Mozilo and Sambol supported the stated mission of Countrywide? Do you think people in Countrywide were guided by the mission? If people in the firm were guided by the mission, they could have corrected even the CEO. Then Countrywide might have avoided disaster. Let's explore the roles of the mission, vision, and values statements in an organization.

The Vision Statement

A **vision statement** is a statement of an organization's overarching aspirations of what it hopes to achieve or to become. Here are some examples of vision statements:

- **Disney**: To make people happy
- **IKEA**: To create a better everyday life for the many people
- **British Broadcasting Company (BBC)**: To be the most creative organization in the world
- **Avon**: To be the company that best understands and satisfies the product, service and self-fulfillment needs of women—globally
- **Sony Corporation**: To be a company that inspires and fulfills your curiosity (Note: O'Donovan, K. (2017, April 16). 20 Inspiring Vision Statement Examples (2017 Updated). Retrieved August 01, 2017, from http://www.lifehack.org/articles/work/20-sample-vision-statement-for-the-new-startup.html)

Disney's vision statement is "To make people happy."

The vision statement does not provide specific targets. Notice that each of the above examples could apply to many different organizations. Instead, the vision is a broad description of the value an organization provides. It is a visual image of what the organization is trying to produce or become. It should inspire people and motivate them to want to be part of and contribute to the organization. Vision statements should be clear and concise, usually not longer than a short paragraph.

The Mission Statement

The vision statement and mission statement are often confused, and many companies use the terms interchangeably. However, they each have a different purpose. The vision statement describes where the organization wants to be in the future; the **mission statement** describes what the organization needs to do now to achieve the vision. The vision and mission statements must support each other, but the mission statement is more specific. It defines how the organization will be different from other organizations in its industry. Here are examples of mission statements from successful businesses:

- **Adidas**: We strive to be the global leader in the sporting goods industry with brands built on a passion for sports and a sporting lifestyle.
- **Amazon**: We seek to be Earth's most customer-centric company for four primary customer sets: consumers, sellers, enterprises, and content creators.
- **Google**: To organize the world's information and make it universally accessible and useful
- **Honest Tea**: To create and promote great-tasting, truly healthy, organic beverages
- **Jet Blue Airways**: To provide superior service in every aspect of our customer's air travel experience
- **The New York Times**: To enhance society by creating, collecting and distributing high-quality news and information (Note: 50 Mission Statement Examples from Businesses That Get It Right. (2014, May 12). Retrieved August 01, 2017, from http://yourbrandvox.com/blog/2014/5/12/business-mission-statement-examples)

Notice that each of these examples indicates where the organization will compete (what industry it is in) and how it will compete (what it will do to be different from other organizations). The mission statement conveys to stakeholders why the organization exists. It explains how it creates value for the market or the larger community.

Because it is more specific, the mission statement is more actionable than the vision statement. The mission statement leads to strategic goals. **Strategic goals** are the broad goals the organization will try to achieve. By describing why the organization exists, and where and how it will compete, the mission statement allows leaders to define a coherent set of goals that fit together to support the mission.

The Values Statement

The **values statement**, also called the **code of ethics**, differs from both the vision and mission statements. The vision and mission state where the organization is going (vision) and what it will do to get there (mission). They direct the efforts of people in the organization toward common goals. The values statement defines what the organization believes in and how people in the organization are expected to behave—with each other, with customers and suppliers, and with other stakeholders. It provides a moral direction for the organization that guides decision making and establishes a standard for assessing actions. It also provides a standard for employees to judge violations.

However, managers cannot just create a values statement and expect it to be followed. For a values statement to be effective, it must be reinforced at all levels of the organization and must be used to guide attitudes and actions. Organizations with strong values follow their values even when it may be easier not to. Levi Strauss & Co is an excellent example of a company that is driven by its values.

When Levis Strauss began to source its manufacturing overseas, the company developed a set of principles called the Global Sourcing and Operating Guidelines for overseas operations and suppliers. One of the principles covered the use of child labor:

> Use of child labor is not permissible. Workers can be no less than 15 years of age and not younger than the compulsory age to be in school. We will not utilize partners who use child labor in any of their facilities. We support the development of legitimate workplace apprenticeship programs for the educational benefit of younger people.

Levi Strauss found that one of its contractors was employing children under 15 in a factory in Bangladesh. The easy solution would be to replace those workers, but in Bangladesh, the children's wages may have supported an entire family. And if they lost their jobs, they may have had to resort to begging on the streets. Levi Strauss came up with a different solution, one that supported its values of empathy, originality, integrity, and courage: it paid the children to go to school. Levi Strauss continued to pay salaries and benefits to the children and paid for tuition, books, and supplies. (Note: Case Study: Child Labor in Bangladesh. (n.d.). Retrieved August 1, 2017, from http://www.levistrauss.com/wp-content/uploads/2014/01/Case-Study_Child-Labor-in-Bangladesh.pdf) Even though it would have been easier to just fire the child laborers and consider the problem settled, Levi Strauss was driven by its values to find a better solution.

Together, the vision, mission, and values statements provide direction for everything that happens in an organization. They keep everyone focused on where the organization is going and what it is trying to achieve. And they define the core values of the organization and how people are expected to behave. They are not intended to be a straitjacket that restricts or inhibits initiative and innovation, but they are intended to guide decisions and behaviors to achieve common ends.

Key Points

The vision, mission, and values statements form the foundation for all activities in an organization. The vision statement describes what the organization will become in the future. It is a broad and inspirational statement intended to engender support from stakeholders. The mission statement defines how the organization differentiates itself from other organizations in its industry. It is more specific than the vision statement and is intended to show how stakeholders' needs will be satisfied. The values statement defines how people in the organization should behave. It provides a guideline for decision making.

INTRODUCTION TO PROS AND CONS OF PLANNING

What you'll learn to do: explain the pros and cons of planning

Of the four management functions—planning, organizing, leading, and controlling—planning is usually the first step. It sets the foundation that everything else rests upon. But planning is also controversial. Why make plans when the environment changes so rapidly that plans are likely to be obsolete before they are completed? In this section we will look at planning and why it helps and possibly hinders organizations.

PROS AND CONS OF PLANNING

Learning Outcomes

- Explain benefits of planning.
- Explain the drawbacks of planning.

Planning is the process of setting goals and defining the actions required to achieve the goals.

Planning begins with goals. Goals are derived from the vision and mission statements, but these statements describe what the organization wants to achieve, not necessarily what it can achieve. The organization is affected both by conditions in its external environment—competitors, laws, availability of resources, etc.—and its internal conditions—the skills and experience of its workforce, its equipment and resources, and the abilities of its management. These conditions are examined through a process called a SWOT analysis. (SWOT will be discussed in greater detail in another module.) Together, the vision and mission statements and the results of the situation analysis determine the goals of the organization. This idea is illustrated by the figure that follows.

Achieving business goals starts with planning.

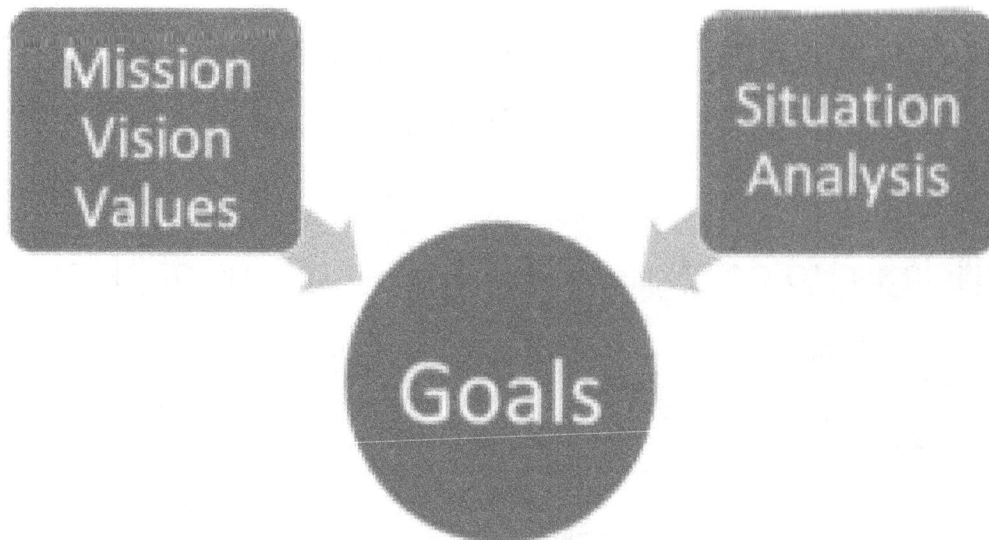

Using the mission, vision, and values of a company, along with situation analysis, can help the company set goals.

The rest of the planning process outlines how the goals are to be met. This includes determining what resources will be needed and how they can be obtained, defining tasks that need to be done, creating a schedule for completing the tasks, and providing milestones to indicate progress toward meeting goals. The planning process will be discussed in more detail in the following section.

Benefits of Planning

In today's chaotic environment, planning more than a few months in advance may seem futile. Progress, however, is rarely made through random activity. Planning does provide benefits that facilitate progress even when faced with uncertainty and a constantly changing environment. Some of the benefits include the following:

- **Planning provides a guide for action.** Plans can direct everyone's actions toward desired outcomes. When actions are coordinated and focused on specific outcomes they are much more effective.
- **Planning improves resource utilization.** Resources are always scarce in organizations, and managers need to make sure the resources they have are used effectively. Planning helps managers determine where resources are most needed so they can be allocated where they will provide the most benefit.
- **Plans provide motivation and commitment.** People are not motivated when they do not have clear goals and do not know what is expected of them. Planning reduces uncertainty and indicates what everyone is expected to accomplish. People are more likely to work toward a goal they know and understand.
- **Plans set performance standards.** Planning defines desired outcomes as well as mileposts to define progress. These provide a standard for assessing when things are progressing and when they need correction.
- **Planning allows flexibility.** Through the goal-setting process, managers identify key resources in the organization as well as critical factors outside the organization that need to be monitored. When changes occur, managers are more likely to detect them and know how to deploy resources to respond.

Drawbacks to Planning

Planning provides clear benefits to organizations, but planning can also harm organizations if is not implemented properly. The following are some drawbacks to planning that can occur:

- **Planning prevents action.** Managers can become so focused on planning and trying to plan for every eventuality that they never get around to implementing the plans. This is called "death by planning." Planning does little good if it does not lead to the other functions.

- Planning leads to complacency. Having a good plan can lead managers to believe they know where the organization is going and how it will get there. This may cause them to fail to monitor the progress of the plan or to detect changes in the environment. As we discussed earlier, planning is not a one-time process. Plans must be continually adjusted as they are implemented.
- Plans prevent flexibility. Although good plans can lead to flexibility, the opposite can also occur. Mid- and lower-level managers may feel that they must follow a plan even when their experience shows it is not working. Instead of reporting problems to upper managers so changes can be made, they will continue to devote time and resources to ineffective actions.
- Plans inhibit creativity. Related to what was said earlier, people in the organization may feel they must carry out the activities defined in the plan. If they feel they will be judged by how well they complete planned tasks, then creativity, initiative, and experimentation will be inhibited. Success often comes from innovation as well as planning, and plans must not prevent creativity in the organization.

Key Points

Goals and plans do not have to be formal documents. In small organizations, they may exist only in the minds of the manager. But research and experience have shown that planning brings clear advantages to an organization, whether through formal procedures or informal intuition. However, when plans become the object instead of a means to an objective, they can have negative consequences for the organization. For example, General Motors missed the opportunity to become the first American automaker to produce an electric car because it was committed to its plan rather than its goals. GM had EV-1 prototypes designed and produced in the 1990s and literally destroyed the cars rather than sell them.

INTRODUCTION TO THE PLANNING CYCLE

What you'll learn to do: explain the stages of the planning cycle

Planning is often viewed as a linear process, with a sequence of steps taken in order. Although this is true, it is also true that at any point in the planning process it may be necessary—because of changing conditions or unexpected results—to go back and change earlier decisions. This section will look at planning with both a sequential and cyclical approach.

THE PLANNING CYCLE

Learning Outcomes

- Explain the stages of the planning cycle.
- Explain why the planning cycle is an essential part of running a business.

Organizations have goals they want to achieve, so they must consider the best way of reaching their goals and must decide the specific steps to be taken. However, this is not a linear, step-by-step process. It is an iterative process with each step reconsidered as more information is gathered. As organizations go through the planning, they may realize that a different approach is better and go back to start again.

Remember that planning is only one of the management functions and that the functions themselves are part of a cycle. Planning, and in fact all of the management functions, is a cycle within a cycle. For most organizations, new goals are continually being made or existing goals get changed, so planning never ends. It is a continuing, iterative process.

In the following discussion, we will look at the steps in the planning cycle as a linear process. But keep in mind that at any point in the process, the planner may go back to an earlier step and start again.

Stages in the Planning Cycle

Define objectives

The first, and most crucial, step in the planning process is to determine what is to be accomplished during the planning period. The vision and mission statements provide long-term, broad guidance on where the organization is going and how it will get there. The planning process should define specific goals and show how the goals support the vision and mission. Goals should be stated in measurable terms where possible. For example, a goal should be "to increase sales by 15 percent in the next quarter" not "increase sales as much as possible."

Develop premises

Planning requires making some assumptions about the future. We know that conditions will change as plans are implemented and managers need to make forecasts about what the changes will be. These include changes in external conditions (laws and regulations,

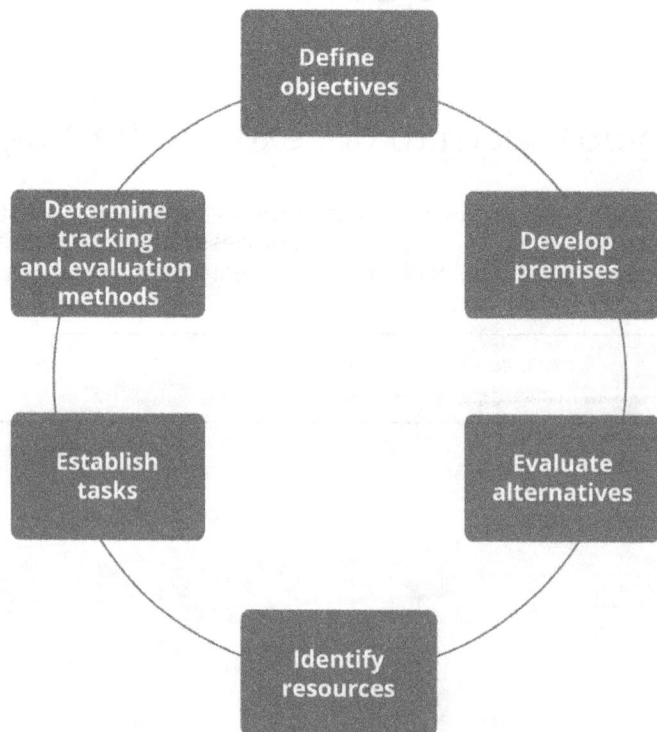

The stages in the planning cycle

competitors' actions, new technology being available) and internal conditions (what the budget will be, the outcome of employee training, a new building being completed). These assumptions are called the plan premises. It is important that these premises be clearly stated at the start of the planning process. Managers need to monitor conditions as the plan is implemented. If the premises are not proven accurate, the plan will likely have to be changed.

Evaluate alternatives

There may be more than one way to achieve a goal. For example, to increase sales by 12 percent, a company could hire more salespeople, lower prices, create a new marketing plan, expand into a new area, or take over a competitor. Managers need to identify possible alternatives and evaluate how difficult it would be to implement each one and how likely each one would lead to success. It is valuable for managers to seek input from different sources when identifying alternatives. Different perspectives can provide different solutions.

Identify resources

Next, managers must determine the resources needed to implement the plan. They must examine the resources the organization currently has, what new resources will be needed, when the resources will be needed, and where they will come from. The resources could include people with particular skills and experience, equipment and machinery, technology, or money. This step needs to be done in conjunction with the previous one, because each alternative requires different resources. Part of the evaluation process is determining the cost and availability of resources.

Plan and implement tasks

Management will next create a road map that takes the organization from where it is to its goal. It will define tasks at different levels in the organizations, the sequence for completing the tasks, and the interdependence of the tasks identified. Techniques such as Gantt charts and critical path planning are often used to help establish and track schedules and priorities.

Determine tracking and evaluation methods

It is very important that managers can track the progress of the plan. The plan should determine which tasks are most critical, which tasks are most likely to encounter problems, and which could cause bottlenecks that could delay the overall plan. Managers can then determine performance and schedule milestones to track progress. Regular monitoring and adjustment as the plan is implemented should be built into the process to assure things stay on track.

The Planning Cycle: Essential Part of Running a Business

Following the planning cycle process assures the essential aspects of running a business are completed. In addition, the planning process itself can have benefits for the organization. The essential activities include the following:

- Maintaining organizational focus: Defining specific goals requires managers to consider the vision, mission, and values of the organization and how these will be operationalized. The methods and selected goals can demonstrate that the vision, mission, and values statements are working documents that are not just for show but prescribe activities.
- Encouraging diverse participation: Planning activities provide an opportunity for input from different functions, departments, and people. Some organizations establish planning committees that intentionally include people from diverse backgrounds to bring new perspectives into the planning process.
- Empowering and motivating employees: When people are involved in developing plans they will be more committed to the plans. Allowing diverse input into the planning cycle empowers people to contribute and motivates them to support the outcomes.

Key Points

There are several stages, or steps, in the planning process. It is not unusual to have to repeat steps as conditions change. This process is essential to a business to maintain focus, gather diverse opinions, and empower and motivate employees.

INTRODUCTION TO TYPES OF PLANS AND COMMON PLANNING TOOLS

What you'll learn to do: list and describe the types of plans and common planning tools

Leo Tolstoy wrote "Happy families are all alike; every unhappy family is unhappy in its own way." The famous author wanted to point out that for a marriage to succeed (be happy), it had to succeed in several key aspects. Organizations are like marriages in this regard. There are key planning tools that every organization must use to ensure success. This section will look closely at these key tools.

TYPES OF PLANS AND COMMON PLANNING TOOLS

Learning Outcomes

- Differentiate between the uses of long-term plans, short-term plans, and operational plans.
- Differentiate between standing plans and single-use plans.
- Explain how policies, procedures, and regulations impact operational plans.
- Explain the role of budgets in the planning process.
- Differentiate between forecasting, scenario planning, and contingency planning.
- Explain the use of "management by objectives" (MBO), SMART goals, and benchmarking in planning.

https://youtu.be/De0HyiqRXIU

Watch the short animated video for a brief overview of the importance of long-term and short-term planning.

Long-term and Short-term Plans

When you decided to attend college, you had a long-term plan in mind. You would spend the next four or five years preparing to become a teacher, a businessperson, or perhaps an ecologist. Or, you may have committed two or three years to become a nurse, a medical technician, or an electrician. Your long-term goal was necessary to make sure that your daily activities would help you achieve your desired outcome. You could have just enrolled in a school and taken classes that looked interesting, but then where would you be in four years? You most likely would not have taken the courses required to qualify you for the job you want. An organization, especially a business, is not so different. It also needs a long-term plan to make sure that the daily activities of its employees are contributing to the mission and value statements of the organization.

A **long-term plan** is crucial to the ultimate success of the organization. A long-term plan for many businesses, such as construction, hospitality, or manufacturing, generally extends four to five years into the future. For other faster-changing industries, especially technology companies, a long-term plan may only look two or three years into the future. After that, it becomes too difficult to predict the future with any degree of certainty.

Top management is responsible for the development of the long-term plan. It is up to the CEO to make sure that changing conditions (both external and internal) are reflected in the organization's long-term plan. The larger and more complex the organization, the larger and more complex the long-term plan will be to include all of the individual departments and functions.

Short-term plans generally allocate resources for a year or less. They may also be referred to as operational plans because they are concerned with daily activities and standard business operations. Like long-term plans, short-term plans must be monitored and updated, and this is the role of middle- and first-level management. Different managerial levels have responsibility for implementing different types of short-term plans. For example, a department manager may be comfortable implementing an operational plan for the entire year for her department. A marketing manager may direct a three- to four-month plan that involves the introduction of a new product line. A team leader may only be comfortable planning and implementing very specific activities over the period of a month.

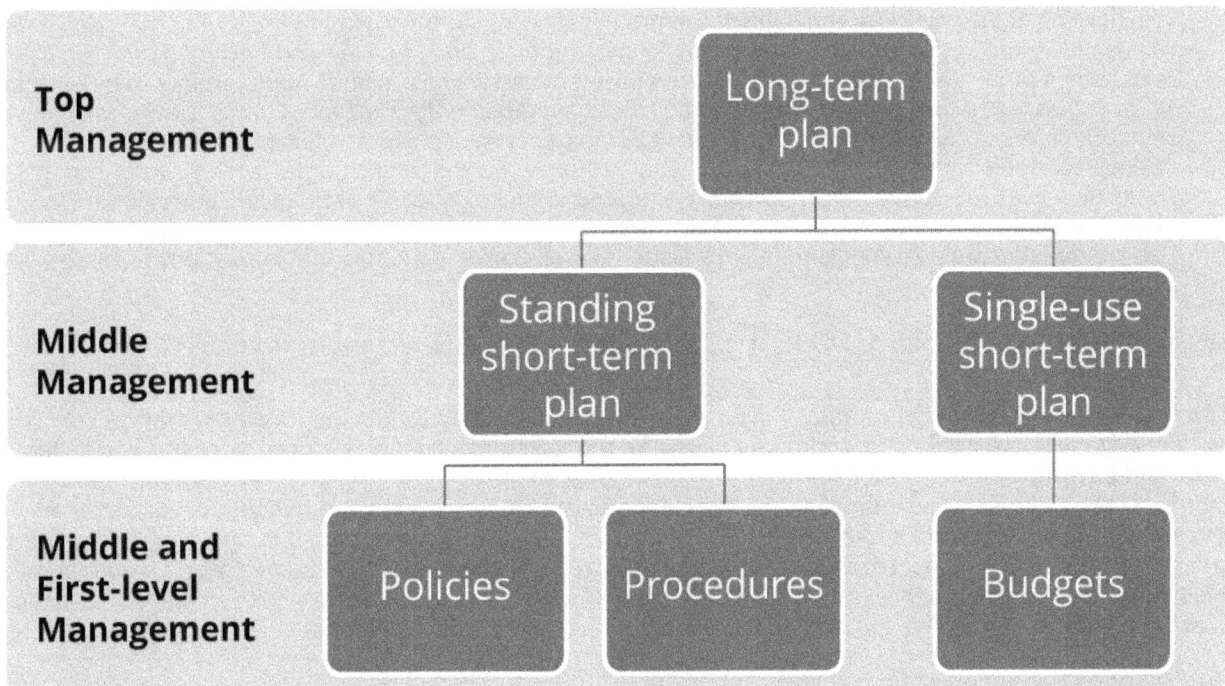

Organizational Plan Hierarchy: The figure above summarizes the relationship between these types of management planning

Operational Plans: Standing Plans and Single-Use Plans

An **operational plan** describes the specific goals and objectives and milestones set by an organization during a specific period. (**Objectives** are specific tasks undertaken to meet broader goals. A goal may be to increase product sales by 3 percent; an objective may be to hire two additional sales agents.) It will allocate the tangible resources (labor, equipment, space) and authorize the financing necessary to meet the objectives of the plan. There are two types of operational plans: standing plans and single-use plans.

- **Standing plans** are plans designed to be used again and again. Examples include policies, procedures, and regulations. The advantage of standing plans is that they foster unity and fairness within an organization and help to support stated organizational values. Managers don't have to make unique decisions already addressed by various organizational policies. Standing plans also save time because managers know in advance how to address common situations. Finally, standing plans aid in the delegation of work, because employees are already familiar with the procedures and regulations followed by the organization.
- **Single-use plans** refer to plans that address a one-time project or event. The length of the plans varies, but the most common types are budgets and project schedules. The obvious advantage of a single-use plan is that it can be very specific in how it addresses the needs of a particular situation.

Policies, Procedures, and Regulations

As stated above, the most common examples of standing use plans are policies, procedures, and regulations. These plans are usually published and handed out to new hires or posted on the organization's employee website for easy reference.

- **Policies** provide broad guidelines for the smooth operation of the organization. They cover things like hiring and firing, performance appraisals, promotions, and discipline. For example, a company may have a policy to encourage recycling in the workplace or a policy that prohibits personal cell phone use in manufacturing areas.
- **Procedures** are steps to be followed in established and repeated operations. Procedures should reflect the policies of the company and support the organization's long-term goals. Procedures may also detail steps that should be followed to ensure employees are disciplined in a fair and unbiased manner. For example, if employees feel that other employees interacted with them in an inappropriate manner, then they should follow the procedure for bringing this to management's attention. Or, the organization may establish procedures for what to do in cases of emergencies, such as a fire or toxic spill.
- **Regulations** refer to what is allowable and what is strictly prohibited in an organization. In other words, a regulation is a kind of rule that addresses general situations. In many hospitals and laboratories, for example, there are safety regulations against wearing open-toed shoes or shoes with slippery soles. State and federal governments frequently issue regulations for industries that impact public safety.

The Role of Budgets in the Planning Process

Refer to the "Organizational Plan Hierarchy" figure earlier and locate the box labeled "Budgets." Notice that budgets are examples of single-use, short-term plans. An organization's budget is a document that details the financial and physical resources allocated to a project or department. They are single-use plans because they are specific to a particular period or event. For example, departments may have a hiring budget that allocates a certain number of positions and a total salary value for a calendar year. Next year, that budget may be the same or it may change, depending upon conditions in the organization. But it cannot be assumed that the budget will stay the same. Zero-based budgets look at each budget as if it were brand new and require managers to justify each of the budgeted items. This process ensures that budgets are closely tied to the latest organizational goals.

Managers deal with a variety of budget types:

- Financial budgets include balance sheets, income/expense statements, and statements of cash flow.
- Operating budgets project revenue against expenditures.
- Nonmonetary budgets allocate resources such as labor, workspace, and equipment use.
- Fixed budgets are budgets that do not change with increased or decreased activities, such as sales revenue. They are also called static budgets.

- Flexible budgets will vary with the level of activity (grow or be reduced according to changing conditions).

Budgets are a very important planning tool, and organizations take their budgeting process very seriously. Some managers spend most of their time making sure that the expenses and projects they control do not exceed authorized spending limits. To routinely "go over budget" is a sign of a poor planning—and planning is one of the basic management functions. In some cases, to routinely come in under budget is also viewed negatively, because with more accurate budgeting those committed resources could have been allocated to other projects. Often, projects compete for limited resources so the best budget is the one that most closely projects actual expenses and revenue.

Forecasting, Scenario Planning, and Contingency Planning

Forecasting is simply making a prediction about the future. Anyone can make a forecast—the trick is to be right or close enough so that important planning decisions can be based on the forecast. Some "botched" forecasts by business leaders follow:

"This telephone has too many shortcomings to be seriously considered as a means of communication." – President of Western Union, 1876

"There is a world market for maybe five computers." – Chairman of IBM, 1943

"Television won't be able to hold on to any market it captures after the first six months. People will soon get tired of staring at a plywood box every night." – Darryl Zanuck, president of 20th Century Fox, 1946

"There is no chance that the iPhone is going to get any significant market share." – Microsoft CEO Steve Ballmer, 2012

Scientific forecasting is using mathematical models, historical data, and statistical analysis to make predictions about what will happen in the future. Businesses use **short-term forecasting** all the time when creating budgets and anticipating expenses. Mostly, these forecasts are based on what they sold and what they paid providers in the recent past. **Long-range forecasting** requires both quantitative numerical data and qualitative data based on expert opinions and insights. Often, organizations will create a number of long-range forecasts based on "best-case" and "worst-case" scenarios. They will then make plans on how they would respond to each situation and, as time goes on, they will update and adapt the long-term plan.

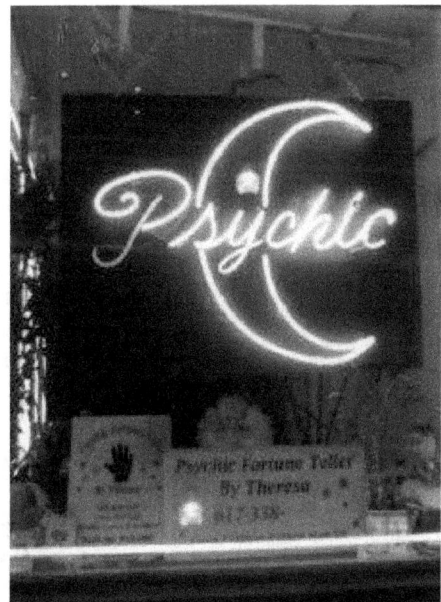

One other important type of planning is the **contingency plan**. A contingency plan describes what will happen in a possible—but not expected—situation. Usually, contingency plans are designed to handle emergency situations. For example, airports have contingency plans for plane crashes on takeoffs or landings, and popular tourist attractions have begun developing contingency plans in case of terrorist threats.

An example of the critical importance of contingency planning involves the Deepwater Horizon oil spill in the Gulf of Mexico in 2010. Eleven people lost their lives and seventeen were badly injured when an explosion on an oil rig released almost five million barrels of oil into the Gulf of Mexico. It was the worst marine oil spill in history, and its effects

There are actually much better ways to predict the future than resorting to fortunetellers.

were even more devastating because BP Oil did not have contingency plans in place for that kind of disaster. The spill went on for months while BP and its partners tried to figure out how to shut off the oil's source. Even though BP spent $62 billion on the response and cleanup activities, there was extensive damage to marine and wildlife habitats and fishing and tourism industries. Getting employees involved in planning may help prevent tragedies similar to this one.

Management By Objectives (MBO) and SMART Goals

Management by objectives, or MBO for short, is a tool that can be used to improve the performance of an organization by creating clearly defined objectives agreed upon by management and by the employees. Peter Drucker, a prolific author and a leader in management theory, coined the phrase "management by objectives" in 1954. The intent of MBO is to improve employee motivation and organizational communication by focusing on aligning individual goals to corporate objectives. In MBO, a manager and an employee do the following:

- jointly set goals and objectives for a period.
- together plan tasks that the employee performs with the support of management.
- agree on the standards for evaluating performance of the task.
- regularly meet to review progress.

MBO must be a top-down management tool, because organizational goals are cascaded down to create the various operational levels. Drucker showed that as long as employee goals support short-term and long-term organizational objectives, MBO will help move the company forward. Critics, however, charge that managers using the approach focus more on creating goals than on helping the employee achieve them.

SMART goals are a technique often paired with MBO. SMART stands for specific, measurable, achievable, realistic, and time-bound. The SMART goal paired well with MBO theory by

1. Providing incentives to employees by rewarding them when they meet key goals.
2. Empowering employees by allowing them to set their own objectives for achieving their individual goal.
3. Communicating honestly about what went well and what did not, and focusing on developing the missing skills.

The chart that follows summarizes the most important characteristics of each part of a SMART goal.

SMART GOAL CRITERIA	
SPECIFIC	Objectives must be specific enough to avoid confusion. They should identify what the objective is in terms of action to be done.
MEASURABLE	The objective should be numerical and quantifiable. Avoid term such as some, most, many, and enough.
ACHIEVABLE	An objective should be able to be met with reasonable effort. They should not be the source of undue physical or emotional stress.
RELEVANT	The objective should contribute in some way to the success of the organization as well as the development of the employee.
TIME-BOUND	Objectives should come with firm dates—not "soon" or "in a timely manner."

For example, let's say you set a goal to become a recognized department expert in a subject relevant to advancement within the organization. How could you turn this into a SMART goal?

- **Specific:** I will learn about the liabilities of six major nonprofit organizations.
- **Measurable:** I will make presentations to the advertising, grant writing, and donor/client committees.
- **Achievable:** I will interview one nonprofit organization every week for six weeks.
- **Relevant:** This expertise will fill a current knowledge gap in the new client department.
- **Time-bound:** I will fulfill this goal before my next scheduled annual performance evaluation.

Benchmarking

The last planning tool we'll discuss in this section is benchmarking. You may think that your organization has an excellent long-term plan and effective short-term plans, but how do you really know? Even if your company is showing growth, is it growing as fast as your competitor? A benchmark is a standard used for comparison purposes. **Benchmarking** is looking at performance levels outside of your organization, or sometimes across departments or divisions inside your organization, to evaluate your own performance. You can benchmark using several different criteria:

- **Industry**: Let's say you produce technology widgets. Benchmarking can answer questions about how your company is doing in comparison to other tech widget makers. This approach is a type of competitive benchmarking.
- **Geography**: Your state is showing a lot of economic growth. You can use benchmarking to determine if your company is sharing in that wealth or underperforming compared to the regional economy.
- **Organization**: You are a small business owner. Benchmarking can help answer questions about whether the economic climate is friendlier to big business than it is to small business, or whether nonprofits are failing whereas for-profits are succeeding.
- **Processes**: You can use benchmarking to determine what processes other firms are using that are helping or hurting them. Are there lessons to be learned from them? This is also called strategic benchmarking or process benchmarking.
- **Innovation**: Benchmarking can help you discover what partners or techniques your competitors are using that are missing in your organization. Are there functions in your products or programs that should be eliminated and others that could be added? Functional benchmarking is key in technology-related organizations.

Internal benchmarking means comparing a department's performance with another department in your company or branch within the same larger organization. The important thing about benchmarking is that it gives you a standard against which to compare your progress.

Key Points

Planning tools are designed to help you determine goals, guide behaviors within the organization, and help you evaluate your performance against external benchmarks. Plans are essential, but good managers know to be flexible when conditions demand.

PUTTING IT TOGETHER: PLANNING AND MISSION

If you don't know where you're going, any road will get you there.

Let's return our attention to Sun City Boards and its owner, Tom Wilson. Dan travelled to Tom's operations on the West Coast and confirmed his suspicions that the problems the organization is facing are due to a lack of planning. Dan is meeting with Tom to report on his findings and to submit his recommendations.

"OK Tom, I've spent the last several days going through your operations and records, and I'm confident that there are actions you can take that will help turn around the business."

Tom lets out a long sigh and says, "Dan, you have no idea how glad I am to hear that. So at a high level, what's the problem?"

"In a nutshell, the problem with Sun City Boards is that you have lost your focus and there is no clear plan for moving forward." Tom looks confused, so Dan explains. "When you started the business, what was your vision?"

Tom answers, "To set people free from the earth … free to ride the waves."

"Perfect!" Dan responds. "And how were you going to do that?"

Tom thinks for a moment and then emphatically declares, "We will strive to provide the absolute best in high-end surfboard design and production!"

Dan tells Tom that he has just created the vision and mission statements for Sun City Boards. He further explains, "You have to start creating a focused plan that will help the organization deliver on its vision and mission. The reason your company is struggling is that there is no clear roadmap to success."

Tom asks, "What do you mean?"

Dan continues, "When you started the company you were very successful because you focused on one key thing—making the best surfboards anyone had seen. As a result, everything your business did revolved around that core idea."

Tom interrupts, "OK Dan, I think I see where you're headed. When we started making money in the early days, I began to start expanding into other areas without a lot of thought. I listened to salespeople who came in and told me that I should branch out into low-end surf gear, then swimwear, then camping gear. Customers don't know what we're all about any more. And neither do my managers and employees."

Dan can see Tom is getting his arms around the concept of vision and mission, so he moves on. Next, he presents his recommendation that Tom and his key leaders should come together regularly to create, review and update Sun City's business plan. This is new to the team, so he gives them a quick example:

1. **Define Objectives**: Sun City Boards should look to reduce noncore product lines and associated inventory. Minimum margin target is 35 percent across all remaining product lines.
2. **Develop Premises**: Monitor competitor's plans to implement a new polymer board and determine potential impact to Sun City's sales.
3. **Evaluate Alternatives**: Evaluate opportunity of opening new retail outlets along the West Coast. Also, explore international sales options for high-end surf boards.
4. **Identify Resources**: Analyze the level of capital necessary to achieve expansion goals and incorporate plan to close financial gaps in the annual budget.
5. **Plan and Implement Tasks**: Create a Gantt chart or other project planning tool that outlines the actions necessary to reach the goals outlined earlier.
6. **Determine Tracking and Evaluation Methods**: Create SMART goals for both managers and employees that align with direction the overall business plan provides.

Finally, Dan reminds Tom that the planning process is only a tool and that the plan should be regularly reviewed and updated. Dan warns him that planning is no substitute for taking action, but it is a guide for him and his team as to what actions should be taken.

This consulting project has reminded Dan how important it is for an organization to have a clear vision and mission to know where it's headed. Likewise, the planning process is critical to know how it's going to get there. The alternative is like trying to take a cross-country trip without a map—you don't know where you might end up!

MODULE 4: ENVIRONMENTS AND STRATEGIC MANAGEMENT

WHY IT MATTERS: ENVIRONMENTS AND STRATEGIC MANAGEMENT

Why does a business need to understand the environment and strategy?

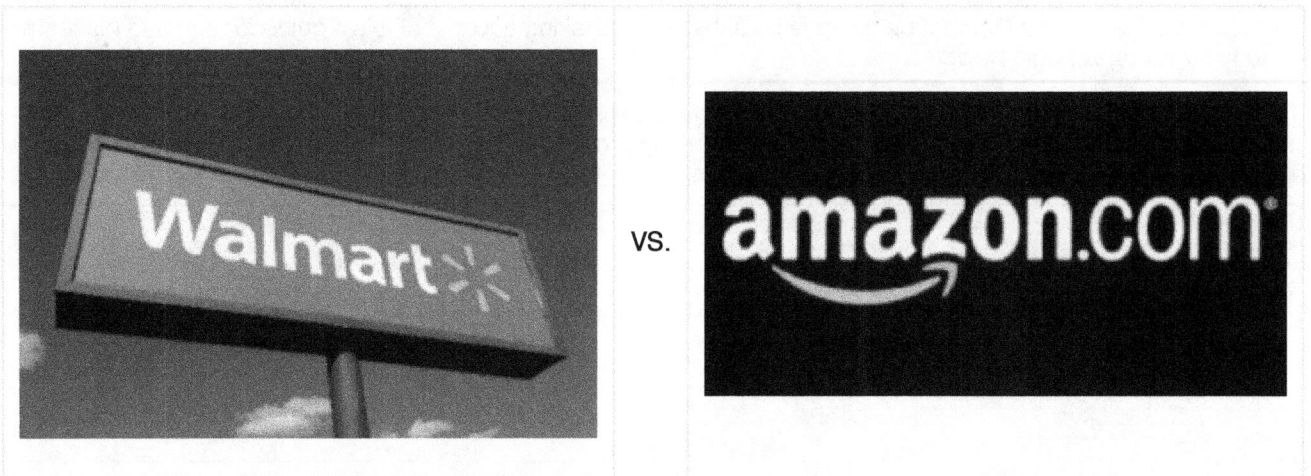

Walmart VS. amazon.com

Imagine you've been working in the business world for a number of years and you have just been promoted to your dream job as head of North American operations for Walmart. As you're settling into your new office, your boss, the CEO, drops by unexpectedly. He sits down and says, "I'm excited to have you in this new role, and I know you're going to do fantastic." Then he pauses briefly and continues, "Now tell me—what are you going to do about Amazon?"

You knew this question was going to come, but you weren't expecting it before you had even unpacked. This is the question on everyone's mind: how are you going to handle the competitive threat posed by Amazon? Stated another way, given the current political, social, and competitive environments, what is your strategy to succeed?

In this module, you will learn about the importance of crafting a well-thought-out strategy in order to be successful in business. You will learn techniques to assess the environments in which your organization operates and how to maneuver within them to achieve a favorable outcome.

INTRODUCTION TO THE ROLE OF STRATEGY IN MANAGEMENT

What you'll learn to do: explain the role of strategy in management

Strategy defines how a firm will achieve long-term success. Why do customers consistently choose to buy one product or service over another? Strategy helps us understand why some companies succeed and others fail. Strategic management is the process of integrating all the functions and activities in an organization into a coherent whole.

THE ROLE OF STRATEGY IN MANAGEMENT

Learning Outcomes

- Explain the concept of competitive advantage.
- Explain the concept of value proposition.
- Explain how strategy relates to the overall management of a business.

Introduction

Businesses do not exist in isolation. They exist as one element of a complex situation that comprises the social, political, economic, and competitive environment. A firm's **strategy** is a comprehensive plan to achieve its goals in the face of these conditions. Strategy defines how a firm will achieve long-term success. Determining the strategy is a critical decision for management because it involves a significant commitment of resources and, once initiated, it is very difficult and costly to change.

In the movie *The Godfather II*, Michael Corleone says: "My father taught me many things. He taught me: keep your friends close, but your enemies closer." This applies in strategy, as well. A company's friends are its customers. Strategy must keep the company aligned with its customers' needs. Its enemies are its competitors. **Competitors** are firms that provide similar products or services and try to attract the same customers. Competitors are likely to have similar business goals in terms of sales, profitability, and market share. To succeed and achieve its goals, a firm has to "beat" its competitors by constantly striving to improve its offerings to customers and to be better than the competitors' alternatives. In this section we look at how companies address competitors in their strategy.

Competitive Advantage

In a competitive environment, businesses try to stand out from their competitors. Consider the following car companies. Is there a particular characteristic or quality that you associate with each of them?

- Porsche
- Volvo
- Hyundai
- Toyota
- Ford

Companies try very hard to create a perception that they are different from their competitors. If you are looking for a high-performance sports car you probably won't go to a Ford dealer. But if you are looking for a durable truck you wouldn't go to a Porsche dealer. Companies strive to provide a product or service that is distinct, or **differentiated**, in some way from their competitors. When customers perceive the distinction as being valuable, they will prefer to purchase the business's product over a competitor's products. This is called a **competitive advantage**. Competitive advantage means that the business outperforms its rivals in the market because customers prefer its products or services.

Businesses can achieve competitive advantages in a number of different ways. Their product may provide superior performance; it may be of higher quality; it may be more durable; or it may have unique features. The businesses may provide better customer service or have better availability. They may advertise and promote their products better, or they may offer their products at a lower price. The best businesses provide a combination of unique attributes that competitors cannot match.

Creating Competitive Advantage

Businesses create competitive advantage by doing some things better than their competitors. For example, look at the companies in the chart that follows. By doing some things much better than competitors, the businesses are able to create a valuable distinction for customers.

Company	How Company Creates Distinction
Apple	Research and development: creates new or improved products with leading-edge technology
Nike	Marketing: uses celebrity endorsements to create a powerful brand image
Walmart	Supply chain management: created a highly integrated system to keep supplier costs low and keep products that customers buy on the shelf
Zappos	Customer service: strives to deliver "Wow!" in the customer's experience
UPS	Logistics: integrates package delivery with customer needs
Zara	Rapid responsiveness: quickly gets the latest styles into stores

It may seem that the best way to create competitive advantage is to do *everything* well. Unfortunately, this is not possible. Generally, resources are limited and it would be much too costly to try to excel at everything. Businesses that try to do too many things well often don't succeed at doing anything extremely well and don't produce distinction. This is referred to as being "stuck in the middle."

Creating competitive advantage is not the only goal of business. Companies also must be able to maintain their competitive advantage. When competitors see a company is doing something that customers value, they will try to copy it. Some things can be copied quickly. For example, when American Airlines introduced the AAdvantage frequent flier program to reward loyal customers, it was copied within months by Delta, United, and British Airways. Other things are more difficult to copy. Walmart, for example, has created a tightly linked supply chain to provide low costs. No other company has figured out how to duplicate this system. The goal of companies is to create competitive advantage in ways that are difficult or costly for competitors to copy. This is called a **sustainable competitive advantage.**

Strategy and Competitive Advantage

Achieving competitive advantage is not likely to be a formal goal of a business. However, having competitive advantage means a company will have resources to pursue its goals. When firms beat their competitors it means they can finance more research and development to improve their products or services; they can spend more on advertising and promotions to attract customers; they can donate to charities to improve community relations; and they can provide greater profits to their owners. In short, competitive advantage is the *means* to meeting organizational goals.

Walmart's supply chain helps to keep its prices low, giving it a competitive advantage over others.

Because strategy is a plan to achieve long-term goals, we can define strategy as a plan to create sustainable competitive advantage.

The Value Proposition

Companies strive to produce a unique product or service that will give them an advantage in the market place. But this produces competitive advantage only if customers perceive the difference and understand why this difference matters to them. A **value proposition** is a statement that a company uses to convince customers that its product or service provides more value to them than a competitor's product or service. The value proposition communicates to the customer the main reason a product or service is the one best suited to their needs.

The value proposition is communicated through a company's webpage, advertising, or social media. It should have a bold headline or graphic that grabs attention and depicts the benefits delivered to the customer. This brief "announcement" can be followed by a short paragraph or a few bullet points that list the key features of the product.

An excellent example is the value statement for the Apple MacBook. It shows an edge-on image of a MacBook with the caption "**MacBook**: Light. Years ahead." This very cleverly conveys the important distinctions of the MacBook. First, it's a really slick design. In the edge-on view the computer almost disappears. Second, it is light. In the laptop market, weight is important. Both the image and the statement emphasize that the MacBook is easy to carry around. Finally, it emphasizes MacBook's advanced technology, "Light years ahead." In a very small space, Apple conveys the main differentiators for the MacBook—its weight and its advanced technology.

Strategic Management

Strategic management is the process of integrating all the functions and activities in an organization into a coherent whole. We previously defined management as the process of planning, organizing, leading, and controlling people in the organization to effectively use resources to meet organizational goals. Strategy management provides the "glue" that holds these processes together. Rather than looking at individual functions or activities, strategic management considers the entire organization and how the pieces fit together. Good strategic management allows an organization to develop **synergy**. That is, the pieces support each other so that the total output is greater than the sum of the output of individual functions.

Strategic management best fits with the planning function, and it involves two broad functions. The first is to determine how the company will create competitive advantage. That is, how will the company produce distinction and value to its customers? The answer to this question is the company's **business strategy**. Management must make sure that all activities in the company support its business strategy. This is called "doing the right things." It means everyone must be focused on excelling at the things that create competitive advantage, making sure that resources are allocated to the departments that create competitive advantage, and closely controlling the activities that create competitive advantage. That doesn't mean they can ignore other things; successful businesses have to do many things well but excel at only a few.

Strategic management's second function is to make sure that the people in the organization support the strategy. As we discussed previously, almost everything an organization accomplishes is achieved by people doing things. Management must make sure that the people in the organization are willing and capable of excelling at the things that create competitive advantage. This is called "doing things right." They can do this by providing training and development opportunities for employees to improve skills that support the strategy, by creating a compensation system that rewards behaviors that support the strategy, and by implementing a supervisory system that encourages and recognizes behaviors that support the strategy. Management can also instill a **culture of excellence** throughout the organization. **Organizational culture** is the shared values and beliefs that guide individual behaviors in the organization. Managers can induce a culture that supports the strategy by communicating and modeling behaviors and values they want to see throughout the organization.

For example, when Tom's of Maine introduced a new deodorant that disappointed customers, company founder Tom Chappell pulled the product from the market and reimbursed the customers who had purchased it. The company lost the money it had put into developing and producing the product, as well as the reimbursement cost. But it reinforced the core values of fairness and honesty that the company espoused, and demonstrated that quality and customer satisfaction were the company's competitive advantage.

In another example, Southwest Airlines' management implemented the "Walk a Mile" program in which managers and executives pitch in to help front-line employees. Executives clean planes, load luggage, and attend gates. Flight attendants were surprised when Herb Kelleher, the company chairman, showed up to help them provision a plane. This program reinforces the family culture at Southwest, where everyone is valued and considered equal. It also emphasizes the company's focus on customer service by demonstrating that everyone has to support activities that directly affect the customer.

Industry Analysis

The purpose of strategic management is to create competitive advantage. But how do companies know they have competitive advantage? In the long term, competitive advantage will lead to greater profitability. But in the shorter term, it is difficult for companies to assess how well they are creating competitive advantage. An **industry analysis** is a method for a company to assess its market position relative to its competitors. An industry analysis is meant to help a company review various market and financial factors in its industry that affect the business, including evaluating the competition. This analysis helps managers understand the important factors of the marketplace and how these factors may be used to gain a competitive advantage. Industry analyses are an important tool for companies to assess their strategy in a shorter time frame.

Because conditions in the business environment are constantly changing, industry analyses need to be done periodically to keep up with developments. This can be a very time-consuming process and, if not done accurately, can lead to bad strategic decisions. For this reason, managers may go to outside firms, either to produce the analysis or to provide data for the company to complete an analysis. A number of companies exist that maintain huge databases of information about particular industries, such as Hoovers and IBIS. These companies have methods for gathering the data and for analyzing the data to produce reports.

INTRODUCTION TO COMMON FRAMEWORKS FOR EVALUATING THE BUSINESS ENVIRONMENT

What you'll learn to do: describe common frameworks used to evaluate the business environment

To set goals, businesses analyze what's going on in the external environment as well as what's happening inside the organization. Frameworks for completing the external analysis help managers process large amounts of data in a rational way. Two widely used management tools are introduced in this section that explain why sound business strategy relies on finding the best possible information.

COMMON FRAMEWORKS FOR EVALUATING THE BUSINESS ENVIRONMENT

Learning Outcomes

- Explain environmental scanning and the PESTEL checklist for a company's general environment.
- Explain the impact of Porter's "five forces" on industry profits.
- Explain competitor analysis.

Introduction

The environment is always changing, and this is just as true for the business environment as it is for the physical world around us. Managers try to avoid being "taken by surprise" by unexpected events that would impact their organizations through an ongoing process called **environmental scanning**. Environmental scanning is a high-level, broad-based process of gathering, analyzing, and dispensing information for purpose of developing strategies or tactics. The process entails getting both factual data and qualitative opinions. Organizations also scan when they are considering whether to enter a particular industry.

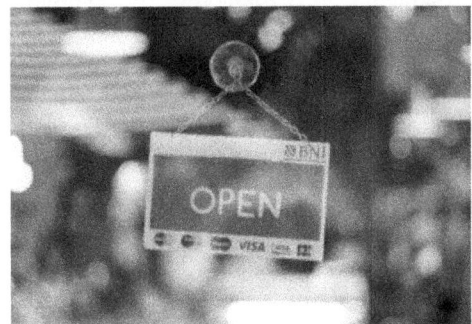

Starting a new business without evaluating the competitive environment is risky, indeed.

PESTEL

You may wonder just how you go about analyzing the total external environment that would affect your company. A commonly used management tool is called PESTEL. PESTEL is an organizing framework that allows decision makers to understand and make connections with a mass of information. (You may sometimes see the name of this tool written as PESTLE or even just PEST in older sources.)

A PESTEL analysis examines six key macro-environmental factors in order to understand their interactions with the organization.

Besides alerting top management to potential threats in the environment, a PESTEL analysis is a part of the external strategic analysis when conducting research into new markets. It gives an overview of the different macro-environmental factors that the company has to take into consideration. Descriptions of the six key PESTEL factors follow.

Political

Political issues are a function of how much the government intrudes or is involved in an organization's operations. In particular, it looks at taxation and tariffs, regulations, political stability, and elections. For example, Google and other Internet providers have financial, legal, and ethical issues relating to operating in countries like China or Iran, where repressive governments want to control the flow of information. In another example, Google was slapped with a $2.7 billion fine by the European Union for

Political

Economical

Social

Technological

Environmental

Legal

P E S T E L

The PESTEL framework organizes information gathered from environmental scans.

antitrust abuses (Google can appeal this decision with the European Court of Justice). Finally, the CEO of Apple is awaiting changes in the tax law before bringing almost $250 billion in foreign reserves back to the United States. Often, decision makers for these organizations must choose between making money or suppressing information critical of the repressive regimes.

Economic

Economic factors start with indicators for the U.S. economy as a whole. These are growth, employment, inflation, and interest rates. Companies with foreign operations will worry about exchange rates. These factors are important in long-range forecasts for revenue and expenses. Businesses in the financial industry may pull back from aggressive strategies in times of rising interest rates.

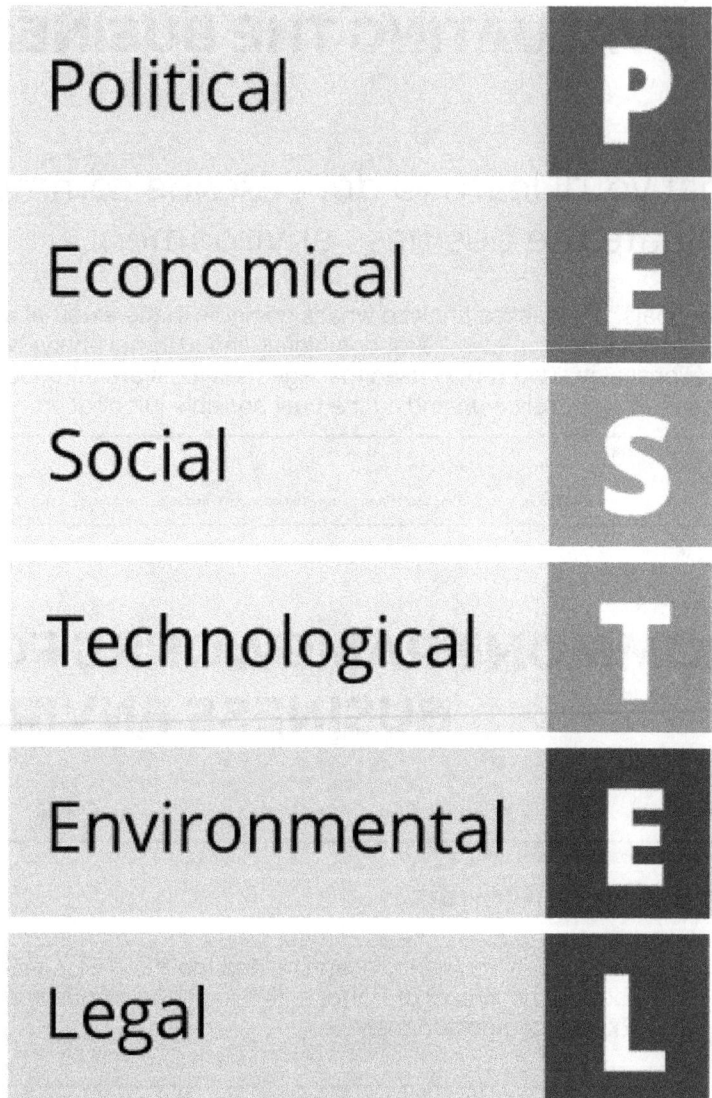

Social

Society and culture have great impacts on the business environment. These factors include demographics like population growth, age distribution, and attitudes toward safety and health consciousness. For example, rising rates of obesity have forced management to look closely at marketing campaigns in giant food corporations such as Nestle and Kraft Foods.

Technological

Technology facts include research and development (R&D), automation and robotics, and technology incentives. The rate of technological change in the business environment is staggering. A term often paired with technology is *disruption*, a description for innovations that completely change the cast of leading competitors in an industry. Many organizations not only scan the technological environment but also monitor closely for new and disruptive processes. Walt Disney and Alphabet (Google's parent corporation) are both investing heavily to become leaders in virtual reality. They are betting billions that augmented reality will have the power to disrupt the gaming and entertainment industries.

Environmental

Weather, climate change, air quality, and natural disasters are all environmental factors. Some industries are especially at risk from changes in the natural environment, including manufacturing, agriculture, tourism and travel, and sports and entertainment. Many pollution regulations limiting water and air pollution have been passed that affect the operation of businesses. Today, the impact of climate control is being debated in Congress, and organizations in many industries are concerned how this latest environmental threat will affect their operations. Recently, Shell Oil spent more than $7 billion exploring parts of the Arctic Circle for oil—a venture that was not possible before global warming increased drilling access in the area. They have since cancelled this initiative due to a lack of results, as well as strong international protests that it may cause further damage to an environmentally sensitive location.

Legal

Legal factors include discrimination laws, consumer protection laws, and employment, health, and safety policies. Antitrust, piracy and copyright laws, as well as immigration issues are also of growing importance in the business environment. All of these factors affect how organizations operate, their costs, and the demand for products. For example, after the collapse of Enron, the government passed the Sarbanes-Oxley Act in 2002. This legislation completely changed accounting and reporting requirements for corporations. These businesses have had to implement rigorous procedures to ensure compliance with the new regulations. After the Great Recession of 2008–2009, Congress passed the Dodd-Frank Act, which greatly increased regulations and oversight for banks and other financial firms. Bank lobbyists successfully slowed the implementation of many rules, but compliance costs doubled and totaled $70 billion in 2016.

Porter's Five Forces

Michael Porter, a well-known business consultant and professor at Harvard University, identified five critical external factors that affect strategies being developed by organizations in any industry. This system, known as **Porter's Five Forces**, has become an important management strategy tool. Managers use the tool to examine opportunities and threats and to facilitate decision making in the context of their company's external environment. It measures the competitiveness of an industry and thus its *attractiveness* or potential profitability. An *unattractive* industry is one in which the combination of these five forces acts to drive down overall profitability.

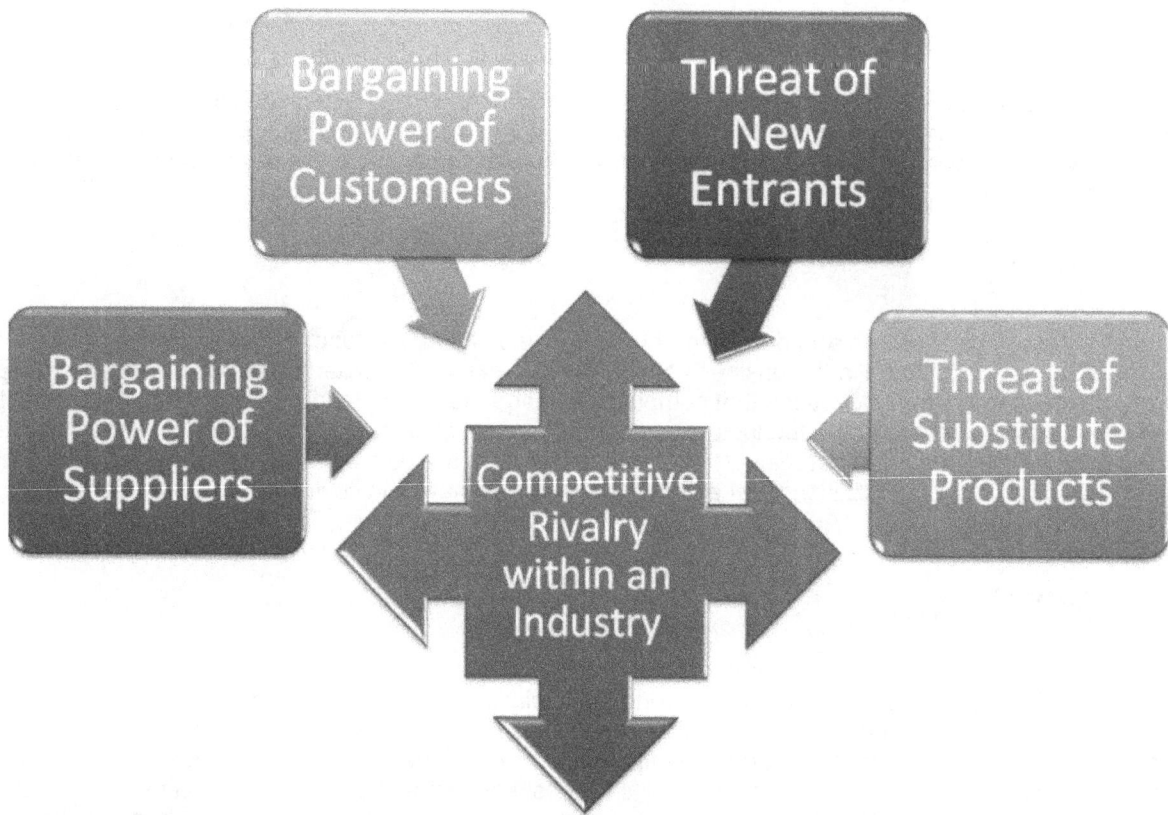

The five forces defined by Porter include:

- The **threat of new entrants (or barriers to entry)**. This refers to the threat that new competitors pose to the existing businesses in an industry. A profitable industry will attract new competitors. If it is easy for new businesses to enter the industry, then the businesses already operating in the industry are at a greater risk. There may be a high threat of new entrants to an industry when brand names are not well-known, when it is easy for customers to switch to a new supplier, and when trademarks or copyrights are not involved in the production process. For example, it would be very hard to enter an industry such as airlines, which requires a huge financial investment to pay for equipment, personnel, and airport gateways.
- The **threat of substitute products or services**. A substitute product is not a similar product from a competitor, but rather a different product or service altogether but that performs the same purpose in the mind of the consumer. For example, a city subway system could be a substitute product to an automobile manufacturer. Likewise, e-mails may substitute for writing letters, olive oil may be a butter substitute, and tea may substitute for coffee. If there are good substitutes to a product, the industry is less profitable.
- **Competitive rivalry within the industry**. Porter believes that the intensity or the level of competition in an industry is one of the main forces that determines the profitability of that industry. A highly competitive market suggests that the competitors are aggressively trying to take market share from their rivals. Intensity can be affected by the number of competitors, the size of the market, the growth of the industry, and how difficult it is to differentiate your product (make it unique in some major feature). The airline and automotive industries are examples of high rivalry industries.
- The **bargaining power of buyers**. Buyer bargaining power refers to the amount of pressure customers can put on a seller. The buyer wants to lower prices, increase service, or improve the quality of the product. From the viewpoint of the seller, an industry where the buyer has high bargaining power is not particularly attractive because competitors will have many possible strategies for easily taking the customer away. High buying bargaining power decreases potential profits if the seller responds to the buyers' tactics. Remember that the buyer is not always a consumer; many businesses sell to other businesses who also have buyer bargaining power. A company like Walmart has a lot of buyer bargaining power because of the extremely high volume of its purchases.
- The **bargaining power of suppliers**. Supplier bargaining power is another force that shapes the competitive measure of an industry because it limits the ability of the seller to make a profit. Powerful

suppliers can pressure buyers by raising prices, lowering quality, or reducing the availability of the supply.

An important thing to remember about Porter's Five Forces is that it is useful at an industry level and not for groups or segments of a market. It is also a "snapshot" of what the industry looks like at a particular time and needs to be updated regularly. And as with any management tool, it is not perfect and infallible. When considered as a starting point for discussion and further investigation, however, Porter's Five Forces is very useful.

Competitive Analysis

Earlier in this module, you read about the concept of competitive advantage. You learned that knowing the strengths and weaknesses of your competitors are key elements in devising organizational goals and determining strategies to meet the goals.

Once the external business environment has been analyzed for its suitability, industry competitors must be profiled to determine who your specific competitors are. Not all "players" in an industry will be in direct competition with your organization. (You don't want to spend valuable resources on an in-depth competitive analysis of BMW and Mercedes if you sell Hyundais.) A robust competitive analysis will allow you to focus on those companies that will compete for customers in your target market.

A competitive analysis looks at competitors and tries to answer such questions as these in the following categories:

- **General Background**: Who are my competitors? Where are they located? Who are the key personalities? What type of organizational structure is it?
- **Financial**: How profitable are they? Have they grown in the recent past? And any other data you can ethically discover.
- **Products**: What products do they sell? Have they introduced new products and what is their success rate? What brands do they carry? Do they hold patents and licenses?
- **Customers**: What market segment do they serve? What is the customer growth rate? How strong is the customer loyalty?
- **Advertising and Sales**: What are their distribution channels? What is their promotional strategy? How large is their sales force? What is their pricing and discount structure?
- **Personnel**: How many employees do they have? What is their compensation package including benefits? What kind of managers and what management style do they show? More importantly, what skills is the competition hiring? If a company is hiring experts in artificial intelligence, it tells the competition quite a bit about the plans for the future.

There are many more questions that would be relevant to this kind of in-depth analysis. The more you know about your competition, the better prepared you will be when you go up against it. The next section will identify industry components that affect your ability to operate. It will introduce tools that allow organizations to focus on only the specific internal and external features that affect them.

INTRODUCTION TO COMMON FRAMEWORKS FOR SITUATIONAL ANALYSIS

What you'll learn to do: describe common frameworks used for situational analysis

Generally, the more data you have on a topic, the better informed a decision on that topic will be. Identifying the most important components focuses the research effort. Organizing information so that it can be used to make valid comparisons is one of the roles of management. Finally, analyzing your resource assets will guide you in creating a sustainable competitive advantage.

COMMON FRAMEWORKS FOR SITUATIONAL ANALYSIS

Learning Outcomes

- Differentiate among five components of industry environment: customers, competitors, suppliers, regulations, and advocacy groups.
- Explain SWOT.
- Explain the resource-based view of strategy.

After the macro, or PESTEL, level analysis has been completed, the next step in goal setting is to do a **situational analysis** that looks more closely at external and internal conditions that affect your particular organization. Five key components of the organization's specific business environment are examined. These are customers, competitors, suppliers, and government and legal issues—including regulations and advocacy or support groups. The analysis looks at what impact these factors may have on a specific organization or business.

Customers

A customer analysis is a critical component of any organizational strategy. You probably would not want to open an extreme sports adventure business in a city where the age of the typical resident is older than fifty. Or, you might be wasting your marketing dollars advertising trendy, designer jeans on the Hallmark TV channel. You might do very well, however, if you opened a combination coffee/book store in a busy college town. If an organization doesn't know who its customers are or what its customers want, it can't meet customer needs.

Some of the things a **customer analysis** should do is to:

Customer analysis should answer questions such as: Who is your target customer today? How will you retain your customers?

- Identify the target customer. Is this customer base growing or is it decreasing? What are your customer demographics (age, income, location, gender, politics, etc.)? What is the revenue of these customers? How much discretionary income do they have?
- Understand the specific customer needs. Why do they buy certain brands? How do make their purchasing decisions? Do they purchase in person or online?
- Show if and how your product or service meets those needs.

Besides determining if a customer base exists in the region, this data can be used in the future to plan effective promotional campaigns, forecast inventory needs, and determine the optimal combination of distribution channels.

Competitors

You read about competitive analysis in the previous section at the macro level. At the situational level, a business needs to identify its specific competitors and assess their potential for taking market share. An organization needs to be aware of future initiatives of the competition (as much as is possible) and examine the competitors' financial and marketing performances.

Suppliers

Another industry component that will greatly impact an organization is its suppliers. Your business may start by buying raw materials and producing finished goods purchased directly by consumers. Or it may process raw materials into products that are part of another company's final consumer goods. Some organizations create services rather than goods but still need materials, such as computer software and hardware or office supplies, to provide those services. Whatever the situation, without raw materials or support products, the organization cannot operate.

In the past, it was common for an organization to choose suppliers that were in the same region or at least the same country. In today's competitive global economy, however, a supplier is likely on the other side of the world. The **supply chain** is a system comprised of organizations, information, resources, people, technology, and activities that bring products or services from a supplier to a consumer. In larger organizations, entire departments may be dedicated to supply chain logistics. Implementing cooperative alliances with key suppliers is also a popular tactic employed by strategic organizations. Although multiple sources of supply helps to guarantee the availability of supplies, creating a cooperative agreement with one supplier can significantly reduce costs. How to handle suppliers is an extremely important factor in setting goals and generating strategies.

Regulations

Governmental and legal environment are part of the PESTEL analysis discussed in the previous section. At the situational level, however, state and local regulations also need to be part of any analysis. The regulatory burden depends largely upon the type of industry and the specific nature of the business. In some industries, regulation is the single biggest uncertainty affecting investment and spending, corporate image, and risk management. These organizations include airlines, utilities, railways, telecommunications, banking, and pharmaceuticals. Often, the regulations have positive impacts on both consumers and businesses. They provide the public with a high level of confidence in the safety and efficacy of the products. They can also prevent competition from businesses with substandard and low-quality goods from trying to enter an industry. Despite the benefits that regulations can provide, any changes in how the product is manufactured, shipped, tested, or provided will greatly affect unit costs and profit margins.

Regulations are lighter for less risky products and businesses, but every company must comply with federal and state payroll, benefits, tax requirements, and following municipal commercial and building codes can present challenges. For example, a decision to expand the size of a fitness center to attract more customers may be thwarted by a local regulation that fixes a ratio of parking spaces to square footage. Or extra time could be added to delivery schedules if truckers must avoid more direct routes to comply with weight regulations on local highways. Some localities will not permit the shipping of dangerous chemicals through their towns. These factors all affect an organization's ability to be competitive.

Regulations are a greater burden on small companies unless they are exempted because of size (some companies with fewer than twenty-five employees are exempt from overtime pay provisions, for example.) However, dealing with regulations can be challenging regardless of the size of the organization. Complying with regulations often involves a trade-off between short-term profits and long-term public relations and social responsibility.

Advocacy Groups

Advocacy groups are also known as special interest groups, public interest groups, environmental groups, or political support groups. Whatever their label, their aim is to influence public opinion, public policy, and company behavior. Advocacy groups use a variety of strategies and tactics to draw attention to their causes, including lobbying, promotions using celebrities, and public information campaigns. They provide a type of check on the business community by exposing unethical or unpopular practices. The Internet—especially social media—has greatly strengthened the ability of these groups to impact an organization.

Advocacy groups represent political, economic, and social interests—all of which affect the business environment. (The PESTEL analysis in a previous section looked at the macro effect of these groups.) Today environmental interest groups are extremely varied, and many hold conflicting views about appropriate strategies for pursuing their interests.

People for the Ethical Treatment of Animals (PETA) is one of the more outspoken activist groups and has targeted many organizations it believes abuse animals. In 2016, after years of PETA campaigns aimed at publicizing its marine operations, SeaWorld announced that it would end its orca whale breeding program. In 2017, a combination of low ticket sales and adverse publicity on the general condition of circus animals led Ringling Bros. and Barnum and Bailey Circus to close after almost a century and a half. PETA had filed more than 130 formal complaints against the circus with the U.S. Department of Agriculture. Regardless of criticisms that some advocacy group charges are not scientifically sound, negative publicity alone may be enough to disrupt business.

SWOT: A Situational Analysis Summary

Once external factors have been thoroughly considered, an organization can look at its own internal resources. A **SWOT analysis** is a method that examines the internal strengths and weaknesses of an organization as well as external opportunities and threats (social, political, economic, legal environmental) that would affect that organization. In fact, a SWOT analysis is really more of a summary of data from various other analyses formulated in a way that allows for comparisons. SWOT stands for strengths, weaknesses, opportunities, and threats.

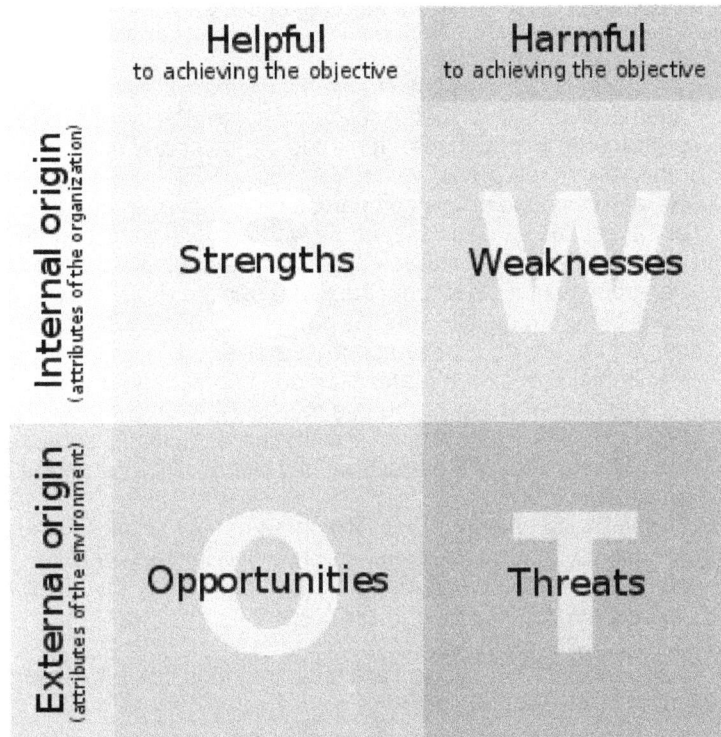

The organization puts together its vision and mission with the SWOT analysis to set its goals.

- **Strengths** are the areas where the organization has particular skills and resources that would allow it to pursue goals effectively. For instance, innovative and collaborative organizational cultures are strengths of Apple and Google.
- **Weaknesses** are areas where the organization is lacking resources and would be prevented from pursuing some goals. For example, when consumers demanded smaller, fuel-efficient cars, many American manufacturers lacked the designs and equipment to make these cars.
- **Opportunities** are conditions that are favorable to the organization and would facilitate its efforts to achieve its goals. Building on the earlier example, Japanese automakers saw an opportunity in the American demand for smaller cars to increase their market share.
- **Threats** are conditions that would prevent the organization from achieving its goals. Many businesses, for instance, are concerned about the threat posed by China's competitive growing manufacturing capability.

Resource-based View (RBV) Strategic Approach

The **resource-based view (RBV)** argues that focusing on an organization's strengths is essential to achieve a sustained competitive advantage. (Remember, the purpose of the SWOT analysis is to help companies identify their strengths.) RBV supporters look for ways to use internal resources (assets) to take advantage of external opportunities. To understand RBV, resources are classified into two groups: tangible and intangible.

- **Tangible assets** are physical things such as land, equipment and machines, and real estate. Although they are necessary, they aren't unique and competitors can fairly easily acquire these kinds of assets.
- **Intangible assets** are anything an organization can own that is not physical. Examples include brand names, intellectual property, and the organization's reputation and goodwill. These kinds of assets are not easily acquired and usually contribute heavily toward a sustained competitive advantage. For

example, Mercedes Benz has a reputation for quality engineering and luxury in its vehicles. People take it as a given that they produce precision, high-quality products

The VRIO Framework

In 1991, J.B. Barney developed the VRIN framework to analyze a firm's internal resources and capabilities to see if they can be used to sustain a competitive advantage. A few years later, he later revised VRIN to VRIO, the current model. VRIO stands for the four key characteristics that a resource must have if it is to produce sustained competitive advantage.

- **Valuable.** A resource is valuable if it enables the company to take advantage of opportunities or defend against threats. A valuable resource allows the company to provide value for its customers by making its product better or cheaper. It means the company can continue to add features or lower the price to maintain the perceived value.
- **Rare.** If only one or two companies can acquire a resource it is considered rare. A resource may be rare because little of it exists, such as workers with particular skills, or because there are few sources for it, such as lithium for batteries. Rare and valuable resources can create a *temporary competitive advantage* because even if other firms duplicate performance, they don't have access to the unique resource (tangible or intangible, such as a patent or unique skill). If the resource is not rare, the best a company can achieve is competitive parity (equality).
- **Inimitable.** If another organization can't copy, buy, or find a replacement for the resource, it is *inimitable*. According to Barney, resources can be inimitable if they (1) developed historically over a long period of time, (2) competitors cannot identify the particular resources that are the cause of competitive advantage, and (3) the resource is a result of the corporate culture and personal dynamics of the organization.
- **Organized to capture value.** The three characteristics listed earlier are "necessary but not sufficient conditions" to achieve a sustained competitive advantage. The missing ingredient is management's ability to develop the strategy to put it all together. The firm must be organized in a way that can capture value by employing the right strategies.

The VRIO and the SWOT analyses are tools that help companies organize to successfully achieve sustained competitive advantages.

INTRODUCTION TO STAGES AND TYPES OF STRATEGY

What you'll learn to do: explain the stages of strategy, and describe the common types of business strategies

The strategic management process starts with knowing the vision and mission, formulating clear goals, implementing plans with precision, and evaluating results to ensure milestone are met. Most business strategies are focused on the competitive environment. Porter's system that classifies generic strategies allows organizations to choose how to situate themselves in the industry environment. Finally, all strategies must include an approach to address the digital world of e-commerce.

STAGES AND TYPES OF STRATEGY

Learning Outcomes

  - Explain the stages of strategy.
  - Explain Porter's general types of competitive strategies.
  - Explain e-commerce strategy.

Introduction

The previous sections have examined the role of strategy in management and looked at common frameworks for analyzing the external and internal environment of business organizations. But what are the specific steps in the strategic management process? How do managers decide what to do, when to do it, and make sure it is happening the way they want? This is what the strategic management process is all about.

The Strategic Management Process

The strategic management process consists of three, four, or five steps depending upon how the different stages are labeled and grouped. But all of the approaches include the same basic actions in the same order. A brief description of these steps follows:

1. **Strategic Objectives and Analysis.** The first step is to define the vision, mission, and values statements of the organization. This is done in combination with the external analysis of the business environment (PESTEL) and internal analysis of the organization (SWOT). An organization's statements may evolve as information is discovered that affects a company's ability to operate in the external environment.
2. **Strategic Formulation.** The information from PESTEL and SWOT analyses should be used to set clear and realistic goals and objectives based on the strengths and weaknesses of the company. Identify if the organization needs to find additional resources and how to obtain them. Formulate targeted plans to achieve the goals. Prioritize the tactics most important to achieving the objectives. Continue to scan the external environment for changes that would affect the chances of achieving the strategic goals.
3. **Strategic Implementation.** Sometimes referred to as *strategic execution*, this stage is when the planning stops and the action begins. The best plans won't make up for sloppy implementation. Everyone in the organization should be aware of his or her particular assignments, responsibilities and authority. Management should provide additional employee training to meet plan objectives during this stage, as well. It should also allocate resources, including funding. Success in this stage depends upon employees being given the tools needed to implement the plan and being motivated to make it work.
4. **Strategic Evaluation and Control.** Because external and internal conditions are always changing, this stage is extremely important. Performance measurements (determined by the nature of the goal) will help determine if key milestones are being met. If actual results vary from the strategic plan, corrective actions will need to be taken. If necessary, reexamine the goals or the measurement criteria. If it becomes apparent that the strategy is not working according to plan, then new plans need to be formulated (see Step 2) or organizational structures adjusted. Personnel may need to be retrained or shifted to other duties. You may even have to repeat the strategic management process from the beginning, including the information and knowledge gained from this first attempt.

Strategic Objectives and Analysis	Vision Mission Values	SWOT and PESTEL Analysis
Strategic Formulation	Plans Gather resources	
Strategic Implementation	Training Allocate resources	
Strategic Evaluation and Control	Evaluation Correction	

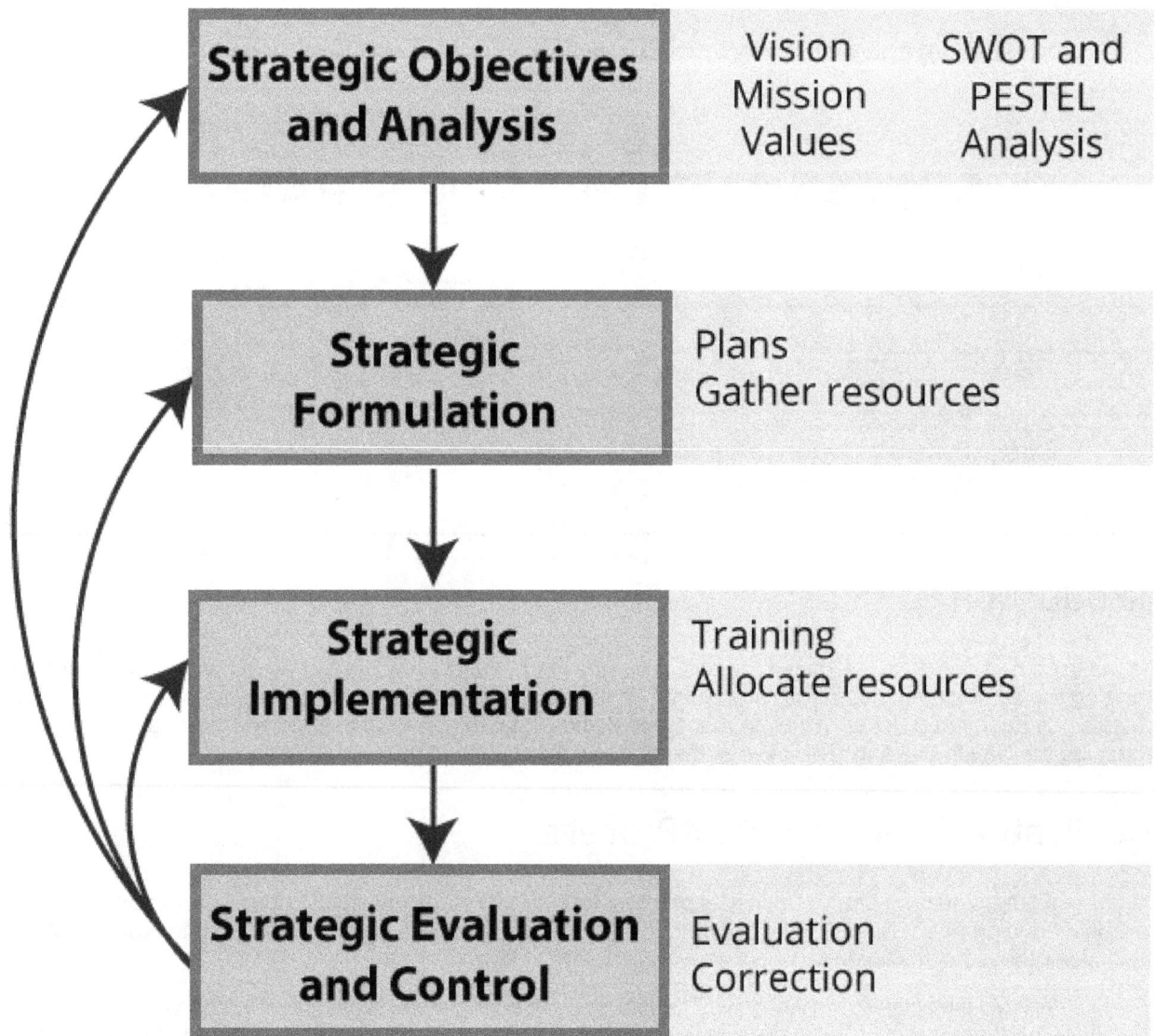

The graphic depicts the basic steps of the strategic management process. Note that analysis, decision making, and action happen in all of the steps and throughout the process.

Porter's Competitive Strategies

The strategic management process described earlier can be successfully used for a wide number of business strategies. In practice, however, most organizations develop strategies that focus on the competition.

Besides studying the nature of industry profits in the Five Forces Theory, Michael Porter is also recognized for his work on four general types of competitive strategies. (More recently, a fifth strategy has been added.) Porter's model describes two ways of achieving competitive advantage, either by differentiation or by cost. It also identifies two ways of targeting the market, by focusing on a particular market segment or appealing to the overall (broad) market. This approach results in four separate competitive strategies: overall differentiation, overall low cost, focused differentiation, and focused low cost. The fifth strategy combines elements of both low cost and differentiation. This is called the integrated approach.

PORTER'S COMPETITIVE STRATEGIES

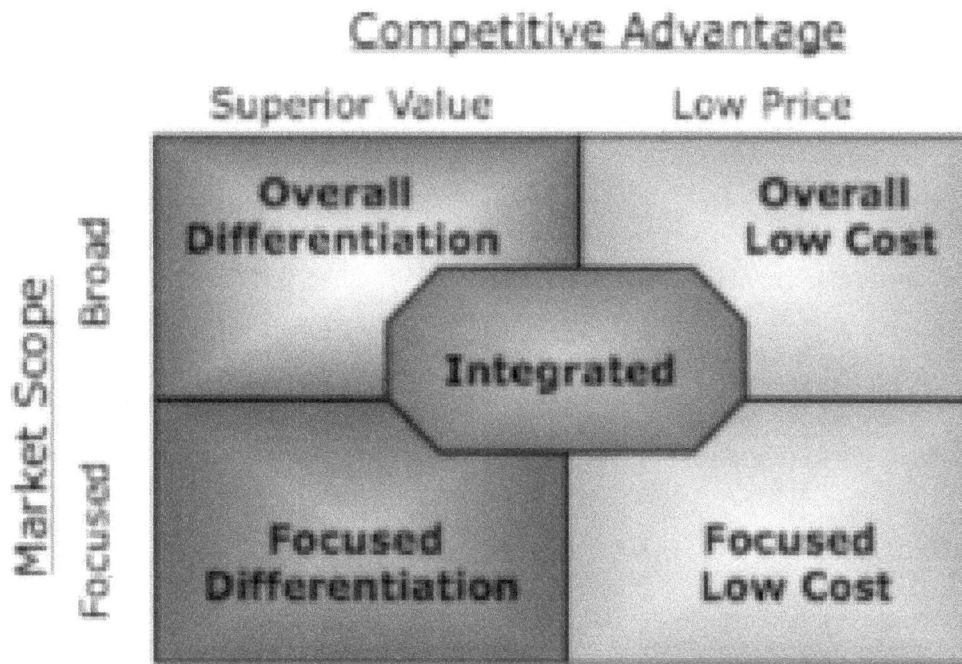

Competitive Advantage

Porter classified competitive strategies by cost and differentiation, with a focused or broad market scope. He later recognized a fifth (integrated) classification.

Low Price Leadership Strategy

An organization seeking a low-cost strategy seeks to become a leader in providing low-cost products to its customers. The strategy is to produce (or purchase) comparable value goods or services at a lower cost than its competitors. The lower cost will attract the majority of customers and allow it to profit by the volume of goods sold. For this strategy to be successful, it requires that only one or two companies can be industry leaders in this position. For example, Walmart and Costco are leaders in the overall low-cost strategy. IKEA is a low-cost leader using a focused low-cost strategy, appealing to a particular segment of the overall market.

ADVANTAGES OF LOW-COST STRATEGY	DISADVANTAGES OF LOW COST-STRATEGY
Reduces buyer bargaining power	Lack of differentiation/value in products and services
Forces out less efficient rivals	Some methods can be easily copied
Makes it hard for new entrants to compete	Focus on cost cutting decreases investment in key activities

Differentiation Leadership Strategy

A strategy based on differentiation (*distinction*) calls for goods and services that offer unique features and that have high value for the target customer. The features must be perceived by the customer to be so much better than what the competition offers that they are worth an additional cost.

The differentiation may be based on the total number of features, quality of the features, customer service, or other criteria. Marketing campaigns are one way to differentiate a product and create a strong emotional attachment to it, supporting premium prices. Examples of companies in the overall market scope that pursue an overall differentiated strategy include Sony and Apple. They produce a large number of quality products that appeal to the wide technology consumer market. Businesses that sell luxury goods in any industry are employing a focused differentiation strategy. Prada, BMW, and Rolex are all companies whose strategy depends upon maintaining a loyal customer base convinced of the superior quality and uniqueness of their products—and who are also willing to pay a premium for the perceived quality value.

ADVANTAGES OF DIFFERENTIATION STRATEGY	DISADVANTAGES OF DIFFERENTIATION STRATEGY
Buyers are less price-sensitive	Costs to produce can be high
Rivalry is reduced (fewer direct competitors)	Distinctive features don't necessarily create value
Difficult for new entrants into the market to copy the product or service	Distinctive features may be easily imitated
Uniqueness makes it hard to find substitutes	Distinction may be erased by innovation

Integrated Strategy

In today's highly competitive market, customers expect distinction and low cost. Some companies have responded by adopting an **integrated strategy**. Porter originally argued that this integrated, or "stuck in the middle," strategy would fail, but other researchers showed real-world examples. Later, Porter modified his view. The organizations strive to provide more value than the average competitor but also focus on keeping costs low. Examples of integrated strategy firms include the automobile companies who manufacture a "luxury" brand, such as the Kia K900. Kia keeps costs down by using many components of its low-cost models but adds additional features comparable to luxury car producers. This approach is risky, because these products run the risk of being too expensive for the economy-driven customer but not having the prestige of the classic luxury brands.

ADVANTAGES OF INTEGRATION STRATEGY	DISADVANTAGES OF INTEGRATION STRATEGY
Provides value to two types of customers	Very difficult to maintain
Forces out less efficient rivals	Possible dilution of brand identity and customer confusion

E-Business and E-Commerce

Businesses today need a strategy for competing with online "upstarts" who can underprice and steal customers. Companies that once thought they were immune to online competition have discovered that the Internet is biting into their profits. Warby-Parker is an online provider of eyeglasses that offers lenses at up to 70 percent off the price opticians charge. The customer only needs to choose frames, pick a lens, and enter the prescription. Returns are guaranteed. Even many routine medical procedures are being addressed digitally as patients meet online with doctors.

E-business can be defined as any business that takes place over digital processes using a computer network rather than in a physical location ("brick and mortar"). Organizations of all types, military and nonprofit, educational and governmental, use e-business strategies. The strategies are geared to three purposes:

- those related to decreasing production costs and increasing efficiency.
- those creating customer focus.
- those addressing internal management.

E-commerce is a more limited term than e-business. It refers specifically to exchanges or transactions that occur electronically. The younger the shopper, the more likely he or she is to conduct "business" using a smart phone. E-commerce strategies rely on the power of the Internet, both in the growing popularity of online purchasing and in shaping marketing strategies. About 8.5 percent of all retail sales were made online in 2016 and this figure is increasing rapidly every year. Many organizations have sales and marketing teams dedicated to devising strategies for capturing their share of the growing online market. Amazon clearly dominates e-commerce with a whopping 33 percent of all online purchases. Its e-commerce strategy is "simply" to make it as easy as possible for the customer to find, order, pay, receive, and return (if necessary) the goods that it buys from the giant corporation. It doesn't wait for the customer to search out a product, but rather pushes products to the customer based on past purchases.

Retailers and manufacturers also use the aspects of the internet such as Twitter, Facebook, and other social media sites to predict trends as they are developing to get a jump on production. First to market can be a key competitive advantage, in part because of the short life span of many fads. Many of the strategies needed to succeed in e-commerce are very different from competing in a nondigital environment. To survive today, organizations need to be present in both environments.

INTRODUCTION TO HOW ENVIRONMENT AFFECTS STRATEGY

What you'll learn to do: explain the key aspects of the environment that can affect strategy

Managers develop strategies to guide their organizations to success. They analyze external and internal conditions to make sure that their assumptions are based as much as possible on solid data. The truth is, however, that the environment today is changing faster than it ever did in the past. And the rate of change is increasing, as well. There are some attributes in the modern environment that make strategic planning a risky business.

HOW ENVIRONMENT AFFECTS STRATEGY

Learning Outcomes

- Explain the key aspects of the environment that can affect strategy (e.g., stability, complexity, resource scarcity, and uncertainty).

Introduction

We've talked about how organizations use strategy to integrate their functions and activities. Strategy also integrates the firm with its external environment. This means that the structure of the firm must align with external conditions. The problem this presents is that the environment constantly changes and the firm has little control over the changes. Strategy and structure must be flexible to adapt to changes in the environment.

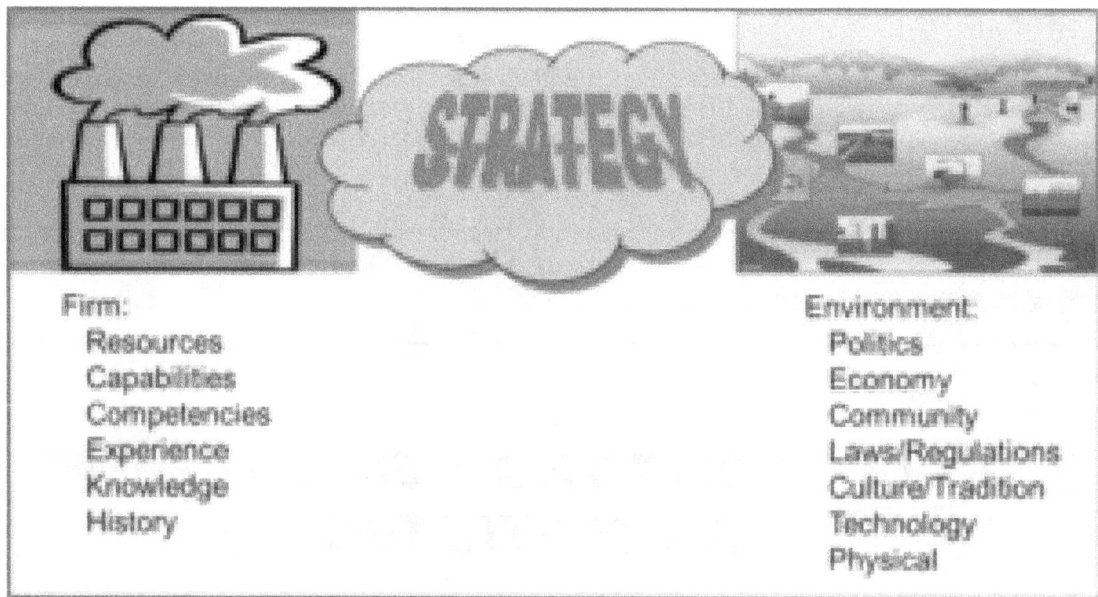

Strategy integrates the organization with its external environment.

Strategy and Change

To determine the appropriate strategic response to changes in the environment, managers must be able to understand the impact of the changes. There are four components that describe the nature of change in the environment: stability, complexity, resource scarcity, and uncertainty.

Stability

Stability refers to the rate at which change occurs. In a **stable environment**, change is slow. Managers have time to monitor and respond to changes in a deliberate manner. The grocery industry is relatively stable. A **dynamic environment** is changing rapidly. Managers must react quickly and organizations must be flexible to respond. Today's business environment is generally very dynamic. Technology, consumer tastes, laws and regulations, political leaders, and international conditions are all changing rapidly and dramatically. Failure to monitor and respond to changing conditions often results in a company's demise. Consider the Nokia example we introduced in an earlier section. Nokia was a market leader just a few years ago (2011). It didn't respond quickly to the emergence of smartphones and has now been acquired by Microsoft. Or we can look at the example of True Religion Jeans, a market leader in fashion jeans very recently. It did not respond to the shift in consumer taste to casual sportswear and the company has filed for bankruptcy.

Complexity

Complexity refers to the number of elements in the organization's environment and their connections. In a highly complex environment there are many variables that can affect the company. The variables are hard to identify and measure and are connected in ways that are hard to understand. Managers must monitor and respond to more sources of change, which makes it more difficult to make decisions. Complexity can be modeled with *chaos theory*, where small changes in one factor can produce a major change in another. For example, the failure of an Ohio power company to trim tree branches near its high-voltage lines lead to the biggest power blackout in US history, affecting more than 50 million people. Should GM, a global auto manufacturer, have anticipated that an increase in default rates on US home mortgages would begin a series of financial crises that would eventually lead to declaring bankruptcy?

Resource Scarcity

Resource scarcity refers to the availability of resources critical to a company or that are in high demand by other companies. Resource scarcity is usually the result of a shortage of supply, but it can also result from demand driving up prices. In conditions of resource scarcity, a company may not be able to acquire the resources it needs to operate or grow. For example, lithium ion batteries are now used extensively in electronic devices, tools, and electric cars. But lithium supplies are in a severe shortage and new sources are slow to arise. Tesla, the US electric car manufacturer, will require about one-third of the available lithium to supply its new battery factory. Its ambitious growth plans could be jeopardized if new sources are not developed.

Uncertainty

Instability, complexity, and resource scarcity all lead to uncertainty. Uncertainty refers to how predictable environmental conditions are. In an uncertain environment it is very difficult for managers to predict where and how change will occur. Instead, managers must make decisions based on assumptions rather than clear facts. Companies that "guess" right benefit from uncertainty and companies that guess wrong suffer. For example, in the 1990s when oil prices were around $50 per barrel, there was no clear information to predict what would happen in the near future. Southwest Airlines bet that fuel prices would go up and hedged against oil price increases. Other airlines bet that prices would be stable or decline. When oil prices soared to more than $100 per barrel, Southwest was able to remain profitable whereas other airlines lost more than $6 billion.

Summary

Nothing stays the same. This simple fact underlies strategic management, which seeks to adapt to and benefit from change. However, in today's environment, it is difficult for managers to identify and understand rapid or unexpected changes in the environment. Conditions of instability, complexity, resource scarcity, and uncertainty make it impossible for managers to anticipate change and make rational decisions. Instead, they must operate with incomplete data and base decisions on assumptions and best guesses. This makes good managers, who use their experience and training to guess right more often, even more important to organizations.

PUTTING IT TOGETHER: ENVIRONMENTS AND STRATEGIC MANAGEMENT

Let's return to the scenario that we considered at the outset of this module. As the new head of North American operations for Walmart, you've been asked by your boss to outline your strategy for dealing with the threat posed by Amazon. Let's apply the strategic management process you just learned about.

Step One: Strategic Objectives and Analysis

You start by reviewing the mission statement to ensure that your strategy is focused appropriately: "We save people money so they can live better." You will want to make sure that your strategy is consistent with this vision.

Next, you will move to an external analysis of the business environment using the PESTEL methodology.

Factor	Analysis of External Environment
Political	Minimum wage pressure Working conditions of international suppliers (child labor)
Economic	GDP growth forecasts are modest Low interest rates, but Fed signaling increases
Social	Aging population Large millennial demographic
Technological	Growth of online shopping (greater consumer acceptance)

| Environmental | Impact of emissions standards on truck fleet |
| Legal | Healthcare regulation impact on large part-time workforce |

Once you have evaluated the external factors impacting Walmart, it's time to look inward. An important tool that you learned about in this module was the SWOT analysis. You decide to use this framework next.

Strengths

- Low-cost supply chain
- Large network of brick and mortar stores
- Large fleet of commercial trucks
- Exceptional logistics
- Database of consumer shopping habits

Weaknesses

- E-commerce presence one-fifth the size of Amazon's
- Negative PR—employee wages
- Low brand acceptance among millennials

Opportunities

- Improvement in HR practices
- Increase investment in technology
- Online shopping growth
- Improve quality standards

Threats

- Aggressive competition (Amazon)
- Ease of entry to online selling
- Intense price competition

Step Two: Strategic Formulation

You have gathered a lot of important information about the organization and the environments in which it operates. Now you need to turn that data into concrete goals consistent with the established vision.

It's becoming clear to you that your competitive advantage lies in three areas.

First, Walmart has the lowest-cost supply chain of any retailer in the world. Walmart's buying power gives it considerable leverage in supplier negotiations. However, in the minds of consumers, Amazon is the low-cost place to shop online.

Strategic Goal: Use the company's low-cost advantage to put financial pressure on Amazon and other competitors and clearly market this differentiation to consumers.

Another clear competitive advantage you have over Amazon is your massive network of distribution centers and fleet of commercial vehicles. One of the things you noticed when studying Amazon's financials is that they spend a lot of money on next day and second-day delivery. If you leverage your network, you can establish a clear advantage.

Strategic Goal: Leverage the distribution centers and commercial fleet to provide excellent delivery service at a fraction of the competition's cost.

Finally, you recognize that although everyone is focused on moving retail online, Walmart's existing brick and mortar stores are an asset that is being underused. Many consumers want to have the option of interacting with both an online and physical presence when shopping. There is a tactile dimension to shopping that is lost in an online transaction.

Strategic Goal: Better integrate the online and physical aspects of shopping that Walmart can offer (for instance, offer in-store pick-up of online purchases) and communicate that experience to consumers.

With these strategic goals in mind, you are ready to move to the next step in the strategic management process.

Step Three: Strategic Implementation

Now it's time to move to action. As the head of North American operations, you pull together your key executives and work on specific goals for each division and functional area. All leaders are aware of their specific responsibilities and deliverables and have been given the necessary authority to execute the plan. As stated earlier in the module, a good plan is not enough—the right action is what will determine success or failure.

Step Four: Strategic Evaluation and Control

As you've learned, internal and external conditions are always changing. Although you feel good about the plan you've constructed, you know environments are fluid. So you implement processes to measure performance and frequently test the plan's assumptions. Doing so helps ensure that the ongoing actions will deliver the desired results.

In this module you have learned the importance of strategic management and how to analyze the factors that impact an organization. The best leaders know that the proper application of these tools can result in lasting competitive advantage.

MODULE 5: DECISION MAKING

WHY IT MATTERS: DECISION MAKING

Why does a manager need to understand the processes and techniques in decision making?

You have been in your new role as a manager for two months, and your boss just asked you to lead a committee in selecting a new data management system for human resources (HR). The current data management process is run on spreadsheets, but the company has grown from fifty to three hundred employees in just three years, and the spreadsheets won't work anymore. You have all the key areas from HR represented on your committee, plus finance and IT. How will you decide which new system to use?

Decision Criteria

In your kickoff meeting, you spend time finding out the important factors, such as what systems it will need to run (payroll, benefits, disability, leave of absence, etc.), how many employees it will need to handle, software compatibility, and the budget. After an extensive list of requirements is compiled on the white board, you label the list "decision criteria."

Weigh Decision Criteria

Next, you ask the members to weigh the importance of each of the criteria. Early on, everyone weighted his criteria as critical, but eventually the group was able to agree on some less critical needs, such as customization of the web interface (brand colors, logos, etc). Comfortable with the group's progress, you task all the members to bring potential solutions to next week's meeting.

Generate Alternatives

Feeling confident from the previous week's successful meeting, you are anxious to hear the replacement solutions. However, there are only two options offered: stay with current system but add staffing, or go with a new vendor in the field, who happens to be run by your boss's daughter.

Evaluate the Alternatives

Besides the obvious landmines that exist in this decision-making process, you know the biggest flaw will be due to the lack of alternatives to evaluate. Although you may be tempted to engage deciding between these two options or neither, you know that the committee needs more alternatives in order to make the best decision.

This scenario represents the types of challenges you may face and decisions you may have to make in a management role. Throughout this module you'll learn about the processes and tools that can help you make the right call when faced with tough decisions.

INTRODUCTION TO BARRIERS TO INDIVIDUAL DECISION MAKING AND STYLES OF DECISION MAKING

What you'll learn to do: describe the barriers to individual decision making and common styles of decision making

Making decisions is easy. Making the right decision is hard. When making decisions, you will face many barriers, including the quality of information you have, the amount of time allowed, and several cognitive biases that will influence your decisions. In addition to these barriers, we'll also look at some common styles of decision making, including satisficing, optimizing, intuitive, rational, combinatorial, and positional.

BARRIERS TO INDIVIDUAL DECISION MAKING

Learning Outcomes

- Describe the barriers to decision making.

Obviously, not all decisions prove to be good ones. Sometimes that is due to unfortunate situations that would have been impossible to foresee. Other times, however, the problem with the decision could have been avoided. What are the potential barriers that we should be aware of during the decision-making process?

Information-Related Barriers

Almost every decision is based at least in part on information that the decision maker trusts. The reliability and use of that information can potentially lead to multiple problems.

One of the most obvious information-related problems occurs when the information is either incorrect or incomplete. Trusting information that is faulty leads to many wrong deductions and conclusions. If information is incomplete, even if the decision maker is aware of that fact, uncertainty is introduced, and any decision based on that partial information could prove to be misguided.

On the other hand, a contrasting problem can arise when there is too much information available. An information overload can make it difficult to grasp the big picture and recognize which pieces of information are most important. Another problem it can create is that large sets of data may contain data that seems contradictory, leading the analyst to confusion or uncertainty and an inability to synthesize it as a whole.

An overabundance of information can also lead to an inability to process everything to the decision maker's satisfaction. The result can be a harmful delay in the decision-making process as the over-abundance of information is being considered for an undue amount of time. Similarly, if the decision maker is excessively concerned to find every possible piece of information, the same problem can arise.

Circumstance and Time-Related Barriers

A variety of difficulties can also arise from the circumstances in the midst of which a decision maker must work. One of the most common issues is stress, which can arise from a great number of sources. If the decision maker is experiencing abnormal levels of stress either in his personal life or work environment, that can often lead him to poor decisions that are out of character. He may be less objective or less disciplined in following the decision-making process he usually trusts. Recognizing high stress levels can provide the opportunity to intentionally protect against those tendencies.

Also, when time is a restricting factor, that often contributes to poor decisions. Unsurprisingly, evidence suggests that when decision makers feel rushed for time, their judgment often suffers. This is true even when there actually is sufficient time for the decision-making process: just the feeling of a lack of time causes problems. It is important to commit to taking sufficient time for decisions if at all possible (and it usually is).

Cognitive Biases

In this optical illusion all lines are parallel. Perceptual distortion makes them seem crooked.

Even when circumstances are conducive to good decisions and a sufficient supply of accurate information is available, there are still a number of ways in which decision makers might be at fault in their manner of judgment. For instance, their perception can be distorted. Understanding how this happens is relevant for managers because they make many decisions daily. They must also deal with many people making assessments and judgments.

Faulty ways of thinking during the analysis stage are often referred to as cognitive biases. A few common ones follow:

Confirmation Bias

Confirmation bias is the tendency to seek out or prefer information and opinions that we believe will confirm our own judgment. We want to be confirmed, so we pay more attention to information that we think supports us, and we ignore or diminish the significance of information to the contrary. We also tend to accept information at face value that confirms our preconceived views while being critical and skeptical of information that challenges these views. For example, if you believe your new diet of bananas and almonds is the healthiest foods to eat, you will search for and accept any supporting information on the virtues of bananas and almonds, and ignore and discount any contradictory information.

Framing Bias

Framing bias is the tendency to be influenced by the way that a situation or problem is presented. Framing a message with a positive outcome has been shown to be more influential than framing a message with a negative outcome. For example, public health messages that depict nonsmokers as happy and popular with sparkling white smiles has proven more effective than displaying a smoker's diseased lung. Numerous studies have demonstrated framing effects in our everyday lives.

- We are more likely to enjoy meat labeled 75 percent lean meat as opposed to 25 percent fat.
- 93 percent of PhD students registered early when the framing was in terms of a penalty fee for late registration, with only 67 percent registering early when the framing was in terms of a discount for earlier registration.
- More people will support an economic policy if the employment rate is emphasized than when the associated unemployment rate is highlighted. (Note: "The Framing Effect Bias: Improving Decision Making Skills for Cognitive Misers." IQ Mindware. http://www.highiqpro.com/willpower-self-control/the-framing-effect-improving-decision-making-skills-with-capacity-strategy-training)

It is important to be aware of this tendency because, depending on how a problem is presented, we might choose an alternative that is disadvantageous simply because of how it is framed.

Hindsight Bias

Hindsight bias is the tendency to believe falsely that we would have accurately predicted the outcome of an event after that outcome is actually known. When something happens and we have accurate feedback on the outcome, we appear to be very good at concluding that this outcome was relatively obvious. For example, a lot more people claim to have been sure about the inevitability of who would win the Super Bowl the day after the game than they were the day before.

What explains hindsight bias? We are very poor at recalling the way an uncertain event appeared before we realize the actual results of the event, but we can be exceptionally talented at overestimating what we actually knew beforehand as we reconstruct the past. Just listen to a call-in sports show after a big game, and hindsight bias will be on full display.

We seek out or prefer information and opinions that we believe will confirm our own judgment. We want to be confirmed, so we pay more attention to information that we think supports us, and we ignore or diminish the significance of information to the contrary.

Anchoring

Anchoring bias is a tendency to fixate on initial information and then fail to adjust for subsequent information. When our opinion becomes anchored to that piece of information, we cannot stray very far from it. For example, in a mock jury trial, one set of jurors was asked to make an award in the range of $15 million to $50 million. Another set of jurors was asked for an award in the range of $50 million and $150 million. The median awards were $15 million and $50 million respectively with each set of jurors.

Halo Effect

Halo effect concerns the preferential attitude that we have toward certain individuals or organizations. Because we are impressed with their knowledge or expertise in a certain area or areas, we unconsciously begin to give their opinions special credence in other areas as well. This would, for example, be exhibited when sports stars express their political opinions and the public gives strong weight to what they say. There is no logical reason to think that they have sound political opinions just because they have great skill in the realm of sports.

Overconfidence Bias

Overconfident bias is particularly easy to understand. It basically amounts to the idea that an individual decision maker trusts his own judgment (usually his intuition) and allows that judgment to override evidence to the contrary. His opinion counts more strongly to him than that of experts who are more knowledgeable and often more than factual data that contradicts his views. From an organizational standpoint, as managers and employees become more knowledgeable about an issue, the less likely they are to display overconfidence. And overconfidence is most likely to arise when employees are considering issues outside of their area of expertise.

Status-Quo Bias

Some decision makers prefer to avoid change and maintain the status quo. This desire, perhaps unrecognized, often leads them to favor ideas that do not lead to significant changes. Evidence and ideas that support change are neglected as a result.

Pro-Innovation Bias

Pro-innovative bias is the opposite of the status-quo bias. Rather than prefer things to stay the same, the innovation bias gives preference to any new and innovative idea simply because it represents something new. The feeling is that new ideas must be better than old ones. Even if no objective evidence supports the new idea as useful and helpful, it is still attractive just by virtue of being new.

Here is an explanatory video that will help you understand some of these biases along with others:

https://www.youtube.com/watch?v=cAbdmV3VOwA

STYLES OF DECISION MAKING

Learning Outcomes

- Identify common styles of decision making.

Optimizing vs. Satisficing

The "fog of war" refers to the uncertainty common on a battlefield. Business is not quite that bad, but there often isn't good information for a full analysis. With limitations on information, thoughtful analysis may be impossible. So what's a decision maker to do? There are two ends of a spectrum from which to approach this: satisficing and optimizing. Satisficing—a combination of the words "satisfy" and "suffice"—means settling for a less-than-perfect solution when working with limited information. Optimizing involves collecting as much data as possible and trying to find the optimal choice. Generally, decision makers don't pick one or the other—you can think of satisficing to optimizing as a spectrum, and each decision starts with an assessment of how critical it is. A branch of management called management science offers methods for solving complex problems.

Intuitive vs. Rational

According to Daniel Kahneman, who you'll read more about in the next section, each of us has two separate minds that compete for influence. One way to describe this is a conscious and a subconscious perspective. The subconscious mind is automatic and **intuitive**, rapidly consolidating data and producing a decision almost immediately. The subconscious mind works best with repeated experiences. The conscious, **rational** mind requires more effort, using logic and reason to make a choice. For example, the subconscious mind throws a ball and hits the target, while the conscious mind slowly describes the physics and forces required to complete the action.

Combinatorial vs. Positional

Aron Katsenelinboigen proposed this description based on how the game of chess is played. A **combinatorial** player has a final outcome in mind, making a series of moves that try to link the initial position with the final outcome in a firm, narrow, and more certain way. The name comes from the rapid increase in the number of moves he must consider for each step he looks ahead. The **positional** decision-making approach is "looser," setting up strong positions on the board and preparing to react to the opponent. A player using this strategy increases flexibility, creating options as opposed to forcing a single sequence.

In business, a market share strategy is positional. A dominant market share gives a firm negotiating power even with lesser product. A complex situation with many players and many solutions might require a more combinatorial strategy. Apple faced a complex environment when it entered the music streaming business. It created an ecosystem that served artists, labels, and customers without dominating the music business.

Like chess players, businesses can use combinatorial or positional strategies to make decisions.

INTRODUCTION TO RATIONAL DECISION MAKING VS. OTHER TYPES OF DECISION MAKING

What you'll learn to do: explain the concept of "rational decision making" and contrast it with prospect theory, bounded rationality, heuristics, and robust decisions

Though everyone makes decisions, not everyone goes about the process in the same way. In fact, not everyone even uses a "process" to make decisions. There are various decision-making styles, and we will focus on the rational decision-making model. We will also become familiar with a common process that many groups and individuals follow when making decisions. Though almost everyone will agree that decision making should be rational, there are also some important contrasting ideas that often balance out the "rational" aspects to the process.

RATIONAL DECISION MAKING VS. OTHER TYPES OF DECISION MAKING

Learning Outcomes

- Summarize the steps in the rational decision-making process.
- Differentiate between prospect theory, bounded rationality, heuristics, and robust decisions.

The Rational Decision-Making Process

The rational decision-making process involves careful, methodical steps. The more carefully and strictly these steps are followed, the more rational the process is. We'll look at each step in closer detail.

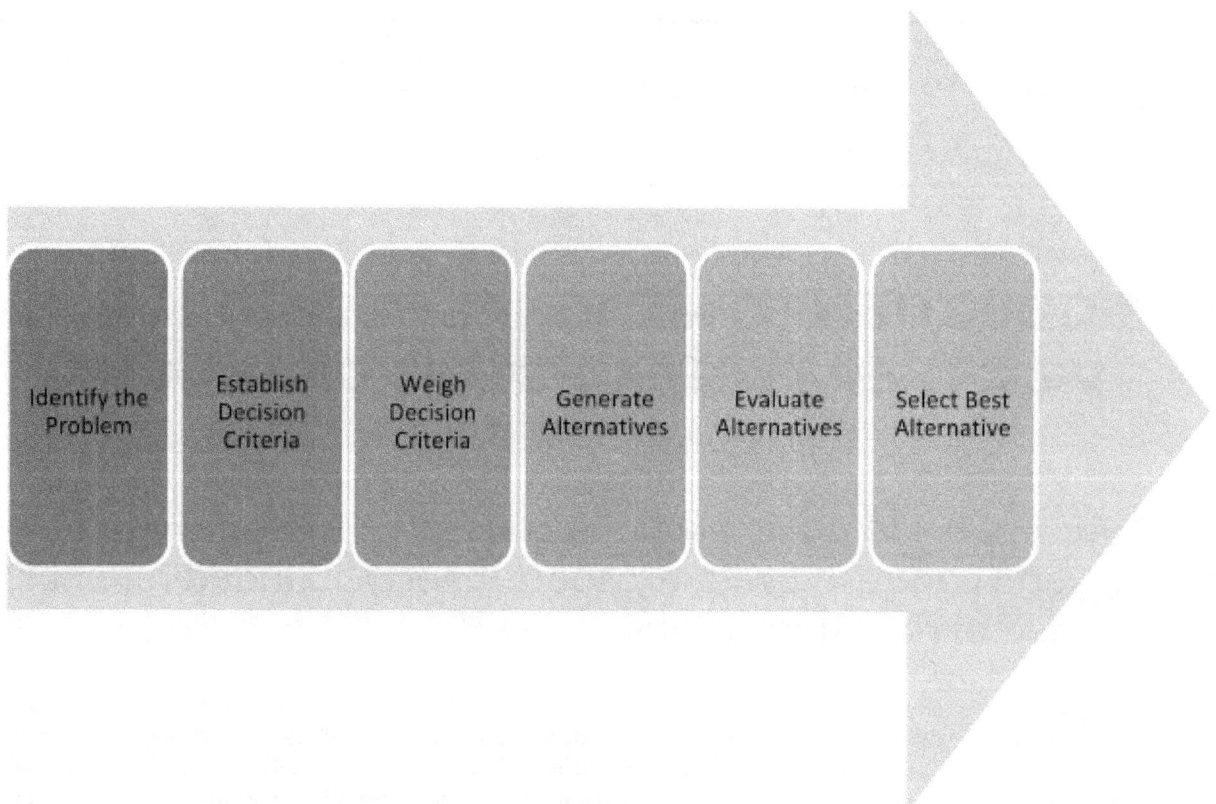

Identify the Problem → Establish Decision Criteria → Weigh Decision Criteria → Generate Alternatives → Evaluate Alternatives → Select Best Alternative

Step 1: Identify the Problem

Though this starting place might seem rather obvious, a failure to identify the problem clearly can derail the entire process. It can sometimes require serious thought to find the central issue that must be addressed. For example, you have taken a new job and you may initially decide you need to find a new car for commuting back and forth from work. However, the central problem is that you need a reliable way to commute to and from work.

Step 2: Establish Decision Criteria

In this step, the decision maker needs to determine what is relevant in making the decision. This step will bring the decision maker's, and any other stakeholder's, interests, values and preferences into the process. To continue our example, let's assume you are married. Some of the criteria identified might include budget, safety, functionality, and reliability.

Step 3: Weigh Decision Criteria

Because the criteria identified will seldom be equally important, you will need to weight the criteria to create the correct priority in the decision. For example, you may have weighted budget, safety, and reliability as the most important criteria to consider, along with several other slightly less critical criteria.

Step 4: Generate Alternatives

Once you have identified the issue and gathered relevant information, now it is time to list potential options for how to decide what to do. Some of those alternatives will be common and fairly obvious options, but it is often helpful to be creative and name unusual solutions as well. The alternatives you generated could include the types of cars, as well as using public transportation, car pooling and a ride-hailing service.

Step 5: Evaluate Alternatives

After creating a somewhat full list of possible alternatives, each alternative can be evaluated. Which choice is most desirable and why? Are all of the options equally feasible, or are some unrealistic or impossible? Now is the time to identify both the merits and the challenges involved in each of the possible solutions.

Step 6: Select the Best Alternative

After a careful evaluation of alternatives, you must choose a solution. You should clearly state your decision so as to avoid confusion or uncertainty. The solution might be one of the particular options that was initially listed, an adaptation of one of those options, or a combination of different aspects from multiple suggestions. It is also possible that an entirely new solution will arise during the evaluation process.

Data, Logic, and Facts

Rational decision making is defined not only by adherence to a careful process, but also by a logical, data-driven manner of following the steps of that process. The process can be time-consuming and costly. It is generally not worthwhile on everyday decisions. It is more useful for big decisions with many criteria that affect many people.

In the evaluation stage, the process usually requires numeric values. The next stage will use these to calculate a score for each alternative. Some properties are not easily measured, and factors that rely on subjective judgment may not be trusted. If they are not fully weighted, the final analysis will lean toward whatever is easiest to measure. In a company, the final decision usually belongs to an executive, who takes the analysis as a guide but makes his own decision.

Ideas that Complement and Contrast with Rational Decision Making

Though most decision makers will recognize much that is commendable in the rational decision-making process, there are also reasons to consider complementary or even contrasting ideas. Taken to its extreme, the rational method might entirely discount factors that are of known and obvious value, such as emotions and feelings, experience, or even ethical principles. This danger, along with other limitations of the rational method, has led to the development of the following concepts to provide a more balanced and holistic approach to decision making:

Prospect Theory

An epoch-making idea in the field of behavioral economics, prospect theory is a complex analysis of how individuals make decisions when there is risk involved. Most strictly rational approaches to questions of financial risk rely on the principle of expected value, where the probability of an event is multiplied by the resulting value should the event occur. Notice the numerical and logical approach to that analysis.

However, Daniel Kahneman and Amos Tversky, the developers of prospect theory, demonstrated through various experiments that most people alter that approach based on their subjective judgments in any given situation. One of the common examples of this is that many individuals think differently about the risk of financial loss than they do when considering situations where different levels of financial gain are concerned. In a purely rational approach, the numbers and calculations involved work the same way regardless of whether the situation is one involving potential gain or potential loss.

Daniel Kahneman is one of the developers of prospect theory.

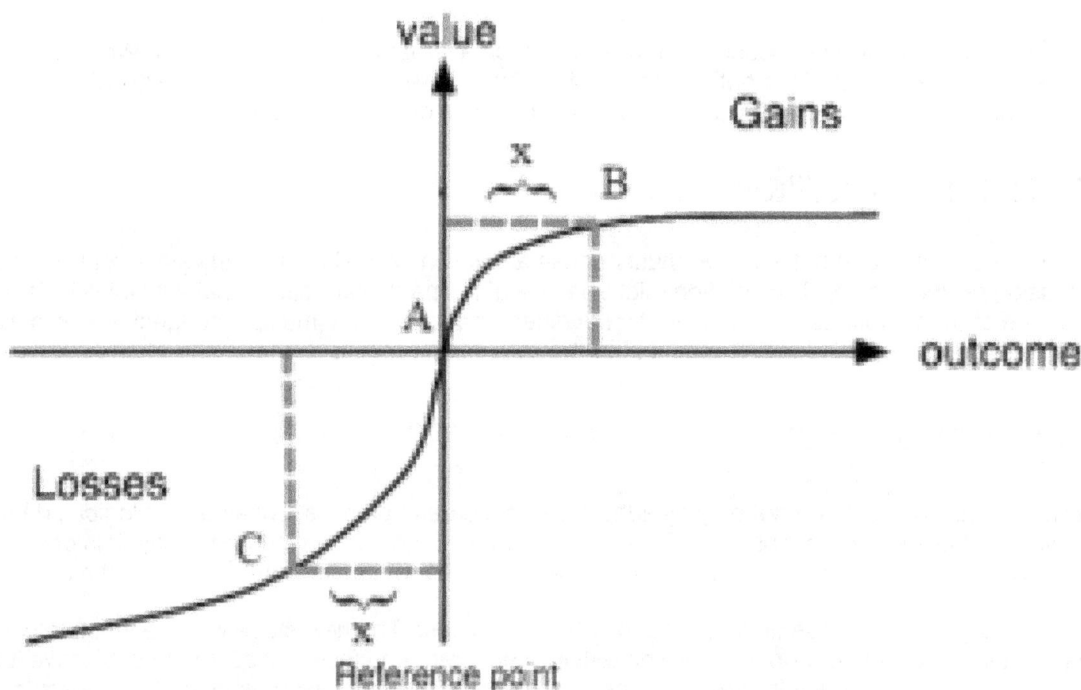

This graph shows how prospect theory describes individuals' subjective valuations of profit and loss. Notice that the value curve is not a straight line and that the positive "gains" section of the curve is not symmetrical to the negative "losses" section of the curve.

Prospect theory is a description of how people made actual decisions in experiments. It doesn't say whether this is right or wrong. It is in the hands of decision makers to determine whether these tendencies are justifiable or if they should be overridden by a rational approach.

Bounded Rationality

Another theory that suggests a modification of pure rationality is known as bounded rationality. This concept revolves on a recognition that human knowledge and capabilities are limited and imperfect. Three specific limitations are generally enumerated:

- Decision makers do not have access to all possible information relevant to the decision, and the information they do have is often flawed and imperfect.
- Decision makers have limited analytical and computational abilities. They are not capable of judging their information and alternatives perfectly. They will inevitably make misjudgments in the evaluation process.
- Decision makers do not have unlimited time to make decisions. Real-life situations provide time constraints in which decisions must be made.

In light of these limitations, the theory of bounded rationality suggests that decision makers must be willing to adapt their rational approach. For example, they must determine how much information is reasonable to pursue during the information-gathering stage; they cannot reasonably expect to gather and analyze all possible information.

Similarly, decision makers must content themselves with a consideration of only a certain number of alternative solutions to the decision.

Also, decision makers being far from perfect in their abilities to evaluate potential solutions must inevitably affect their approach. They must be aware of the possibility that their analysis is wrong and be willing to accept evidence to this effect. This especially includes situations in which they're relying on predictions of an uncertain future. Uncertainty and inaccuracy often arise in efforts to predict the future. For example, your career decision is fraught with uncertainty as you don't know if you will like the work or the work environment. What are decision makers to do when they are uncertain about potential results from their actions? This makes a strictly rational approach difficult and less reliable.

Heuristics

One of the approaches that might stem from a recognition of bounded rationality is the use of heuristics. These are analytical and decision-making tools that help simplify the analysis process by relying on tried and tested rules of thumb. A heuristic simplifies a complex situation and allows the decision maker to focus only on the most important pieces of information.

For example, a business might use their proven experiences and that of many other companies to conclude that a new product line requires a certain amount of time to gain market share and become profitable. Though there are many complex factors involved in market analysis, the business might use this proven rule to guide its decision making. When a proposed decision contradicts this rule, the company might discard it even if a complex and seemingly rational analysis might seem to support it.

Of course, there are exceptions to most rules, and the use of heuristics might prevent a company from following courses of action that would be beneficial. Likewise, heuristics that were once reliable rules might become obsolete because of changing markets and environments. Nonetheless, most analysts recognize heuristics as useful tools when used properly.

Robust Decisions

One final adaptation of the rational process that is becoming more prominent, especially in areas such as energy production and natural resource preservation, is the practice of making "robust" decisions.

Robust decisions revolve around the inability to predict the future with certainty. Rather than rely on an imperfect analysis to determine the "best" decision, a robust decision provides a plan that will work in light of numerous uncertainties. It supposes that a number of situations are all possible and provides a solution pathway that will be successful if any of those situations should arise. This pathway could potentially be a single solution that works in any of the likely future scenarios, or it might provide separate responses to be enacted depending on how the future uncertainties unfold.

INTRODUCTION TO EVIDENCE-BASED DECISION MAKING

What you'll learn to do: explain evidence-based decision making and its tools

We have seen how the rational decision-making process is valuable but also can be improved by useful modifications. We are ready now to learn about another emphasis that might provide improvement on the strictly rational model. In one sense, however, an emphasis on "evidence-based" decision making is only an extension and refinement of rational principles. As its name suggests, this approach relies on actual evidence of effectiveness in evaluating alternative approaches to a decision.

EVIDENCE-BASED DECISION MAKING

Learning Outcomes

- Explain evidence-based decision making.
- Explain the uses of descriptive and predictive analytics.

Using objective facts as the supporting basis for decisions seems like a sensible approach. However, there is a way to do this that still leaves far too much room for error. Having looked at objective data, it is still far too easy and common to posit unproven theories to explain the data, identify causes, and predict future outcomes. Even if the data itself is reliable, how that data is used remains a key consideration. This is where the idea of "evidence-based" decision making becomes central.

Proof of Success

The emphasis of evidence-based thinking is relying on actual experimentation to demonstrate that a plan does indeed provide a likelihood of success. Suppose an analysis of data and trends leads a decision maker to propose a potential course of action. The decision maker believes the course of action should resolve a particular problem and lead to a desirable outcome. An evidence-based approach asks a key question: has such a course of action been proven to be effective for others in similar situations?

This calls for a different type of data collection and analysis. There is today an increased focus on scientific experimentation—or at least as close to scientific as circumstances will allow—to test theories and provide evidence about the effectiveness of different approaches to problems and different business strategies.

The medical field provides an example of an area where evidence-based decision making is clearly valuable. Medical professionals work with much scientific and objective data about the health conditions of their patients, but many professionals believe that many medical practices have too long been subjective in nature. Given the same set of conditions, one doctor might prescribe one treatment whereas another doctor might prefer another. The question becomes that of which treatment has been shown to be most effective in actual practice. By relying on actual evidence of this sort, much of the uncertainty about treatment practices can be removed.

Of course, physical health is a complex matter that involves many factors, just as business situations are. Identifying the significance of all the factors involved and finding parallel situations to use as evidence can remain very challenging. Still, evidence-based principles provide one more helpful tool in guiding the decision-making process.

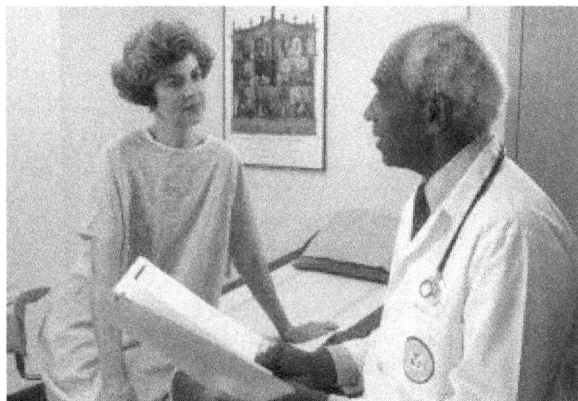

A doctor consults with a patient

Data Collection, Sharing, and Analytics

In today's business environment, those who take an analytical and evidence-based approach have at least one significant advantage: there is plenty of material for them to work with. One of the main reasons people have not relied on evidence-based decision making as strongly over the years is that the evidence simply did not exist or was not accessible. Today, however, the advance of technology has resulted in previously unparalleled amounts of data that can be collected, shared, organized, and analyzed in ways never before imaginable.

Descriptive Analytics

This dramatic increase in the availability of data has led to the rapid development and maturation of the field of data analytics. Much attention has been given to the science of how to analyze this data in a useful way.

The most basic type of data analytics is known as descriptive analytics. The focus of this type of analytics is simply to understand and describe what has taken place as revealed by data sets. The analyst attempts to explain what the data reveals about the events that have occurred, the relationships between different events and market forces, and why the numbers are what they are.

Though this sounds simple enough, the vastness of the data sets makes it rather a tall order to accomplish. Turning almost endless matrixes of numerical data into sensible patterns of interrelated and explainable trends can be a daunting task. However, the same technological power that has made the collecting of such data sets possible has also been harnessed to aid in analyzing that data.

Today's massive sets of data are commonly referred to as "big data."

Predictive Analytics

There is another step beyond the basic analytical goal of explaining what the data reveals, though. What if an understanding of past events and trends could be used to predict the most likely outcomes of future data sets and events? If current trends are identified and projected to continue in the future, decision makers will have access to rich insight that can aid their cause. This work of projecting future trends is known as predictive analytics, and although it still obviously remains only a best guess about the future, it is grounded in objective facts and trends and can provide a greater degree of likelihood as a result.

The practice of predictive analytics should also be subjected to the discipline of evidence-based principles. That is, not only should guesses be made about the likelihood of future outcomes based on present trends, but also those predictions should be verified by actual examples from similar situations in the past—as much as possible, at least. When data from many situations has common trends that end up leading to similar outcomes, the consistent pattern provides strong evidence for future results under similar conditions and trends.

INTRODUCTION TO USING A DECISION TREE

What you'll learn to do: describe the components and use of a decision tree

Despite the limitations of strict rational decision making, there is no doubt that it still has significant value—especially as we refine and improve our abilities to predict costs and market outcomes for our potential actions. When a business feels it has a reasonably accurate measurement of potential costs and a reasonable prediction of likely future outcomes, that data can be used to calculate the likely value of decision pathways. A useful tool for this is the decision tree, which we are going to learn about now.

USING A DECISION TREE

Learning Outcomes

- Describe the components and use of a decision tree.

Decision trees are useful tools, particularly for situations where financial data and probability of outcomes are relatively reliable. They are used to compare the costs and likely values of decision pathways that a business might take. They often include decision alternatives that lead to multiple possible outcomes, with the likelihood of each outcome being measured numerically.

How to Construct a Decision Tree

A decision tree is a branched flowchart showing multiple pathways for potential decisions and outcomes. The tree starts with what is called a decision node, which signifies that a decision must be made.

| | | DECISION 3 | OUTCOMES |

An example of a decision tree

From the decision node, a branch is created for each of the alternative choices under consideration. The initial decision might lead to another decision, in which case a new decision node is created and new branches are added to show each alternative pathway for the new decision. The result is a series of decision pathways. The flowchart might include only one or two decisions with only one or two alternatives, or it can become a complex sequence of many decisions with many alternatives at each node.

Along the decision pathway, there is usually some point at which a decision leads to an uncertain outcome. That is, a decision could result in multiple possible outcomes, so an uncertainty node is added to the tree at that point. Branches come from that uncertainty node showing the different possible outcomes.

Eventually, each pathway reaches a final outcome. The decision tree, then, is a combination of decision nodes, uncertainty nodes, branches coming from each of these nodes, and final outcomes as the result of the pathways.

How to Make Calculations with a Decision Tree

Even in only this simple form, a decision tree is useful to show the possibilities for a decision. However, a decision tree becomes especially useful when numerical data is added.

First, each decision usually involves costs. If a company decides to produce a product, engage in market research, advertise, or any other number of activities, the predicted costs for those decisions are written on the appropriate branch of the decision tree. Also, each pathway eventually leads to an outcome that usually results in income. The predicted amount of income provided by each outcome is added to that branch of the decision tree.

The other numerical data that needs to be provided is the probability of each outcome from the uncertainty nodes. If an uncertainty node has two branches that are both equally likely, each should be labeled with a 50 percent, or 0.5, probability. Alternatively, an uncertainty node might have three branches with respective probabilities of 60 percent, 30 percent, and 10 percent. In each case, the total of the percentages at each uncertainty node will be 100 percent, representing all possibilities for that node.

With this numerical data, decision makers can calculate the likely return value for each decision pathway. The value of each final outcome must be multiplied by the probability that the outcome occurs. The total of the possibilities along each branch represent the total predicted value for that decision pathway. The costs involved in that decision pathway must be subtracted to see the final profit that pathway represents.

INTRODUCTION TO MANAGING GROUP DECISION MAKING

What you'll learn to do: explain common techniques used to manage group decision making

Thus far in our study, we have not distinguished strongly between the decision-making process from the standpoint of the individual and that of the group. Many business decisions, however, are made in groups. Though many of the principles we have learned about apply to group decision making, there are unique advantages, disadvantages, and techniques for group settings that should also be considered.

MANAGING GROUP DECISION MAKING

Learning Outcomes

   •   Identify the advantages of group decision making.
   •   Identify the disadvantages of group decision making.
   •   Describe techniques managers can use to guide and reach consensus in groups.

Decision making in group settings is quite common because most businesses recognize the potential benefits of group participation in the process. In that group setting, the same basic decision-making process can be followed, the same decision-making styles might be favored, and many of the same techniques and biases can still be identified. There are also significant differences, however. What unique aspects to decision making arise when decisions are made in groups?

Advantages of Group Decision Making

Involving multiple participants in the decision-making process provides unmistakable benefits. To begin with, the sum of the knowledge, skills, creativity, and expertise in a group setting will always be greater than that of any individual member. If this greater resource base can be properly accessed and harnessed, the result should be a greater number of more diverse and higher-quality solution ideas. Also, the ability to evaluate those ideas should be improved by group collaboration.

In addition to this primary and most important advantage, group participation also provides the significant benefit of increased understanding of the issue and the decision amongst the team members. If an individual works through the decision-making process alone, arrives at a decision, and communicates that decision to employees who were not involved in the process, those employees might not understand or appreciate the nature, importance, or propriety of the decision. When a decision is made as a group, all the members will have a far greater understanding of the issues and the reasons behind the decision.

Similarly, if group members have a legitimate opportunity to participate in the decision-making process, they will be far more likely to support the decision. They were a part of the process, had the opportunity to help shape the decision, and will probably take greater "ownership" of and exhibit more "buy-in" to the decision.

Disadvantages of Group Decision Making

The advantages of group decision making are clear, but there are certainly potential drawbacks to consider as well.

To begin with, even when the advantages of group decisions are used, there is no way around the process being slower and more expensive than individual decision making. All the group members must invest their time in the process, and the group discussion and interaction is more time-consuming than individual decision-making processes. The number of man-hours involved can be relatively high, and the larger the group, the higher that number. Further, many group members involved in business meetings report that they find the meetings to be inefficient and wasteful of time.

If groups lead to wiser, better decisions, however, these higher resource investments will almost certainly be more than repaid. There are ways, though, in which group involvement can actually become a hindrance to making good decisions if not managed properly.

One common pitfall is groupthink. This is the tendency of group members to conform to and support a proposed group position. Perhaps an outspoken individual strongly favors a decision, and other group members allow themselves to be persuaded simply because of his forcefulness. Alternatively, perhaps a segment of the group shares a common perspective and common biases. Together, they propose a course of action, and because multiple voices are already supporting the decision it makes it easy for the rest of the group to fall in line. This negates the whole purpose of group involvement, which is to bring a variety of perspectives and ideas to the decision-making process.

Groups can also sometimes exhibit a tendency to polarization, meaning their decisions move toward extremes that the individuals alone might not be comfortable supporting. The group setting can cause individuals to feed on the excitement or enthusiasm of one another and move toward those extreme positions.

On the other hand, there is also the danger that groups with sharply divergent perspectives can struggle to agree on a course of action that they can all support. This can lead to a loss of time when no decision is reached. Pressure to resolve this situation and make a decision can then lead to a compromise decision where all sides take a middle ground. Too often, this middle ground represents a solution that none of the group members support wholeheartedly. The end result is often a far from optimal solution.

Lastly, to compound the situation, if a group does make a decision that is not optimal, who bears the responsibility? In one sense, the entire group is accountable, but this also means that no individual will be personally and directly accountable, which can be problematic at times.

Ways to Facilitate Group Decision Making

In light of the potential advantages and potential dangers involved in group decision making, it is important to have a plan to direct and facilitate the group process so it is carried out effectively. This usually requires one individual to take some form of leadership within the group, even if only to help organize and direct meetings. A number of things can be done to pursue smooth and effective group meetings.

Brainstorming is an idea-generating process that specifically encourages all alternatives while withholding any criticism of those alternatives. Therefore, this technique can help build a group's cohesiveness because all members are encouraged to contribute and participate in the process without fear of judgment. In a typical brainstorming session, a small group of people respond to questions or problems posed by a facilitator. All responses are recorded and there is no discussion or analysis at this point. After a set amount of time, the group then selects the ideas or alternatives it would like to explore, but there is no pressure to commit to selecting a solution during brainstorming.

Brainstorming can indeed generate new ideas, but research consistently shows that individuals working alone actually generate more ideas than group sessions because of "production blocking." (Note: Paul B. Paulus and Huei-Chuan Yang, "Idea Generation in Groups: A Basis for Creativity in Organizations," Organizational Behavior and Human Decision Processes 82, no. 1 (May 2000): 77.) When people are generating ideas in a group, many people are talking at once, which distracts the thought process and impedes the sharing of ideas.

The **nominal group technique** is similar to brainstorming, in that it encourages all members to contribute their ideas. However, it is different from brainstorming in that it limits discussion during the decision-making process. Group members are all present but members operate independently and use the following four-step process in idea generating:

1. Members independently write down ideas on a given problem.
2. Each member presents one idea to the group. Each member takes a turn, presenting a single idea, until all ideas have been shared.
3. The group engages in discussion on the ideas for clarity and evaluation.
4. Each member independently rank-orders the ideas. The idea with the highest aggregate ranking determines the final decision.

A major advantage of the nominal group technique is it alleviates the fear of those people who are concerned about having their ideas criticized and who do not like to engage in conflict. But because of the highly structured format, it lacks the flexibility to address more than one idea at a time. Another disadvantage to the nominal group technique is the amount of time needed to present each idea and the resulting discussion on each and every idea proposed.

A new variation is **e-brainstorming**, where people respond to issues via their computers in real time. The responses and rankings are all anonymous and displayed for everyone to view and to add further comments. The advantages of e-brainstorming are the possibility of lots of generated ideas, anonymity, honesty, and speed. The major disadvantage is the reduction in group cohesiveness.

The **devil's advocacy** decision-making technique is where an individual or a group is selected to become the critic in the proposed decision. The biggest strength to using the devil's advocate technique is the ability to prevent groupthink. (Note: Charles Schwenk. "Devil's Advocacy in Managerial Decision Making," Journal of Managerial Studies, 21, no. 2, 1984.) The devil's advocate technique allows for in-depth dialogue on a range of ideas and can help bridge seemingly irreconcilable opposites. (Note: Thomas L. Wheelen and J. David Hunger, Concepts in Strategic Management and Business Policy: Achieving sustainability. (Upper Saddle River, NJ: Prentice Hall, 2010).) This process can help the group refine its thinking and produce high-quality ideas. Any leader using this technique must be aware that it is designed to generate conflict and will require the leader to actively manage the meetings.

For an in-depth discussion on an issue, a neutral **facilitator** or **referee** can be used to separate participant and leadership roles or groups with opposing ideas. The facilitator manages group processes and dynamics and calls for a high degree of neutrality about content issues and a focus on group needs. The facilitator is focused on what needs to be accomplished and appropriate levels of participation, all in an effort to ensure quality decisions are made. The advantage to a facilitated technique is that it can produce innovative, creative and high-quality decisions. (Note: Thomas L. Wheelen and J. David Hunger, Concepts in Strategic Management and Business Policy.) The facilitated model does require a skilled facilitator and a significant amount of time.

In the **Delphi technique** (named after the Oracle at Delphi), experts respond to questionnaires in a number of rounds. Questions narrow in on a specific topic as the rounds progress. The first questionnaire consists of open-ended questions and aims to identify broad issues related to the issue at hand. The responses are analyzed qualitatively by sorting, categorizing, and searching for common themes. These responses are then used to construct the second questionnaire, which is more specific and aims to rate or rank the items in terms of their significance. Subsequent questionnaires can narrow down responses further. As the facilitator feeds back results from the previous rounds, there tends to be convergence to a consensus of opinion. The Delphi technique is useful if convening the participants face-to-face is not practical. The disadvantage is that it takes days to complete and it requires a large amount of work by the leader.

Within all of these group decision-making techniques, you will need to watch for affective conflict and strive for healthy cognitive conflict. **Affective conflict** is when the dialogue becomes "personal" and people become more aggressive or start to disengage. The mindset moves from "we have a problem" to "you are the problem." Opposition is seen as something to be thwarted rather than explored. The goal becomes winning for its own sake rather than the best possible solution. (Note: Satyanarayana Parayitam and Robert S. Dooley, "The interplay between cognitive- and affective conflict and cognition- and affect-based trust in influencing decision outcomes," Journal of Business Research 62, no. 8 (August 2009): 789–796) **Cognitive conflict** is where people focus on the tasks or issues and debate and thrash these out and come to a creative solution. The parties might argue and exchange views vigorously, yet there is two-way communication and an openness to hearing each other. The goal is to find the best possible solution rather than to win the argument. Alternative perspectives are seen as valuable rather than threatening.

The Final Decision

One of the basic requirements is to make the decision-making process clear. There are different options, of course, and different settings and preferences might lead to selecting one of three options: command, democratic, or consensus. When an organization has a centralized decision-making structure, the "command" preference will dictate that the leader will make the final decision. Also, it could be that the group will actively participate in the discussion and thought process, but the final decision will be made by an individual leader. The **democratic method** is when all group members are given equal authority in a formal voting system. Even then, there are choices. A decision might be accepted by a simple majority or unanimity might be required. The most favored method currently is through **consensus**. Each one of the decision-making processes detailed here is predicated on the involvement of everyone in the group. The consensus process enables the discussion of current and potential obstacles, already known to participants, resulting in work-arounds to be built into a decision in advance. Defining that process from the start will help everyone know what to expect.

Strengths and Weaknesses of Group Decision-Making Techniques

Each of these group decision-making techniques has its own strengths and weaknesses. The choice of one technique will depend on what criteria you want to emphasize and the cost/benefit trade-off. For instance, as illustrated in the figure that follows, e-brainstorming is good for generating lots of ideas, the nominal group technique minimizes conflicts, the devil's advocate generates high quality ideas, and brainstorming builds a group's cohesiveness. Remember that group performance varies significantly, no matter which techniques you use.

Evaluating Group Decision-Making Techniques

Effectiveness Criteria	Brainstorming	Nominal	e-Brainstorming	Delphi	Devil's Advocate	Referee/Facilitator

Number of ideas	Moderate	High	High	High	Low	Low
Quality of ideas	Moderate	High	Moderate	Moderate	High	High
Speed	Moderate	Moderate	High	Low	Moderate	High
Potential for interpersonal conflict	Low	Moderate	Moderate	Low	High	Moderate
Commitment to solution	Not applicable	Moderate	Moderate	High	Moderate	High
Group cohesiveness	High	Moderate	Low	Low	Moderate	High

It is also essential to manage the process of the group meeting time to make it productive. There must be a concerted effort to keep the discussion on topic. All group members must also feel free to contribute their thoughts. Sometimes there are rules in place that prohibit any criticism of ideas during the brainstorming sessions so all ideas can be voiced without fear of a negative reception.

At some point, however, ideas need to be evaluated together. Finding the right way for that to happen with a good spirit and environment is important. An effective group leader will find the system that works best for each particular group and setting. If at any point interpersonal conflict or tension arises, the group leader must be prepared with a plan to diffuse the situation and bring the group back to productive cooperation.

PUTTING IT TOGETHER: DECISION MAKING

Let's apply what you've learned in this module to the scenario that we considered at the beginning. As you will recall, you were assigned to lead a team to come up with a new data management system for the human resources department. You started by following the steps in the rational decision-making model.

1. **Identify the Problem:** The current data management system of spreadsheets is ineffective.
2. **Establish Decision Criteria:** Key criteria were established in the first meeting related to areas such as what systems need to be run, how many employees it must handle, compatibility issues, and financial considerations.
3. **Weigh Decision Criteria:** With some guidance, the team was able to settle on which criteria were truly the most important.
4. **Generate Alternatives:** Only two alternatives were presented by the team: stay with the current system or use a firm run by the boss's daughter.
5. **Evaluate Alternatives:** The process essentially stalled here because of the results of Step 4.
6. **Select the Best Alternative:** Not completed yet.

The process was going well until the group came to Step 4 and only generated two alternatives: staying with the current, inadequate system or employing a vendor that also happens to be the boss's daughter. You realize that these aren't enough viable alternatives to generate an ideal solution, but what are you going to do now?

As you will recall from this module, there are many benefits associated with group decision making, but there are times when facilitation is required to realize these benefits. There are options you might select to improve the quality and quantity of alternatives generated. In order to reach a robust decision, you decide to employ two techniques that you've learned.

Brainstorming

You want the group to generate significantly more alternatives for consideration, so you decide to facilitate a brainstorming session. You follow the nominal group technique, which employs the following process:

1. Everyone independently comes up with alternatives to the current data management system.
2. You go around the group and each member presents one alternative.
3. Group members discuss each of the alternatives, but only after they have all been presented.
4. Finally, each person rank orders the alternatives. The ideas with the highest aggregate ranking move to your next step.

Devil's Advocacy

As a second step, you take the ideas with the highest aggregate ranking from the brainstorming session and subject them to the devil's advocacy method. Rotating members of the group are selected to be the critic for the alternatives that made it through the brainstorming round. You choose this method to ensure that groupthink hasn't settled into the decision-making process.

The end result of this process is that numerous alternatives were suggested and evaluated. Ultimately, you were able to present a solution to your boss that was well thought-out and has the support of the rest of the team.

It bears repeating that this scenario represents the types of challenges you may face and decisions you may have to make in a management role. This module has equipped you with the processes and tools that can help you make the right call when faced with tough decisions.

MODULE 6: ORGANIZATIONAL STRUCTURES

WHY IT MATTERS: ORGANIZATIONAL STRUCTURES

Why does a manager need to understand organizational structure?

IBM Credit Corporation is the finance arm of parent company IBM Corp. and is responsible for providing customer financing to facilitate the sale of computers, software, and services. To be successful in this industry, it is important that approvals for credit be timely so sales aren't lost to competitors and their finance subsidiaries. In other words, speedy credit approval serves as a competitive advantage to a business.

Unfortunately, the approval turnaround time at IBM Credit was dreadfully slow. It took six days to weeks from the time an application was submitted to reaching a final credit decision. As you can imagine, this was a significant impediment to IBM salespeople tasked with growing the company's revenues.

Why did it take so long for credit decisions to be made? It turns out that it was not a function of the effort involved in reaching a decision. Rather, it was a result of the organizational structure in place at the time.

How could the organizational structure have such a significant impact on IBM Corporation's success? We will look at the answer to that question at the conclusion of this module. First, it is important that you begin to understand the fundamentals of various structures, which is what you will be learning in this module.

INTRODUCTION TO THE PURPOSE OF ORGANIZATION

What you'll learn to do: explain the purpose of organization

If you have a job now or you've had one in the past, you have some understanding of organizational structure—you know who your manager is, and you probably know who your manager reports to. You might also know who your company's CEO is. But where did this organizational structure come from? There are reasons behind an organization's structure, and understanding them at your current or next job will help you recognize how specialized your work will need to be, who you can talk to when you have questions, and what internal and external elements may impact your work.

THE PURPOSE OF ORGANIZATION

Learning Outcomes

- Explain the efficiencies created by specialization and the division of labor.
- Describe characteristics of organizational structures.
- List Edgar Schein's four common elements of an organization.

Common Elements of an Organization

From a manager's perspective, operations will be successful if a common purpose is made clear across the organization to create a coordinated effort of resources. Edgar Schein, a prominent organizational psychologist, identified four key elements of an organization's structure: **common purpose, coordinated effort, division of labor,** and **hierarchy of authority**. Each of the four elements represents an essential component of an effective structure. Further, Schein proposes that these elements are instrumental in defining the organization's culture.

Common Purpose

An organization with a clear purpose or mission is one that is easy to understand and manage. A common purpose unifies employees and helps them understand the organization's direction. Any employee working at the NASA Space Center in the 1960s knew that that organization's common purpose was to put a man on the moon. Included with the common purpose would be the business and company strategy, mission statement, company values, and the organization's short- and long-term objectives. The role of communicating all of these components most likely falls to managers through the company.

Coordinated Effort

Arguably, a manager's most important responsibility is to coordinate the effort of work in a way that maximizes resources with the common purpose in mind. Managers will need to leverage the employees' skill sets, experience, and personalities in a way that consistently adds value. Managers must also take into account employees' preferences as they relate to job satisfaction and engagement.

Specialization and the Division of Labor

Early in the twentieth century, every employee on the Ford Motor Company assembly line had a specific, repetitive task. For instance, one person would install the wheels on the left side of the car, and another employee only installed the front bumper. By breaking the whole job down to specific standardized tasks and repeating them over and over, Ford could produce one car every ten seconds.

Ford, and many other factories, demonstrated that **specialization** made work more efficient. Management saw this as the most efficient use of the relative skills of its employees. Employee skills at performing a task improve through repetition. Less time is spent changing tasks, in putting away tools from a prior task and getting the necessary tools for the next task. A second, and equally important, efficiency with specialization is the ease and low cost of finding and training people to do specific and repetitive tasks.

Specialization continued to be used for maximum efficiency by McDonald's, which invented the fast-food industry by specializing the work of every employee in the cooking, preparing and delivering of every meal. This model continues with newer companies such as Chipotle and Starbucks.

The **division of labor** describes the degree to which a task is divided into separate jobs or departments in order to improve efficiency. Larger firms, such as Fortune 100 companies, tend to have a high degree of division of labor; smaller entrepreneurial ventures tend to have more informal divisions of labor. For example, a large financial firm will have accountants in one department that only work on internal audits and another department where they focus on budgets and forecasting. An accountant in a small firm, however, needs to be more of a generalist and take on many different things (e.g., internal auditing, plus payroll, accounts receivable, financial planning, and taxes).

Workers are on the job on an assembly line at a Ford Motor Company plant in Long Beach, California, in 1930.

Specialization requires a trade-off between breadth and depth of knowledge. Although a high degree of specialization can increase productivity, it usually has undesirable side effects such as reduced employee job satisfaction because of the repetitiveness of certain tasks. Specialization limits the agility of a workforce, as employees cannot fill in for people in other areas of the business, and employees take longer to qualify for managerial positions. Fewer job improvements will occur because employees do not get the opportunity to work on other tasks.

Hierarchy of Authority

Hierarchy determines the formal, position-based reporting lines and expresses *who reports to whom.* The U.S. Army has a tall hierarchy with about twenty ranks between a private and a general. On the other hand, Valve, an independent game developer, has a flat organization. Officially, it has no managers. With about 2.2 million employees, Walmart has a tall hierarchy, with twenty-nine senior managers all reporting to the top executive level, illustrated in the figure that follows.

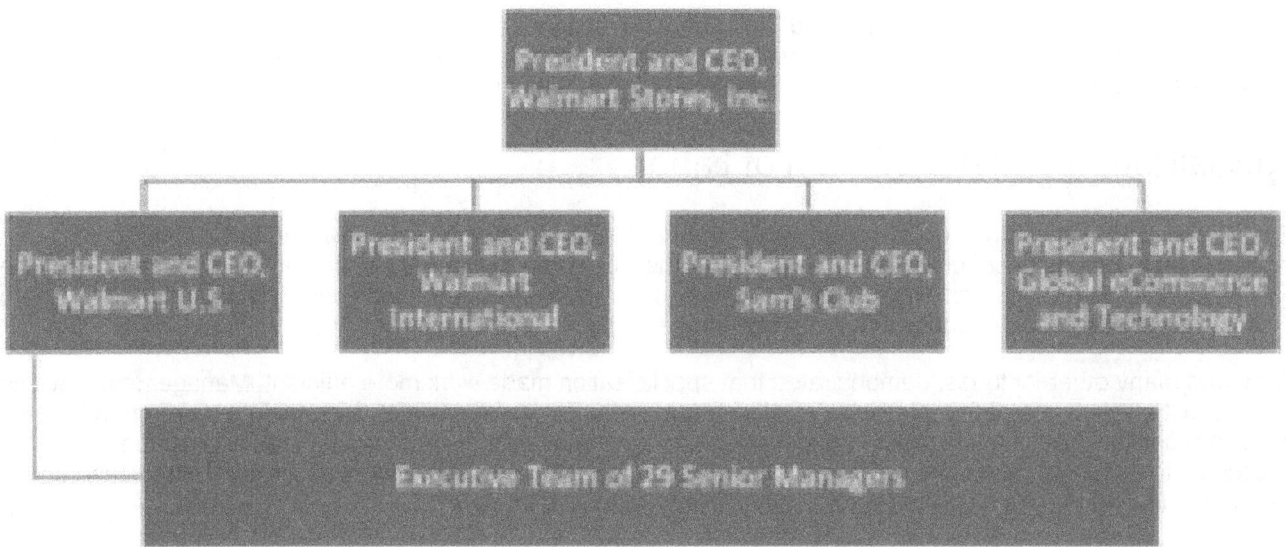

The top of Walmart's organizational structure, which consists of ten additional layers.

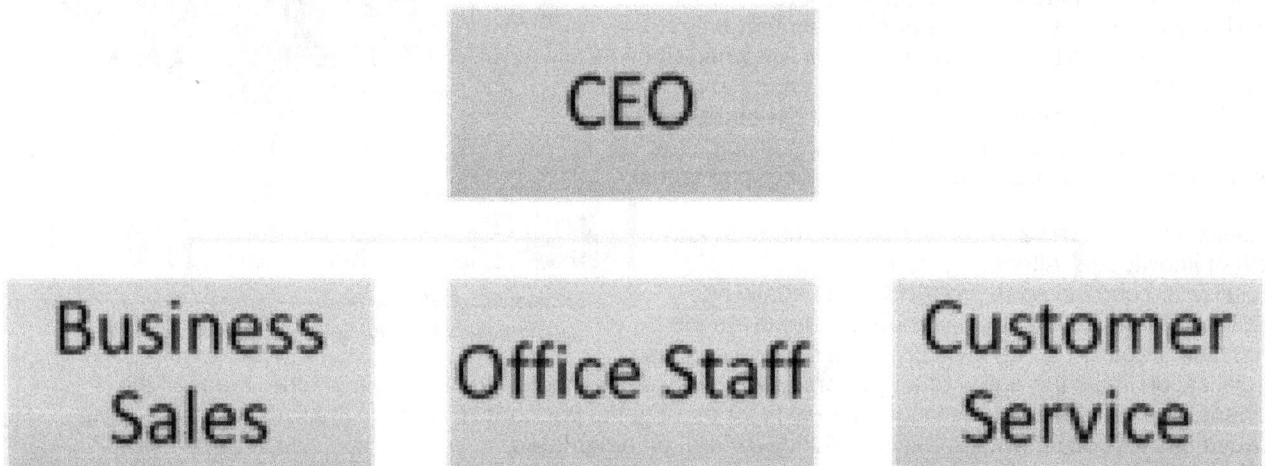

An example of a flat organizational structure, which only has two levels of employees: the owner/CEO at the top and all other types of employees below.

The number of levels of hierarchy, in turn, determines the managers' **span of control**—how many employees directly report to a manager. In tall organizational structures, the span of control is narrow. In flat structures, the span of control is wide, meaning one manager supervises many employees. In recent years, firms have delayered by reducing the headcount (often middle managers), making themselves flatter and more nimble. This, however, puts more pressure on the remaining managers who have to supervise and monitor more direct reports because of an increased span of control. Recent research recommends a span of control between fifteen and twenty direct reports.

Additional Characteristics of Organizational Structures

In addition to Schein's four key elements of an organizational structure, there are a few other characteristics to consider when determining the best structure for a business.

Centralization and Decentralization

In centralized organizations, only the top managers make decisions, whereas the lower-level managers are tasked with carrying out the directives. The military is a prime example, as generals give the orders and each successive rank passes on these orders for following. In decentralized organizations, the decision making is pushed down to the managers who are the closest to the work or client.

The term **centralization** refers to the degree to that decision making is concentrated to the top of the organization. To be clear, this refers to key decisions with potential impact on the business. If all proposals and decisions are made exclusively by the executive team, it is a highly centralized structure. However, if managers are allowed to make significant decisions affecting their areas of the business, it is a decentralized structure.

Formalization

Formalization refers to the degree to which positions in an organization are standardized. If a job is highly formalized, then the employee has little to no discretion over what to do, when to do it, and how to do it. People sometimes confuse formalization with specialization, but they aren't the same thing. Airline pilots have highly formalized jobs, dictated by FAA regulations that must be followed before, during and after every flight. Although the captain and co-pilot do have specialized tasks to perform, they are both involved in the entire delivery of service, and are able to function in each other's roles if needed. Further, the training required for pilots is extensive, with regular flight simulator testing for enforcement of formalized responses for known situations and challenges that can be encountered in flight.

Certain jobs will have much less formalization of duties. Pharmaceutical representatives—the employees of pharmaceutical companies who call on medical offices to inform doctors of their drug's effectiveness—have a great deal of freedom in their jobs. They each develop their own practices for gaining access to the doctors (starting with the medical office front desk staff) and generally only report on the number of physician conversations per week.

INTRODUCTION TO COMMON ORGANIZATIONAL STRUCTURES

What you'll learn to do: describe common organizational structures and their advantages and disadvantages

Three primary variables interact to explain much of an organization's structure: size, age, and industry. Organizations will typically start the structure process by clarifying what it will take to do the work, meet goals, grow sales, etc. And you will see great consistencies in the structure that develops across organizations in many different industries.

COMMON ORGANIZATIONAL STRUCTURES

Learning Outcomes

- Differentiate between the four basic types of departmentalization (function, product, customer, and geography).
- Distinguish matrix organizations from traditional departments.
- Differentiate between team-based structures, networks, and modular organizations.

Departmentalization

Based on an organization's application of the common elements—common purpose, coordinated effort, division of labor, hierarchy of authority, as well as centralization/decentralization and formalization—the resulting structure will typically exhibit one of four broad departmental structures: functional, product, customer, and geographic.

Functional Structure

As sales increase, organizations generally adopt a functional structure. This structure groups employees into functional areas based on their expertise. These functional areas often correspond to stages in the value chain such as operations, research and development, and marketing and sales. They also include support areas such as accounting, finance, and human resources. The graphic that follows shows a functional structure, with the lines indicating reporting and authority relationships. The department head of each functional area reports to the CEO; the CEO then coordinates and integrates the work of each function.

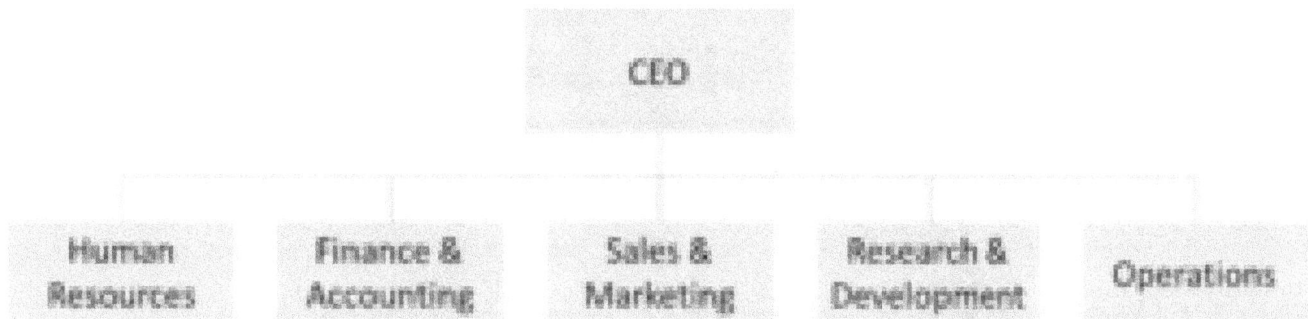

Functional structure organizational chart.

A functional structure allows for a higher degree of specialization and deeper domain expertise than a simple structure. Higher specialization also allows for a greater division of labor, which is linked to higher productivity. (Note: Andrew J. Epstein, Jonathan D Ketcham, and Sean Nicholson, "Specialization and Matching in Professional Services Firm," RAND Journal of Economics. 41, no. 4 (Winter 2010) 811–834. p. 824.) Although work in a functional structure tends to be specialized, it is centrally coordinated by the CEO, as in the earlier graphic. A functional structure allows for an efficient top-down and bottom-up communication chain between the CEO and the functional departments, and thus relies on a relatively tall structure. The disadvantage inherent to a functional structure is that the emphasis on specialization can cause high levels of job dissatisfaction and fewer process improvements for the business.

Product Structure

Companies with diversified product lines frequently structure based on the product or service. GE, for example, has structured six product-specific divisions supported by six centralized service divisions. (1) Energy, (2) Capital (3) Home & Business Solutions, (4) Healthcare, (5) Aviation, and (6) Transportation. Product divisions work well where products are more technical and require more specialized knowledge. These product divisions are supported by centralized services, which include: public relations, business development, legal, global research, human resources, and finance.

This type of structure is ideal for organizations with multiple products and can help shorten product development cycles. One disadvantage is that it can be difficult to scale. Another disadvantage is that the organization may end up with duplicate resources as different divisions strive for autonomy.

Customer Structure

Companies that offer services, such as health care, tend to use a customer-based structure. While similar to the product structure, the different business segments at the bottom are each split into a specific customer group — for example, outpatient, urgent care, and emergency care patients. Since the customers differ significantly, it makes sense to customize the service. Employees can specialize around the type of customer and be more productive with that type of customer. The directors of each customer center would report directly to the chief medical officer and/or the hospital CEO. This is also designed to avoid overlap, confusion, and redundancies. The customer structure is appropriate when the organization's product or service needs to be tailored to specific customers.

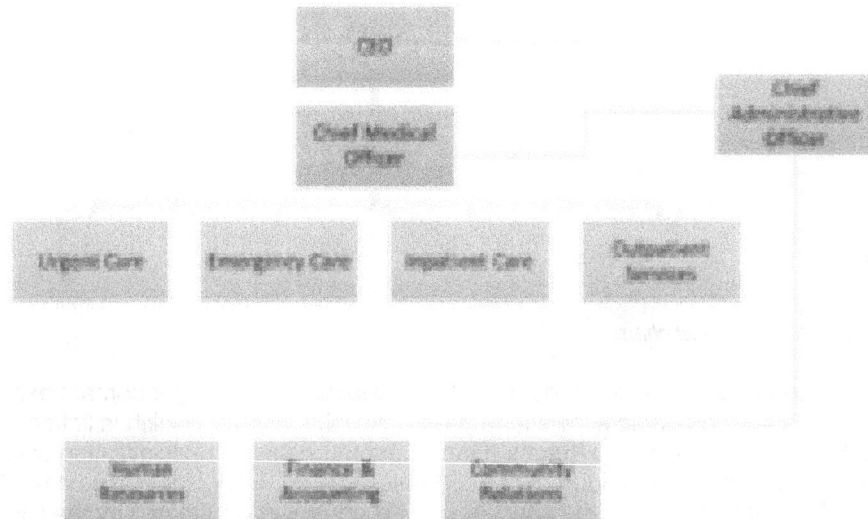

Customer structure organizational chart.

The customer-based structure is ideal for an organization that has products or services unique to specific market segments, especially if that organization has advanced knowledge of those segments. However, there are disadvantages to this structure, too. If there is too much autonomy across the divisions, incompatible systems may develop. Or divisions may end up inadvertently duplicating activities that other divisions are already managing.

Geography Structure

If an organization spans multiple geographic regions, and the product or service needs to be **localized**, it often requires organization by region. Geographic structuring involves grouping activities based on geography, such as a Latin American division. Geographic structuring is especially important if tastes and brand responses differ across regions, as it allows for flexibility in product offerings and marketing strategies. Also, geographic structuring may be necessary because of cost and availability of resources, distribution strategies, and laws in foreign countries. Coca Cola structures geographically because of the cost of transporting water. NetJets, a private aviation company, had to create a separate company in Portugal to operate NetJets Europe, because the entity had to be owned by a European Union carrier.

McDonald's is well-known for its geographic structure and localization strategy for food preferences. The McDonald's in Malaysia is certified halal (no pork products) and you can order the McD Chicken Porridge: chicken and onions in porridge. Other examples are Brie Nuggets (fried brie) in Russia; the Ebi Filet-O (shrimp patty) in Japan; and in Canada, you can get poutine (fries and cheese curds smothered in gravy).

This type of structure is best for organizations that need to be near sources of supply and/or customers. The main disadvantage of a geographical organizational structure is that it can be easy for decision making to become decentralized; geographic divisions can sometimes be hundreds, if not thousands, of miles away from corporate headquarters, allowing them to have a high degree of autonomy.

Matrix Organizations

Where two dimensions are critical, companies will use a matrix structure. Employees may be organized according to product and geography, for example, and have two bosses. The idea behind this type of matrix structure is to combine the localization benefits of the geography structure with those of the functional structure (responsiveness and decentralized focus).

CEO

| CEO SBU 1 | CEO SBU 2 | CEO SBU 3 | CEO SB4 |

North America

South America

Europe

Middle East & Africa

Asia

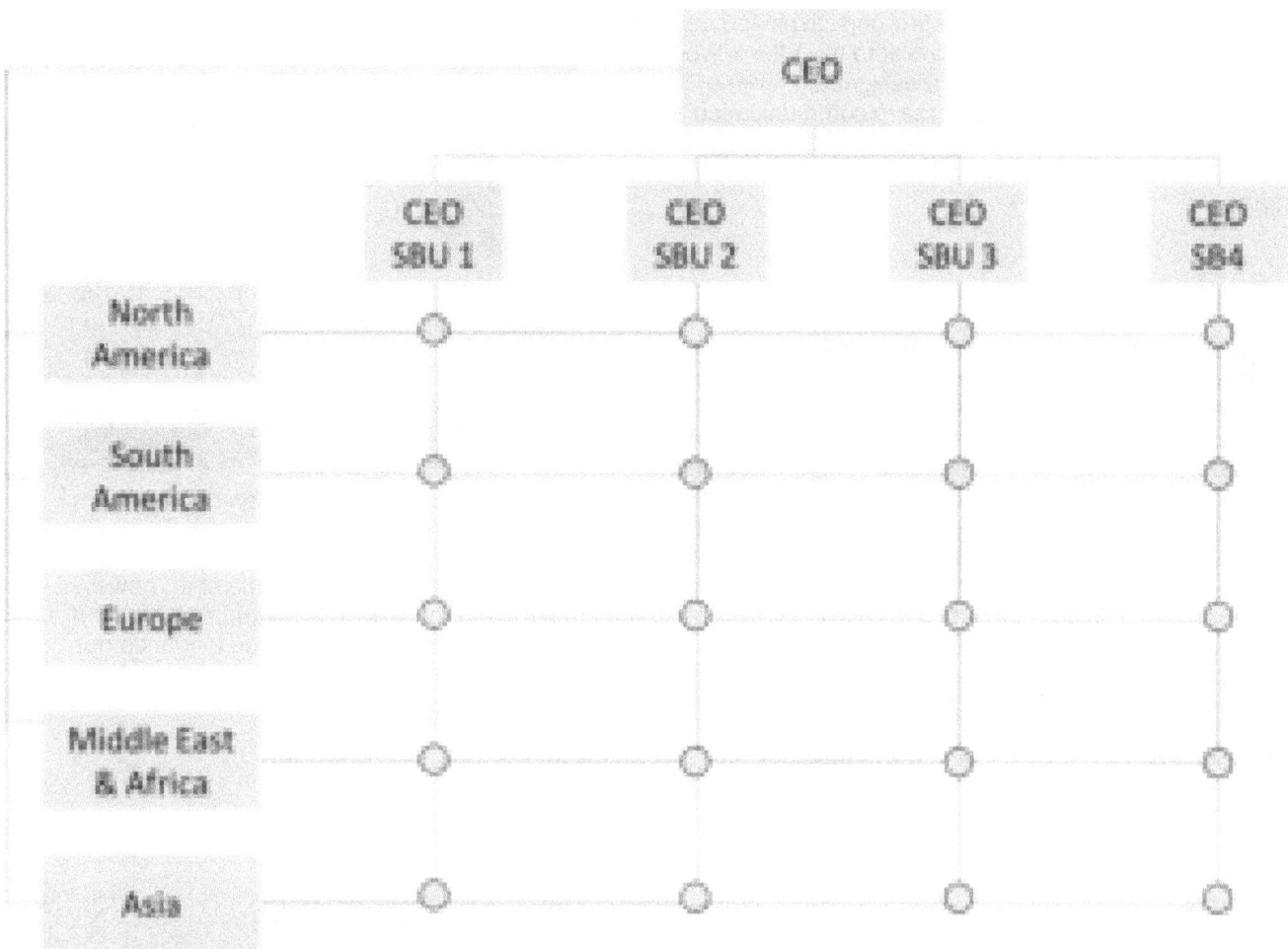

Matrix structure with geographic and product (SBU) structure.

The advantage of the matrix structure is that it can provide both flexibility and more balanced decision making (because two chains of command exist instead of just one). Its primary disadvantage: complexity, which can lead to confused employees.

Team-based Structures, Networks, and Modular Organizations

The reality is that if an organization is successful enough to survive and grow, it will eventually need some form of integration. Poor communication between siloed departments often leads to a crisis that inspires efforts to integrate—efforts such as teams, networks, and modular structures.

Team-based Structure

Over the last several decades, team-based structures of some variation have become common in almost every industry. Lockheed Martin Aircraft Corporation started its "Skunk Works" project in 1943 in response to the U.S. Army's need for a jet fighter. Based on a handshake, a small team of engineers worked secretly in a tent to design and build the XP-80 Shooting Star Jet Fighter in 143 days—seven days less than was required. The level of secrecy needed for this type of a project team is extremely rare in most organizations, yet it did spawn the modern-day project team.

Project teams are focused on a few objectives and usually disbanded at a project's end. Similar to the Skunk Works® model, this team may locate in a designated room or building with the intention to increase communication and collaboration and minimize distractions. Although project teams are less hierarchical, they typically still include a manager.

Team

In general, a team is made up of people with complementary skills who are working toward a common purpose. Organizations create teams by grouping employees in a way that generates a variety of expertise and addresses a specific operational component of the organization. Teams that include members from different functions are known as cross-functional teams. Because of the success of early project teams, the belief is that a team

A picture of the Skunk Works® hangar in Palmdale, California

will be a more creative and productive structure to face new challenges. It is important to remember, however, that every team is a group but not every group is a team. A team structure must be less hierarchical, share the leadership, and be more fluid than traditional structures (such as functional or divisional). True teams do not disband after a project. Rather, they continue to change and adapt to fulfill group and organizational objectives over several years.

The following table lists some of the differences between teams and groups.

	Teams	Groups
Purpose	Distinct, specific to the team's charter	Indistinguishable from, or parallels that of, the organization
Work	Interdependent with a collective work product	Independent tasks with individual work products
Performance	Synergy – collectively we achieve more than the sum of individual efforts	Additive – the sum of the individual efforts
Skills	Complementary	Job-specific
Leadership	Shared	One leader
Accountability	Mutual accountability, responsibility for the collective work product	Individuals: For their own products Leader: For group product
Communication	Performance conversations	Hierarchical

Source: Information derived from Katzenbach and Smith (1993)

Team structures can eliminate layers of management, which allows employees to make decisions without getting multiple approvals. This streamlines processes and lowers administrative costs. However, motivating individuals in a team-based organization can be more challenging as team accomplishments are rewarded rather than individual achievements.

Network Structure

The newest, and most divergent, team structure is commonly known as a network structure. A network structure has little bureaucracy and features decentralized decision making. Managers coordinate and control relations both internal and external to the firm. A social structure of interactions is fostered to build and manage formal and informal relationships. The goal of this structure is to achieve rapid organizational evolution and adaptation to constantly changing external and internal environments.

Zappos has embraced this model and labeled it holacracy. Rather than relying on a traditional top-down hierarchical management structure, **holacracy** attempts to achieve control and coordination by distributing power and authority to self-organizing groups (so-called circles) of employees. Circles of employees are meant to self-organize and own a specific task, such as confirming online orders or authorizing a customer's credit card. Order is supposed to emerge from the bottom up, rather than rely on top-down command and control as in traditional organizational structures. Rules are explicit in a so-called constitution, which defines the power and authority of each circle. For coordination, the employee circles overlap horizontally and without vertical hierarchy. Once the teams are in place, the CEO effectively relinquishes all executive powers.

A network structure is meant to promote communication and the free flow of information between different parts of the organization as needed. However, the circular structure can be confusing, especially for new employees. (Note: Devaney, Erik. "The Pros & Cons of 7 Popular Organizational Structures [Diagrams]." HubSpot Marketing. Dec. 23, 2014 (updated Aug. 3, 2017). https://blog.hubspot.com/marketing/team-structure-diagrams)

The following video explores Zappos' work culture and organizational structure.

https://www.youtube.com/watch?v=5mknIg_Abfw

Modular Organizations

A business that has areas or departments that can be easily separated from the company without jeopardizing the company are considered to have a modular organizational structure. The key lies in the ability to identify which modules, or departments, of a business are effective and which can be outsourced to create a tighter organization.

Organizations that want to remain flexible and streamlined must know when it is time to remove a module and allow the job to be done outside the company. For example, a small specialty T-Shirt company may recognize that its design, production, and customer service modules are at peak form and working well together but that its website design and maintenance department is slowing it down. The shop may externalize that module and send the work to an outside business. (Note: Sparks, Dana. "Modularity Organization Structure." Houston Chron. http://smallbusiness.chron.com/modularity-organization-structure-12822.html)

INTRODUCTION TO FACTORS IMPACTING ORGANIZATIONAL DESIGN

What you'll learn to do: identify important factors for consideration in organizational design

Now that you are familiar with the elements of organizational structure and the various forms, we will dive into the environmental forces to consider when designing an organization's structure. Further, you will learn how a business growth cycle affects organizational choices.

FACTORS IMPACTING ORGANIZATIONAL DESIGN

Learning Outcomes

- Identify aspects of the external environment that influence the design of an organization's structure.
- Identify aspects of the internal environment that influence the design of an organization's structure.
- Explain how business growth cycle affects organizational choices.

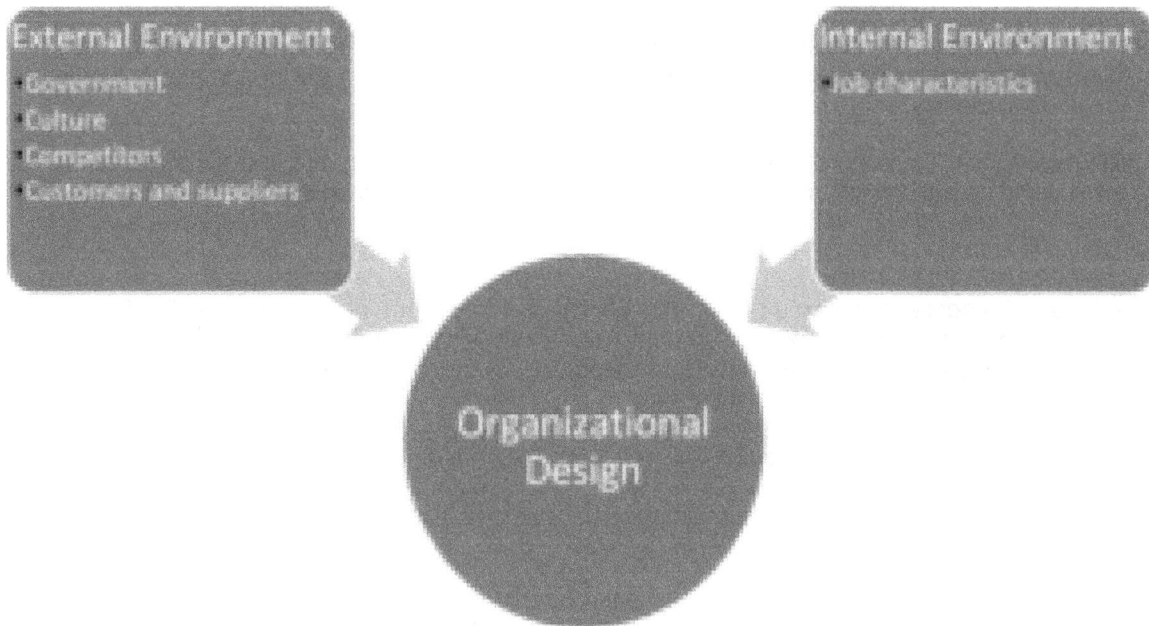

External Environment
- Government
- Culture
- Competitors
- Customers and suppliers

Internal Environment
- Job characteristics

Organizational Design

External Environment

The first factor to influence an organization's design will be that of the external environment. The external environment consists of everything outside of organizations that can affect their performance and outcomes. Availability and need for raw materials, human resources, and financial resources are elements of the environment. Further key elements include customers and suppliers, competitors, cultural factors, and the types of regulatory frameworks or governmental influences on the organization.

The greater the number of external forces, the greater the complexity of the external environment. A pharmaceutical company operates in a very complex environment dealing with many groups such as doctors, hospitals, pharmacists, external research establishments, regulators, health insurance providers, labor markets, and many suppliers. In addition, a pharmaceutical company would deal with these groups in many countries with varying local economic conditions, health care arrangements, and regulatory regimes.

Environmental stability refers to how stable all of the environmental forces are over time. There was a time when certain external forces were considered stable, such as governmental regulations and laws, which could continue for many years, even with new political administrations in place. However, the financial crisis of 2008 and political changes in the United States have added volatility. The high-tech and software industries would be considered unstable because of the relative ease for new software and technology companies to enter and take over an existing market.

Internal Environment

The internal environment is influenced by the jobs and the employees as they relate to those jobs. The employees' influence on the internal environment is directly related to their level of engagement, or job satisfaction. The job characteristics model, proposed by Richard Hackman and Greg Oldham in 1980, proposes that the right combination of skill variety, task identity, task significance, autonomy, and feedback can lead to high-quality performance, high internal motivation, and high satisfaction.

Skill variety: This is the degree to which the job requires a person to use multiple high-level skills. A department store greeter whose job consists of greeting customers and giving them a shopping cart demonstrates low levels of skill variety, whereas the employee who acts as a cashier, stocks shelves, and manages the inventory of outdoor furniture demonstrates high skill variety.

Task identity: This is the degree to which a person is responsible for completing an identifiable task from start to finish. A graphic designer who creates images for a website might have low task identity. This is because the designer's work is only part of a larger whole; other designers and coders contribute their work to completing the website. However, a graphic designer who creates a brochure for a client from the idea phase to the final proof will have a high task identity.

Task significance: This is the degree to which a person's job affects customers or other people's work. A nurse handling the diverse needs patients in the intensive care unit may score high on significance, whereas new nurses aiding in the same department may feel that they perform only busy work and feel a low level of significance.

Autonomy: This is the degree to which a person can decide how to perform his or her tasks. For instance, a grocery store clerk who is given a list of tasks to complete by the end of the day has greater autonomy than a clerk who is given that same list and told that the list needs to be completed in a particular order, with certain tasks needing to be done by certain times of the day.

Feedback: This is the degree to which people learn whether they are doing their job well. Feedback may come from other people, such as managers, peers, subordinates, and customers, or it may come from the job itself. For instance, a customer service representative might receive feedback from a supervisor, as well as from the customers he or she has tried to help.

Taken all together, the job characteristics model links the task itself to employee motivation. More specifically, a job that is challenging will improve employee motivation but a job that is boring and repetitive will hamper employee motivation. To make a job challenging, managers can ensure the following:

- There are a variety of tasks for the employee to complete.
- The employee feels a sense of autonomy.
- The employee is empowered to make certain decisions.

Growth Cycle

Larry Greiner's model of growth offers an organic view of the business life cycle. Like people, organizations change as they age and grow. Each growth stage encompasses an evolutionary phase of growth and a revolutionary phase where an organizational crisis will occur, and the business's ability to handle these crises can determine its future.

Phase 1 – Creativity

The creativity phase is marked by early growth of a company due to an emphasis on creating a product or service. The founders of the company are usually technically or entrepreneurially oriented, and they generally disdain management activities. As the complexity of the business increases, the founders will struggle to both grow and manage the business.

Phase 2 – Direction

A strong business manager will be brought in to install a functional organizational structure, with formal communication channels and hierarchy. A strong focus on accounting and capital management will drive most business decisions. Top management's control of all operations diminishes the autonomy that middle-level managers enjoyed, despite their superior knowledge of markets and products.

Phase 3 – Delegation

The delegation phase is marked by the application of a decentralized organizational structure. Middle managers are freed up to make decisions and executives monitor the operation and focus on bigger issues, such as mergers or acquisitions. Better coordination of all the operations will be required as the executives feel a loss of control over the middle managers.

Phase 4 – Coordination

The coordination of the business structure involves the merging of local units into product groups, a centralization of support functions, and establishment of formal planning procedures. Although resource use becomes more efficient and growth occurs, managers become frustrated with the bureaucratic red tape. The rules and procedures appear more important than productivity and innovation. In turn, corporate staff becomes frustrated with the uncooperative and uninformed managers.

Phase 5 – Collaboration

All parts of the organization criticize the resulting bureaucratic structure, and it will take all the key leaders, managers, and employees to collaborate in an attempt to create a better structure. The formal systems and procedures will have to give way to social control and self-discipline. A shift to a problem solving-based approach is needed as teams combine across various business functions and previous systems are simplified.

INTRODUCTION TO CURRENT TRENDS IN ORGANIZATION AND JOB DESIGN

What you'll learn to do: describe current trends in organization and job design

The Industrial Revolution model of structure, which was largely modeled after military structure, has been fading in popularity and prevalence over the last twenty years. The move to flatter organizational structure with greater autonomy given to employees is highlighted by companies such as Apple and Microsoft. Ironically, the U.S. military is also moving to highly autonomous, self-organizing teams.

CURRENT TRENDS IN ORGANIZATION AND JOB DESIGN

Learning Outcomes

- Explain the advantages of flatter organizational structures.
- Explain the benefits of employee empowerment.

Flatter Organizational Structures

When Gen. Stanley McChrystal took charge of the U.S. Joint Special Operations Task Force in 2003, he recognized that traditional tactics of warfare were failing in Iraq. McChrystal wrote in his book Team of Teams that "To defeat a network, we had to become a network." A network in this context is a collection of small cross-functional teams that have been empowered to self-organize, self-manage, and self-execute.

The traditional career ladder follows a hierarchical path; entry-level position followed by promotions up the chain with broader responsibilities and less job or skill specificity. A flat structure model focuses on horizontal growth, digging deeper, expanding knowledge and getting better at core competencies. The benefit to employees is greater autonomy, as they have the freedom to work amongst each other without the titles of hierarchy slowing down communication.

Employee Empowerment

At the core of all of the trends in organizational structure is employee empowerment. The traditional hierarchical structure took away most of an employee's power to make decisions. The movement is to trust the employee's ability and to give him or her the authority to make decisions, even mistakes. The benefit to organizations can be greater productivity, innovation, and customer service. The responsibility of the organization is to clearly lay out the roles and responsibilities to decrease ambiguity.

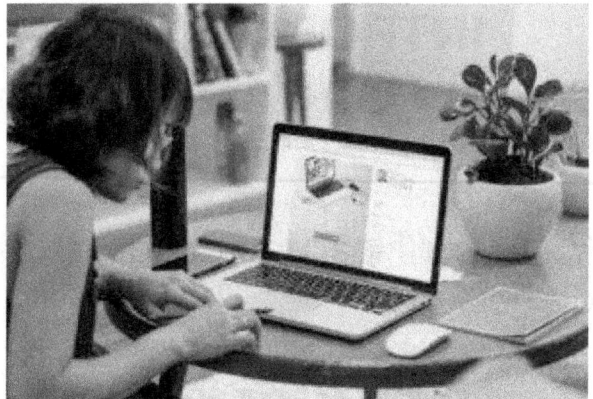

In many industries, the option to work from home is becoming increasingly popular.

A good example of empowerment is flexible work arrangements (FWAs). FWAs include reduced workload (part time), compressed work weeks, and remote work (telework). The most important aspect of a FWA policy is that the organization believes that the employees and their managers know best as to how, when, and where to complete their work. Remote work is prevalent throughout most industries and can range from working from home on certain days when needed to fully remote workers with no corporate office. These arrangements will work only if the organization values productivity over face time.

114

PUTTING IT TOGETHER: ORGANIZATIONAL STRUCTURES

Back to IBM Credit Corporation

Let's return to our case study of IBM's credit arm that we considered at the outset of this module. You'll recall that credit applications could take six days to several weeks to be processed, during which time sales were being lost to competitors. So what did IBM do?

Two senior managers with the company decided to follow a credit application throughout the entire process. When they did, they were surprised to discover that the actual processing time for each application was only ninety minutes! It quickly became evident that the delays were not a result of the amount of work that needed to be completed. Instead, it was a function of the structure the company had implemented. Each step in the approval process was routed to a different specialist to be completed.

Step 1	Central office operator receives a finance request from a salesperson and records it on an input form → form is routed to the credit department
Step 2	Credit specialist reviews the customer and makes a credit decision → result is recorded on the form, which is routed to the business practices department
Step 3	Business practices approves any customer-requested changes to the standard loan covenants → changes are noted on the form and it is sent to the pricing department
Step 4	Pricing specialist determines the appropriate rate to charge based on the customer's credit and specific loan covenants → form moves to the administration department
Step 5	Administration specialist turns all information recorded on the form into a quote letter → quote letter is routed to the sales specialist for delivery to the customer

Based on what you learned in this module, how would you describe IBM Credit's organizational structure? Thinking back to Schein's four key elements of an organization, where do you see opportunities for improvement?

- **Common Purpose** – Do the specialists understand their role in the overall purpose of the credit arm's goal to support the sale of IBM computers, software, and equipment?
- **Coordinated Effort** – Has management coordinated the effort of work in a way that best adds value to the organization?
- **Specialization and Division of Labor** – Has management broken down the tasks into optimum sizes to allow maximum efficiency?
- **Hierarchy of Authority** – Is the optimal reporting structure in place?

In the end, the company realized that it had done a poor job of coordinating the efforts of the organization. Although each of the specialists was working hard, the structure did not support the overall goal of maximizing IBM Corp's sales. In fact, the problem was based on an erroneous assumption that every request that was received was unique and difficult. In reality, the majority of credit requests were straightforward and easy to process. It generally did not require someone with the in-depth knowledge of a specialist. The organization had divided the labor too narrowly.

The company changed its structure, and instead of using specialists, it assigned generalists trained to handle a standard credit request. They would own the request from start to finish and would only engage the help of a specialist if the situation was more complex than they could handle. The result? The new turnaround time was closer to four hours compared with six days or weeks!

This example clearly illustrates the need for managers to carefully analyze their organizational structure to ensure that it is capable of delivering the desired results.

MODULE 7: HUMAN RESOURCE MANAGEMENT

WHY IT MATTERS: HUMAN RESOURCE MANAGEMENT

Why does a manager need to understand HR management and its legal constraints?

You're the manager of marketing, and you've just learned you can hire a new person to help with a major project. That's great news—but how do you select the right person for the job? How much can you pay that person? Is there money in the budget for training your new hire to use your company's special software system? This isn't part of your normal job, so how do you know what to do?

Now your new hire has started, and she's doing a great job. There's a deadline coming up, and you need her to work extra hours to get the job done on time. Is it legal to ask her to stay late to meet a deadline? Will you need to pay her extra for the extra hours—or can you offer her different options, such as time off, once the project is completed? Again, these questions don't have anything to do with your role in marketing, so how will you proceed?

The answers fall into the area known as human resources management (HR). Although managers may work in marketing, finance, or some other functional area, it is vital that they understand the basic principles of HR as they interact with their employees. HR covers a broad spectrum of laws and regulations designed to protect the employee, and even though it is not necessary for all managers to be HR specialists, it is important for them to have a general understanding of HR practices.

In this module you will learn about the options, requirements, rules, and laws related to human resources management.

INTRODUCTION TO PURPOSE OF HUMAN RESOURCE MANAGEMENT

What you'll learn to do: explain the purpose of human resource management for both the organization and individuals

In this section, you'll discover how human resources functions within a corporation. You'll find out how HR decisions help the company to meet its goals, and how HR management can make or break a company's reputation. You'll also learn about the laws and policies companies must follow when making decisions about HR policies.

PURPOSE OF HUMAN RESOURCE MANAGEMENT

Learning Outcomes

- List the functions of human resource management.
- Explain how HR decisions reflect the corporate strategy.

Susan Fowler is an engineer who writes a blog about her experiences. She used to work at Uber, the popular ride-share company. But although Uber did interesting work and she liked her job, her boss was harassing her.

After many attempts to change the situation by going to the Human Resources department at Uber, Susan realized that HR was not interested in supporting her. It was willing to break the law and allow her boss to get away with sexual harassment. But Susan wasn't willing to accept this behavior from her employer. She spoke up and got others to speak up with her.

The result: Uber not only lost a great employee but also lost the respect of the public. Since Fowler started writing about her experiences, Uber has lost money, employees, and opportunities to grow.

Here is some of what Susan Fowler says about her experience at Uber:

> On my first official day rotating on the team, my new manager sent me a string of messages over company chat. He was in an open relationship, he said, and his girlfriend was having an easy time finding new partners but he wasn't. He was trying to stay out of trouble at work, he said, but he couldn't help getting in trouble, because he was looking for women to have sex with. It was clear that he was trying to get me to have sex with him, and it was so clearly out of line that I immediately took screenshots of these chat messages and reported him to HR.

After reporting the situation, Fowler assumed HR would do the right thing. At the very least, it would reprimand the manager for breaking the company's code of ethics. Instead, says Fowler, HR did the opposite:

I was told by both HR and upper management that even though this was clearly sexual harassment and he was propositioning me, it was this man's first offense, and that they wouldn't feel comfortable giving him anything other than a warning and a stern talking-to. Upper management told me that he "was a high performer" (i.e. had stellar performance reviews from his superiors) and they wouldn't feel comfortable punishing him for what was probably just an innocent mistake on his part.

Instead of confronting the manager, HR told Fowler she could leave the team. Her other option was to stay on the team—but if she stuck with it, she should expect a poor performance review, even if she did a good job. Fowler left the team but started asking other women about their experience at Uber. Over and over, she heard stories similar to her own. She even learned that HR had lied to her: her manager had been reported for sexual harassment many times but had never been disciplined for his behavior.

Finally, after trying and failing to get an appropriate response from upper management, Fowler quit her job. She then went on to write about her experience, sharing the details of Uber's poor management with the world. (Note: Susan J. Fowler, "Reflecting on One Very, Very Strange Year at Uber," Susan J. Fowler (blog), Feb. 19, 2017, accessed July 26, 2017, https://www.susanjfowler.com/blog/2017/2/19/reflecting-on-one-very-strange-year-at-uber.)

A good HR department could have handled all of Susan's concerns legally and appropriately, and Uber could have avoided a great deal of trouble. Investors voted with their feet, and Uber's stock lost $10 billion, according to CNBC. (Note: Anita Balakrishnan, "Scandals may have knocked $10 billion off Uber's value, a report says," CNBC, April 25, 2017, accessed July 26, 2017, http://www.cnbc.com/2017/04/25/uber-stock-price-drops-amid-sexism-investigation-greyballing-and-apple-run-in--the-information.html.) At best, this is a lost opportunity that will cost the company far more than managing within the law.

The Functions of Human Resource Management

Managing employee conflicts and legal issues is only part of HR's function. In fact, HR is a key department in any company, and it is responsible for many areas. Each of these areas can be categorized into the main functions of human resource management:

Function	What It Is
Recruitment and Selection	• Finding and hiring qualified employees and/or contractors • Using recruitment tools and technology • Preparing employee contracts and negotiating salaries and benefits • Meeting legal requirements related to hiring and adhering to ethical practices
Training and Development	• Onboarding training for new employees and ongoing training and development for current employees • Trainings and development activities may include internal meetings, conferences, or external educational courses • Opportunities for employee evaluation
Compensation	• Setting appropriate and competitive wages or salaries for employees • Researching and negotiating insurance and retirement plans, as well as other types of benefits, with third-party providers
Safety and Health	• Ensuring that employees have a safe work environment and that the organization is complying with legal requirements set forth by the Occupational Safety and Health Administration (OSHA)

	• Implementing new safety measures when laws change in a given industry • Discussing safety and compliance with relevant government departments • Discussing safety and compliance with unions
Employee and Labor Relations	• Mediating disputes between employees and employers, as well as between employees and other employees • Ensuring employees understand their rights with regard to unions and unionizing
Terminate employee contracts when necessary	• Helping to document employee problems in order to justify firing • Terminating employees for various reasons and following up with appropriate paperwork and legal actions

Human resources management can also play an important role in strategic planning and company growth. For example, HR professionals take part in:

• Planning to hire or transfer employees when a company grows.
• Training new employees as the company makes changes or expands.
• Developing incentive programs to help the company compete with other employers.
• Researching laws and policies related to employees in other states or countries.
• Setting up employee transportation, moves, and other logistics as needed.

Why is all this important? HR is a specialty that involves a great many legal details. Mistakes in employee benefits, mismanaging sensitive employee records, or glossing over company ethics policies could land a company in legal trouble. Lawsuits that go to court have incurred a median cost of $200,000. (Note: Andrea G. Simpson, "What Are Chances a U.S. Business Will Face an Employee Lawsuit?" Oct. 28, 2015, accessed July 26, 2017, http://www.insurancejournal.com/news/national/2015/10/28/386321.htm.) HR professionals are the people who have the knowledge, time, and responsibility to ensure that employees receive the services, resources, and support they need to be successful at work.

A recent trend is more part-time and contract workers. HR professionals source and hire both and handle the contracts and legal risks.

The following video highlights some of the important work HR managers do in a company, as in this example of the human resources director at Quiksilver.

https://www.youtube.com/watch?v=bb4RGuQu2Pk

HR and Corporate Strategy

You might think of HR management as a somewhat standard part of every business–the HR department deals with hiring, training, compensation, safety issues, and so on. But successful businesses don't take a one-size-fits-all approach to HR management. Instead, they use their HR policies to support the business's strategic goals and increase their competitive advantage.

In practice, that means making sure the key elements of HR are aligned with the organization's strategy. For example, if one of your organizational goals is to create innovative products, your HR policies might allow employees a certain amount of time to work on their own ideas. Google does this with its famous "20 percent time" policy that allows employees to spend one-fifth of their time working on a project of their own choosing that they think will most benefit Google. 3M had a similar policy before Google, and it resulted in one of the company's most successful products: the Post-It Note. Allowing employees time to be creative on the job not only helps attract the types of employees these companies want, but also benefits the company when employees come up with innovative ideas and strategies.

Today's HR managers need to think less about enforcing compliance rules and tracking simple metrics and more about how policies will help achieve strategic goals. They must align the organization's people with the desired outcomes. Depending on the business's strategy, this might mean using a very selective hiring process to find the candidate with the right skills for the job, or using contractors instead of full-time employees to keep costs low. The goal of HR is to ensure that an organization has the right skills, abilities, and knowledge to implement its strategy.

High-performing organizations use HR elements such as job design and diversity management to maximize employee performance. **Job design** (also referred to as work design or task design) is a core function of human resource management. It's related to the specification of contents, methods, and relationship of jobs in order to satisfy technological and organizational requirements as well as the social and personal requirements of the job holder. Its principles are geared towards how the nature of a person's job affects their attitudes and behavior at work, particularly relating to characteristics such as skill variety and autonomy. The aim of a job design is to improve job satisfaction, to improve throughput, to improve quality, and to reduce employee problems (e.g., grievances, absenteeism).

HR managers are also concerned with diversity in the workplace. In a global economy, employing a diverse workforce and celebrating multiculturalism can create or strengthen an organization's competitive advantage.

INTRODUCTION TO LAWS AFFECTING HUMAN RESOURCE PRACTICES

What you'll learn to do: summarize the key laws affecting human resource practices

In the United States, federal, state, and local laws exist that affect employees and employers. They help protect workers from unsafe work settings, discrimination, harassment, and unfair business practices. Every business must abide by these laws or face fines and other legal consequences. Human resources professionals are the people who must learn about these laws, implement policies to follow them, and keep up with changes in the laws. Managers, too, must understand the laws and policies and follow them as they make decisions that affect hiring, firing, work conditions, and other issues.

LAWS AFFECTING HUMAN RESOURCE PRACTICES

Learning Outcomes
• List the protected employee classes in the United States. • Summarize the key laws related to employee discrimination. • Explain what HR managers can do to protect the company against discrimination lawsuits. • Explain HR's role in workplace safety. • Explain collective bargaining and the law that governs it.

Protected Classes of Employees

Certain groups of employees are legally protected from discrimination. In other words, if an employee belongs to a protected group and is discriminated against because of his or her status as a member of that group, that employee can take legal action against the employer. But being part of a protected group does not mean an employee can never be disciplined or fired.

For example, imagine a female employee who shows up late, meets few of her goals, and receives a poor evaluation. She applies for promotion but loses out to a white man who has worked hard, met his goals, and received a very positive evaluation. In this case, the woman was not discriminated against because of her gender; rather, she was denied promotion because of poor work performance. As a result, she would not have legal cause for action.

On the other hand, imagine a Latino employee who has a stellar work record. He is laid off, whereas a Caucasian worker with a poor work record is kept on. In this case, there is a good chance the Latino employee could win a legal case against his employer for racial discrimination.

HR managers can protect the company against discrimination lawsuits by understanding discrimination law and putting policies into place to avoid discrimination. Should discrimination occur despite workplace policies against it, HR managers can work with upper management to quickly address individual issues, compensate employees, and discipline managers who discriminate. The Equal Employment Opportunity Commission (EEOC) is responsible for interpreting and enforcing the laws against discrimination in the workplace.

Employers may not discriminate against employees because of:

1. **Race or Color:** This category includes blacks, whites, people of Latino or Asian origin or descent, and indigenous Americans (Eskimos, Native Hawaiians, Native Americans).
2. **National Origin:** This means employers may not discriminate based on the country where a person was born or the country from which his or her ancestors came—unless language or other requirements make it impossible for the individual to do the job effectively. For example, a native Russian speaker with no English language skills could reasonably be denied a job as a lecturer in a U.S. college.
3. **Sex:** This means an employer cannot discriminate against either men or women as a result of their gender. In some states, laws also apply to transgender individuals.

4. **Religion:** According to the EEOC, protections "include moral or ethical beliefs as to what is right and wrong which are sincerely held with the strength of traditional religious views." Employers must "reasonably accommodate to an employee's or prospective employee's religious observance or practice" unless doing so would impose an "undue hardship on the conduct of the employer's business."

Key Laws Related to Employee Discrimination

Employee discrimination has been the focus of several important laws. They include the following:

Equal Pay Act of 1963: This law makes it illegal to pay men more than women for the same work.

Civil Rights Act of 1964: This act is intended to protect people who were often discriminated against because of their race, national origin, gender, color, or religion. The Title VII of the act relates specifically to employment. The law, which applies to any company with more than fifteen employees, also makes it illegal to discriminate against an employee because she is pregnant or coping with conditions (such as morning sickness) caused by pregnancy. New rules also provide some protections to transgender individuals. Title VII also created the EEOC to implement the law.

Age Discrimination in Employment Act of 1967: This law, which applies to companies with twenty-plus employees, makes it illegal to discriminate against employees because they are more than forty years old.

Pregnancy Discrimination Act of 1978: This act amended Title VII of the Civil Rights Act to also prohibit discrimination on the basis of pregnancy.

Americans with Disabilities Act of 1990: According to this act, employers must make "reasonable" workplace modifications to accommodate the needs of a person with a disability. Examples include addition of ramps for wheelchairs, adjustments to work schedules, etc.

Family Medical Leave Act of 1993: This law offers job protections to individuals for parental leave and medical leave. For covered employers, a parent may take up to 12 weeks after the birth of a child.

Uniformed Services Employment and Reemployment Rights Act of 1994 (USERRA): This law offers job protections to individuals when they are called to uniformed service.

Genetic Information Nondiscrimination Act of 2008: According to this act, genetic information cannot be used to make employment or health insurance decisions.

In addition to these laws, there are also several that relate only to federal government employees. These include sections 501 and 505 of the Rehabilitation Act of 1973 and the Civil Service Reform Act of 1978. Individual states also have their own employee protection laws; for example, some states forbid discrimination based on sexual orientation, weight, marital status, etc.

Workplace Safety

There are a number of laws in place in the United States that require employers to provide a safe workplace. These laws are administered by OSHA, but HR must be sure the laws are followed. In some occupations, however, safety can't be guaranteed. For example, when employees work with hazardous chemicals, large machinery, transportation vehicles, etc., there are risks. Workers have the right to refuse to work in dangerous conditions without risking their jobs.

To lower risk, management and HR can work together to substitute less dangerous procedures or materials when both options can get the job done, isolate dangerous materials or machines from employees who do not need to work with them, ensure that proper safety equipment and

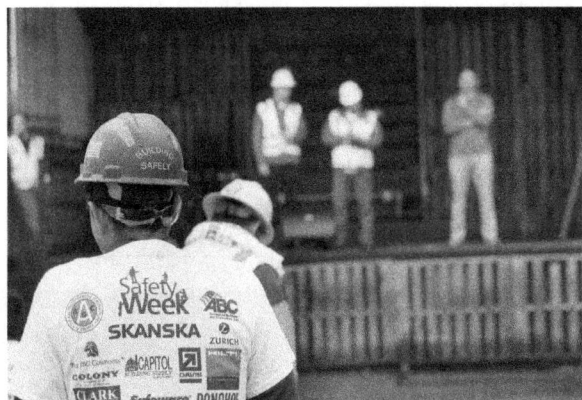

ventilation are used in all hazardous situations, put policies in place that decrease risk by taking required safety precautions, and require employees to use appropriate safety equipment such as goggles, gloves, and hard hats.

Worker safety is the focus of many training activities and initiatives.

All these positive changes can help the company by keeping employees on the job, thus increasing productivity. Research shows that safety programs more than pay for themselves. (Note: David Machles, "Evaluating the Effectiveness of Safety Training," June 01, 2003, accessed July 26, 2017, https://ohsonline.com/Articles/2003/06/Evaluating-the-Effectiveness-of-Safety-Training.aspx.)

Collective Bargaining

A 2004 story in the *New York Times* describes how, until recently, workers were locked into a building while working at night for Sam's Club:

> *Looking back to that night, Michael Rodriguez still has trouble believing the situation he faced when he was stocking shelves on the overnight shift at the Sam's Club in Corpus Christi, Tex.*
>
> *It was 3 a.m., Mr. Rodriguez recalled, some heavy machinery had just smashed into his ankle, and he had no idea how he would get to the hospital.*
>
> *The Sam's Club, a Wal-Mart subsidiary, had locked its overnight workers in, as it always did, to keep robbers out and, as some managers say, to prevent employee theft. As usual, there was no manager with a key to let Mr. Rodriguez out. The fire exit, he said, was hardly an option – management had drummed into the overnight workers that if they ever used that exit for anything but a fire, they would lose their jobs. (Note: Steven Greenhouse, "Workers Assail Night Lock-Ins By Wal-Mart," Jan. 18, 2004, accessed July 26, 2017, http://www.nytimes.com/2004/01/18/us/workers-assail-night-lock-ins-by-wal-mart.html?mcubz=2.)*

How could employees respond to such a terrible situation? Individual employees have few choices: they can stay and cope with the situation, they can complain and face the possibility of being fired, or they can quit. Labor unions—groups of employees acting together—can give employees more leverage. Although one worker had little power to make change, large groups in unions could threaten strikes or slowdowns to force change.

Today, labor unions and employers make agreements through a process called collective bargaining. Collective bargaining is the process by which employers work with union representatives to decide on policies, wages, and benefits. Union representatives are empowered to speak on behalf of the entire union. If the union representative negotiates a raise for its members, all members get more money.

Labor unions gained much of their power through the Wagner Act of 1935. The act made it legal for most workers to organize or join labor unions. It also made it possible for labor unions to negotiate contracts for their members. To help labor unions become more effective, the act set up the National Labor Relations Board (NLRB).

The NLRB oversees the rules and policies related to collective bargaining. According to the NLRB: "If a union is selected as the representative of employees, the employer and union are required to meet at reasonable times to bargain in good faith about wages, hours, and other mandatory subjects. Even after a contract expires, the parties must bargain in good faith for a successor contract, or the termination of the agreement, while terms of the expired contract continue." The NLRB also provides many specific rules for negotiation, mediation, and arbitration in the case of a disagreement between employer and labor.

INTRODUCTION TO RECRUITING AND SELECTING QUALIFIED JOB APPLICANTS

What you'll learn to do: describe effective strategies for recruiting and selecting qualified job applicants

If you've ever applied for a job, you've probably interacted with the human resources department. HR decides that a position is open, helps to write the job description, recruits candidates for the job, and (with the help of the hiring manager) helps decide which candidate will be hired. This can be a complex process, involving several important steps.

RECRUITING AND SELECTING QUALIFIED JOB APPLICANTS

Learning Outcomes

   •   Describe effective strategies for recruiting and selecting qualified job applicants.

There are several steps in the recruitment and selection process. They include advertising for and sourcing candidates, reviewing applications, screening candidates, conducting interviews, and making an offer. HR works closely with hiring managers during the interviewing process.

Managers know more than anyone else about what a particular position involves and what kinds of skills an employee needs to do the job effectively. They may be the one to request the creation of a new position. They are very likely to be asked to help define an existing job or a new job. They, with the help of HR professionals, will describe the tasks and responsibilities of the position, as well as the qualifications required.

First, HR professionals go through a process of job analysis. They ask questions, observe workers, conduct surveys, and determine what, exactly, is required to do the job well. What qualifications will an employee need for the job? What skills are necessary? Are there physical skills or requirements?

Job analysis is a first step toward creating a job description and job specification. The job specification is a statement of employee characteristics and qualifications required for satisfactory performance of defined duties and tasks comprising a specific job or function. A job description is more than just a paragraph describing the responsibilities of the job; it's also an important document that should contain specific information and statements. For example, a job description should state that the employer does not discriminate against potential employees based on age, race, gender, or other personal qualities. In addition, the job description should describe the level of education, experience, and knowledge required for the position. These types of statements are important for several reasons. First, they make it easier to decide whether a particular candidate is really a good match for the job. Second, they provide documentation to show why one candidate might be chosen over another. Discrimination lawsuits that go to court are very expensive, so well-crafted job descriptions can save an employer a great deal of money.

Now the HR department takes over. It's up to them to reach out to find qualified candidates, screen possible applicants, and select individuals who meet your needs. You will then interview a small number of highly qualified individuals and choose the person who best fits your department's needs.

Here is the process of recruitment and selection that starts once a job description has been finalized:

Advertising Openings and Recruiting Candidates

How do you find the perfect candidate for a job opening? There are several techniques. Advertising in newspapers and trade publications can be effective. Most recruiters also use online sources to find job candidates. For example, sites such as Indeed, Monster, and CareerBuilder are very popular. Employers can list jobs on these sites and can search through resumes to find potential employees.

Social sites are also a good way to seek out qualified candidates. LinkedIn is a website that allows employers and potential employees to share information about themselves. Facebook offers opportunities for employers and potential employees to find one another. Often, recruiters search these sites to find qualified candidates, and reach out to selected individuals about job openings. HR also considers candidates suggested by existing employees, talks to people who walk in to inquire about jobs, reaches out through college recruitment events and job fairs, and contacts individuals who have received certification through programs such as Udacity. Another option is to work through recruiters called "head hunters" who find individuals with the right skills and invite them to apply for a particular position.

In many cases, jobs are opened up to internal candidates before they are advertised to the wider world. When that happens, jobs are advertised through company newsletters and bulletin boards and candidates go to HR to apply for the job.

Screening Applicants

Very often, people apply for jobs for which they are not fully qualified. To narrow down the applicants, HR screens applications. They look carefully at resumes, skills, and level of experience to be sure the individual really meets the criteria for the job. They also do background checks on applicants who appear promising, checking on possible criminal records or other serious issues. They may also use keyword filters to review large numbers of resumes for mention of specific skills, educational levels, or management experience. Keyword filters are necessary—but at the same time they can be a problem. Software may eliminate individuals who really are qualified for a job or include individuals who use the right keywords but don't really have the skills they need to jump in and do the job right.

Watch the following interview between Peter Cappelli of the Wharton Business School and *The Wall Street Journal* to find out more about why qualified applicants have a hard time getting through some screening tools.

Preliminary Phone Interview

Quite a few job applicants look "good on paper," meaning that their resumes are impressive. Once you actually speak with them, however, it may become obvious that they don't really meet the requirements of the job. Alternatively, a moderately attractive applicant might turn out to have personal qualities and abilities that are better than they appeared on paper. Preliminary phone interviews allow the HR department to select only the most promising candidates for in-person interviews with the hiring manager and other members of the hiring team.

Face-to-Face Interview and Selection

After preliminary interviews are completed, HR can provide the hiring manager with a set of promising applicants who have the skills, credentials, and background to fit the manager's needs. Now the hiring manager can sit down with each candidate and get to know her through a personal interview. Often, hiring managers will conduct a second interview after narrowing down their options to just a few candidates. They may also include other team members in the interviewing process and/or conduct tests to determine whether candidates have the level of technical skill they need for the job.

It takes some skill and knowledge to interview a job applicant effectively. It's important to do the job right, though, because the costs of hiring someone are substantial, and many hires leave within one year. Some effective interviewing techniques includes the following:

Planning and preparation. Before starting an interview, it's important for a manager to have read the applicant's resume, prepare questions, and know what he wants to learn during the interview. It's also helpful to set a time limit for the interview.

Understanding the job. In some cases, managers don't have direct experience doing the job for which they're hiring. When that happens, it's important for the manager to talk with people who are doing the job now as well as direct supervisors and teammates. What are the most important qualities, skills, and qualifications required for the job? Are there specific situations for which the new hire should be prepared? Knowing about the job makes it easier to ask the right questions.

Connecting with the applicant. Most people are nervous at job interviews, and it's important to set the applicant at ease so she can put her best foot forward. Instead of just saying "Don't be nervous," good managers spend some time chatting with the candidate and explaining the interview process.

Active listening. Managers want to learn about the candidate, so active listening is very important. Managers need to show that they're interested by nodding, asking follow-up questions, smiling, or otherwise using body language to encourage the candidate to share more information.

The Job Offer

Once the hiring manager decides who she'd like to hire, the HR department makes an offer. Typically, a job offer includes information about salary and benefits as well as details about the job requirements. If the candidate is interested, he will need to sign a contract or otherwise accept in writing before taking the job—usually a letter or email is acceptable until the employee's first day.

Because the process can be complicated, it's important to have very concrete reasons for choosing one candidate over another. For example, saying "Mary fits into the team better than Sally" is likely to lead to Mary's feeling that she has lost a popularity contest. A better option is to have a checklist of qualifications that can be shared with job candidates. If you can show Sally that Mary has stronger IT skills, more management experience, and important marketing knowledge, it will help Sally understand why Mary really is the better person for the job.

INTRODUCTION TO EMPLOYEE ORIENTATION AND TRAINING

What you'll learn to do: describe employee orientation and training approaches

Not even the best-qualified employee will arrive without any questions or training needs. That's because every company (and every department) has its own policies, customs, systems, software, and expectations. Before getting to work, therefore, employees go through a process or orientation and training. Usually the human resources department takes the lead in this process, but it's likely that you and your team will need to help new employees get settled in.

EMPLOYEE ORIENTATION AND TRAINING

Learning Outcomes

- Describe employee orientation approaches.
- Describe employee training approaches.

Before any employee can get to work, he or she must go through a process of onboarding that includes:

- Filling out legal and financial paperwork
- Learning about and signing up for eligible benefits
- Reviewing the employee handbook and policies
- Receiving any necessary training in job-specific technology, procedures, etc.

Sometimes, corporations believe that they can hand new employees a stack of paperwork and assume they will fill it out correctly and figure out how to fit in with their new employer. This is rarely a good idea, as every employer has its own systems and expectations—and being the "new kid on the block" is tough enough without adding a laundry list of do-it-yourself tasks.

Why Orientation and Training Are Important

When a new employee arrives, he or she is likely to have preconceived ideas about what is expected of him or her, and are likely to be anxious about making a good impression. Often, those ideas are based either on prior experience, on word of mouth, or on information the new employees have gathered through the media. None of these sources will help a new employee if his expectations don't match reality.

Orientation and training can serve many positive purposes. For example, they can:

1. Lower costs by helping the employee get up to speed quickly and avoid time- or money-consuming mistakes.
2. Help the employee to gain confidence and feel valued because he or she knows the company's system, people, and expectations.
3. Improve the employee's performance by helping him or her to build skills and relationships quickly.

Employees who know what they're doing can save their employer a huge amount of money. Almost half of Walmart's workers turn over each year, (Note: Rachel Abrams, "Walmart Worker Advocates Express Skepticism Over Raises," June 3, 2016, accessed July 27, 2017, https://www.nytimes.com/2016/06/04/business/walmart-worker-advocates-express-skepticism-over-raises.html.) which could be why it often scores poorly for customer service. Walmart said inept shelf-stocking cost $3 billion in 2014. (Note: "Serfs up," The Economist, March 26, 2015, accessed July 27, 2017, https://www.economist.com/news/business/21647320-american-firms-are-having-get-back-habit-granting-pay-rises-serfs-up.) Costco pays more to have happier staff who quit less and build up skills. Margins are higher as a result. (Note: Wayne F. Cascio, "The High Cost of Low Wages," December 2006, accessed July 27, 2017, https://hbr.org/2006/12/the-high-cost-of-low-wages.)

Even an employee who makes $8 per hour can end up costing a company around $3,500 in turnover costs, both direct and indirect. (Note: The Build Network, "Try Fixing the Problem Before Replacing It," Inc., Feb. 27, 2014, accessed July 27, 2017, https://www.inc.com/the-build-network/turnover-costs.html.) Some studies have put the costs of employee turnover in certain industries even higher—one report from Cornell University's Center for Hospitality Research estimated an overall turnover rate of 120 percent in the quick-service restaurant industry, with turnover costs averaging $5,864 per employee. (Note: J. B. Tracey and Timothy R. Hinkin. "The Costs of Employee Turnover: When the Devil Is in the Details." Cornell Hospitality Report 6, no. 15 (2006), 6, 8. http://scholarship.sha.cornell.edu/cgi/viewcontent.cgi?article=1148&context=chrpubs.)

How Human Resources Onboards Employees

Human resources professionals are usually in charge of ensuring new hires have completed all necessary paperwork, signed up for benefits, reviewed safety and ethics policies, and received a comprehensive tour of the workplace. Before getting into the details of the workplace, most HR managers will ensure that employees have filled out and signed paperwork that proves their eligibility to work in the United States, as well as tax forms and other important documents.

Together with the hiring manager, HR may also set up and implement training, introduce new hires to key staff, provide keys or codes, and explain (for example) how mail is sent and received, when and where to get lunch, where to park, and whether it's okay to use social media during work hours.

How Managers Welcome New Employees

Even though HR will (or should) walk a new employee through necessary paperwork and training, it's important for managers to make their new hires feel welcome. It's equally important to help new hires acclimate to a new work setting. To do this, many managers will:

- Send a welcome letter to their new hire before they arrive, providing information about what to expect on their first day at the new job. Sometimes this letter will include suggestions for appropriate attire, parking information, and other key details.
- Meet with HR to discuss exactly when and how the new hire will learn about company policies and benefits.

- Meet with team members to set up the new hire's work space, passwords, telephones, and access to necessary systems.
- Assign one individual to serve as the new employee's mentor or buddy (usually someone who knows the ropes and can provide answers to most reasonable questions).
- Plan for the new hire's schedule and initial set of tasks, as well as a process for helping the new hire to ask questions, review procedures, and ensure that he or she is off to a good start.
- Plan for any training the new hire will need (in collaboration with HR and department members).
- Set up a lunch with the new hire and other members of the working team as a way to get to know one another, answer questions, and make personal connections.

Options for New Employee Training

Training can take many forms, depending upon the type of work for which the employee is hired and the employee's existing level of skill. Training may be more critical if the company uses proprietary software or systems that don't exist in other locations or if procedures or policies are unusual, involve industrial or official secrets, require specialized knowledge, or are legally complex.

Some types of training techniques include:

- Self-paced online training in areas such as software skills, safety procedures, or other technical skills.
- Hands-on training in the use of equipment or machines ranging from copiers to heavy equipment.
- Leader-led group training programs to teach "soft" skills such as coaching, team-building, customer service, client management.
- Formal business courses through outside vendors.
- "Shadowing" or following a skilled employee to observe and learn skills and procedures.
- Mentoring or one-on-one meetings to review work, discuss options, and provide feedback.

The key to successful training is to ensure that the employee truly understands and can use the information provided. Evaluation can involve formal testing or informal conversations. It's important to let the new hire know that questions are welcome—and there is no such thing as a "dumb question."

INTRODUCTION TO EMPLOYEE DEVELOPMENT AND PERFORMANCE EVALUATIONS

What you'll learn to do: describe employee development and performance evaluations

Good managers know that employees are the company's most valuable assets. Employee development is the process by which employees become even more valuable by building their skills and expanding their capabilities.

The better their skills and abilities, the more likely it is that employees will succeed in their jobs and progress in their careers.

Performance evaluations are a tool for determining how quickly and well an employee is developing. They are also an opportunity to discover employees' untapped strengths and interests, and to fill gaps in employee training that can lead to mistakes or lower productivity.

EMPLOYEE DEVELOPMENT AND PERFORMANCE EVALUATIONS

Learning Outcomes

- Describe employee development approaches.
- Describe performance evaluation approaches.

The best, most loyal employees are often people who started near the bottom of the organizational chart and worked their way up the ladder with the help, support, and encouragement of their manager and their employer. That help, support, and encouragement are all part of employee development. In a well-managed company, there are systems in place to provide appropriate development opportunities and resources. In addition, managers are trained to support their team members with coaching, meaningful feedback, and—in some cases—mentorship.

Managers have an important role to play in ensuring that their employees develop their potential. Some of the most important things a manager can do for their team members are:

- Delegating responsibility rather than fixing problems before they arise.
- Being aware of development opportunities as they become available and sharing information with team members.
- Offering or suggesting specific appropriate development opportunities to employees and/or human resources when and as they are appropriate.
- Providing meaningful, actionable feedback to team members regularly.
- Including "up and coming" employees in meetings, conferences, and other events where they can contribute ideas, learn about opportunities, and ask questions.

Formal Employee Development Strategies

In any company, there are employees who are satisfied with entry-level work and those who are eager to learn, grow, and build their careers. Although training programs are appropriate for both groups, certain types of training are particularly important for individuals willing to work hard to improve their career opportunities. These include training opportunities in areas such as leadership, management, negotiation, and other areas likely to be useful to a new manager.

Formal employee development strategies are often planned and implemented by HR and/or consultants, online training companies, and universities. Topics taught range from "soft" skills (interpersonal communication, public speaking, negotiation, leadership skills, etc.) to "hard" technical skills (coding, accounting, systems administration, etc.). Options include:

- On-site or off-site workshops to train employees in areas such as business ethics, communication, management skills, business writing, public speaking, and management techniques.
- Online training programs to build skills in areas such as international business law, marketing or sales techniques.
- Certification programs in areas ranging from software proficiency to legal knowledge to management in specific areas such as human resources and manufacturing.
- Funding for formal coursework in pursuit of postsecondary degrees or certifications in areas such as business administration, finance, or related fields.
- Opportunities to attend conventions and conferences at which employees may attend workshops and build their professional networks (or in some industries, present their research, products, or ideas).

Informal Employee Development Strategies

In addition to formal employee development, many corporations offer informal development options. These often take the form of on-the-job training, shadowing, mentorship, or similar experiences that allow newer employees to learn from senior staff. In addition, managers may choose to coach promising employees to prepare them for more challenging opportunities.

- **On the job training** may involve a newer employee watching and then imitating a more experienced colleague. On-the-job training is fairly standard in hands-on work such as manufacturing, trades, and restaurant work—but it is also effective in many business situations. In sales, for example, a more experienced representative might make a sale using specific techniques and then allow the newer representative to try using that same technique with another potential client. After the interaction is complete, the more experienced individual might provide constructive feedback.
- **Shadowing** is a technique in which a newer employee literally "shadows" or follows a more experienced colleague to watch and learn from his or her techniques. As with on-the-job training, a day of shadowing is usually followed by a conversation during which the learner asks questions to better understand the techniques demonstrated. Shadowing works well when a specific skill is being demonstrated; mediation and negotiation, for example, are best understood in a real-world setting.
- **Mentorship and coaching** are generally offered not by peers but by managers who have the experience and knowledge to advise promising employees. Some corporations offer formal mentorship programs that match individual employees with mentors who have greater experience and higher-level positions in a similar field. Other corporations encourage informal mentoring. Coaching is usually provided by a direct manager who may, for example, wish to support an employee so that he or she can successfully navigate a tricky or challenging project.

Performance Evaluations

Most companies perform annual performance evaluations. These high-stakes reviews can have a profound influence on an employee's career, as they are often the basis on which decisions are made regarding raises, promotions, and even retention. As a result, they create a great deal of anxiety, both for employees and for their managers.

Fortunately, it is possible to craft the performance evaluation so that it is relatively painless. At the same time, a well-crafted evaluation process can also help both managers and employees to review job descriptions with an eye to making appropriate changes, set goals, and address unnecessary roadblocks and challenges that sabotage high performance.

The following list covers some of the most popular approaches to performance evaluations. Each of these has its pros and cons, depending on the type of job and the purpose of the evaluation. Often, managers use multiple techniques to gain a fuller picture of each employee.

- **Checklists** are helpful in that they allow managers to quickly check off skills, achievements, and behaviors as they are accomplished. The downside is that checklists provide little meaningful information about the quality of the accomplishments or any challenges an employee might have encountered when attempting to complete a task. For example, an employee might have legitimate difficulty arriving on time if a public transit strike occurred—but a checklist would simply note that the employee was tardy. Because they're so quick and easy, though, it's possible to use a checklist regularly and compare outcomes over time.
- **Rating Scales** allow managers to rate the quality of an employee's performance or skills; generally, the rating scales are 1 to 5 or 1 to 10. This allows a little more flexibility than a checklist, and it can suggest opportunities for improvement over time. For example, an employee who earns 6 out of 10 for punctuality in January can earn 8 out of 10 in February—thus showing both motivation and improvement.
- **Comparative Techniques** allow managers to compare individual employees head to head for specific goals and outcomes. For example, managers might compare the number of sales made, customers served, income generated, etc. Comparative techniques make it possible to see whether an individual employee is falling far behind or leaping out in front of his or her peers. Of course, comparative techniques only apply to groups of employees who have identical goals, resources, opportunities, and training.
- **Narrative Techniques** are essays describing employee performance. These are generally written by the employees' direct managers, though they are sometimes written by the employee himself or herself. On the one hand, narrative essays take time and energy away from the manager's (or employee's) daily tasks. On the other hand, they can provide the most detailed and meaningful evaluations, as they are flexible enough to describe individuals' strengths, challenges, obstacles, and opportunities.
- **360 Feedback** asks employees' managers, subordinates, and peers to provide feedback about performance from every angle. This can be a very useful form of evaluation, as some individuals can be wonderful managers but have a difficult time interacting with peers or vice versa. By gathering a wide range of perspectives, managers can pinpoint areas of strength and opportunities for growth. On the other hand, this approach can be problematic if the employee in question is less popular for any reason or if a supervisee is unhappy about being disciplined.
- **Cost Accounting** is an approach that is most appropriate for individuals who make direct sales, produce a manufactured product, or provide direct service. The question asked is: how does the cost of the employee's salary and benefits compare to the income this individual generates? By making a direct cost/benefit analysis, the manager can determine whether the employee is worth the amount being spent on him or her by the corporation. This type of accounting, however, rarely provides a complete story about the employee's abilities or assets. For example, a sales person who takes his or her time getting to know the client may make fewer sales per week but may generate more goodwill and recommendations over the long term.
- **Management by Objectives** is a personalized evaluation technique that measures the individual employee's achievement by comparing the employee to objectives agreed upon the prior year. For example, the employee and manager may have agreed on a particular sales objective; at the end of the year, the employee's actual sales can be compared positively or negatively to the individualized objective.

INTRODUCTION TO EMPLOYEE COMPENSATION, INCENTIVE, AND BENEFITS STRATEGIES

What you'll learn to do: describe common employee compensation, incentive, and benefits strategies

Most people work to make a living. In other words, our jobs make it possible for us to buy a home, food, transportation, clothing, and the extras that make life fun. For most of us, the idea of making more rather than less money is compelling—and may draw us to a job or keep us in a job.

But for many people, money is just part of the larger picture. Some of us choose a particular job because we care about the products, services, or goals of the company. Or we need the generous health and education benefits provided to employees. Some people may choose a job because of its flexible hours, ample paid vacation, or opportunities to grow.

Employee compensation, incentives, and benefits can be combined in many different ways to suit the needs, desires, and challenges of each company and employee.

EMPLOYEE COMPENSATION, INCENTIVE, AND BENEFITS STRATEGIES

Learning Outcomes

- Describe common employee compensation and incentive strategies.
- Describe common benefits strategies.

Most companies want to hire the most qualified employees and keep those employees loyal and productive. To attract and keep their best employees, companies provide a "package" that includes compensation (money), incentives (special perks or rewards for good work), and benefits (valuable options such as health insurance and paid vacation).

Because each employee is unique, larger corporations offer a wide range of mix-and-match options to suit individual needs and preferences. As a manager, you may have the option of offering your team members specific incentives based on their type of work and particular areas of interest and need.

Compensation

Compensation is just another word for wages. Managers work with human resources to set and raise wages based on a number of factors:

- Competitive analysis (what are people in similar jobs making per hour, week, or year?).
- Cost of living (it's more expensive to live in New York City than, for example, in most rural areas).
- Labor negotiations (if the person is a member of a labor union, collective bargaining may apply).
- Personal qualifications (Audrey may command a higher salary than Joe because she has more years of experience or a higher level of education).
- Supply and demand (if your company must find a person with specific qualifications and there are very few people with those qualifications, your company may need to spend more to attract qualified candidates).

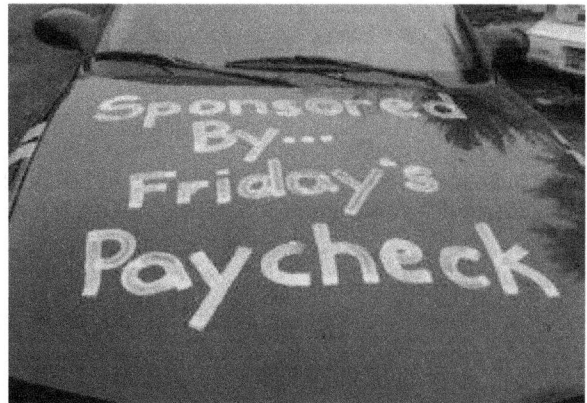

As a manager, you may need to negotiate compensation both within your corporation and with your new hire. For example, you may need to make the case for paying Audrey more than Joe would have demanded by explaining why Audrey's skills will make a positive difference to the bottom line. The reasons behind compensation are complex; as a manager, you will need to keep your eyes on the competition and changing trends to be sure your employees receive fair and equitable pay.

Payroll Management

Compensation is usually provided through a payroll system that manages and records payment of wages to each employee. Payroll systems are set up and managed by HR or by a contracted payroll company. Payroll involves:

- Collecting employee information such as W-4 and I-9 tax forms and proof of legal work status.
- Tracking work hours for employees eligible for overtime pay or comp time (extra time off to pay back overtime hours).
- Record keeping related to payment for benefits and bonuses.
- Management of state and federal taxes.

Incentives

If you want to encourage people to work hard, you should offer them both a reward for good work and a consequence for poor performance. The consequence is often that if you do poor work, you will get fired and lose your income and benefits. But how do you encourage (or incentivize) a person to do their best work? The answer depends on the culture of the business, the needs or preferences of the individual, and the options available.

One industry that offers an incredible range of perks and incentives to its employees is software development. Silicon Valley is loaded with companies that provide everything from free food to massages to its employees. Google, in particular, is well-known for making its employees happy and providing resources to lower stress. Free haircuts and dry cleaning, gyms and swimming pools with personal trainers, nap pods, subsidized massages, and on-site doctors are just a few of the perks it offers.

Watch the following news clip to find out more about perks at Google.

https://youtu.be/PA54HWLZ2e4

Other companies offer completely different kinds of perks. Home Depot, for example, has a terrific on-site childcare program called Little Apron that is good enough to be highlighted by the magazine *Working Mother*.

Little Apron Academy has a learning-based curriculum and offers programs such as Language Works, Math Counts, Science Rocks and ArtSmart, as well as kindergarten prep and school-age programs, and programs geared toward infants, toddlers and preschoolers. It has a capacity for 326 children including 278 enrolled full-time and 48 school age kids who attend for summer camp and school breaks. The center also provides back-up care services for families of The Home Depot. (Note: Santos, M. (2016, December 16). 5 Fabulous and Inspiring Onsite Daycares. Retrieved August 16, 2017, from http://www.workingmother.com/5-fabulous-onsite-daycares#page-5)

It's easy to guess which types of employees would be attracted by foosball (young single men) and which by a childcare program (working mothers and fathers). But there are also incentives that can motivate people with completely different needs and goals. For example:

- Many companies offer low-cost, fun perks such as catered lunches, free snacks and coffee, and Employee of the Month awards.
- It's common for companies to include employees' families in special events such as picnics, ballgames, and outings.
- To encourage employees who make direct sales, some companies offer significant incentives for meeting or exceeding goals. For example, Huntington National Bank offered sales teams a program that allowed them to earn points toward an all-expenses-paid trip to the World Series.
- Some employees are more motivated by opportunities than by "prizes." For these individuals, it may be more motivating to offer trips to trade conferences and conventions, plum assignments, or inclusion in upper-level meetings.

Benefits

Benefits are a part of the compensation package, and they are often worth a great deal to employees. Health insurance and retirement, in particular, are valuable and coveted benefits. So too are paid vacations, sick days, life insurance, and retirement packages. Because these benefits are so valuable, it's important for managers to make their employees aware of what's available to them—and to work with HR to provide training in how to access and use benefits.

In most companies, employees can choose among different benefits. There is a cost associated with many benefits, so some employees will opt out (so they can have more in their paycheck) whereas others will opt in (for better health benefits or a greater sense of security in case of disaster).

- **Healthcare:** Health benefits are usually offered in the form of health insurance, but many companies also offer on-site exercise facilities and programs for reducing stress. Health insurance comes in many "flavors"; often employees can choose among several levels of HMOs, PPOs, health savings accounts, and even on-site clinics.
- **Paid vacations:** Outside of national holidays, corporations are under no obligation to offer paid vacation or sick days. Some offer very minimal vacation—and hourly or part time workers may get no vacation at all. To compete for highly qualified workers, however, the majority of companies do offer at least some paid vacation. Usually the number of vacation days increases over time—one reason for employees to stay loyal to their employer.
- **Retirement:** Retirement programs give employees regular income after they leave the company. For many people, a good retirement plan is enough reason to stick with a job, even if the job is less than thrilling. There are two major types of retirement plans: pensions and contribution plans (usually 401(k) plans). Pensions offer regular, guaranteed income to retired employees for the rest of their lives; retirement benefits may also be offered to surviving spouses. Although pensions were popular for many years, most employers no longer offer them. Contribution plans invest funds provided by both the employee and the employer. Funds are invested, and they may grow or shrink depending upon the market. These days, contribution plans are much more common than pensions.
- **Stock and Stock Options:** If a corporation is large enough, it may offer stock (shares in the company) as one benefit of employment. If the corporation is doing well, stocks can become increasingly valuable. For some employees, stock options are a good way to share in their employer's success.

INTRODUCTION TO EMPLOYEE SEPARATION AND TERMINATION

What you'll learn to do: describe the options for employee separation/termination

At some point, management must also plan for departures: retirements and separations. Sometimes employees retire, but they may also be fired or laid off.

EMPLOYEE SEPARATION AND TERMINATION

Learning Outcomes

- Describe the options for employee separation/termination.

There are really only two reasons for employees to leave a job: they are asked to leave or they leave voluntarily. There are very different ways to handle voluntary and involuntary termination; in some cases, the manager is very involved with the process, but in other cases separation or termination is managed by human resources.

Watch the following video to find out some of the most common things managers do that make good employees quit.

https://youtu.be/5La2Hfw-g2g

Voluntary Separation

Why would an employee leave his job? The most obvious reason is that the employee is ready to retire. But the fact is that there are as many reasons for quitting as there are employees. Sometimes, poor management can be the reason your employees are walking out the door. In many cases, managers can make changes to improve the situation and help employees make the decision to stay; in other cases, though, it just makes sense to say goodbye. Some reasons for voluntary separation include:

- **Better opportunities:** Many people leave jobs because there is better job available elsewhere. When that happens, employees may offer their managers the opportunity to top the better job offer. If your employee is really extraordinary, you may want to discuss options with upper management and HR. Can you improve on the employee's compensation and benefits package? How can you make it worth their while to stay?
- **A family move:** Bill just got married, and he and his new wife are moving to California to be closer to her family. In this case, it may be tough to make Bill a better offer. In some cases, however, it might be possible to transfer Bill to another division of the company that's closer to his new home.
- **Illness or disability:** In some instances, illness or disability can force an employee to resign. Sometimes it is possible to accommodate an employee with a physical challenge by making minor changes to the workplace or schedule. In other cases, however, the problem is significant enough or affects productivity to such a degree that the employer can't accommodate the worker. For example, a graphic artist who is unable to walk can still do her job with accommodations for a wheelchair, but a waiter who can't walk is unlikely to be able to continue in his job. When the illness or disability relates to someone else in the family (an elderly parent, for example), the employer may be able to help with a more flexible schedule or options for working from home. Often, though, the employee's job requires them to be on the spot for specific working hours.
- **Job dissatisfaction:** It's not unusual for employees to leave a job because they're unhappy in their work and believe they can be happier elsewhere. There are many reasons why this can be the case; sometimes the manager is the problem, and often the manager can help, but just as often they can't. For example, an employee might leave because he sees no opportunity for advancement. In some cases, managers can find, create, or point out ways in which the employee really can advance in the company. In other cases, an employee might decide that the job is not as interesting or fulfilling as he had anticipated; again, managers can sometimes (but not always) help make changes to suit the employee's needs.
- **Changing circumstances:** Very often, jobs that were perfect for a period of time are no longer appropriate. For example, a traveling sales position may have been exciting and fun for a single woman who is now married and wants to settle down. A strenuous job may have been ideal for a younger man who is now getting older and wants something a little less exhausting. A low-paying position may have been acceptable for a person just getting started but may pay too little when the employee wants to own a home. Again, managers may be able to help employees figure out options within the company—but it may also be the case that the employee really needs to make a more radical change.

When an employee leaves voluntarily—and the employee and manager agree that it's time for a change—most of the process of separation is handled by HR. Typically, the employee gives at least two weeks' notice, fills out paperwork acknowledging the separation, and turns over keys, IDs, and equipment. In some cases, clearance may be revoked. Most companies ask employees to sit down for an exit interview, which is a chance for the employee to provide feedback about their employment.

Many companies have a tradition of honoring people who are leaving voluntarily. Retirees who have been with the company for a long time may be honored with a special dinner, an award, or a party. Going-away parties are also popular. From a management point of view, it's important for the employees who are not leaving to see that their colleague's work and time were of value to the company.

Involuntary Termination

The word "termination" sounds unpleasantly like "extermination," but of course it simply means that an employee has been asked to leave the job. There are two general reasons for termination: layoffs and firing. When employees are laid off, they are being asked to leave because their position will no longer exist but they have done nothing personally to deserve termination. When an employee is fired, it is for "cause," meaning that something they did (or didn't do) led to being fired.

- **Layoffs:** Layoffs are the unfortunate outcome of changes in industries or problems with individual corporations. In rare cases, people are laid off simply because their project has ended. More often, though, they are laid off because their employer has been forced to close stores, stop producing certain products, or simply save money. Managers can sometimes step in and help individual employees to stay with the company by building new skills or shifting into different departments or divisions. Often, though, there are no feasible ways to avoid layoffs.
- **Firing:** There are quite a few reasons why people are fired from their jobs, but in general people are fired because they (1) broke company rules or laws; (2) were unable or unwilling to do their jobs; (3) created

problems for the company because of their behavior. Occasionally, people are fired for "political" reasons. For example, a top manager might be let go to make room for the boss's son-in-law. In such cases, however, the employee might well be able to sue the employee, so such firings are rare.

It is almost always the manager who decides that a person should be fired. Before making that decision, though, the manager will need to go through a number of steps to document problems with the employee. The steps vary depending upon the corporation, the situation, and whether or not the employee is a member of a labor union. At the very least, the manager should:

- Address problems directly with the employee, providing feedback and support as needed so that the employee can respond and make changes.
- If the problem persists, the manager should work with human resources to determine whether there are other options for making change. For example, if an employee is unable to do his work because he simply can't master the systems required, there may be a different job he can do.
- If the problem still persists, HR will need to get involved. Most companies have systems for putting problem employees on probation or giving formal warnings.
- If the employee's issues do not improve, and the manager has taken every appropriate step to change the situation, it may be time to hand the employee the proverbial "pink slip."

Of course, if the employee has actually broken the law or behaved unethically, firing is usually immediate and automatic. Embezzlers and thieves rarely get a second chance in any corporation.

INTRODUCTION TO CURRENT TRENDS AND CHALLENGES IN HR MANAGEMENT

What you'll learn to do: describe current trends and challenges in HR management

In the past, many people went to work for a corporation when they graduated from high school or college—and retired from the same corporation forty years later with a pension. They went to work in the morning and didn't communicate with their friends or family until they returned home in the evening. Many were union members and relied on union representatives to manage their contracts, wages, and benefits.

Today, things have changed. People change jobs often, and many people work part time. Social media has changed the way we communicate during the day, and it can even change the way we spend our working hours. Labor unions are on the decline, which means that individual workers are now working out contracts with their employers—sometimes with negative consequences.

CURRENT TRENDS AND CHALLENGES IN HR MANAGEMENT

Learning Outcomes

- Describe common effects of instant communication on motivation and work-life balance.
- Describe the advantages of part-time employees.
- Describe the disadvantages of part-time employees.
- Explain the decline in union membership and the impact on labor relations.

As the workplace changes, managers must change too. Sometimes managers are caught in the middle, seeing changes that negatively affect their team members but having no ability to stop the changes from happening. Sometimes, though, managers can make a positive difference.

Part-Time Employees

According to a study by a research group called Fieldglass, in 2015 the average company's workforce consisted of 54 percent traditional, full-time employees, 20 percent contingent workers (freelancers, interns, and contractors), and 26 percent that existed in a gray area somewhere between the two (including remote and part-time workers). The researchers predicted that by 2017, the share of "nontraditional" workers would grow to 25 percent contingent, 34 percent gray area, and 41 percent traditional workers. (Note: Dwyer, C. J. (2015, October). The State of Contingent Workforce Management 2015-2016: The Future of Work Is Here. Retrieved August 17, 2017, from http://resources.fieldglass.com/rs/655-SDM-567/images/ Ardent_Partners_The_State_of_CWM_2015_Fieldglass.pdf?mkt_tok=3RkMMJWWfF9wsRoivKzLZKXonjHpfsX67%2BQ 0ER3fOvrPUfGjI4ES8RnI%2BSLDwEYGJlv6SgFTLXAMbNk17gIXRY%3D)

This means that a very large number of the people you're likely to be managing are not full-time employees at your place of business. They may work for themselves or for consulting firms, or they may be employees of a contractor for whom your business is the client.

Upside of Part-Time and Contingent Employees

From the point of view of a manager, part-time and contingent employees can be a flexible, budget-friendly resource. Imagine selecting only the most experienced employees for a project, bringing them on board without the need to provide training or benefits, and letting them go with no drama when the project is completed. Even better, in many cases, part-time and contingent employees are provided through firms who manage payroll, handle any disciplinary issues, and take care of finding substitutes should an individual employee be unable to fulfill his obligations.

Part-time and contingent employees are usually brought on board for specific types of jobs or projects. For example:

- Providing staff for a project that is normally handled in-house but is too big, falls at the wrong time, or coincides with another major deadline.
- Helping to meet a large deadline that requires more staff than you have in-house.
- Supporting a staff member whose load is too large for one person but not significant enough to warrant a second full-time hire.

- Implementing projects, events, or programs that are seasonal in nature (e.g., staffing up a restaurant in a beach town during the summer; providing additional landscaping personnel in the spring; staffing a "pop-up" Halloween store in the fall; offering gift wrapping services during the Christmas rush).
- Working with staff on a unique or unusual project (planning and implementing a celebration of the 100th anniversary of the corporation; creating and implementing training modules for a new division; setting up offices and hiring staff for a new office).

Downside of Part-Time and Contingent Employees

Part-time and contingent staff may be paid through a contracting agency, but on a day-to-day basis they are overseen by on-site managers. This can be very tricky for managers: it is difficult to manage someone who doesn't exactly work for you, hasn't been trained in your policies and procedures, and who will be gone is a few months. Typical procedures such as onboarding, training, shadowing, and on-the-job training cost a good deal of money—and are irrelevant if staff members are unlikely to stay on the job for a significant period of time. Yet untrained staff can be more of a liability than a help!

Another serious downside to outsourcing is the reality that contracted staff can learn your business and then leave. They can even learn inside information or business secrets and then use what they've learned to start their own business—or sell what they've learned to a competitor. The consulting firm Booz Allen faced this problem when its contractor, Edward Snowden, stole and revealed secrets damaging to the Defense Department and the United States. (Note: Brett LoGiurato. "Why A 29-Year-Old Contractor Had Access To Government Secrets," Business Insider, June 9, 2013, accessed July 26, 2017, http://www.businessinsider.com/edward-snowden-nsa-leak-booz-allen-hamilton-2013-6.)

Part-time staff can be equally difficult to manage. Yes, they are part of the team—but because their available time is so short, it can be hard to determine which tasks and responsibilities are appropriate for them. Often, part timers are not included on all-staff memos, invited to events, or offered the same bonuses or perks offered to full-time employees. This creates a sort of caste system that can be frustrating and demoralizing. Managers need to think through exactly how they will include (or exclude) part-time staff, and explain their reasoning and policies so no one feels unfairly treated.

Pros and Cons of Social Media and Instant Communication

With a smartphone in your pocket you can manage your bank account while you wait on hold for tech support. You can check in with your kids while you sit at a boring meeting. You can respond to an "emergency" at home by texting the location of the extra set of keys to your partner. You can respond to client queries, manage projects, and handle transactions even when you're watching your child's ballgame, attending a wedding, or on vacation.

Do social media and instant communication add to or detract from our ability to work and keep a balance between home and work? The answer is … both.

According to a CNBC study in 2014, "access to business and leisure content everywhere via mobile devices is blurring the parameters between the working week and weekend. Seventy percent of executives surveyed, more than ever before, now agree that mobile technology use invades time between work and leisure, with six in ten accessing business content via their mobile device over the weekend." In other words, it's getting increasingly difficult to leave work at work or to leave home at home.

On the other hand, social and mobile media are making a huge positive difference in our ability to reach clients and manage business transactions. According to the CNBC study: "The importance of social media in business continues to grow and is highest in Asia. In Europe 61% claim to use social media for a variety of business related functions (vs. 58% in 2013 and 53% in 2012). Top scoring business applications include interacting with clients and customers (37% vs. 31% in 2013), building brand presence among social network communities (34% vs. 27% in 2013) and tracking industry trends." (Note: "New Study Shows How Mobile Technology Is Disrupting Work-Life Balance," CNBC, Dec. 11, 2014, accessed July 26,

Meanwhile, social communication is draining time and energy away from productivity. It's impossible to stay focused on work while sharing adorable videos of kittens with workmates. It's even harder when workers are using their smartphone technology to interact with partners and children, plan trips, look up recipes, or buy birthday gifts.

To help reduce the amount of time and energy spent on social media and instant communication, many corporations have created technology policies. In addition to limiting access to smartphones and tablets during work hours, these policies also ensure that employees do not share company images, information, or ideas. Although these policies are helpful in theory, they can be very difficult to enforce. Managers need to be aware of the ways in which technology is helping and hurting their team, and be willing to enforce technology policies. Of course, to be effective in managing other peoples' technology use, managers must be willing to put their own smartphones away during work hours.

Labor Relations

According to Forbes Magazine: "In 2013 the unionized workforce in America hit a 97-year low. Only 11.3% of all workers were unionized. In the private sector unionization fell to 6.6%, down from a peak of 35% in the 1950s. American corporations have made a concerted effort to get rid of unions and reduce labor costs since 1980, and they have been very successful." (Note: Mike Collins, "The Decline of Unions Is a Middle Class Problem," Forbes, March 23, 2015, accessed .July 26, 2017, available by subscription only, https://www.forbes.com/sites/mikecollins/2015/03/19/the-decline-of-unions-is-a-middle-class-problem/#a2795e77f2db.) This trend continues: only 10.7 percent of employees were unionized in 2016. (Note: "Union Members Summary," U.S. Bureau of Labor Statistics, Jan. 26, 2017, accessed July 26, 2017, https://www.bls.gov/news.release/union2.nr0.htm.)

Is this a good thing or a bad thing? It depends on who you ask.

Watch the following video from grassroots progressive activist group MoveOn.org to get an idea of some of the things American unions have been responsible for over the years. While you watch, think about who might benefit from and who might be hurt by the decline of unions.

https://www.youtube.com/watch?v=iObqguaNDdA

For working men who would have belonged to a labor union during the 1950s, unionization meant higher wages. Unions were created to give workers the ability to bargain collectively with their employers—and employers had no choice but to work with the union. If the union called a strike, the employer would have to stop business. In the last century, laws have required or companies have adapted many of the policies for which unions fought. This has weakened the support and the need for unions. And workers find it easier to switch jobs now than in the heyday of unions. Transportation to get to a job and the ease of finding a job have improved.

For corporations in general, fewer unionized workers means more ability to hire contingent and part-time workers, pay lower wages, ship jobs overseas to cut costs, and increase profits. Business-oriented politicians have worked hard to decrease the power of labor unions, and this has resulted in positive outcomes for U.S. businesses. It also makes it easier for U.S. manufacturers to compete with overseas manufacturers because U.S. businesses can pay lower wages to nonunion workers. German unions have taken a different approach: they have allowed flexibility in exchange for promises for continued employment, which companies honored in the recession. (Note: "Why Germany's current-account surplus is bad for the world economy," The Economist, July 8, 2017, accessed July 26, 2017, https://www.economist.com/news/leaders/21724810-country-saves-too-much-and-spends-too-little-why-germanys-current-account-surplus-bad.)

The trend toward deunionization has slowed, but it hasn't stopped. Nevertheless, public service labor unions are still strong, and rising inequality may drive new support for unions.

PUTTING IT TOGETHER: HUMAN RESOURCE MANAGEMENT

Now that you've completed your study of this module, let's return to the situation we introduced at beginning. You're a marketing manager faced with hiring a new team member to help complete a major project. When we started this module, you had a lot of human resource questions and didn't know how to proceed. Based on what you know now, let's see how you could put the information into practice.

Preparing to Recruit

You start by developing a strong recruiting plan. You understand that people are the organization's greatest asset, so you want to ensure you hire the right person for the role. You start by working with your company recruiter on an advertising plan to let people know about the job. You then develop a strong list of interview questions. You're careful not to ask any questions that would violate discrimination laws such as the Civil Rights Act of 1964 or the Age Discrimination Act of 1967. You've also decided that you are going to start with telephone interviews so that you can narrow down the candidates to a handful that will come in for face-to-face interviews.

Starting Out Right

Your search is successful—your top candidate has accepted your job offer! Now that you've hired a great candidate, it's important to get her prepared for the job so that she starts out confidently. Your organization has a standard onboarding process for new employees that does a good job of grounding them in the company's history and values. Likewise, your new hire will understand more about the culture of the business. However, you want to provide every opportunity for her to be successful so you develop training that is specific to your department. This includes a variety of computer-based training, but it will also provide an opportunity for job shadowing. By partnering your new hire with someone more experienced, she should be able to ramp into her role more quickly and with greater job satisfaction.

Ongoing Development

You've also been thinking about the need for ongoing development for your entire team. With the learning you have completed in this module, you understand how important it is for your team to get regular feedback against specific objectives. Additionally, you have begun to think about other training that would benefit them.

Although they may not become HR specialists, every manager needs to understand certain fundamentals to maximize the value of the organization's most important asset—its people. The material you have covered in this module is something that you will likely come back to many times during your career and will help you become more successful as a manager.

MODULE 8: GROUPS, TEAMS, AND TEAMWORK

WHY IT MATTERS: GROUPS, TEAMS, AND TEAMWORK

Why does a manager need to understand groups, teams, and teamwork?

Lisa is a project manager with IT Solutions, and she was recently given an assignment to deliver a new customer relationship management database for the organization's largest client. When Lisa met with her boss, she received information about the members of her team. Here are the notes she took on each person's background:

- Paul – Ten years of experience with various types of projects; expertise in budgets and scheduling.
- Susan – Five years of experience as a programmer; limited exposure to this type of project.
- Tim – Seven years of experience; excellent problem-solving skills.
- Dan – Two years of experience; no exposure to this type of project.
- Wendy – Eight years of experience; strong programming and project management experience; significant exposure to these types of projects.

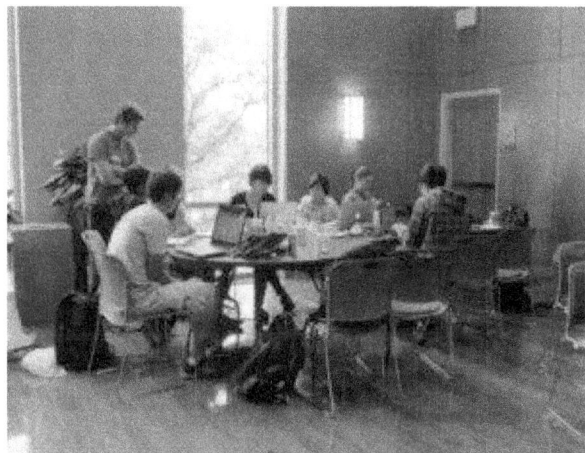

How does a manager get a group of individuals to function as a team?

As Lisa reviews the specifics of the project, she realizes she has a lot to accomplish, and the deadlines are really tight. As mentioned earlier, this is IT Solutions' largest client, so it is vital that the team be successful. To do this, its members will need to function well together—and work quickly.

Unfortunately, this is a team that is being brought together specifically for this project. Lisa has worked with Susan and Tim briefly on a couple of earlier projects. Tim has worked with Dan in the past, but otherwise, this is a brand new team.

How would you start building a team from this group of individuals? What problems do you think you might have along the way, and how will you deal with them? Managers need to understand the nature of teams and how to build them effectively. In this module, you will learn why teams are important, how to develop effective teams, and how to deal with common conflicts that might arise.

INTRODUCTION TO COMMON GROUP BEHAVIORS

What you'll learn to do: describe common group behaviors that can help or hurt organization goals

People are social animals and function best when they work with others in groups or teams. Some human behaviors show up repeatedly among groups. In the workplace, it is important to understand how these behaviors affect performance. Social cohesion and collective efficacy benefit team functions, whereas social loafing reduces team effectiveness. This section will examine these common behaviors.

COMMON GROUP BEHAVIORS

Learning Outcomes

   • Discuss social cohesion, social loafing, and collective efficacy.

Introduction

Moneyball is a popular movie about the Oakland Athletics baseball team during the 2002 season. The film shows how the team's general manager, Billy Beane (played by Brad Pitt), and the assistant general manager, Peter Brand (Jonah Hill), defy conventional wisdom that says they should look for standout stars for the team. Instead, they use statistics to select players based on their overall performance and how well their skills will fit into the team. They bet that a well-functioning team could be better than the sum of its parts. The Oakland A's did not win the pennant in 2002, but they did win a record twenty straight games.

The movie is really more about the A's management team than it is the players. It shows how Beane puts his trust in Brand to choose players for the team, and how they overcome resistance to their ideas and methods from scouts, the manager, and the owner. They eventually are able to put together a high-performing team of managers and players. It is an excellent portrayal of how teams go from initial formation, through resistance and conflict, into high performance. They did not achieve the ultimate goal of winning a World Series pennant, but they did change the way teams evaluate baseball players throughout professional. As you study how teams work in this module, keep this example in mind and consider what it reveals about the team formation process.

146

What Is a Team?

A team is a unit of two or more people who regularly interact to accomplish common goals and who hold themselves mutually accountable for meeting performance results. There are several important elements to this definition.

1. It involves two or more people who interact regularly.
2. People on the team share a goal and are committed to achieving the goal.
3. The people on the team hold each other mutually accountable for the performance of the team.

Note that a group of people, such as people waiting for a train, is not a team. Even though they might have a common goal—to get on the train—they do not interact regularly, and they are not accountable to each other for reaching the goal. A team implies a commitment to a shared objective and collective responsibility for achieving it.

All of these people inside the train station are part of a group, but they are not part of a team.

Teams are very common in larger organizations, and they benefit both the company and the employees. People who feel they are part of a team are often mutually supportive and report greater job satisfaction. However, not all teams are successful. In one survey, only 14 percent of the companies rated their teams as highly effective (Note: Traci Purdum, "Teaming, Take 2," Industry Week 254, no. 5 (May 2005): 41–44.), around 50 percent rated them as somewhat effective, and 15 percent rated them not effective at all. In this module, we look at teams and how effective teams are developed. We start by looking at common behaviors that can help or hurt efforts to meet organizational goals.

Common Team Behaviors

There is a fundamental dilemma in working in teams: each individual contributes, but the result is attributed to the team. If the team is successful, individual contributions may not be recognized, regardless of how hard the individual worked. On the other hand, if the team fails, it is likely that the leader or other important members of the team will receive the blame. This leads to some behaviors that can either help or hurt a team effort. Although some of these behaviors are characteristic of groups in general, they all apply to teams in the business environment.

Social Cohesiveness

Social cohesion is defined as the willingness of members of a society to cooperate with each other to survive and prosper. In work teams, social cohesiveness means the members want to be part of the team and want to contribute to its success. Members of cohesive teams have social and emotional bonds to each other and to the overall team, which motivates higher commitment and performance. Southwest Airlines, for instance, works hard to develop cohesiveness in its organization. As a result, everyone is willing to work toward the success of the organization. That is why it is not unusual to see people pitch in, even when it is not part of their job. For example, pilots may help to load luggage if it helps maintain on-time performance.

The main influential factors of cohesion are size of the group, similarities among its members, and team success. Small groups tend to be more cohesive than larger ones because people can interact with each other more. Similarity among group members contributes to team cohesiveness because people with similar backgrounds are more likely to have fewer communication barriers and share views on what constitutes appropriate behaviors. People are generally more trusting of others when they share some important background experiences. In substance abuse recovery groups, for example, members know that everyone has had the same ailment and is dealing with similar experiences. When a team experiences success early in its development, members get reinforcement that their efforts can produce results. They are more likely to be motivated to continue to contribute. Success also creates a sense of pride that fosters feelings of belonging and mutual attraction in the team.

Social Loafing

Social loafing is when one or more group members fail to do their fair share of work within the group. You may have witnessed this behavior firsthand on a team or school project. One group member finds an excuse for not doing his or her job. There are two main consequences of social loafing. The free-rider effect is when one or more team members do not put in their share of the work, assuming others will cover their shortfall. The other is the sucker effect, where other team members reduce their effort in response to the free rider's behavior.

Several causes exist for social loafing. A member may not be motivated by a goal and may not want to work to achieve it. Or a member may feel that his or her contribution to the team will not be recognized, so the member is not motivated to contribute. Both of these causes are more pronounced in large teams. Social loafing is also more likely when there isn't an individual evaluations system where the performance and contributions of members are regularly reviewed. Finally, if there is unequal compensation and the members of the team feel the compensation is unfair, they will be more likely to lessen their effort.

A good manager should monitor employees to watch out for these social loafers or "slackers." The manager is responsible for making sure all team members are carrying their fair share of the work they have been assigned. If the manager doesn't deal with social loafing, it can create a stressful work environment that may turn into conflicts among coworkers.

Collective Efficacy

Collective efficacy is the team's belief that it is capable of organizing and working together to reach its goals. Creating collective efficacy is a bit of a balancing act. If goals are perceived as being too easy to reach, members may not feel they have to put in their full effort. On the other hand, if goals are perceived to be too difficult, members may feel their effort doesn't matter because the goal cannot be reached regardless of how hard they work. In either case, social loafing may result. But when the goal is "just right," difficult but not impossible, the team will believe it can reach it only if it works hard together.

Psychologist Albert Bandura researched the relationship between efficacy and job performance and found that each affects the other. When a team achieves some success, it can build self-confidence and the belief that it can achieve more. The resulting collective efficacy, in turn, makes it more likely that the team will be successful. But a downward spiral can occur when both performance and collective efficacy are low. Poor performance makes team members question ability, and the decrease in collective efficacy leads to more poor performance. (Note: Shauna Geraghty, "How Self-Efficacy Affects Workplace Performance," Talkdesk, March 23, 2013, accessed Aug. 2, 2017, https://www.talkdesk.com/blog/the-relationship-between-self-efficacy-and-workplace-performance.)

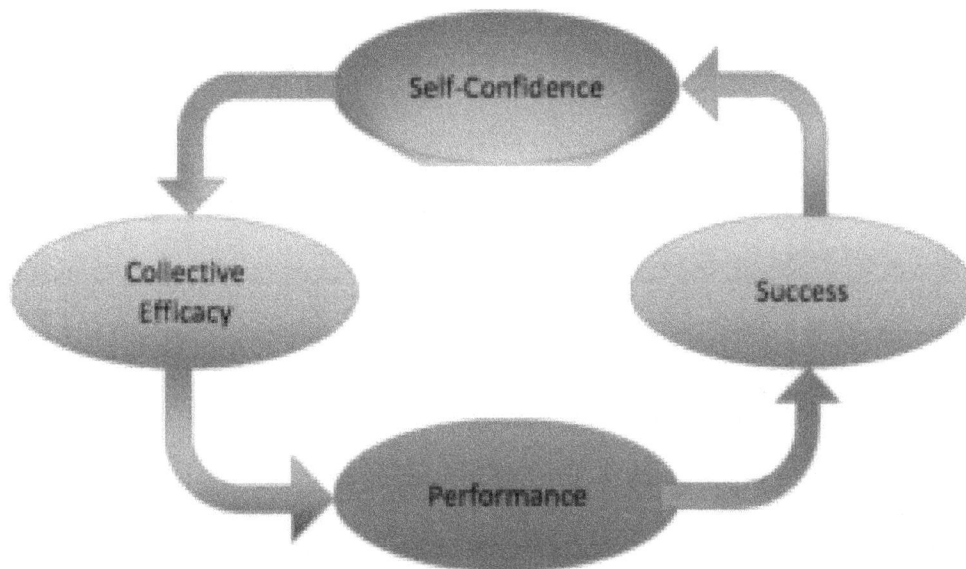

The relationship between success and collective efficacy is affected by self-confidence and performance.

Good planning and good leadership can both improve collective efficacy. When the tasks needed to reach the team's goals are being planned, initial activities should lead to demonstrable team achievements. When teams experience successes early in their development, they are more likely to build collective efficacy. Good leadership provides a clear vision for the team and articulates why the goals are important. The leader provides guidance, feedback, and encouragement. When timely feedback is given to teams, they are more likely to understand the relationship between their effort and their performance.

INTRODUCTION TO TYPES OF TEAMS

What you'll learn to do: describe the types of teams found in business organizations

You hear a lot about teams every day—sports teams, disaster and rescue teams, and medical support teams. Teams exist because they are effective in achieving goals, especially when the goal is well-defined. In the business environment, the reliance on teams has been growing in the last few decades as organizations become more virtual (operating over distance) and more structurally complex. Businesses rely on teams to perform tasks not well-suited to more traditional organizational structures. The most common types of teams are discussed in this section.

TYPES OF TEAMS

Learning Outcomes

- Describe the advantages of teams.
- Describe the disadvantages of teams.
- Differentiate between task forces and cross-functional teams.
- Differentiate between virtual teams and self-managing teams.

Business organizations have both groups and teams. A group is formed around a common interest or purpose with the goal of sharing information, but there is no collective accountability. Work groups may consist of social clubs or volunteer efforts. A team's focus is collective performance, with both individual and mutual accountability. For example, all of the people who work in accounting constitute a group, but people from each functional department who meet regularly to standardize financial procedures are a team. Before we look more closely at what constitutes an effective (high-performing) team, we will review the advantages and disadvantages of using teams in the workplace.

Advantages of Teams in the Workplace

Teams bring together people with diverse skills and make something that nobody could do alone. A well-planned team improves **motivation**. Communication is higher on teams, and the diverse skill set means teams can discover new approaches. Because teams have specific shared goals, team members usually enjoy greater autonomy, variety, task identity, task significance, and feedback. Teams often enjoy the social support for difficult tasks, improving morale and motivation.

Another benefit of teams is to improve product and service quality. Each Whole Foods grocery store operates with an average of ten "self-managed" teams, including produce, prepared foods, groceries, etc. Each store also has a team made up of just the team leaders from each team to facilitate communication and sharing. Each team takes responsibility for the quality of the products and service in its area.

Efficiency in product development is another advantage to building teams within the traditional hierarchy. Teams can analyze and identify dependent tasks in a nonlinear process, sometimes realizing startling improvements.

Employees also benefit from participating on teams. They develop relationships to people from other areas of the business and learn more about what is happening across functional department lines (**cross training**). A 2009 study by CG and WHU-Otto Beisheim School of Management of eighty global software development teams showed that members of effective teams are more motivated and report greater job satisfaction, which leads to fewer employees quitting.

Disadvantages of Teams

Not all teams are wildly successful. When companies do not make adequate efforts to create, build, and support strong teams, employees may initially become discouraged and leave the firm. You read in the first section about some of the behavioral problems related to teams, including **social loafing**. Another phenomenon that can happen in groups is **groupthink**. We'll discuss this in more detail in the next section, but it involves the reluctance to speak out against the majority opinion in fear of upsetting other members and disrupting social cohesion. When a few people begin to speak for the whole team, individual members may not feel as responsible for the team's success.

Teams are also ineffective when they lack leadership, when the decision making is not democratic, and when the team lacks expertise and necessary skills. Eventually, team members don't feel accountable, and the team fails. Finally, some teams fail because the members are not adequately prepared or supported. Teams can't perform well if they have no clear purpose, are not given autonomy, and don't have the resources required.

Some individuals are not compatible with teamwork. Workers must be selected to fit the team as well as requisite job skills. Conflict will develop between team members, so leaders must be able to step in. And teams can be time-consuming due to the need for coordination and consensus.

Types of Teams

A cross-functional team is just what it sounds like—a team that pulls its members from across the different functional areas of an organization. For example, cross-functional teams may be composed of representatives from production, sales, marketing, finance, and legal. The strength of this type of team lies in its members having different functional backgrounds, education, and experience. The diversity of experience aids innovative problem solving and decision making.

Unfortunately, the very factors that give cross-functional teams strength can also lead to weaknesses. Without a strong leader and very specific goals, it may be hard to foster social cohesion in cross-functional teams and to create a system of accountability. A cross-functional team might be brought together to review and make recommendations on potential acquisitions or mergers.

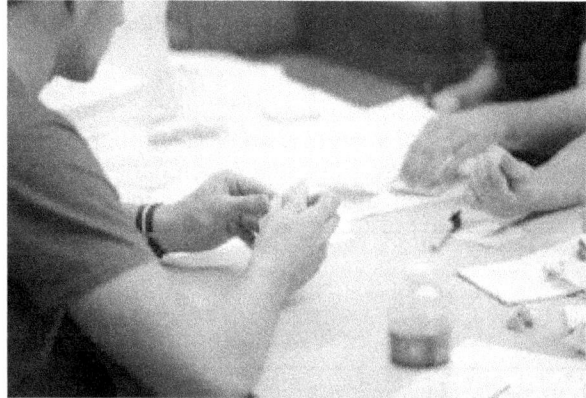

Companies create different types of teams for different purposes.

A task force is a group or committee, usually of experts or specialists, formed for analyzing, investigating, or solving a specific problem. Quite often, a task force is formed in reaction to a problem or specific event, and once the job is done, the task force is disbanded. The goal of a task force is to offer solutions, support, and, if possible, create preventive measures for issues. Types of concerns that may generate task forces in the workplace include bullying, health and wellness, employee training, increasing customer sales, or improving employee job satisfaction. A project team is similar to a task force, but a project team is often ongoing and covers a wider range of tasks.

Virtual teams are groups of individuals working together with a common purpose but from different locations. People may be in different time zones or even different organizations. The obvious advantage of a virtual team is the low cost, both in time and money to maintain it. Meeting in virtual time increases flexibility for the members (no need to get dressed before the meeting!) and allows the organization to use the talent of people from around the globe. The idea of virtual teams is relatively new. However, according to the IQVIS management consulting firm, virtual teams have grown 80 percent in business use from 2005 to 2015. Virtual teams are possible thanks to advances in communications and technology, such as e-mail, the World Wide Web (Internet), videoconferencing, and other products.

Working across cultures can be as challenging as working cross-functionally. Working with different cultures means working with very different leadership styles and decision-making processes. In the United States, managers tend to gather data, make a quick decision, and move forward, making corrections as need. Northern Europeans prefer to slowly build consensus, whereas French schoolchildren are trained to debate and confront. Some business consultants will tell you that decisions in Japan are made in small, informal conversations before the formal meeting ever takes place.

In spite of these barriers, many companies have been adapting virtual teams. SAP is the world's largest inter-enterprise software company with more than thirty thousand employees in sixty countries. It relies on virtual teams to survive. It has five headquarters around the globe, each one with a specific area of expertise shared via virtual meetings. IBM and General Electric are corporations that also depend on virtual team strategies.

Self-Managing Teams

A **self-managed** team is a group of employees that's responsible and accountable for all or most aspects of producing a product or delivering a service. It could be thought of as a mini-company within a larger organization. Traditional organizations assign tasks to employees depending on their skills or the functional department (sales, finance, production). A self-managed team carries out the supporting tasks as well, such as planning and scheduling the technical workflow tasks, and human resource tasks such as managing vacations and absences. Team members may take turns leading and assuming technical responsibilities.

Because of the autonomy given to self-managed teams, these teams have greater ownership of the jobs they perform. Some benefits of self-managed teams are: team members share accountability for what they accomplish, which can be a great motivator; individuals have greater commitment to the task because they're directly responsible for its results; and they take on some of a manager's work so he can continue on other tasks.

However, self-managed teams are not without problems. Groupthink occurs more frequently with these teams. Members may struggle during the transition from supervisor-led management to self-management, possibly because of lack of interpersonal skills or poor implementation by the company. Not surprisingly, the most effective self-managing teams are found in companies where the corporate culture supports democratic decision making and the employees are generally well-educated.

INTRODUCTION TO BUILDING EFFECTIVE TEAMS

What you'll learn to do: describe common techniques used to build effective teams

We have previously discussed some of the advantages and disadvantages of working in teams and types of teams commonly found in business organizations. Next, we'll describe key characteristics of effective teams and how organizations can build teams that produce high performance results.

BUILDING EFFECTIVE TEAMS

Learning Outcomes

• Explain the importance of communication in teams.
• Explain how team goals and accountability differ from individual goals and accountability.

Characteristics of Effective Teams

Many studies have been completed on the topic of what effective teams look like. They agree on key characteristics that effective teams share. The chart that follows identifies skills and attitudes that help teams function effectively.

Members of an effective team help each other achieve goals.

KEY CHARACTERISTICS OF EFFECTIVE TEAMS

Clarity of Purpose	The purpose of the team must be clearly defined in concrete and measurable objectives. Effective teams know how their work contributes toward an organizational goal. The team leader reminds members of how each team member makes business success possible.
Good Communication	Open and accurate communication both between the team members and between the team and the larger organization is critical to keep members informed, motivated and focused. Part of the communication process involves establishing roles, making plans, and following standard business protocols and procedures.
Positive Role for Conflict	We will look at the role of positive and negative conflict in more detail later in this module, but generally effective teams use conflict to improve decision-making and problem solving processes.
Accountability and Commitment	Each member of the team understands his role on the team and takes responsibility for his actions. Team members take proactive measures to ensure that they can complete tasks, and they alert management when a problem arises. Members of effective teams not only know the team's purpose but are committed to achieving it and demonstrate the behavior needed to meet the goals. Team members have the authority to do what they need to do without being checked every step along the way. Finally, members must be incentivized and rewarded on both an individual and team basis.
Shared Leadership	Effective team members are willing to assume leadership roles when appropriate. Shared leadership reinforces a sense of shared responsibility and increases morale and team performance.
Positive Group Dynamics	Interpersonal relationships in effective teams are built on trust, respect, honesty, and acceptance. Conflict will still occur, but a positive group dynamic will focus the conflict productively.

Check out the following video to discover what Cisco has found to be the key tips for building effective teams:

https://youtu.be/K6ppysmJZbE

Common Techniques for Team Building

Once you know the characteristics of effective teams, how do you go about building those qualities into a group? When initially forming the team, follow these procedures and techniques to help create the environment needed for the development of those characteristics.

- **Set team goals and priorities.** This step supports the key characteristic of clear goals. Team members need detailed explanations of how their individual actions contribute to the achievement of the team goals. Team priorities should be established so that members can understand when and where to provide additional help if needed. Individuals need to understand how their personal SMART goals support the team goals and how supporting the team also allows them to meet their own personal goals. If personal goals and team goals are not interdependent (for example, if a team goal is not specifically tied to a personal goal), then the employee most likely will focus on her own needs to the detriment of the team. Good communication skills are required to make sure that the goals are written clearly and that team members know their performances will affect the team goal and thus each other's performance.
- **Select team members carefully.** Three factors should be considered when selecting people for a team: individualism, the average level of experience and ability, and the degree of diversity.
  - It's a fact that some people make better team members than others. It's also a fact that with determination, anyone can learn to function on a team. **Individualists** generally put their personal welfare and interests first, and they prefer independent tasks in which they work alone. On the opposite end of the spectrum is the **collectivist**, who prefers cooperation to competition and is happiest working in a group. Although collectivists generally make better team members, there are many instances when independent tasks are part of a larger team effort. It may take more effort to communicate with the individualists, however.
  - The experience and ability levels of team members should be balanced so tasks can be distributed with high expectations of the work being done. At the same time, newer employees need to become a fully functioning part of the workforce, and this can happen by teaming them with the more experienced people. It is also important to select people based on their skills and leadership potential.
  - Team **diversity** represents not only the mix of skills and experiences, but also how people of varying culture, ethnicity, race or gender work together. Diversity is a good defense against groupthink because of a different outlook and belief system that challenges common assumptions.

Optimal Team Size

There seems to be no question about the right size of many teams. Basketball teams have five players (on the court), football is played with eleven members on the field, and a bridge team is made up of only two players. Businesses don't have rules for the proper size of a team. Jeff Bezos, CEO and founder of Amazon, has his own rule for the right-sized teams: the team should only be as big as can be fed with two pizzas. By normal standards, that would suggest five to eight people on a team. Bezos is said to have followed this guide when he created the innovative and decentralized start-up that has grown into one of the most successful companies in the country.

When in doubt about the right size of your team, you can always fall back on the "two-pizza rule."

The ideal size, according to most management experts, falls within the range of five to nine people. The reason the size is so important that it is the focus of research studies has to do with processes and outcomes. Too few people and the team may not have enough resources or skills. Too many people and communication becomes more challenging. Groupthink and social loafing may occur and negatively affect team performance. In one study, it was determined that teams with more than twelve people had greater conflict and formed subgroups that disrupted the team cohesiveness. (Note: "Choosing Team Size and Team Members," Boundless Open Textbook, May 26, 2016, accessed Aug. 2, 2017, https://www.boundless.com/management/textbooks/boundless-management-textbook/groups-teams-and-teamwork-6/building-successful-teams-53/choosing-team-size-and-team-members-268-3956/)

Experts also agree that the optimal size of the team is driven by other factors: what type of task the team will perform, what skills the team requires to complete the task, and the time provided to complete the task. Answers to those questions will often determine the best size for a team. If the task, for example, is a sales function, then one individual may do most of the work until the very end, when a finance and delivery/inventory manager gets involved. One business may be fortunate to have four employees with multiple skill sets whereas another company would have to include six or seven people to reach the same level of abilities. Finally, the shorter the timeframe to complete the task, the fewer the people should be on the team. Larger numbers increase complexity of communication and administration.

INTRODUCTION TO THE FIVE STAGES OF TEAM DEVELOPMENT

What you'll learn to do: describe the five stages of team development

Effective teams don't just happen. They are the result of a development process through which members learn to work together and support team goals. Teams become high performing when the members have worked through their individual differences and have agreed on standard values that control behaviors. Teams are effective when the development process results in strong relationships and high performance.

THE FIVE STAGES OF TEAM DEVELOPMENT

Learning Outcomes

- Describe the five stages of team development.
- Explain how team norms and cohesiveness affect performance.

Introduction

Our discussion so far has focused mostly on a team as an entity, not on the individuals inside the team. This is like describing a car by its model and color without considering what is under the hood. External characteristics are what we see and interact with, but internal characteristics are what make it work. In teams, the internal characteristics are the people in the team and how they interact with each other.

For teams to be effective, the people in the team must be able to work together to contribute collectively to team outcomes. But this does not happen automatically: it develops as the team works together. You have probably had an experience when you have been put on a team to work on a school assignment or project. When your team first gets together, you likely sit around and look at each other, not knowing how to begin. Initially you are not a team; you are just individuals assigned to work together. Over time you get to know each other, to know what to expect from each other, to know how to divide the labor and assign tasks, and to know how you will coordinate your work. Through this process, you begin to operate as a team instead of a collection of individuals.

Stages of Team Development

This process of learning to work together effectively is known as team development. Research has shown that teams go through definitive stages during development. Bruce Tuckman, an educational psychologist, identified a five-stage development process that most teams follow to become high performing. He called the stages: forming, storming, norming, performing, and adjourning. Team progress through the stages is shown in the following diagram.

Forming stage

The forming stage involves a period of orientation and getting acquainted. Uncertainty is high during this stage, and people are looking for leadership and authority. A member who asserts authority or is knowledgeable may be looked to take control. Team members are asking such questions as "What does the team offer me?" "What is expected of me?" "Will I fit in?" Most interactions are social as members get to know each other.

Storming stage

The storming stage is the most difficult and critical stage to pass through. It is a period marked by conflict and competition as individual personalities emerge. Team performance may actually decrease in this stage because energy is put into unproductive activities. Members may disagree on team goals, and subgroups and cliques may form around strong personalities or areas of agreement. To get through this stage, members must work to overcome obstacles, to accept individual differences, and to work through conflicting ideas on team tasks and goals. Teams can get bogged down in this stage. Failure to address conflicts may result in long-term problems.

Norming stage

If teams get through the storming stage, conflict is resolved and some degree of unity emerges. In the norming stage, consensus develops around who the leader or leaders are, and individual member's roles. Interpersonal differences begin to be resolved, and a sense of cohesion and unity emerges. Team performance increases during this stage as members learn to cooperate and begin to focus on team goals. However, the harmony is precarious, and if disagreements re-emerge the team can slide back into storming.

Performing stage

In the performing stage, consensus and cooperation have been well-established and the team is mature, organized, and well-functioning. There is a clear and stable structure, and members are committed to the team's mission. Problems and conflicts still emerge, but they are dealt with constructively. (We will discuss the role of conflict and conflict resolution in the next section). The team is focused on problem solving and meeting team goals.

Adjourning stage

In the adjourning stage, most of the team's goals have been accomplished. The emphasis is on wrapping up final tasks and documenting the effort and results. As the work load is diminished, individual members may be reassigned to other teams, and the team disbands. There may be regret as the team ends, so a ceremonial acknowledgement of the work and success of the team can be helpful. If the team is a standing committee with ongoing responsibility, members may be replaced by new people and the team can go back to a forming or storming stage and repeat the development process.

Team Norms and Cohesiveness

When you have been on a team, how did you know how to act? How did you know what behaviors were acceptable or what level of performance was required? Teams usually develop **norms** that guide the activities of team members. Team norms set a standard for behavior, attitude, and performance that all team members are expected to follow. Norms are like rules but they are not written down. Instead, all the team members implicitly understand them. Norms are effective because team members want to support the team and preserve relationships in the team, and when norms are violated, there is peer pressure or sanctions to enforce compliance.

Norms result from the interaction of team members during the development process. Initially, during the forming and storming stages, norms focus on expectations for attendance and commitment. Later, during the norming and performing stages, norms focus on relationships and levels of performance. Performance norms are very important because they define the level of work effort and standards that determine the success of the team. As you might expect, leaders play an important part in establishing productive norms by acting as role models and by rewarding desired behaviors.

Norms are only effective in controlling behaviors when they are accepted by team members. The level of **cohesiveness** on the team primarily determines whether team members accept and conform to norms. Team cohesiveness is the extent that members are attracted to the team and are motivated to remain in the team. Members of highly cohesive teams value their membership, are committed to team activities, and gain satisfaction from team success. They try to conform to norms because they want to maintain their relationships in the team and they want to meet team expectations. Teams with strong performance norms and high cohesiveness are high performing.

For example, the seven-member executive team at Whole Foods spends time together outside of work. Its members frequently socialize and even take group vacations. According to co-CEO John Mackey, they have developed a high degree of trust that results in better communication and a willingness to work out problems and disagreements when they occur. (Note: Jennifer Alsever, Jessi Hempel, Alex Taylor III, and Daniel Roberts, "6 Great Teams that Take Care of Business," Fortune, April 10, 2014, http://fortune.com/2014/04/10/6-great-teams-that-take-care-of-business/)

INTRODUCTION TO CONFLICT WITHIN TEAMS

What you'll learn to do: describe common types and causes of conflict that arise within teams

Conflict has both positive and negative connotations in businesses. A moderate amount of controlled conflict can stimulate innovation and creativity. But too often, conflict is allowed to escalate because managers and team members don't understand conflict-resolution techniques. Unresolved negative conflict can shut down even the highest-performing teams.

CONFLICT WITHIN TEAMS

Learning Outcomes

- Describe common types and causes of conflict that arise within teams.

Common Types of Team Conflict

Conflict is a common occurrence on teams. Conflict itself can be defined as antagonistic interactions in which one party tries to block the actions or decisions of another party. Bringing conflicts out into the open where they can be resolved is an important part of the team leader's or manager's job.

Smart managers know how to handle team conflict.

There are two basic types of team conflict: substantive (sometimes called task) and emotional (or relationship).

- **Substantive conflicts** arise over things such as goals, tasks, and the allocation of resources. When deciding how to track a project, for example, a software engineer may want to use a certain software program for its user interface and customization capabilities. The project manager may want to use a different program because it produces more detailed reports. Conflict will arise if neither party is willing to give way or compromise on his position.
- **Emotional conflicts** arise from things such as jealousy, insecurity, annoyance, envy, or personality conflicts. It is emotional conflict when two people always seem to find themselves holding opposing viewpoints and have a hard time hiding their personal animosity. Different working styles are also a common cause of emotional conflicts. Julia needs peace and quiet to concentrate, but her office mate swears that playing music stimulates his creativity. Both end up being frustrated if they can't reach a workable resolution.

Conflict Can Be Beneficial

Not all conflict is negative. Just as some forms of stress can be beneficial, so can some types of conflict. Eustress is a positive reaction to stress that generates a desire to achieve and overcome challenges. For instance, some people find that they produce their best work when a deadline is looming and the pressure to produce gets the adrenaline flowing. Team conflicts can also produce positive results when the conflict centers on substantive issues. Conflict can spark new ideas and generate creativity.

On the other hand, when people feel they cannot disagree or offer different opinions, new ideas cannot emerge. **Groupthink** is the mindset that develops when people put too much value on team consensus and harmony. It is common when individuals are afraid to go against what most group members—especially dominant members—think. Some degree of conflict helps teams avoid groupthink and forces the group to make choices based on rational decision making.

If there is too much cooperation, the best ideas may never get shared and team effectiveness is sacrificed for the sake of efficiency. For the same reasons that diversity bestows benefits on a workforce, a mix of ideas and opinions improves team performance and decision making. If there is too much conflict, however, then nothing can get done. Employees on the team become less satisfied and motivated and may turn to social loafing or may even work against other members out of sheer frustration.

Common Causes of Conflict

Some common causes of negative conflict in teams are identified as follows:

- Conflict often arises when team members focus on **personal (emotional) issues** rather than work (substantive) issues. Enrico is attending night school to get his degree, but he comes to work late and spends time doing research instead of focusing on the job. The other team members have to pick up his slack. They can confront Enrico and demand his full participation, they can ignore him while tensions continue to grow, or they can complain to the manager. All the options will lower team performance.
- **Competition over resources**, such as information, money, supplies or access to technology, can also cause conflict. Maria is supposed to have use of the laboratory in the afternoons, but Jason regularly overstays his allotted time, and Maria's work suffers. Maria might try to "get even" by denying Jason something he needs, such as information, or by complaining to other team members.
- **Communication breakdowns** cause conflict—and misunderstandings are exacerbated in virtual teams and teams with cross-cultural members. The project manager should be precise in his expectations from all team members and be easily accessible. When members work independently, it is critical that they understand how their contributions affect the big picture in order to stay motivated. Carl couldn't understand why Latisha was angry with him when he was late with his reports—he didn't report to her. He didn't realize that she needed his data to complete her assignments. She eventually quit, and the team lost a good worker.
- Team morale can be low because of **external work conditions** such as rumors of downsizing or fears that the competition is beating them to market. A manager needs to understand what external conditions are influencing team performance.

Common Approaches to Conflict Resolution

There are five common approaches, or styles, to handling negative conflict. Each of the approaches combines some degree of cooperation and assertiveness. Each of them is more likely to be effective in certain cases and not in others. A manager has the responsibility to make sure that the conflict resolution process—whichever approach is followed—is executed impartially and with respect for all the parties involved. Finally, experts agree that it is better to address conflict sooner rather than later to prevent escalation that would affect team performance. The five approaches are described in the following text. An easy way to remember these approaches are as "no way, my way, halfway, your way, and our way."

Avoiding (no way)

Rarely, but occasionally, the best approach to conflict is to ignore it. When the reason for the conflict is trivial (as when someone was inadvertently left off an e-mail) or when waiting for more information would help resolve the conflict, the avoidance approach is appropriate. The manager may also want to avoid the conflict if she wants team members to handle it informally, on their own—and if the conflict does not significantly interfere with team performance. A manager may also decide to avoid an issue if there could be no possible resolution to addressing the conflict (a "lose-lose" situation). Consider the case of a well-liked foreman in the inventory department of a major retailing firm with fewer than three months until his retirement. He had been leaving early and generally not meeting his responsibilities. His direct reports made excuses and covered for him. The manager felt conflicted because the foreman was setting a bad example, but she decided that team morale would suffer if the foreman were disciplined. It was a "no-win" scenario.

Dominating (my way)

The dominating style ("my way or the highway") may actually be an appropriate response in emergency situations or when quick, decisive action is needed. It may also be the only effective approach for unpopular decisions or when individual team members are personally affected. Again, imagine that a popular and senior team member has been making disparaging and offensive remarks about another individual on the team. The target is not the type to complain, but you have heard that he is unhappy and thinking about leaving the team. You may be tempted to get them together to hash out the problems, but a better approach might be to tell the senior team member that his behavior is affecting team performance, that you are relying on him to behave more professionally, and that you will be monitoring the situation.

Compromising (halfway)

Compromising can be an effective approach

- when the arguments on both sides are equally rationale.
- when the participants are fairly equal in status.
- when both sides are willing to give something up.
- when time or expediency is a factor.

The example at the beginning of this section referred to a software engineer who favored a certain software program to track a project for its user interface and customization capabilities. The project manager wanted to use a different program because it produced more detailed reports. As a compromise, the software engineer agreed to customize the software to produce two key reports, and the project manager agreed to support the engineer's choice of program.

Accommodating (your way)

Accommodating a team member may be an effective strategy for resolving conflict when you agree that the team member is, in fact, right. It can also be a good approach if you don't feel strongly about the result, if you want to gain goodwill from the team member, or if it is more important at that particular time to keep the whole team functioning and cooperating.

Collaborating (our way)

The collaborative approach is also known as the win-win approach. It is mostly used in high-stakes conflicts when getting a resolution is too important for the issues not to be carefully examined. It requires a great deal of skill to use the collaborative approach successfully. Negotiation and mediation are types of collaboration, usually in formal situations such as labor negotiations or creating employment contracts for senior level management. Negotiation and mediation are most effective when both parties have something to gain and something to lose, and when there is great amount of interdependence.

PUTTING IT TOGETHER: GROUPS, TEAMS, AND TEAMWORK

Do you remember our scenario to start this module? Lisa, with IT Solutions, has been given a major project and five individuals to get it done with. She has tight deadlines, and the project is for a major client—so the pressure is on. Lisa knows she needs to get the most out of this team, and she is familiar with the five stages of team development covered in this module. Let's see how she manages through the stages.

It is fun to be part of a winning team!

Forming

Lisa brings everyone together for a face-to-face meeting on day one of the project. She knows that during this first stage of team development, everyone is getting to know each other. To facilitate this process, she opens the meeting with some icebreakers and a "getting to know you" time. As expected, they all try to find their particular place on the team given the skills and experiences of the others. As time passes, Lisa can see that they are starting to open up and share more about themselves. They are successfully transitioning to stage two.

Storming

Lisa has anxiously awaited this moment. From her study of management and team dynamics, she understands that the storming phase is critical to manage. She begins to see signs of friction between team members. Wendy and Paul begin to jockey for position because both have strong project management backgrounds. Additionally, Dan begins to feel like the team is ignoring his opinions given that he has the least amount of experience.

It is important that Lisa exert influence at this crucial time in the team's formation. She patiently waits for a little while to see if things resolve, but she acts when they don't. She pulls everyone back together and reminds them of the project's importance and each person's agreed upon scope of responsibility. She also establishes a process for dealing with any differences of opinion going forward.

By stepping in and giving firm guidance, Lisa is able to bring the team together under her leadership. As a result, she begins to gain confidence in the outcome of the project.

Norming

The project is moving along now, and the team is working together very well. The disputes that arose in stage two are a thing of the past, and the team is becoming a cohesive unit. Each team member is sharing his or her knowledge, which serves to both bind the team and develop it. On a personal level, the team members are becoming good friends. They are socializing outside of work and truly enjoy one another's company. Lisa is excited because she knows what's coming next!

Performing

As the deadline nears, the team is performing at an amazingly high level. The work is being completed ahead of schedule and exceeds the requirements the customer established. Paul told Lisa that in all his years of experience, he has never had so much fun while working so hard. Lisa's boss is happy because all of this is being done well under budget, so IT Solutions is going to have a good year financially as a result.

Adjourning

Now that the project is over, Lisa gets everyone together again so that they can celebrate the win and say proper good-byes. Because the project was so successful, each member of the team has already been given their choice of next assignments in the organization. Similarly, Lisa has been identified as a rising star, and the executive team has big plans for her. They all exchange contact information and make plans to stay in touch as they move their separate ways. This has been an amazing experience for them all.

Learning to lead a team is important no matter what functional area of business you enter. A key role of management is to deliver results through others—and the strategies you have learned in this module will serve you well throughout your career.

MODULE 9: CULTURE AND DIVERSITY

WHY IT MATTERS: CULTURE AND DIVERSITY

Why does a manager need to understand organizational culture and employee diversity?

"If you get the culture right, most of the other stuff will just take care of itself" – Tony Hsieh, CEO of Zappos.com

Imagine for a moment that you have just been promoted to CEO of Zappos.com, a major online shoe and clothing shop. Where should you immediately focus your attention? Finance? Marketing? Maybe improving supply chain operations? Although all of these areas are important, Tony Hsieh, the current CEO of Zappos.com, believes that defining and maintaining the organizational culture is key. In fact, as you read in the earlier quote, he believes that the right culture will enable the other functional areas of business to succeed.

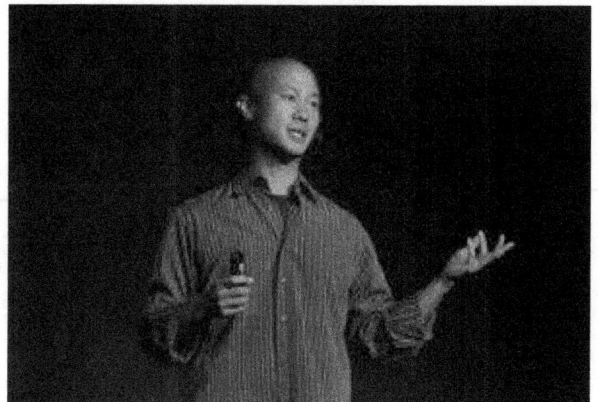

Zappos.com CEO Tony Hsieh believes organizational culture is key to a company's success.

Why is culture so important? Think for a moment about teams that you have been a part of in the past. These could be teams at work, school, or even sports. Also think about how you felt as a member of the team. Now consider two questions: Did you share the same goals, desires, and values as the other members of the team? Did you feel like an important part of the team, and were you committed to its success?

There is a high probability that you had the same answer to both questions, whether yes or no. For example, if you shared the same values as others on the team, then you likely were highly committed to the group's goals.

This is the strategic advantage of having a culture that resonates throughout the entire organization. It leads to a highly motivated team that is success-focused. It's so important that Zappos.com lists on its corporate web page the Zappos 10 Core Values. It includes the following:

- Deliver WOW Through Service
- Embrace and Drive Change
- Create Fun and A Little Weirdness
- Be Adventurous, Creative, and Open-Minded
- Pursue Growth and Learning
- Build Open and Honest Relationships With Communication
- Build a Positive Team and Family Spirit
- Do More With Less
- Be Passionate and Determined
- Be Humble

By clearly defining its culture, Zappos.com is able to recruit the right people and have them focus on the right things. As you work through this module, you will gain a better understanding of the importance of an organization's culture as a competitive advantage. Additionally, you will understand how to maintain culture over time or how implement cultural change if needed. Finally, you will come to see both the opportunities and challenges faced by promoting diversity within the culture.

INTRODUCTION TO ORGANIZATIONAL CULTURE

What you'll learn to do: describe organizational culture, and explain how culture can be a competitive advantage

Organizational culture is a term that describes the shared values and goals of an organization. When everyone in a corporation shares the same values and goals, it's possible to create a culture of mutual respect, collaboration, and support. Companies that have a strong, supportive culture are more likely to attract highly qualified, loyal employees who understand and work toward the company's best interests.

WHAT IS ORGANIZATIONAL CULTURE?

Learning Outcomes

  • Define culture for a business.
  • Explain how culture can be a competitive advantage for a business.
  • List the levels of culture.

Organizational culture is a term that can relate to any organization at all, from a church to a university. When talking about the culture of a business, you'll often hear the term "corporate culture." Corporate culture is, according to *INC Magazine*:

> the shared values, attitudes, standards, and beliefs that characterize members of an organization and define its nature. Corporate culture is rooted in an organization's goals, strategies, structure, and approaches to labor, customers, investors, and the greater community. As such, it is an essential component in any business's ultimate success or failure. (Note: "Corporate Culture," Inc. 2017. https://www.inc.com/encyclopedia/corporate-culture.html.)

Like families (or nations), corporations have cultures. Sometimes those cultures "just happen." All too often, when corporate culture is not intentionally created, the culture winds up being disjointed or even antagonistic.

Employees are all working toward different goals, in different ways, with different approaches. For instance, although Bob is dedicated to the idea of crafting quality products, Suzanne is eager to sell as much product as possible (even if the quality is only so-so). Meanwhile, Brad thinks the company should start making a wider range of products and is trying to push his ideas forward during sales meetings.

The idea of corporate culture developed from our knowledge of national, regional, and family cultures, and many theories exist about what makes a good (or poor) corporate culture. To get an idea of what a corporate culture looks like, think about families you know well. Some are formal whereas others are easygoing. Some work together toward shared goals whereas others encourage individuality and independence. Some are always having fun whereas others seem to be in a permanent state of internal conflict. We can describe corporate cultures in similar ways.

Although some businesses give little thought to corporate culture, many successful companies have cultures that are intentionally created or tweaked. Sometimes corporate cultures are the result of a founder's personal vision. But just as often, corporate cultures are created through a collaborative effort that involves not only upper management but also managers and employees.

What Do Corporate Cultures Look Like?

Perhaps the best way to get an idea of what we're talking about when we talk about corporate culture is to consider some examples. Let's take a look at the cultures inside a few well-known companies.

IBM

IBM's founder Thomas Watson was one of the great developers of corporate culture. Based on a very different worldview than the one we have today, it encouraged morality, temperance, and consistency. Men who worked for IBM were expected to dress in a certain style (dark suits, white shirts) and behave conservatively. The "IBM Spirit" was even represented in corporate songs such as "Ever Onward" that employees were required to sing at gatherings and conventions.

The lyrics to "Ever Onward," captured in a songbook from 1937, are a great way to understand the original culture of a company that became one of the truly great icons of American business. Read one verse of the song that follows.

> EVER ONWARD – EVER ONWARD!
> That's the spirit that has brought us fame!
> We're big, but bigger we will be
> We can't fail for all can see
> That to serve humanity has been our aim!
> Our products now are known, in every zone,
> Our reputation sparkles like a gem!
> We've fought our way through – and new
> Fields we're sure to conquer too
> For the EVER ONWARD I.B.M. (Note: "IBM Rally Song, Ever Onward," IBM, https://www-03.ibm.com/ibm/history/multimedia/everonward_trans.html)

Watch the following video to hear the song and find out more about IBM's early corporate culture:

https://www.youtube.com/watch?v=YBpNzxz1XgU

Google

One business that has revolutionized the way of work and its vision about it is Google. Google has become known as the company with endless perks for its valued employees. Some of these include coffee bars, free meals, lounge breaks, and even the option to bring your pet to work! Google has locations worldwide, and management embraces the idea that a happy employee leads to a productive workplace. The company's long-term success ties back to its corporate culture and values. Here's a list of Google's core values, around which it builds its corporate culture:

1. We want to work with great people.
2. Technology innovation is our lifeblood.
3. Working at Google is fun.
4. Be actively involved; you are Google.
5. Don't take success for granted.
6. Do the right thing; don't be evil.
7. Earn customer and user loyalty and respect every day.
8. Sustainable long-term growth and profitability are key to our success.
9. Google cares about and supports the communities where we work and live.

Apple

Google likes to make sure its employees are having fun, but Apple's corporate culture is a bit more focused on getting things done. Its founder, Steve Jobs, passed along a set of core values that make it clear that competition, focus, and hard work are part of the organizational culture:

1. We believe that we're on the face of the Earth to make great products.
2. We believe in the simple, not the complex.
3. We believe that we need to own and control the primary technologies behind the products we make.
4. We participate only in markets where we can make a significant contribution.
5. We believe in saying no to thousands of projects so that we can really focus on the few that are truly important and meaningful to us..
6. We believe in deep collaboration and cross-pollination of our groups, which allow us to innovate in a way that others cannot.
7. We don't settle for anything less than excellence in every group in the company, and we have the self-honesty to admit when we're wrong and the courage to change. (Note: Have you ever read about Apple's core values? (2017, May 25). Retrieved September 15, 2017, from https://thinkmarketingmagazine.com/apple-core-values/)

Compare Apple's values to those of Google. Apple focuses on competition, outcomes, and excellence, whereas Google emphasizes values such as having fun, behaving ethically, serving the customer, and engaging with the wider world. Both companies make digital products, both have seen great success, and both attract plenty of dedicated employees. But because the corporate cultures are so different, Apple and Google attract different people who have different personal goals, work styles, and expectations.

Corporate Culture as a Competitive Advantage

Why is it so important to have a strong, positive corporate culture? There are three good reasons:

- A strong culture helps employees, customers, and the general public to identify your corporate values. Say, for example, that your company culture values innovation. In that case, your employees will know that they will be encouraged to come up with new ideas—and your customers will know that your products and services are likely to have a creative or unique quality.
- Companies with strong, coherent cultures attract high-quality employees who believe in the same values as the corporation. Once those employees come on board, they start to feel that they "belong" because they are part of a shared culture. Employees who feel that their jobs are a great match for their personal values are more likely to be loyal to their employers. After all, they are doing what they enjoy doing for an organization that shares their ideals and goals.
- A strong corporate culture can help a corporation to build its brand. For example, Starbucks has built a culture and brand that includes very public dedication to international fair trade. Customers who care about fair trade are more likely to buy from—and stay loyal to—Starbucks.

Levels of Corporate Culture

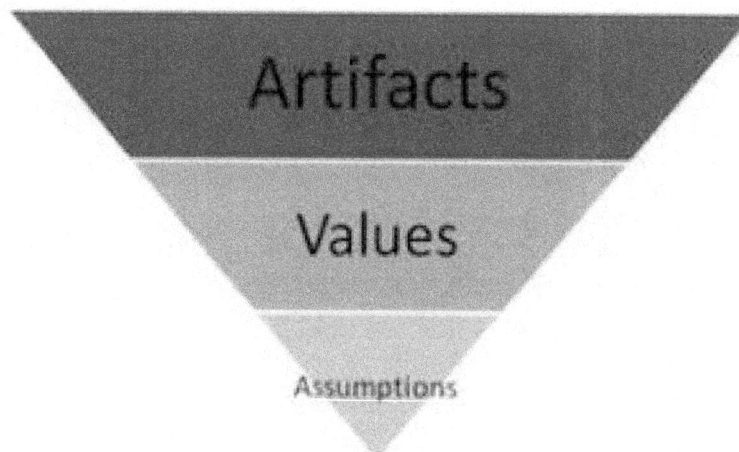

E.H. Schein's model of corporate culture includes artifacts, values, and assumptions

E.H. Schein is a theorist who studies corporate culture. In 1992, he wrote a book titled Organizational Culture and Leadership, which suggests that there are three levels of corporate culture. At the core of a culture are basic **assumptions** about human behavior, which are usually so ingrained into the culture that they're difficult to pinpoint. Surrounding the assumptions are expressed **values** drawn from those assumptions. These usually appear in the form of standards, rules, and public expressions of the organization's philosophy. At the surface level are **artifacts** that are the outcome of the assumptions and values—these appear as actions, policies, the physical environment, office jokes, and so on.

For example, when Home Depot, under the leadership of a new CEO, needed to return the company to its customer-centric roots in 2007, it quickly introduced artifacts—buttons and awards—to remind everyone who came first: customers. Sales associates began wearing buttons that invited customers to ask for help. Associates were rewarded for outstanding customer reviews and recognized in meetings with sales plaques and more buttons. With a renewed focus on its stated value of providing excellent customer service, Home Depot began hiring people who loved serving customers instead of worrying about costs and profits. Management did not completely abandon the cost discipline of its previous CEO, but it loosened the reins substantially. The underlying assumption was that profits would return if the company took care of customers. Profits did return, although the competition from Lowe's has been stiff.

There is no right or wrong set of assumptions and values, and companies can be successful no matter which values they embrace. You are, however, most likely to do well with a company that shares your beliefs. Just looking around a workplace can help you to determine whether a company values hierarchy or shared authority, individual achievement or teamwork.

INTRODUCTION TO KEY DIMENSIONS OF ORGANIZATIONAL CULTURE

What you'll learn to do: identify key dimensions of organizational culture

Every corporation has its own organizational culture. It turns out, though, that the vast majority of corporations fall into just seven cultural categories. When employees' personal styles, values, and assumptions match those of their employers, there's a good chance that the outcome will be positive. When they don't match, problems can ensue.

KEY DIMENSIONS OF ORGANIZATIONAL CULTURE

Learning Outcomes

- Discuss seven dimensions of culture in the Organizational Culture Profile.

Understanding a set of values that might be used to describe an organization's culture helps us identify, measure, and manage that culture more effectively. One framework that provides insight into the different types of organizational culture is the seven-dimension **Organizational Culture Profile (OCP)**. The OCP is an instrument initially developed by consultants Charles A. O'Reilly III, Jennifer Chatman, and David F. Caldwell to assess person-organization fit. In theory, employees should have the same basic cultural assumptions and values as the company for which they work.

According to the OCP, every corporation can be described as one of the following:

A general assumption is that employees should have the same basic values as the company for which they work.

Detail-oriented

Not surprisingly, detail-oriented companies are all about meticulous attention to details. These companies tend to be in customer-oriented industries in which such precision is valued. For example, Four Seasons hotels are dedicated to providing customers with exactly the service they prefer, and they keep records on each guest's experiences, preferences, and expectations. Employees working for Four Seasons must have an eye for detail and thrive on keeping meticulous records.

Innovative

Individuals who want opportunities to invent new products or services should consider working for companies such as W.L. Gore and Associates, maker of GORE-TEX, or 3M. These companies not only encourage innovation but give employees company time to work on their own projects. This approach can result in a wide range of exciting new products developed by engineers or scientists working on their own.

Aggressive

Although some companies value cooperation, others value aggressive competition. Stratasys, a maker of 3D printers, has been willing to make enemies in order to survive and thrive. Stratasys expanded rapidly through growth, takeovers, and mergers to gain a dominant position in the 3D printer industry. Sometimes, Stratasys' aggressive approach has gotten the company into legal battles—but the company has continued to perform well.

Outcome-oriented

Outcome-oriented businesses are all about results. At RE/MAX, for example, employees are trained to sell products, and they are evaluated on their sales performance. RE/MAX, short for "Real Estate Maximums," is an American international real estate company that operates through a franchise system. The company has held the number-one market share in the United States and Canada since 1999.

Stable

Employees at a stable corporation know exactly who is in charge, who to report to, and what they are expected to accomplish. Kraft Foods, for example, is a very stable organization with a strong bureaucracy. Although it is consistent, however, Kraft is not known for innovation or creativity.

People-oriented

If you work for a people-oriented corporation, you can expect the company to care about you. They value fairness and are supportive of individuals' rights and dignity. Software company SAS is a good example of a people-oriented company that offers employees a wide range of individualized benefits, including on-site childcare. CEO Jim Goodnight's philosophy is, "Treat employees like they make a difference, and they will." The result: a loyal and dedicated workforce.

Team-oriented

Employees who like to collaborate and cooperate with team members do well in team-oriented companies. Whole Foods, for example, expects its employees to function as members of teams—and to support other members of the team when necessary. This creates strong, solid relationships within working groups.

There is no one "best" type of corporate culture, and many larger corporations actually exhibit more than one culture. For example, the sales department may have an aggressive culture, whereas marketing is more team-oriented. In general, however, corporations can be grouped into the categories mentioned earlier.

INTRODUCTION TO INFLUENCES ON ORGANIZATIONAL CULTURE

What you'll learn to do: identify the main influences on organizational culture and explain how culture is maintained

Where does organizational culture come from? How is it maintained? How can you recognize it when you see it? In this section, we'll investigate the sources of culture in an organization, as well as the methods for maintaining it. And we'll talk about how to spot the signs of an organization's culture even when you're an outsider looking in.

INFLUENCES ON ORGANIZATIONAL CULTURE

Learning Outcomes

- Discuss the sources of culture in an organization.
- Explain the methods for maintaining a culture.
- List the visible signs of culture.

No matter where you work, you will experience organizational culture. Employees can usually tell from the get-go if their place of employment is serious or fun, people-oriented or results-oriented. But how did the culture get started? How do employees get to know about the corporate culture and help to keep it in place?

Sources of Culture in an Organization

Founders

When a company is founded, there is usually a single individual or group of individuals involved. The founder or founders have a vision for their new company—and that vision helps to form the corporate culture. In some cases, the founder is very intentional about creating a particular culture; he or she may actually want to create a business in which, for example, innovation or teamwork is valued. in other cases, the founder's personality unintentionally forms the culture.

Some individual founders have such strong personalities and values that the company continues to reflect their goals even as it grows—and even after the founder dies. Walt Disney, for example, modeled leadership, teamwork, and innovation so that, even today, the Disney Corporation is built around the values and assumptions of its founder.

Another good example of the way that founders' values create corporate culture is Ben and Jerry's Ice Cream. Founders Ben Cohen and Jerry Greenfield started out to create a company with strong social values—and they succeeded. The company started in 1978, but even today the company continues to focus on sustainability, environmental activism, social activism, and charity.

Industry

It's one thing to be creative, innovative, and fun in the hospitality or entertainment business. But that type of culture won't work well in an industry that's built around regulations and policies that cannot be changed or bent. Industries such as pharmaceuticals and nuclear power require attention to detail and cannot tolerate a "creative" approach to following rules. True, a pharmaceutical company can be people-oriented to a degree, but its willingness to support the individual needs of employees must be secondary to its absolute compliance with regulations and the law.

Methods for Maintaining Corporate Culture

Why do some companies maintain their culture whereas others see it fall apart? The answer lies in how the company goes about recruiting, hiring, onboarding, and training its employees.

- **Recruiting.** To find employees who will fit into the corporate culture, recruiters must look in the right places. When looking for upper-level managers, recruiters should look at corporations with a similar culture to their own. When looking for entry-level employees, recruiters should tap college programs or websites that reflect their corporate culture.
- **Hiring.** When interviewing job candidates, managers and human resources managers must spend some time assessing the candidate's assumptions and values. Is this person a collaborator or a competitor? Are candidates detail-oriented or innovative? Candidates whose personal assumptions and values match the corporate culture are much more likely to help maintain that culture over time.
- **Onboarding.** The "onboarding" process is really a new employee orientation process. During onboarding, human resources personnel help the new employee get to know company policies and practices. It's during onboarding, for example, that a new employee may learn that each team puts together a skit for the company holiday party or that bonuses can be earned as a result of exceeding sales goals.
- **Training.** Training can be both formal and informal. Whereas formal training may teach new employees how to use company software or systems, informal training may involve one-on-one conversations with peers and managers. During those conversations, new employees learn how the company culture manifests itself in the workplace. For example, they may learn that everyone—even bad players—take part in departmental softball games, or that recycling is a "must" in the lunchroom. All these subtle bits of information add up to an understanding of corporate culture.

Once an employee is hired, he or she may feel comfortable or uncomfortable in the new workplace. Typically, those employees who feel "at home" in the corporate culture tend to stick around, whereas those who feel like outsiders tend to leave at the first good opportunity.

Visible Signs of Culture

When you walk into a business setting, you should be able to see visible signs of the business's organizational culture. If you spend a few weeks on the job, you should see even more. Here are just a few things to look out for:

What does having a large space for informal employee meetings and encounters say about an organization's culture?

- **How employees dress.** Most employers have some kind of dress code. Some are quite casual whereas others require more formal clothing. In a minority of businesses there is no dress code at all, and employees are welcome to wear short, sleeveless tops, and even flip-flops to work.
- **Snack areas and candy jars.** How people-oriented is your business? In some workplaces, employees have all-day access to snack bars, free soft drinks, coffee, and other goodies. Candy jars are also a sign that a business is open to people-oriented treats.
- **Plaques and awards.** In some businesses, plaques and awards honoring employees are placed front and center. Some honor individuals as "employee of the month," whereas others recognize specific achievements such as "most sales made in a month."
- **Mission statement.** In many corporations, the organizational mission is posted on every floor. The mission is intended to remind employees why they are there and what their goals and attitudes should be.
- **Events and rituals.** Many workplaces have customs or rituals that become obvious within just a couple of weeks on the job. Whether it's "happy hour Friday," "dress down Tuesday," or weekly update meetings, employees quickly learn the routines.
- **Physical layout and décor.** When you walk into a workplace, what do you see? In some offices, gray cubicles dominate; in others, the workspace is wide open. In some businesses, individuals are encouraged to bring in and show off photos, posters, and plants; in others employees are asked to keep personal items to a minimum.

Recognizing the culture is the beginning of adapting to it and, perhaps, using it to persuade management to your ideas.

INTRODUCTION TO CULTURAL CHANGE

What you'll learn to do: describe the key techniques for initiating and fostering cultural change

Times change, and often corporate cultures must change to keep pace with technology and social norms. Ideally, cultural change is the result of a strategic plan that supports the process and provides resources for overcoming inevitable challenges.

INITIATING AND FOSTERING CULTURAL CHANGE

When times change, corporations may need to change as well. Many factors can make change necessary, ranging from social norms to technology to new ways of doing business. No matter why cultural change is needed, it's never easy. That's because human beings, in general, resist change. To make cultural change successful, therefore, companies must create change management strategies and stick to them over time.

Smart managers and leaders know when a change is needed within their organization.

Initiating Change

Although there are many ways to initiate change, the most effective methods come from the top down. One of the keys to making change happen is the actions of the corporate leader.

- **Create a sense of urgency.** Why should employees change their habits, systems, or ways of doing business? If there's no emergency, employees are likely to resist change. But what if your business is likely to fail if you don't reinvent some of your culture and practices? In 1993, IBM was facing just such a crisis. Lou Gerstner, IBM's CEO, made it clear to employees that the situation was truly dire: change or die. In a short time, IBM shifted from being an old-fashioned, stuck-in-the-past footnote to a future-facing, innovative organization.
- **Role modeling.** If the need for organizational change is communicated from the top down, it must be modeled from the top down as well. When a corporate leader is truly committed to change, he or she becomes a guiding light for the entire organization. A leader can model change through public actions such as press conferences or presentations. More significant, however, are actions that show that the leader is truly taking his or her own ideas to heart. Not only is it inspiring to see a leader taking his or her own advice to heart, but it's also helpful to see what the change really looks like. Robert Iger, who became CEO of Disney, was concerned that innovation was fading. To show his commitment to cultural change, he jumped in to provide hands-on help with game creation.
- **Changing leaders.** Once a company has made a commitment to change, it's important that all members of the senior management team understand and embrace the change. In some cases, individuals may dig in their heels and refuse to change their practices. When this happens, the company has little choice but to terminate their employment.

Managing Change

As is often the reality, it's easy to start a process—but much more difficult to manage it over time. The following techniques can help ensure that change is institutionalized:

- **Excellent communication.** That's the key conclusion of a 2016 study, "Where Change Management Fails," from Robert Half Management Resources. This survey of 300 senior managers found that most change efforts failed in the implementation stage—on shoals of broken or inadequate communication. (Note: "Where Change Management Fails," Robert Half Management Resources. Feb. 3, 2016, accessed Aug. 8, 2017, http://rhmr.mediaroom.com/where-change-management-fails)
- **Changing leaders who present barriers to change.** It's hard for employees to make change when their own managers are resistant to new ideas. When leadership is standing in the way of positive change, upper management may have to "clean house" by dismissing managers who, for personal or political reasons, are unwilling to bend.
- **Training programs.** When organizational culture is the source of unethical or unsafe practices, training can be the key to change. The same is true for changes related to customer service. The Midas auto repair chain, for example, used training to help employees better empathize with customers' needs and concerns.
- **Changing reward systems and corporate symbols.** To let employees know things have really changed, it may be necessary to change incentives. For example, if a company has rewarded individual achievement but wants to see a cultural switch to teamwork, it may need to reward team accomplishments. Similarly, the company may need to change the visual symbols it uses to reflect the new organizational culture.
- **Changing the look and feel of the workplace.** A workplace "makeover" can have a profound impact on change. Visual cues can quickly and effectively let employees know that they are encouraged to gather around a large table in a shared work area, or that managers in an open environment are available for questions and collaboration.

Changing a firm's culture is hard, and many attempts fail. CEOs have lost their jobs because they tried and failed. It generally takes years and may require replacing people. College administrators joke that their ideas for OER (open educational resources, such as this online course) advance slowly, one retirement at a time. But change is possible with the right approach.

INTRODUCTION TO EMPLOYEE DIVERSITY

What you'll learn to do: identify the advantages and challenges of employee diversity within organizations

America is an incredibly diverse country, with residents and citizens from virtually every part of the world. Colleges and universities are perhaps even more diverse than communities. Undergraduate and graduate students travel from Asia, Europe, Africa, and South America to study in the United States. American workplaces are also increasingly diverse, particularly when companies work with or have divisions in other countries. There are great benefits to diversity, but differences can also create challenges.

EMPLOYEE DIVERSITY

Learning Outcomes

- Explain the concept of diversity within organizations.
- Explain the advantages of employee diversity within organizations.
- Explain the challenges of employee diversity within organizations.

A manager who oversees a diverse workforce may find certain advantages and challenges in her job.

What Is Diversity in the Workplace?

Until the 1950s and 1960s, diversity was not associated with the workplace in the United States. In general, people were hired based on their gender, race, social status, and religion. Women were often asked to leave their jobs if they married or became pregnant. No accommodation was made for disability except by special arrangement.

But there were a few exceptions, particularly in fields in which qualified employees were scarce. The computer industry was one such field.

IBM, one of the most strait-laced companies in the United States, was also one of the most diverse. In 1953, for example, IBM's president wrote a letter to his managers stating: "It is the policy of this organization to hire people who have the personality, talent and background necessary to fill a given job, regardless of race, color or creed." Even in the Deep South, where segregation was a reality in restaurants, hotels, and even at water fountains, IBM employees of all races and backgrounds ate together in the cafeteria.

Fast-forward to the twenty-first century, and diversity in the workplace is not just a matter of ethics. Diversity is required by law and is a recommended strategy. Federal protected classes include race, color, religion or creed, national origin or ancestry, gender, age, disability, veteran status, and, in two cases, genetic information. The law creates a minimum response to discrimination, but diversity is also an asset in running a business.

Many experts, including the Boston Consulting Group, recommend diversity as a long-term strategy. They use a broader meaning of diversity, which adds personality, cognitive style, education, social background, and more. For example, the largest companies make a point of hiring from many colleges. Even if Harvard produced the best individual candidates, companies would still hire from many colleges. The diversity of training and connections are strengths, not shortcomings.

A diverse workplace isn't always easy to achieve, as some locations, industries, and positions tend to attract people of certain backgrounds. To diversify the workplace, some companies make a significant effort to reach out to diverse communities. For example, they might reach out to the veterans community, which includes thousands of individuals of all backgrounds, many of whom have solid training and experience.

The explosive growth in global trade means that large corporations began sending more Americans abroad, outsourcing work to other countries, and hiring non-American workers to come to the United States. Meanwhile, changing norms and laws improved the status of women in the workplace, and made it both acceptable and legal to be out, gay, and married. Finally, the Americans with Disabilities Act made it necessary for businesses to accommodate individuals with disabilities through the addition of elevators, ramps, Braille signage, flexible work settings and hours, and more.

With so many requirements for diversity, most US businesses now employ a very wide range of people. A diverse workplace brings both challenges and opportunities.

Advantages of Employee Diversity

The Boston Consulting Group, a management consulting firm, takes an approach to diversity that borrows from ecology. First, diversity builds resilience. Enduring systems comprise a broad variety of agents, which behave and respond to external stimuli in varying ways. As a result, a challenge to the system is less likely to break it. Second, diversity is the basis of adaptiveness. Diversity of problem-solving heuristics and behavior permits a system to evolve and learn from experience. Internal variety—diversity—provides the grist for the system to test ideas and actions and select the most effective in each environment. (Note: Miki Tsusaka et al., "Diversity at Work," Boston Consulting Group, 2017, http://image-src.bcg.com/Images/BCG-Diversity-at-Work-July-2017_tcm9-165880.pdf)

When a workplace employs only people of similar background, education, and lifestyle, it's easy for employees to reinforce one another's preconceptions and prejudices. When people of different cultures and backgrounds are valued and heard, however, new ideas and opportunities emerge. The Peterson Institute for International Economics studied the impact of female executives in ninety-one countries and almost twenty-two thousand firms. The firms with more women in corporate leadership did better. (Note: "New Peterson Institute Research on over 21,000 Companies Globally Finds Women in Corporate Leadership Can Significantly Increase Profitability," Feb. 8, 2016, accessed Aug. 8, 2017, https://piie.com/newsroom/press-releases/new-peterson-institute-research-over-21000-companies-globally-finds-women) A study of this kind cannot determine cause and effect. For example, better performance may result from the nondiscrimination policies and a more open culture, but diversity is a winning strategy either way. Here are some ways that diversity can positively impact an organization:

- **Diversity enhances creativity.** People from different places, ethnicities, and lifestyles can bring fresh ideas to an older corporation. Could a product be made to appeal to a whole new demographic? How might a particular service be advertised to a new ethnic market or the disabled community? By including people of different backgrounds in the conversation, managers get valuable insights into different points of view.
- **Diversity enhances image.** Today's marketplace is diverse; so, too, are customers. When a company can present itself as diverse, clients and buyers respond positively.
- **Diversity improves outreach.** Employees from different parts of the world or different communities can help a corporation to understand and reach out to new markets.
- **Diversity improves morale.** When employees of all backgrounds and abilities feel valued, they are more likely to be loyal, engaged, and productive. Employees are also more likely to feel a sense of pride and belonging when they are associated with an employer that clearly cares about the well-being of all.

Challenges of Employee Diversity

Differences fuel battles and even wars. That's true in the political arena, and it can also be true in the workplace. Problems that can arise with a diverse workplace include difficulty with communication, different work styles or work ethics. Small issues, such as different smells in the lunchroom, can quickly escalate if not managed appropriately.

Differences in culture can also lead to miscommunication. For example, Americans value eye contact—even with members of the opposite sex. But in many Asian and Middle Eastern countries, direct eye contact is considered to be disrespectful. Direct eye contact with someone of the opposite sex may even be seen as flirting. It's very important, therefore, to provide diversity training to avoid serious social gaffes and challenges.

Work styles can also vary from culture to culture. Although many Asians and Central Americans work in groups and value consensus, most Germans and Americans prefer to work independently. Some cultures place a high value on order, organization, and method whereas others emphasize spontaneity and flexible thinking.

Another serious challenge lies in diversity in management. Typically, top leadership is white and male whereas lower level workers may be female or nonwhite. To be seriously considered for promotion to a top-level management position in many US companies, individuals must assimilate to the point where they are virtually indistinguishable from existing leadership. This, of course, negates the advantages of diversity—and raises the bar for promotion.

Fortunately, many of the challenges of employee diversity can be foreseen and managed through employee training and diversity-oriented company policies. It's important, however, for management to think ahead rather than assume that a diverse workforce will work well without any intervention.

PUTTING IT TOGETHER: CULTURE AND DIVERSITY

Think back to the beginning of this module and the quote from Tony Hsieh that "If you get the culture right, most of the other stuff will just take care of itself." Given what you've learned in this module, do you agree with him? Consider also this quote from legendary management consultant Peter Drucker that "Culture eats strategy for breakfast." This module has equipped you to evaluate these statements and understand why exceptional leaders consider culture to be central to organizational success.

Zappos CEO Tony Hsieh highly values his company's culture.

Let's consider the example of Zappos in greater detail. Based on experiences earlier in his career, CEO Tony Hsieh became committed to the idea that culture matters most in an organization. So how does that manifest itself in Zappos?

One of the topics covered in this module was how to integrate culture into the recruiting and hiring processes. This is very important at Zappos. In the early days of the organization, Hsieh or another key executive would participate in every interview. If they didn't feel the candidate was a good culture fit, they would look for someone else. It didn't matter how talented the candidate was—if the culture fit was wrong, they wouldn't make the hire. As the company grew, Hsieh knew that the leaders he had hired would follow his example. As a result, culture fit remains the primary focus in both recruiting and hiring. This has resulted in a team that is focused on the same values and wants to achieve the same goals.

In the following video, Hsieh discusses the importance of cultural fit in the hiring process at Zappos:

https://www.youtube.com/watch?v=9C36EYM-mWQ

This laser focus on culture has proven to be a tremendous competitive advantage for Zappos. The entire organization shares the same core value—please the customer! As an example of this focus, Zappos telephone customer service representatives (CSRs) are not measured on average call time, which is a standard in the industry. Zappos doesn't worry about how long a CSR is on the call with a customer. One caller took 10.5 hours, and Zappos praised the CSR. (Note: Caroline Fairchild, "Zappos' 10-Hour Long Customer Service Call Sets Record," The Huffington Post, Dec. 21, 2012, accessed Aug. 8, 2017, http://www.huffingtonpost.com/2012/12/21/zappos-10-hour-call_n_2345467.html)

Instead, what managers care about is how the customer feels when the call is over. Was their issue resolved? Were they happy with the overall experience? Zappos wants its CSRs to spend as much time as necessary to make customers happy. This is a radically different approach than most organizations, and it results from the organization's culture.

As a testament to the success of its focus on culture, more than 75 percent of sales at Zappos are from repeat customers. This is an amazing statistic, much higher than the industry average of 48 percent. (Note: Andrew Meola, "Returning customers are far more valuable to online retailers than new customers," Business Insider, March 30, 2016, accessed Aug. 8, 2017, http://www.businessinsider.com/e-commerce-report-shows-returning-customers-are-more-valuable-than-new-ones-2016-3) Focusing on creating and maintaining the right culture will help you be successful as a manager and give your organization a unique competitive advantage.

MODULE 10: LEADERSHIP

WHY IT MATTERS: LEADERSHIP

Why does a manager need to understand leadership, leadership theories, and the difference between effective and poor leadership?

What makes someone such as Winston Churchill, England's prime minister during World War II, a great leader?

What's the difference between being a manager and a leader? Why does it matter? When we look at examples from the past, why do we lift up Winston Churchill, Indira Gandhi, Martin Luther King Jr., and others as great leaders—not simply as great managers?

Let's consider a more recent example. Jeff Bezos is the founder and CEO of Amazon.com. Although it's absolutely clear that Amazon is changing the face of business and redefining the way many of us shop, what is it about the man, Bezos, that moves the company ever-forward? Many start-ups have attempted to redefine e-commerce, but none have had the disruptive force of Amazon. Why has Bezos succeeded where so many others have failed? What can we learn from his example? We will consider such questions in more detail at the end of this module.

In this module, you are going to learn about leadership. You'll recognize the differences between management and leadership, and you'll discover some common traits that leaders share. You'll study several of the major theories of leadership and how to analyze leadership skill in others. Ultimately, you'll want to study these lessons with a thought toward your own leadership development and how you might apply these lessons in both your career and personal life.

INTRODUCTION TO LEADERSHIP

What you'll learn to do: differentiate between leadership and management

What is the difference between "management" and "leadership"? Sometimes the terms are used almost interchangeably, but there is an important difference between them. Management includes various aspects, one of which is the leadership function. Learning to distinguish between the two can help individuals evaluate and develop their leadership skills.

WHAT IS LEADERSHIP?

Learning Outcomes

  • Differentiate between leadership and management.

"EVERYTHING RISES AND FALLS ON LEADERSHIP."
John Maxwell

Two Related but Distinct Ideas

Brendan has recently been hired as the general manager of a local athletic club. The club has been struggling financially for the past few years, and part of Brendan's job is to address that issue. As he analyzes the problem, he finds that there is a significant lack of efficiency in the club's operations, so he makes a number of changes to take control of the situation. He organizes the work to be done by employees, creates more consistent schedules, plans an official budget, writes and implements an employee dress code and code of conduct, and provides the shift managers with much clearer instructions as to their responsibilities. Before long, the club's operations are once again profitable and smooth.

Terence has also recently accepted a managerial role with a local catering business. Though the catering business has excellent food, good service, and reasonable prices, it is struggling to gain adequate market share. Terence believes that the company lacks a key identity to distinguish itself from its competitors, and he is determined to provide a new and innovative identity. He works with the entire staff to create a new long-term focus and vision for what the company could become. His enthusiasm is inspiring and motivating to the entire catering team, which embraces the new direction of the company.

Although both Brendan and Terence were successful, there is a difference in the approaches each took to his situation. Brendan's activities were focused strongly on the management aspects of his role. His club needed organization and structure. His task was to take control and help the club become more efficient in how it carried out its current activities—a very important accomplishment!

On the other hand, Terence's emphasis of creating an entirely new vision and direction for the catering company was a demonstration of his leadership abilities. Those abilities were further displayed by the way in which he inspired and motivated the catering team to follow him in pursuing that new direction.

Leadership is about establishing a direction and influencing others to follow. **Management** is about successfully administering the many complex details involved in a business's operations. Leadership pursues change and challenges the status quo, whereas management seeks to control and provide stability within the existing circumstances.

Both management and leadership are necessary skills, and they often overlap with one another. In most settings, the role of a manager includes both leadership and management functions. Leadership skills are needed to set the vision, and management skills are needed to implement a plan to achieve that vision. Recognizing the difference between leadership and management, however, can help individuals focus on developing their skills in both arenas. The greatest success comes when strong leadership is paired with effective management.

To help distinguish between leadership and management, consider the following sets of terms associated with each category:

Leadership	Management
<ul><li>Influencing</li><li>Change</li><li>Direction</li><li>Vision</li><li>Innovating</li><li>Developing</li><li>Long-term</li><li>Originating</li><li>Creating</li><li>Motivating</li><li>Inspiring</li><li>People</li><li>Big Ideas</li></ul>	<ul><li>Planning</li><li>Organizing</li><li>Controlling</li><li>Stability</li><li>Administering</li><li>Maintaining</li><li>Implementing</li><li>Instructing</li><li>Resources</li><li>Budgeting</li><li>Scheduling</li><li>Details</li></ul>

Formal vs. Informal Leadership

As we attempt to understand what leadership is all about, it is worth noting that not all leadership is based on official position. That is, the title and official role of an individual within an organization do not always correspond to his actual leadership influence.

Generally speaking, individuals who are assigned titles and positions of authority are expected to provide leadership. Because that leadership role is officially recognized, this is known as **formal leadership**. Unfortunately, there are plenty of individuals who have formal leadership positions but do not actually provide strong leadership. This is often problematic and can leave the organization lacking direction and purpose.

However, there are also individuals who do not have official positions of leadership but who do exhibit leadership qualities and practices. They help create the company vision with innovative ideas, and they inspire and motivate their coworkers. When leadership is exhibited without an official position, it is known as **informal leadership**. This is a valuable trait for an employee to have.

INTRODUCTION TO WHAT MAKES AN EFFECTIVE LEADER

What you'll learn to do: identify the traits, dimensions, and styles of effective leaders

Leadership is a desirable quality, so it comes as no surprise that much study has been done in attempts to identify the key elements of an effective leader. Much of that study has focused on the specific character, personality, or behavioral traits that most effective leaders have in common. The evidence is mixed on whether traits or personality can predict leadership potential. In the following section, we will examine some of the commonly identified leadership traits along with some of the leadership styles individuals display.

WHAT MAKES AN EFFECTIVE LEADER?

Learning Outcomes

- Identify the traits of effective leaders.
- Differentiate between task-centered and employee-centered leadership behavior.
- Differentiate between autocratic, democratic, and laissez-faire styles of leadership.

Introduction

As people have pursued an understanding of what makes an effective leader, their attention has often moved to the key personal traits those leaders exhibit. The idea is that identifying those common traits will help businesses identify effective leaders and help individuals know how to become better leaders. What are some of those common traits?

Research on traits has many critics. One example that follows will illustrate that someone perceived as a leader may not be the most effective leader in the long run. Nevertheless, some companies will use traits or personality in making hiring or promotion decisions.

Leadership Traits

LEADERSHIP TRAITS

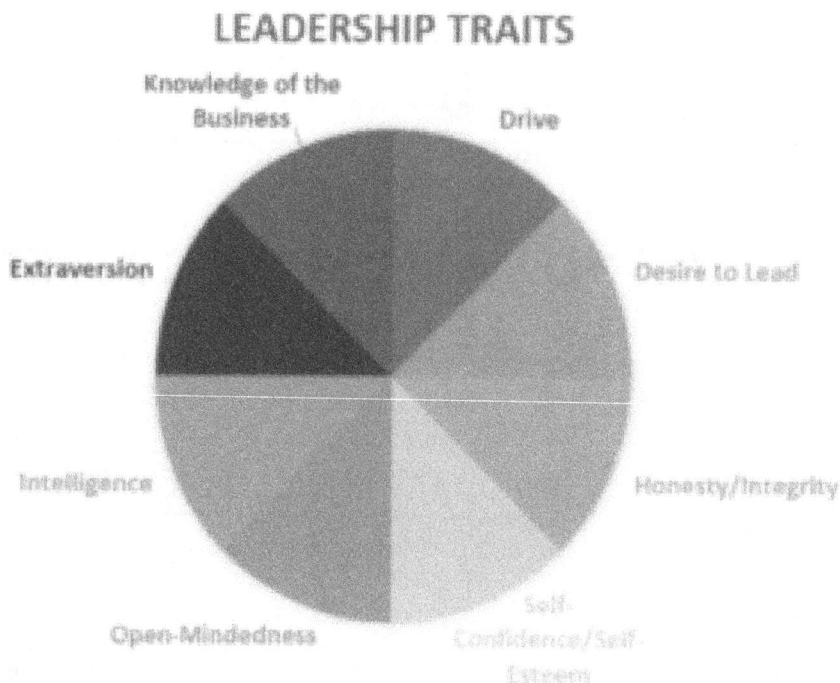

Drive

Leaders tend to be highly motivated individuals. This inner drive is reflected in a number of common ways. They reflect a greater effort level in general, they strive for achievement, they have greater ambition, they work with greater energy, they are often tenacious, and they are more likely to take the initiative rather than wait for someone else to do so.

Desire to Lead

Effective leaders also tend to have a strong desire toward leadership roles and functions. Although others are happier to allow others to take the lead, leaders want to do so themselves.

Honesty/Integrity

The moral aspect of leadership is highly significant. Effective leaders must demonstrate high levels of honesty and integrity. This is essential to inspiring confidence and trust from employees and other followers, without which a leader is not likely to be effective. Dishonesty may not always be revealed at first, but it usually is with time. There are many stories of business leaders who are successful for a period of time but later find themselves in serious trouble due to dishonest or unethical practices. For example, Martin Winterkorn became embroiled in ethical and legal controversy after a period of strong success as CEO of Volkswagen.

Self-Esteem /Self-Confidence

These two elements, self-esteem and self-confidence, are closely related and tend to be prominent in leaders. Perhaps it is best to view these traits in terms of the negative perspective. A lack of self-esteem and self-confidence is very problematic for a leader. When these traits are lacking, doubts arise and insecurities plague a leader's activities. The leader tends to be confident that his beliefs, plans, and actions are correct (hopefully with good reason). This confidence is important in that it enables the leader to persist steadfastly in the right course even when there are obstacles and doubts from others.

184

Open-Mindedness

At the same time, effective leaders also tend to be open-minded to new ideas and experiences. They recognize that innovation is often valuable, and they also tend to consider ideas and suggestions from others. Self-confidence and self-esteem do not have to conflict with this spirit of open-mindedness. When they do, the result is generally harmful.

Intelligence

One obvious trait that many people look for in leaders is intelligence. Studies have shown that this is indeed an important qualification. It has been suggested, however, that pure cognitive ability is a "threshold" qualification. That is, it is important for the entrance into leadership roles. However, once within the leadership circle, most individuals have relatively high intelligence levels, so mere cognitive ability is not enough to distinguish a leader from other leaders.

Further, pure cognitive ability is only one type of intelligence. Relational and emotional intelligence are also important aspects for leaders to develop. An over-reliance on strict cognitive intelligence can be very inhibiting to effective leadership.

Extraversion

Mark Zuckerberg, Facebook

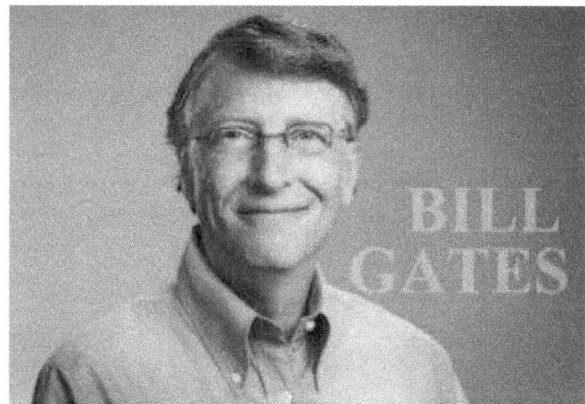

Bill Gates, Microsoft

Another unsurprising personality trait that is commonly associated with leadership is being an extrovert. Leaders tend to be outgoing and social in their personalities, which helps them take the lead and act with initiative. It also helps them with the important aspect of connecting to and inspiring others through relationships.

Though many leaders are extraverts, there are certainly examples of successful leaders who are not. Sometimes other strengths are sufficient to compensate for not being an extravert, or sometimes a leader who is not naturally an extravert is able to train himself to be more outgoing in behavior when needed, though this still does not generally change the leader's basic personality. Bill Gates of Microsoft and Mark Zuckerberg of Facebook are two prominent examples of extremely successful leaders who are introverts by personality.

Knowledge of the Business

Another key ingredient in the leadership trait mix is knowledge of the business. Even if an individual has all the natural personality traits desired of leaders, a lack of knowledge and experience is usually impossible to overcome. A leader must be competent in his field, and the most effective leaders are usually experts with deep insight.

Styles of Leadership

Though a trait-based analysis of leaders is a common approach, another way to evaluate leaders is to analyze their behavioral leadership styles.

Task-Centered or Employee-Centered

Most behavioral leadership styles fall within two broad categories: task-centered styles and employee-centered styles.

Task-centered styles of leadership focus on giving instructions and directions to group members to reach achievement and accomplishment goals more efficiently and effectively. The focus is on the objective analysis of what needs done and the specific course of actions that should be taken to meet those needs. Employees are seen as resources to be used to accomplish the goals.

Employee-centered styles of leadership focus less on objective actions or plans and more on building the relationships between themselves and their followers. By encouraging and supporting them, the leader hopes to make them more qualified, confident, and productive. His focus is on developing his employees and inspiring them to follow the vision he has provided. Employee-centered styles are also often referred to as people-centered or relationship-centered.

Of course, many leaders would hope to combine qualities from both of these styles, but the tendency is for individual leaders to focus more strongly on one or the other.

Autocratic, Democratic, or Laissez-faire

A leader's style can often be identified by the manner in which he makes decisions, especially the degree to which he involves his employees. This aspect of leadership is often divided into a spectrum with three broad categories: autocratic, democratic, and laissez-faire.

"A good leader inspires people to have confidence in the leader. A great leader inspires people to have confidence in themselves."

Eleanor Roosevelt

An **autocratic** leader makes decisions without significant employee involvement in the process. He works from an authoritarian perspective. This approach often corresponds to a task-centered style. This approach can be faster and more efficient than more discursive approaches.

A **democratic** approach strongly involves the employee team in the decision-making process. This can take a variety of forms. For example, the employees may discuss the issue together as a group, followed by the leader making the final decision. Alternatively, the leader might agree to allow the employees a final vote in the matter. In any case, employees have a significant role to play in the process.

A **laissez-faire** approach is a very hands-off approach to leadership. Instead, employees make decisions on their own. This approach generally leads to lower productivity, but it may be the best where employees are experts or where creativity is needed.

INTRODUCTION TO EFFECTIVE VS. POOR LEADERSHIP

What you'll learn to do: compare examples of effective and poor leadership

What do these different leadership traits and styles look like in practice? Looking at real-world examples of good—and bad—leadership will help deepen your understanding of them.

EFFECTIVE VS. POOR LEADERSHIP

Learning Outcomes

  • Compare examples of effective and poor leadership.

Warren Buffett, Berkshire Hathaway

Warren Buffett has become one of the wealthiest men in the world through his leadership of the investment and holdings company Berkshire Hathaway Inc. As chairman, president, and CEO, Buffett is the obvious formal leader at Berkshire Hathaway, but his effective leadership is perhaps better demonstrated by the devoted following he has outside of the official structure of the company. Thousands of individuals travel to hear him at his annual investor meetings, follow his activities and advice, and read his annual shareholder letter (Note: Hamilton Nolan, "Warren Buffett Is the Best Argument for Capitalism. Is It Good Enough?" Gawker, May 5, 2016, accessed July 27, 2017, http://gawker.com/warren-buffett-is-the-best-argument-for-capitalism-is-1774678180.).

Warren Buffett of Berkshire Hathaway

One of the easily identifiable reasons for this is his unparalleled success as an investor, which has led to his becoming one of the wealthiest individuals in the world (Note: "Playing out the last hand," The Economist, May 1, 2014, accessed July 27, 2017, https://www.economist.com/news/briefing/21601240-warren-buffetts-50-years-running-berkshire-hathaway-have-been-one-businesss-most-impressive.). However, there are also a number of key features of his leadership style that have strongly contributed to his effectiveness and influence with his followers.

One interesting fact about Buffett is his "light touch" as a manager. His work is to identify companies for purchase that he believes are well-managed and situated for success. As a rule, he buys only companies whose directors and direction he trusts. Because he has confidence in them and their direction, he is happy to leave them to their work with as little interference as possible, which is a trait that appeals to many companies looking for a potential buyer.

If we look at Buffett's informal leadership influence, a number of traits stand out as contributing forces for his effectiveness. To begin with, he is an excellent example of a leader who presents a vision, stands firmly behind it, and inspires others to confidence and enthusiasm about that vision (Note: "Playing out the last hand," The Economist, May 1, 2014, accessed July 27, 2017, https://www.economist.com/news/briefing/21601240-warren-buffetts-50-years-running-berkshire-hathaway-have-been-one-businesss-most-impressive.). His approach to investing is starkly different from that of many others. He emphasizes a deep understanding of companies and their industries, even refusing for the most part to involve himself in the tech sector simply because he feels he doesn't understand that realm well enough to make wise investing decisions. He urges the wisdom of buying solid, successful companies and trusting in their long-term success. This approach contrasts sharply with an eager obsession to discover an unknown company that is about to explode in value and provide quick riches. This patient, steady approach to long-term investing has proven effective in the extreme, and many others have placed their confidence in Buffett's message and vision. As an important ingredient in this vision-casting, many have attested to Buffett's skill in presenting his approach with a great simplicity that enables his followers to understand the vision easily and deeply, inspiring further confidence.

Two other aspects of Buffett's leadership style call for comment: his truthfulness and his optimism (Note: Zameena Mejia, "Why Warren Buffett is such an influential leader, according to data," CNBC, June 6, 2017, accessed July 27, 2017, http://www.cnbc.com/2017/06/06/why-warren-buffett-is-such-an-influential-leader-according-to-data.html.). He represents what many consider the "honest" way to achieve investing success. He has not sought quick riches through questionable means. He has been transparent and straightforward about his activities. He has also been quick to recognize his mistakes in investing when he has made them. This honesty and transparency are appreciated, especially in contrast with the opposite feeling that surrounds too many in the investment world.

Buffett's optimism and positivity also contribute to his overall effectiveness as a leader. He sees the future as one of bright potential and focuses on that potential rather than dwelling on mistakes and other negative aspects of life. Though he certainly recognizes problems and is straightforward about negative situations, he does not allow them to control his outlook. He challenges others to adopt that same positive mindset, and many have responded to that challenge.

Martin Winterkorn, Volkswagen

At one point in Martin Winterkorn's tenure as CEO of Volkswagen, the auto manufacturer was in the midst of a historically impressive run of increased market share and revenue gains. Winterkorn had set ambitious goals to dominate the world auto market by 2018. The forecast for achieving those goals was very positive based on the progress the company was experiencing (Note: Joann Muller, "How Volkswagen Will Rule the World," July 8, 2013, accessed July 27, 2017, https://www.forbes.com/sites/joannmuller/2013/04/17/volkswagens-mission-to-dominate-global-auto-industry-gets-noticeably-harder/#a48b0b83c464.). Winterkorn's ambition and dedication to success were hailed as vital leadership ingredients propelling Volkswagen forward.

However, shocking news of a widespread scandal within the company disrupted that upward trajectory. The manufacturer was found to have installed secret software that would falsify emissions readings for vehicles when tested (Note: Russell Hotten, "Volkswagen: The scandal explained," BBC News, Dec. 10, 2015, accessed July 27, 2017, http://www.bbc.com/news/business-34324772.). As a result of this scandal, Winterkorn's name now stands as a prominent example of leadership that is not to be imitated. The most significant feature of his legacy as leader of Volkswagen will always be the scandal that led to his resignation. Consider the negative tone that dominates the issue in the following brief video:

https://www.youtube.com/watch?v=To-9u3eyALk

Many people have evaluated the culture of the Volkswagen company under Winterkorn's care in light of the scandal. In the midst of a highly successful period for the company, Winterkorn remained doggedly determined to push for more. Winterkorn was known for his exacting standards and perfectionism. The internal climate at Volkswagen was demanding in the extreme. Even if Winterkorn was indeed ignorant of the unethical goings-on, it has been suggested that his approach fostered an environment where the illegal activities would be seen as an acceptable risk to take in the pursuit of success. In the resultant climate, failure simply was not an option, even if it meant these illegal steps. A leader must consider the impact that his leadership style and demeanor have on his subordinates.

Carrie Tolstedt, Wells Fargo

Another leadership lesson can be learned from the career of Carrie Tolstedt of Wells Fargo. Rising to prominence from humble beginnings, Tolstedt was highly praised as a leading businesswoman both by those within her company and those outside. She earned numerous awards and was seen as a trailblazer for women within the banking industry. Her vision of retail banking was so successful that under her management as head of community banking, Wells Fargo quickly

Executive Carrie Tolstedt is viewed as largely responsible for the fraudulent accounts scandal at Wells Fargo.

became an industry leader in many areas, such as retail deposit volume and customer loyalty. She espoused her belief that banking was all about serving others, helping them succeed financially. Her rise to success in the banking world has been described as something out the storybooks (Note: Associated Press, "The hard fall of Wells Fargo's Carrie Tolstedt," CBS News, April 11, 2017, accessed July 27, 2017, http://www.cbsnews.com/news/the-hard-fall-of-wells-fargos-carrie-tolstedt/.).

The narrative quickly changed, however, when revelations were made of widespread fraudulent account creations within the bank. There are many similarities to Winterkorn's case with VW. Tolstedt was renowned for her ambitious goals for sales and customer account creations. She pushed managers and employees to reach goals that many thought were unrealistic, and she encouraged them to find their own creative ways to achieve those goals. Even when dishonest activity was reported, Tolstedt and others judged this an acceptable cost for the growth. The climate created by the high demands once again fostered the fraudulent activity.

Further criticism has suggested that Tolstedt did not show significant concern for the harm done to customers through the fraudulent activities taking place. An internal investigation found she was resistant to change and inflexible. The failure to address the fraud became a huge problem for both her and the company (Note: Jen Wieczner, "How Wells Fargo's Carrie Tolstedt Went from Fortune Most Powerful Woman to Villain," April 10, 2017, accessed July 27, 2017, http://fortune.com/2017/04/10/wells-fargo-carrie-tolstedt-clawback-net-worth-fortune-mpw/.).

Negative stories such as these remind us of the complexity of leadership and management. Tolstedt set a simple growth goal and paid meaningful rewards to those who met it. The next module discusses the dangers of simple goals. Employees will ignore the negative consequences and pursue the goal single-mindedly. Leadership is responsible for seeing the big picture, not just the simple measures embedded in the incentive system.

Ginni Rometty, IBM

Ginni Rometty, CEO of IBM

The positive leadership example of Ginni Rometty of IBM provides some unique and interesting lessons. As Rometty has pointed out, IBM has been a successful, publicly-traded tech company for more than one hundred years, which is an extremely lengthy heritage in a field that changes quickly. Much of IBM's legacy business is in the field of computer hardware systems, and the changing technology market has led Rometty to the conclusion that IBM must transform itself as a company to keep up with the evolving times. For a number of years now, she has been overseeing a significant shift of focus for the company. She has indeed cast a vision for IBM to make "cognitive computing" the mainstay of their operations, placing large emphasis on the development of their artificial intelligence entity known as "Watson." (Note: Elizabeth Gurdus, " IBM 'woke up the A.I. world,' CEO Ginni Rometty says," June 20, 2017, accessed July 27, 2017, http://www.cnbc.com/2017/06/20/ibm-woke-up-the-a-i-world-ceo-ginni-rometty-says.html.)

Rometty's democratic, soft-spoken, and generally popular leadership style has enabled her to continue as an effective leader thus far despite the less than exciting trends for the company. Many analysts consider her to be moving the company in the right direction, and they recognize that the changing technological environment makes things difficult for IBM and requires this transition. She continues to have the trust of those who have accepted her vision.

Larry Page, Google

Larry Page, cofounder and CEO of Google, provides an interesting contrast in leadership styles to many other successful leaders. Page is certainly considered demanding and highly motivated, and the success of Google under his guidance has been outstanding. His approach to leadership, however, has fostered a very different atmosphere than in some of the previous examples. Google's employees rate their work environment highly, and Page himself receives some of the highest approval ratings for CEOs in the business realm (Note: Kurt Blazek, "An Inspiring Leadership Style – Google CEO Larry Page," The Booth Company, Feb. 3, 2015, accessed July 27, 2017, http://www.boothco.com/360-feedback-resources/inspiring-leadership-style-google-ceo-larry-page/.).

One of Page's outstanding traits is his commitment to pursing innovation. He believes that outlandish and seemingly impossible ideas should be cultivated and encouraged, not rejected. These are the ideas, he says, that can change the world (Note: Vickie Elmer, "What would Larry Page do? Leadership lessons from Google's doyen," Fortune, April 18, 2011, accessed July 27, 2017, http://fortune.com/2011/04/18/what-would-larry-page-do-leadership-lessons-from-googles-doyen/.).

Larry Page, cofounder of Google

The "demanding" aspect of his leadership arises from this desire to pursue innovation. Page is able to inspire his team to seek that innovation with him, rather than drive them to fear of failure. Employees and executives who have worked for and with Page have attested to the fact that he invites open discussion of ideas, even if they might contradict his own thoughts. When Page visits meetings and teams of researchers and engineers, as he often does, his visits are not dreaded but welcomed. His persistent questioning is received as a team effort to improve and strive for new ideas rather than seen as an effort to find problems that will be the basis for rebuke. Even though Page's personality tends toward the reserved and introverted end of the spectrum, he has found the right approach to connecting with and inspiring his team members.

INTRODUCTION TO SITUATIONAL THEORIES OF LEADERSHIP

What you'll learn to do: summarize the situational theories of leadership

Though much attention has been given to the traits and styles of effective leaders, another approach to the question has been developed in recent years. Rather than seeking out universal traits or behaviors that are always effective, many theorists now suggest that flexibility in leadership style is key to success. Situational theories of leadership promote the idea that the most effective style of leadership differs from situation to situation.

SITUATIONAL THEORIES OF LEADERSHIP

Learning Outcomes

- Summarize the situational theories of leadership.

Introduction

Situational theories of leadership work on the assumption that the most effective style of leadership changes from situation to situation. To be most effective and successful, a leader must be able to adapt his style and approach to diverse circumstances.

For example, some employees function better under a leader who is more autocratic and directive. For others, success will be more likely if the leader can step back and trust his team to make decisions and carry out plans without the leader's direct involvement. On a similar note, not all types of industries and business settings require the same skills and leadership traits in equal measure. Some fields demand a large measure of innovation, whereas in others, personal charisma and relational connection with clients are far more important.

Different theories have been developed that recognize the situational aspects of leadership. Each theory attempts to provide its own analysis of how leadership can be most successful in various situations. Let's consider a few of the key theories.

Hersey and Blanchard's Situational Leadership Theory

The term "situational leadership" is most commonly derived from and connected with Paul Hersey and Ken Blanchard's **Situational Leadership Theory**. This approach to leadership suggests the need to match two key elements appropriately: the leader's leadership style and the followers' maturity or preparedness levels.

The theory identifies four main leadership approaches:

- **Telling**: Directive and authoritative approach. The leader makes decisions and tells employees what to do.
- **Selling**: The leader is still the decision maker, but he communicates and works to persuade the employees rather than simply directing them.
- **Participating**: The leader works with the team members to make decisions together. He supports and encourages them and is more democratic.
- **Delegating**: The leader assigns decision-making responsibility to team members but oversees their work.

In addition to these four approaches to leadership, there are also four levels of follower maturity:

- **Level M1**: Followers have low competence and low commitment.
- **Level M2**: Followers have low competence, but high commitment.
- **Level M3**: Followers have high competence, but low commitment and confidence.
- **Level M4**: Followers have high competence and high commitment and confidence.

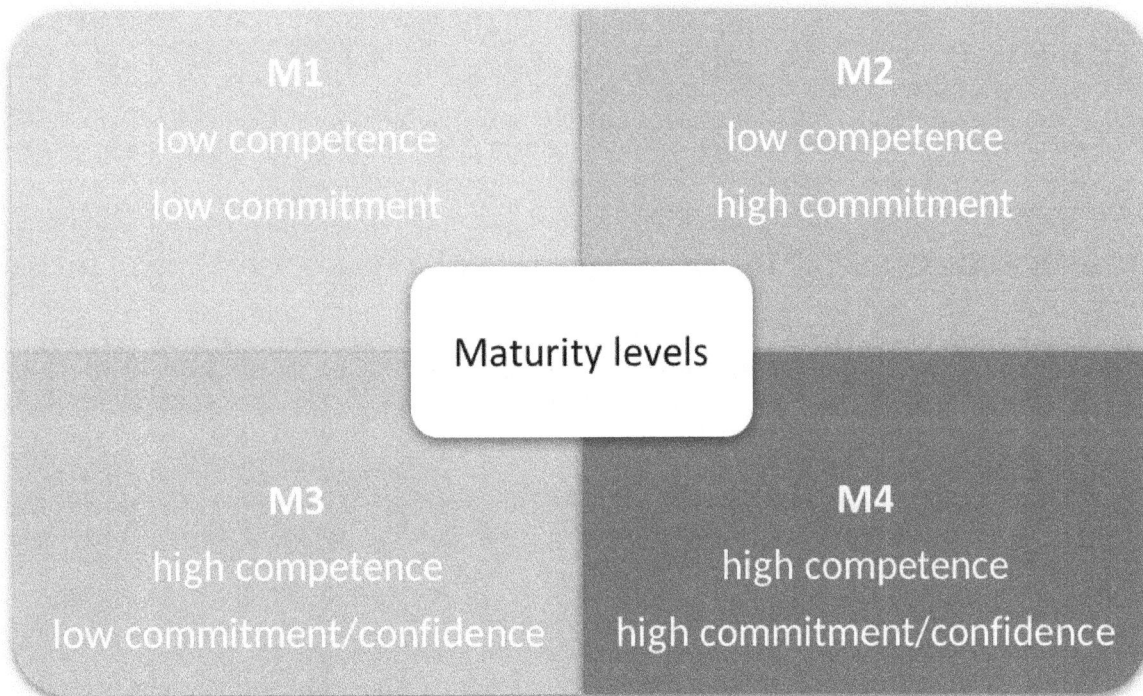

In Hersey and Blanchard's approach, the key to successful leadership is matching the proper leadership style to the corresponding maturity level of the employees. As a general rule, each of the four leadership styles is appropriate for the corresponding employee maturity level:

- Telling style works best for leading employees at the M1 level (low competence, low commitment).
- Selling style works best for leading employees at the M2 level (low competence, high commitment).
- Participating style works best for leading employees at the M3 level (high competence, low commitment/confidence).
- Delegating style works best for leading employees at the M4 level (high competence, high commitment/confidence).

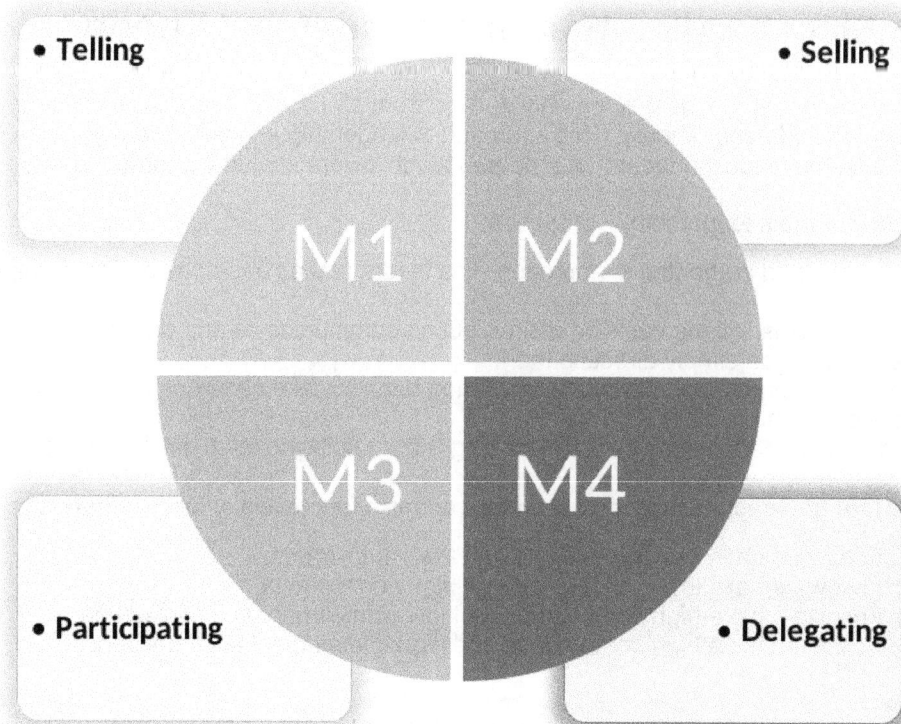

Maturity levels and leadership styles

Identifying the employee maturity level becomes a very important part of the process, and the leader must have the willingness and ability to use any of the four leadership styles as needed.

Goleman's Model of Situational Leadership

Another situational theory of leadership has been developed by Daniel Goleman. His theory incorporates his development of the concept of **emotional intelligence**. He develops that idea into six categories of situational leadership, describing the leadership style and suggesting when each style is most appropriate and likely to be successful:

Pacesetting Leader	The leader sets aggressive goals and standards and drives employees to reach them. This works with highly motivated and competent employees, but can lead to burnout due to the high energy demands and stress levels.
Authoritative Leader	The leader authoritatively provides a direction and goals for the team, expecting the team to follow his lead. The details are often left up to the team members. This works well when clear direction is needed, but can be problematic if the team members are highly experienced and knowledgeable and might resent being dictated to.
Affiliative Leader	A positive reinforcement and morale-boosting style. The leader praises and encourages the employees, refraining from criticism or reprimand. The goal is to foster team bonding and connectedness, along with a sense of belonging. This approach works best in times of stress and trauma or when trust needs to be rebuilt. It is not likely to be sufficient as a long-term or exclusive strategy.
Coaching Leader	The leader focuses on helping individual employees build their skills and develop their talents. This approach works best when employees are receptive to guidance and willing to hear about their weaknesses and where they need to improve.

Democratic Leader	The leader intentionally involves followers in the decision-making process by seeking their opinion and allowing them a voice in the final decision. This works well when the leader is in need of guidance and/or the employees are highly qualified to contribute and there are not strenuous time constraints that require quick decisions.
Coercive Leader	The leader acts as the ultimate authority and demands immediate compliance with directions, even applying pressure as needed. This can be appropriate in times of crisis or disaster, but is not advisable in healthy situations.

Normative Decision Theory

One final theory we will look at is Vroom and Yetton's **Normative Decision Theory**. This approach is intended as a guide in determining the optimum amount of time and group input that should be committed to a decision. A leader has a number of options available to him in this regard:

- He can make a decision entirely by himself.
- He can use information from team members to make decisions.
- He can consult team members individually and ask their advice before making the decision.
- He can consult team members as a group before making the decision.
- He can consult the team as a group and allow the team as a whole to make the decision.

Victor Vroom and Phillip Yetton provide a model that helps leaders decide when to use each approach. The model walks leaders through a series of questions about the decision to be made, and the answers will lead the decision maker to the suggested approach. The questions focus on a few key factors:

- Is decision quality highly important?
- Does the leader have sufficient information to make the decision?
- Is it highly important for team members to accept the decision?
- Are the team members likely to accept the leader's decision if he makes it individually? What if he makes it with their consultation?
- Do the team members' goals match those of the leader and organization?
- Is the problem structured and easily analyzed?
- Do team members have high levels of expertise in the matter to be decided?
- Do team members have high levels of competence in working together as a group?

Leaders are challenged not only to make good decisions, but to decide who decides. At times, the best choice is to involve others in the decision.

INTRODUCTION TO TRANSFORMATIONAL AND TRANSACTIONAL THEORIES OF LEADERSHIP

What you'll learn to do: summarize transformational and transactional theories of leadership

One further way to categorize types of leadership is the contrast between transformational leadership and transactional leadership approaches. These two classes of leadership theories differ primarily in what source of motivation is used with employees.

TRANSFORMATIONAL AND TRANSACTIONAL THEORIES OF LEADERSHIP

Learning Outcomes

- Summarize transformational theories of leadership.
- Summarize transactional theories of leadership.

Transactional Leadership

Every form of leadership involves some method for motivating employees. With transactional leadership, motivation is derived from an arrangement whereby employees are rewarded for accomplishing goals set for them or tasks assigned to them.

This system is extremely common and familiar. One basic form is when sales representatives are paid on commission or given performance bonuses for the numbers of sales they complete. The leader or organization wants the employee to secure sales, so the motivation is provided in the form of money. This transaction of performance for compensation satisfies the wants of both parties—leader and follower.

Many people are motivated by transactional arrangements to sell beauty products or other items.

Transformational Leadership

Transactional leadership theories assume that the desires of the leader and the desires of the follower are not the same. Because of this, the leader must provide some form of extrinsic motivation for the follower. Without this, the follower will not want to do what the leader desires.

The concept of transformational leadership takes a different approach to solving the dilemma. Rather than providing an extrinsic motivation that appeals to the follower's different desires, transformational leadership is committed to changing the desires of the follower so that they match the desires of the leader. If the leader can transform the follower's wants so that he himself shares the leader's vision and desires, the follower will have a greater source of motivation to pursue that vision and goal.

Transforming the follower's desires is not always an easy task, of course. It is generally easier to provide some form of external compensation. What tools can transformational leadership use to accomplish this task? There are four main categories that are usually identified:

- Idealized influence
- Inspirational motivation
- Intellectual stimulation
- Individualized consideration

The following video provides insight into the nature of these four categories and gives some information about the development of both transactional and transformational leadership theories.

https://youtu.be/FtnFKLqhL-Y?t=3m52s

PUTTING IT TOGETHER: LEADERSHIP

In what ways has Jeff Bezos, founder and CEO of Amazon, demonstrated that he's a transformational leader?

Now that you've completed this module, let's return to our question of what makes Amazon founder and CEO Jeff Bezos a great leader. One contemporary approach to the study of leadership that you learned about was the difference between transformational and transactional leadership. Let's consider Bezos in light of what you now know about transformational leaders.

Transformational leaders are those who are able to shape individuals, and even society, to align their goals with those of the leader. There are several attributes of transformational leaders that have been identified, so let's see if these are consistent with what we know about Bezos.

Charisma is one of the key elements we find in leaders who transform industry and society. Charismatic leaders are able to inspire confidence and secure the commitment of others to their vision. From the beginning of Amazon's history, Bezos has been able to lure talent and investors to move his vision forward. The Economist magazine once published an article on the company that featured an astronaut on the moon delivering a package from Amazon. The caption read, "How far will Amazon go?" Beyond a doubt, Bezos has inspired many with his vision of what Amazon can become.

Amazon quickly expanded from being a book retailer to offering more than fifteen million product options today. Additionally, the company has expanded into offering cloud services, the Prime membership program, Kindle reading devices, and many other areas. One would be hard-pressed to come up with any organization in modern history that has transformed the face of business more than Amazon. But behind Amazon's success, we find the vision of one man, Bezos.

Transformational leaders also challenge the status quo and help people expand the way they think. Amazon started as a disruptive force in retail book sales by selling online, but Bezos inspired his team to think much broader. A few years after launching, Amazon began to expand the ways product was delivered to consumers. Two-day delivery quickly became a standard for online delivery. Today Amazon continues to push the boundaries and delivers in some markets within hours of an order being placed. In the near future, you might see Amazon drones overhead rapidly delivering packages.

In this module, you have learned about leadership and its importance in business. With these skills, you can begin to evaluate the leaders that you work with during your career. But more importantly, you should consider your own leadership style and how best to grow and develop it.

MODULE 11: MOTIVATION

WHY IT MATTERS: MOTIVATION

Why does a manager need to understand employee motivation and motivational theories?

There are many different ways to motivate employees

Carol is a new manager who was recently given responsibility over the financial reporting team for her division. She is having lunch with Sam, who is a more experienced manager, and she starts to share some of her recent frustrations.

"Let me tell you what happened today, Sam," she begins. "I had a meeting with my VP at 9:00 a.m. to review our monthly financial results. I needed to go over some of the information with Bill on my team, and he showed up late again. As a result, my monthly review did not go very well."

Sam asks, "Is this the first time Bill has been late?" Carol responds, "No, it's been happening a lot lately. In fact, several individuals on my team are starting to be late more frequently. It seems like they don't care about getting to work on time."

"Well," Sam pauses before continuing. "It sounds like the team's motivation levels are low. You need to do something about that quickly."

Carol is concerned and asks Sam, "Can you help me out? I agree this needs to be addressed now." She and Sam agree to get together soon to brainstorm ideas.

Motivation is a key factor impacting performance, so it's an important concept for leaders to grasp. In this module we will be covering key theories of motivation, and you'll learn how managers can establish goals for their team to increase the odds of success.

INTRODUCTION TO THE IMPORTANCE OF EMPLOYEE MOTIVATION

What you'll learn to do: explain the importance of employee motivation in an organization

Motivation is one of the most frequently researched topics in management. One reason for its popularity is that only about 33 percent of US employees are engaged and thriving in their work. Gallup estimates that actively disengaged employees cost US businesses $483 billion to $605 billion each year in lost productivity. (Note: "State of the American Workplace: Employee Engagement Insights for US Business Leaders," Gallup, 2017). Clearly, this suggests a problem. The good news is that a considerable amount of research now provides us with solid insights into how to improve motivation.

In this section, we will take a closer look at why motivation is so important in an organization, and we'll talk about the two major types of motivation.

THE IMPORTANCE OF EMPLOYEE MOTIVATION

Learning Outcomes

- Explain the importance of employee motivation in an organization.
- Distinguish between internal and external motivation.

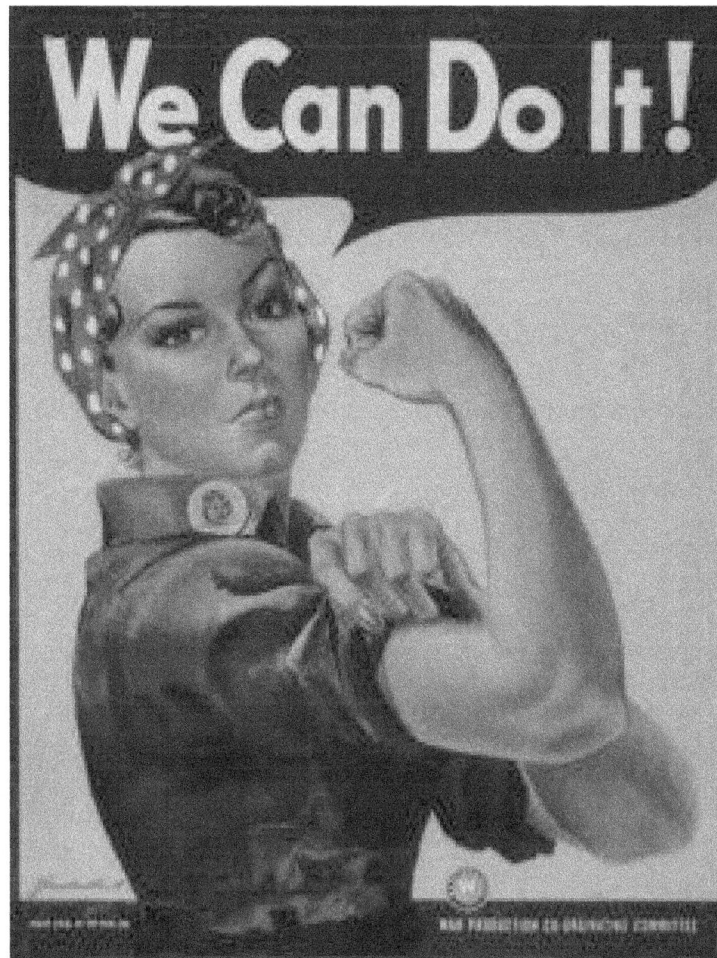

Introduction

Employee motivation is of great concern to any organization. Gallup's 2017 survey on employee engagement shows that "the ratio of disengaged to actively engaged employees is 2-to-1, meaning that the vast majority of U.S. workers (67%) are not reaching their full potential." (Note: "State of the American Workplace: Employee Engagement Insights for U.S. Business Leaders," Gallup, 2017) Research has shown that companies with higher ratios of engaged employees experience higher earnings per share (EPS) compared with their competition. (Note: Gallup, 2017)

Think about what motivates you to get your homework done. Maybe you want to get an A in the class so you can make the dean's list this term. Or maybe you want to learn all about management so you can start your own successful business one day. Because we are not all motivated by the same things, a manager's ability to motivate employees requires gaining an understanding of the different types of motivation. A better understanding will enable you to better identify the best ways to motivate others—and possibly even yourself.

Types of Motivation

Motivation is the collection of factors that affect what people choose to do, and how much time and effort they put into doing it. There are two forms of motivation: **intrinsic** and **extrinsic**. These forms refer to the origin of the motivation. Intrinsic motivation exists within a person; extrinsic motivation comes from external or outside sources.

Intrinsic Motivation

Intrinsic motivation includes many internal sources of motivation. These might include:

- interests
- beliefs
- personal enjoyment and pleasure
- sense of accomplishment
- personal pride
- skill development and competency
- social status
- power

You should notice that these intrinsic rewards are not tangible, meaning that they can't be easily measured or quantified. Over time, however, the outgrowth may be tangible via promotions, better projects to work on, and the power to influence decisions.

Extrinsic Motivation

Extrinsic motivation includes motivational stimuli that come from outside the individual. These stimuli take the form of tangible rewards, such as commissions, bonuses, raises, promotions, and additional time off from work. For example, an employee who will take on extra work, provided there is a sufficient reward for this extra effort, is extrinsically motivated. Extrinsically motivated people may also value the intrinsic rewards, but only if the extrinsic reward is sufficient.

Seldom is anyone exclusively intrinsically or extrinsically motivated. Even though someone may have strong preferences, they can overlap depending on the circumstances.

INTRODUCTION TO NEEDS-BASED THEORIES OF MOTIVATION

What you'll learn to do: explain needs-based theories of motivation

Several motivational theories state that employee performance and satisfaction is based on how well the company meets the needs of the employee. There are four major theories in the needs-based category: Abraham Maslow's hierarchy of needs, Frederick Herzberg's dual factor theory, Clayton Alderfer's existence-relatedness-growth (ERG) theory, and David McClelland's acquired needs theory.

NEEDS-BASED THEORIES OF MOTIVATION

Learning Outcomes

- Differentiate between Maslow's hierarchy of needs and Herzberger's two-factor theory of needs.
- Explain Alderfer's existence-relatedness-growth theory.
- Explain McClelland's acquired-needs theory.

Maslow's Hierarchy of Needs

Abraham Maslow, one of the most prominent psychologists of the twentieth century, created a hierarchy of needs, illustrated by a pyramid representing how human needs are ranked. Maslow's theory is based on the premise that human beings are motivated by needs ranked in order hierarchically. Some of these needs are simply essential to all human beings. When a basic need is satisfied, we begin to seek higher-order needs.

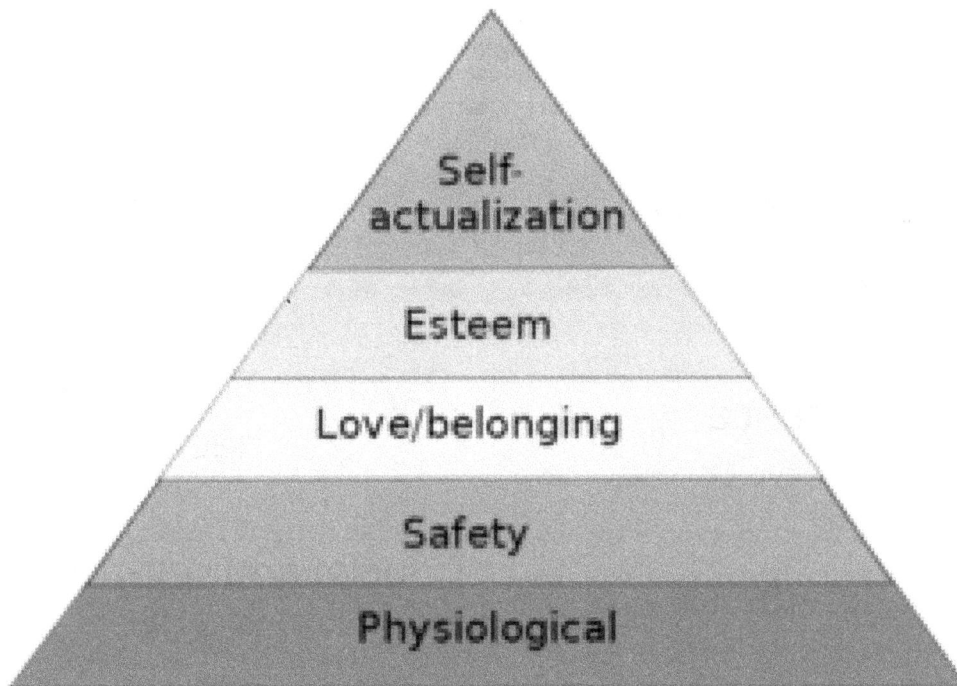

Abraham Maslow's hierarchy of needs shows physiological needs as the most essential.

The first essential motivational needs, according to Maslow, are our physiological needs, such as air, food, and water. Once our physiological needs are satisfied, we become concerned about safety, which includes our own physical safety and security, as well as our employment security. The next need to fill is social: our need to bond with other human beings. The need for love, friendship, and family is considered to be a fundamental human motivation. When we have achieved a sense of belonging, our need for esteem—the desire to be respected by one's peers, feel important, and be appreciated—becomes more salient. The highest level of the hierarchy is the need for self-actualization, which refers to "becoming all you are capable of becoming." (Note: Abraham H.

Maslow, "A Theory of Human Motivation," Psychological Review 50 (1943): 370–396) People can fulfill this need by learning new skills, taking on new challenges, and taking action to pursue their life goals. (Note: Abraham H. Maslow, Motivation and personality, New York: Harper, 1054)

Two-Factor Theory

When studying motivation, Frederick Herzberg started by asking employees what was satisfying and dissatisfying on the job. Herzberg found that certain factors just had to be met and did not raise satisfaction. However, if these factors, called hygiene factors, were not met, it led to strong dissatisfaction. The **hygiene factors** causing dissatisfaction were part of the context in which the job was performed. Company policies, supervision, working conditions, salary, safety, and security on the job are some examples of hygiene factors. For example, you may not link your satisfaction to your office having good lighting, but you would be very dissatisfied if the lighting was too poor to read.

Motivators are the factors that employees need in order to give higher levels of effort. According to Herzberg, the strongest motivators are interesting work, responsibility, achievement, recognition, growth, and advancement.

ERG Theory

Clayton Alderfer modified Maslow's hierarchy of needs into three categories: existence, relatedness, and growth (ERG). The figure below illustrates how the ERG needs correspond to Maslow's five levels. **Existence** corresponds to psychological and safety needs; **relatedness** corresponds to social and self-esteem needs; and **growth** corresponds to self-actualization needs. The ERG theory does not force the order of needs fulfillment, and it supports the pursuit of different levels simultaneously. As a manager, you may notice some people regressing, which shows up when they continue to put effort into lower-level needs rather than pursuing the higher-level needs. The theory suggests that managers will need to help regressing employees see the importance of their pursuit of higher needs to their personal growth. This is referred to as the **frustration-regression principle**.

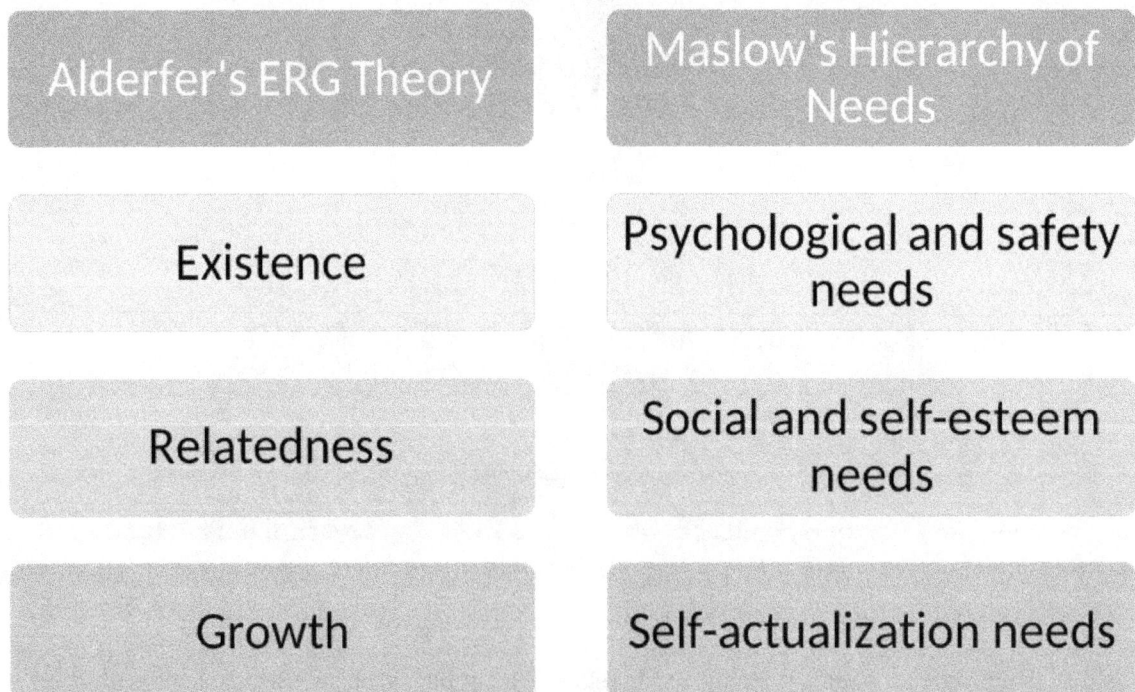

Alderfer's ERG Theory	Maslow's Hierarchy of Needs
Existence	Psychological and safety needs
Relatedness	Social and self-esteem needs
Growth	Self-actualization needs

Clayton Alderfer's ERG theory modifies Abraham Maslow's hierarchy of needs theory

Acquired Needs Theory

Some studies have found that David McClelland's acquired needs theory can predict success in management. The need for achievement, affiliation, and power all operate in combination and are the result of a person's life experiences.

People who have a strong need to be successful have a high need for **achievement**. A high need for achievement results in a high level of satisfaction when that person completes projects on time, closes sales with prospects, or drives new and innovative ideas. Jobs that have very explicit goals to be reached are ideal for individuals who have a high need for achievement. Feedback must be regularly available and easy to understand, as they need feedback to determine their next steps in pursuit of the goal. However, a high need for achievement can be problematic as a person is promoted into management. Instead of relentlessly pursuing his or her own goals, this manager must now get the work done by motivating others. It is not uncommon for a manager with a high need for achievement to view coaching and meeting with subordinates as unnecessary. This type of manager will need to resist micromanaging or trying to do the work himself.

People with a high need for **affiliation** value building relationships. The affiliation-driven employee will be effective in team settings, a strong collaborator, and eager to work with new people.

Managers with a high need for affiliation may find it difficult to deliver unpleasant news and critical feedback. The affiliation-driven manager will need to see the value of providing feedback that will help poor-performing subordinates improve.

People with a high need for **power** are motivated to influence others and control their environment. Their focus is on the larger strategy, the "big picture." The need for power can be positive in improving the way work is done, negotiating for more resources for a department, or gaining more responsibility for a team. The need for power can be a negative for the firm when it means beating someone else. Of the three acquired needs, the need for power is strongly correlated with effectiveness in managerial and leadership positions. (Note: David C. McClelland and Richard E. Boyatzis, "Leadership Motive Pattern and Long-Term Success in Management," Journal of Applied Psychology 67 (1982): 737–743)

As a manager, you will be wise to understand employees' different needs and how that will translate into motivation. Clearly defined goals, timelines, and feedback will be attractive to those with a high need for achievement. Providing and encouraging acknowledgment of good work will motivate people with a high need for affiliation. Employees with a high need for power will be looking for opportunities with more influence and decision making.

INTRODUCTION TO PROCESS-BASED THEORIES OF MOTIVATION

What you'll learn to do: explain process-based theories of motivation

In contrast to needs-based theories, process-based theories see motivation as a rational process: individuals perceive their environment, analyze it, develop reactions and feelings, and respond in certain ways. Two main process-based theories are equity theory and expectancy theory.

PROCESS-BASED THEORIES OF MOTIVATION

Learning Outcomes

- Explain equity theory.
- Differentiate between procedural justice and interactional justice.
- Explain expectancy theory.

In general, process-based theories take the mental processes of employees into account as a way to understand their motivation.

Equity Theory

Equity theory is about perceived fairness. The theory says motivation depends on a comparison to others, called a referent. The employee compares his input and output to colleagues, someone at another firm, or a cousin in another state. If an employee feels he is putting more into a job than what he gets out of the job, relative to the referent, he will become demotivated, disgruntled, and even disruptive.

Here's an example of the role equity plays in motivation:

> A friend graduated from your current college last year with a degree in accounting. After several interviews, she accepted a position with a top accounting firm. She was pleased with the offer: challenging work and an opportunity to gain valuable experience, and the highest salary of any accounting major from your school that was offered last year—$6,500 a month.
>
> Twelve months have passed. You graduated with an accounting degree as well, and got hired by the same firm as your friend. Your friend has enjoyed the challenges, worked hard and performed very well, and even received a $200-a-month raise. However, when she found out you received $7,000 a month, she won't talk to you, and you found out she was actively looking for another job.

In this example, the relevant **inputs** would be the hard work your friend was providing, the number of months she has worked there, and her loyalty to the organization. The **outputs** are the rewards your friend receives from the situation. The $6,700 a month your friend is receiving is a salient output. Other outputs could include benefits or the positive working relationship she has with her supervisor. In fact, your friend may reason as follows: "I have been working here for an entire year. I am loyal and I work hard (inputs). I am paid $6,700 a month for this (outputs). You do not have any experience here (referent's inputs) but will be paid $300 a month more (referent's outcomes). This situation is unfair."

Your friend's referent is you. In other instances, the referent may be a specific person or an entire category of people. In order for the comparison to be meaningful, referents must be comparable to us. For instance, it wouldn't be meaningful for your friend to compare herself to the CEO of the company; the nature of inputs and outputs between these two people is too disparate. Instead, she could make a more meaningful comparison by looking at coworkers who perform similar tasks within the same firm.

According to equity theory, perceived unfairness can cause distress for both the person who feels slighted and the person who gets more than she deserves. In the above example, you might feel guilty when you find out you're making more money than your friend despite just starting with the firm. Equity theory asserts that people will try to restore equity no matter which side they're on to eliminate the negative emotions they're feeling. Research, however, has shown that when people are overcompensated for their efforts, they tend to overestimate the value of their inputs to justify the overcompensation in their minds. So while you may feel a pang of guilt about being paid more than your friend, you would likely rationalize your higher salary by telling yourself that you received better grades than she did and were more qualified than her.

Procedural and Interactional Justice

Fairness means different things at different times and to different people. Companies generally strive for procedural justice and interactional justice. A third type, distributive justice, will be discussed in Module 13.

Procedural justice refers to the degree to which fair decision-making procedures are used. Let's assume that your friend asked for a promotion and presented all her accomplishments and addressed how she would handle the increased responsibilities. For example, if she received a promotion and believed it was a result of being recognized for her hard work, she would have a positive sense of procedural justice.

Interactional justice focuses on employees' perceptions of the quality of the interpersonal treatment received during the enactment of organizational procedures. (Note: R.J. Bies, "Identifying Principles of Interactional Justice: The Case of Corporate Recruiting." In R. J. Bies (Chair), Moving Beyond Equity Theory: New Directions in Research on Justice in Organizations, symposium conducted August 1986 at the meeting of the Academy of Management, Chicago) A manager's display of social sensitivity, such as the level of respect and dignity shown to employees, will have a positive effect on employees' level of engagement. A rude manager will have a negative effect. The higher the level of interactional injustice employees feel, the more likely they are to display resentment and engage in counterproductive work behavior. (Note: Robert A. Baron and Joel H. Neuman, "Workplace Violence and Workplace Aggression: Evidence on Their Relative Frequency and Potential Causes," Aggressive Behavior 22, no. 3 (1996): 161–173)

In 2017, James Damore wrote an open letter to Google employees, titled "Google's Ideological Echo Chamber." Damore argued that basic biological and psychological differences between men and women explain why women are underrepresented in tech, discounting any bias or discrimination that women might face in the workplace. This caused an uproar, and Damore was fired for creating a hostile work environment for women. Both sides claim interactional injustice.

Damore asserted that Google management shames employees into silence. "This silencing has created an ideological echo chamber where some ideas are too sacred to be honestly discussed," he wrote. "The lack of discussion fosters the most extreme and authoritarian elements of this ideology." (Note: James Damore, "Google's Ideological Echo Chamber," 2017, http://gizmodo.com/exclusive-heres-the-full-10-page-anti-diversity-screed-1797564320) One rebuttal says, "The problem here is that this was disrespectful disagreement—and there really is no respectful way to say 'I think you and people like you aren't as qualified to do your job as people like me.'" (Note: Daisuke Wakabayashi, "Google Fires Engineer Who Wrote Memo Questioning Women in Tech" New York Times, Aug. 7, 2017, https://www.nytimes.com/2017/08/07/business/google-women-engineer-fired-memo.html?_i=0)

Expectancy Theory

Expectancy theory focuses on the cognitive process. It argues that motivation depends on the strength of the expectation that the activity will result in a consistent and favorable outcome for an individual. Expectancy theory is comprised of three components: expectancy, instrumentality, and valence. **Expectancy** is the belief or expectation that the employee can accomplish the goal. **Instrumentality** asks if management will honor the bargain. Instrumentality is high if the employee believes success will be rewarded. **Valence** is the degree to which an employee values the rewards, such as a promotion or pay raise. Let's take a look at some examples.

Joel signed up for a required business statistics class. In the early weeks, he is diligent but sees that he is already struggling. Because he is working full time and cannot put more time into it, he decides to drop the class. He did not expect to pass, so his expectancy was low. Mirabel is also struggling and asks a lot of questions. She is taking fifteen to thirty minutes out of each class to get answers to her questions. She is afraid the professor is mad at her. After she does poorly on the midterm, she decides to drop the class because the professor won't give her a fair break. Her instrumentality is low. Peter is doing poorly as well but he already has a good job. He decides he doesn't need the class or the degree and drops out. His valence is low.

Expectancy theory can explain why workers may be motivated to work hard in their job or provide the minimal effort to simply get by. Employees will want to know if the performance appraisal will reflect any extra effort to perform a job, whether strong performance appraisals will lead to rewards, and whether the rewards are attractive. You can see how potentially motivating a large bonus would be, as well as how demotivating only receiving the "employee of the month" plaque can be.

INTRODUCTION TO JOB CHARACTERISTICS THAT AFFECT MOTIVATION

What you'll learn to do: describe the job characteristics that affect motivation

The motivational approach to job design considers the characteristics of a job that affect motivation, satisfaction, engagement, absenteeism, and turnover.

JOB CHARACTERISTICS THAT AFFECT MOTIVATION

Learning outcome

- Describe the job characteristics that affect motivation.

When we covered organizational structure, you learned that the way characteristics of a job are organized can act to increase or decrease effort (job characteristics model). Building on that model, you will learn how job rotation, job enlargement, and job enrichment can have a major impact on motivation.

Job Rotation

Job rotation involves periodically shifting an employee from one task or job to another in an effort to decrease boredom. By cross-training employees, companies have also found reductions in repetitive motion injuries and turnover. Lincoln Electric, a manufacturer of welding and cutting parts company, regularly cross-trains all its employees, including salaried management, to weld and operate production machines. This cross-training effort has helped minimize layoffs during downturns and increased job satisfaction.

McDonald's, the fast food restaurant, uses job rotation. According to a manager in McDonald's Hong Kong locations, the young staff wants flexible working hours and is easily bored. But McDonald's job rotation policy makes workers feel like they can learn something new every day. (Note: Liana Cafolla. "McDonald's top recipe for loyalty," cpjobs, June 21, 2011, accessed Aug. 9, 2017, https://www.cpjobs.com/hk/article/mcdonalds-top-recipe-loyalty)

McDonald's uses job rotation to keep employees engaged

Job Enlargement

Expanding jobs horizontally by increasing the number and variety of tasks that an individual performs is known as job enlargement. It seeks to motivate workers through reversing specialization. For example, replacing an assembly line with modular work gives each worker more variety and responsibility. Audi, for instance, is experimenting with modular assembly for its cars. (Note: "Modular Assembly," Smart Factory illustrated. https://audi-illustrated.com/en/smart-factory/Die-Modulare-Montage)

Although some employees may welcome the opportunity to take on more work, a 1993 study had mixed results. The study looked at job enlargement efforts among clerical staff and managers in the financial services industry. For most employees, the extra work resulted in less satisfaction and efficiency, and stressful overload and errors. (Note: Michael A. Campion and Carol L. McClelland, "Follow-Up and Extension of the Interdisciplinary Costs and Benefits of Enlarged Jobs," Journal of Applied Psychology 78, no. 3 (1993): 339–351)

Job Enrichment

Job enrichment refers to the vertical expansion of jobs. It increases the degree to which an employee also controls the planning and evaluation of the work that she executes. An enriched job increases the employee's independence and responsibility. It also provides feedback, making it possible for employees to evaluate and improve their own performance. (Note: J. Richard Hackman and Greg R. Oldham, Work Redesign, Reading, MA: Addison Wesley, 1980)

INTRODUCTION TO GOAL-SETTING THEORY

What you'll learn to do: explain goal-setting theory

In this section, you will learn about one of the most influential and practical theories of motivation: goal-setting theory.

GOAL-SETTING THEORY

Learning Outcome

- Explain goal-setting theory.

In the 1960s, Edwin Locke proposed that intentions to work toward a goal are a major source of work motivation. This theory has been supported in more than one thousand studies with all types and levels of employees. To motivate, goals must have **specificity, commitment, challenge, and feedback.**

Goals need to be **specific** enough to answer the who, what, when, where, why, and how of any expectations of the goal. Employees perform better when given specific goals than they do when given vague or abstract goals. For instance, a manager tells a stockroom worker to aim to unpack ten boxes by lunchtime rather than telling the worker to do as much as he can. The specificity of the goal now acts as an internal stimulus, and the stockroom worker has a specific objective to attain. One common approach is SMART goals. SMART stands for specific, measurable, achievable, realistic, and time-bound.

The first step in creating motivation is creating commitment to a goal. Goal **commitment** is the degree of determination a person uses to achieve an accepted goal, and there are two main factors that determine it: importance and self-efficacy. The reasons a person has for attaining a goal, including expecting certain outcomes, comprise importance. A person's belief that he or she can achieve a goal is self-efficacy. If you commit to a goal, your performance will always be higher.

A goal is meant to present a **challenge** to an individual, but it should still be attainable. The level of challenge should be specific to each person to increase their motivation. The more challenging a goal is, the more focused you become on the task and the easier it is to avoid unnecessary distractions. You will be energized to work harder toward the difficult goal. For example, imagine a high jumper training for the Olympics. With one month left before the trials, her personal best is one-quarter inch away from the qualifying height. With the goal in sight, she's energized to train hard over the next month. People persist longer to attain difficult goals. Finally, and most importantly, difficult goals will allow us to develop strategies that help us perform more effectively.

Committing to a goal is one way athletes motivate themselves.

Feedback on a goal is an ongoing requirement to be aware of progression or regression. An employee will require feedback on how well he or she is progressing toward his or her goals. Feedback can help an employee determine what she has done and what she wants to do. The easier it is for an individual to monitor his or her own progress, the quicker the individual will be able to make adjustments, if needed, or continue without hesitating for feedback.

INTRODUCTION TO REINFORCEMENT THEORY

What you'll learn to do: explain reinforcement theory

In this section, you will learn about reinforcement theory, the counterpoint to goal-setting theory. Reinforcement theory is a behavioristic approach that says reinforcement conditions behavior.

REINFORCEMENT THEORY

Learning Outcome

- Explain reinforcement theory

In contrast to some other motivational theories, reinforcement theory ignores the inner state of the individual. Instead it focuses on what happens to an individual when he or she performs some task or action. Reinforcement theorists see behavior as being environmentally controlled. Rather than internal thoughts or desires, the theory is that behaviors are controlled by reinforcers—any consequence that, when immediately following a response, increases the probability that the behavior will be repeated. For example, you decided to work over the weekend to finish a project early for your boss. When your boss finds out about your extra effort, she thanks you and buys you lunch. Assuming your boss's reactions were favorable to you, you will be more likely to do similar deeds in the future. If your boss said or did nothing to acknowledge your extra work, you would be less likely to demonstrate similar behavior in the future.

Regardless of the simplicity of reinforcement theory, there are lessons to be learned from proper and improper reward or recognition for behavior. Think of how you would react if you consistently went above and beyond at work and received no reinforcement. Is it possible that you might start believing that you were wasting your time? Or what if a teammate is consistently disruptive and disrespectful, even to the boss, yet is never reprimanded? Might that teammate continue, even increase, his or her disruptive behavior?

Reinforcement theory can be useful if you think of it in combination with other theories, such as goal-setting. If you worked on a team at Microsoft in the 1990s, you were given difficult tasks to create and ship software on a very strict deadline. Because you knew the requirements of working there, and you loved the opportunity to challenge yourself, you were energized to perform. Because Microsoft valued shipping software on time, you were "fabulously rewarded," which could mean hundreds or even thousands of stock options, if you completed your work.

Although reinforcement theory seems straightforward, a manager who uses reinforcement risks offending his employees. Employees might feel the manager is treating them like children or dogs and not giving them the respect due an adult. This video clip from the *Big Bang Theory* television show illustrates reinforcement. Notice that Leonard forbids Sheldon from using reinforcement on Penny and himself.

http://www.youtube.com/watch?v=JA96Fba-WHk

INTRODUCTION TO A MANAGER'S ROLE IN MOTIVATING EMPLOYEES

What you'll learn to do: explain the manager's role in promoting motivation

Motivation in the workplace consists of three factors: the employee, the organization, and the manager. In this section, we will address how organizations address employee's needs, and how managers can individualize motivation strategies.

MANAGER'S ROLE IN PROMOTING MOTIVATION

Learning Outcomes

- Explain how companies address basic needs.
- Explain how managers can individualize motivation strategies.

Addressing Basic Needs

Managers have a critical role to find out what each employee cares about. A mother may need flexible hours. Another person's motivation may be mostly intrinsic, and he needs space (autonomy) to work his way. Someone else may need rules and structure. The work environment may not allow much flexibility, but just recognizing an individual's preferences is a strong first step.

Looking again at Maslow's hierarchy of needs, an organization starts by providing a safe workplace and job security. In turn, an employee can be self-motivated to fulfill his or her higher-level needs. However, each of the organizational structures can pose challenges to employees in reaching their full potential. A strict hierarchical structure will minimize a person's stress from ambiguity about their responsibility and may provide job security. However, that person's need for more challenge, broader interaction throughout the company, and professional growth may take longer than the employee would like. A team-based structure will address the need for more challenge and broader interaction, but it can lead to job insecurity if a person's role is not clear when the team project is completed.

All of the needs- and process-based theories of motivation can be addressed within any organizational structure. First, companies can start by paying their people an appropriate, livable wage. Salary should be enough that employees are not distracted by pending mortgage payments or taking a second job to make ends meet. Many firms offer both salary and incentive pay. Second, a sense of belonging can be fulfilled by having jobs aligned to a clear common purpose of the company. Social interactions can be formal and informal, and rewards and recognition need to be clearly and consistently applied to increase motivation and engagement. Managers need to be held accountable for tracking their employees' personal and career growth within the company.

Managers Are Motivators

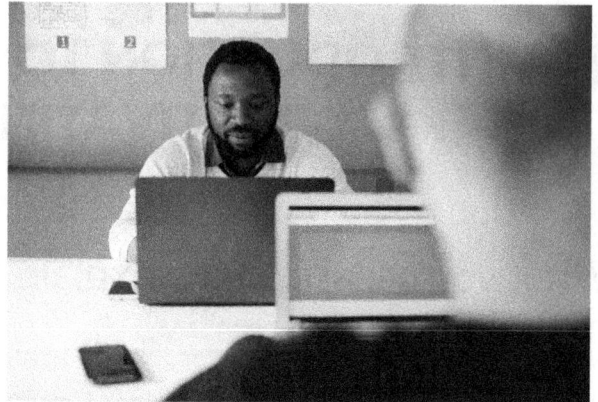

Ultimately, managers have the greatest influence on an employee's motivation. Even though someone's manager can't substantially affect the company's structure, culture and reward systems, the manager can link performance to recognition, bonuses and good work assignments. It is your manager who most directly promotes and implements any of the organization's policies and procedures. The best managers are able meet each subordinate's most important needs. All employees will have varying needs for autonomy and what areas of work they would like to specialize or master. And all employees need to see that their work is tied to the common purpose of the team and the company.

The best managers learn their employees' needs and make an effort to meet them

PUTTING IT TOGETHER: MOTIVATION

Do you remember Carol from the beginning of the module? She is seeing signs of low motivation from her team as several members are starting to regularly be late getting into the office. She is meeting with Sam to discuss what she should do.

"Sam, I've thought a lot about our earlier conversation, and I am concerned that if I don't do something about my team's tardiness, I could have a real problem on my hands."

Sam agrees and says, "Carol, have you addressed anyone on your team for coming in late?"

She thinks for a minute. "No, I guess not. I've been so concerned about being accepted as a manager that I was afraid of the team's response."

It's important to understand the theories of motivation and when to use them

After discussing the situation in greater depth, Sam suggests that Carol pull out her notes from business school related to goal-setting theory. The two of them decide to apply this theory to not only motivate employees to be on time for work but also to reach for more challenging goals. The idea is that if employees are motivated and excited to work hard toward goals that make work interesting and challenging, they will be more likely to put in the effort to show up for work on time.

They come up with a plan for Carol to meet with each employee to discuss the employee's individual goals, as well as the company's goals for the employee. In these meetings, Carol is able to explain the effect that tardiness has on the employee's performance, as well as how it negatively affects other employees and the company as a whole. Carol works with the employees to help them see how being on time for work can lead to greater success in the workplace, which can lead to rewards such as bonuses and promotions.

In meeting with her employees, Carol and the employee set up specific, realistic goals. She then sets up periodic check-ins with the employees to see how they are progressing toward their goals, as well as to offer assistance and support. After a few months, Carol happily reports to Sam that her employee tardiness problem has been resolved.

In this module you've learned about the theories of motivation and how to apply them to influence behavior. One of the key aspects of management is getting work done through others, so it's vitally important that you be able to motivate your team to respond appropriately. This module has provided you with the tools to be successful in these endeavors.

MODULE 12: THE INDIVIDUAL AND THE ORGANIZATION

WHY IT MATTERS: THE INDIVIDUAL AND THE ORGANIZATION

Why is it important for managers to understand the individual's role within the organization?

Samantha is an operations manager with Tech Corp, and she is meeting with William, a senior executive who is mentoring her. They are discussing the recent company-sponsored personality test that Samantha took. She is not convinced that it was worth her time to take. Let's listen in on part of their conversation.

"I just don't see how the results will be useful," complained Samantha. "The test was fun and reading what makes me tick is interesting, but I don't see how this was worth the time and money the company spent on it."

William responded, "I think you'll be surprised just how important it is to understand the various personalities that make up an organization. Knowing how to use that information can be a powerful factor in your success as a leader."

It takes various personalities, joining together, to make a team.

"Really?" she responded looking doubtful. "How can I use this information to my advantage? It just doesn't seem possible."

William smiled and said, "Samantha, you and I are going to cross an 'OCEAN' together."

Understanding how personality and attitude can affect organizational fit is important to leaders at all levels. How do companies like Zappos and Adobe create and maintain their widely acknowledged, exceptional cultures? How do they recruit and hire employees who will be both successful and a good fit? By the time you get through this module, you will begin to acquire some of this important information.

INTRODUCTION TO PERSONAL VALUES AND PERSONALITY AT WORK

What you'll learn to do: recognize the role of personal values and personality at work

Because organizations are made up of individuals, the attributes and characteristics of those individuals must be considered, understood, and appreciated. Two key areas of individuality that we want to consider are personality and values.

PERSONAL VALUES AND PERSONALITY AT WORK

Learning Outcomes

- Describe Goldberg's "Big Five" personality traits.
- Evaluate whether personality tests can predict performance.
- Explain how work expresses individual values.

Personality

Employees are individuals. How does their individuality affect their participation within an organization?

That is a big question, and there are different perspectives on how to answer it. Most answers place at least some emphasis on an individual's personality. Though there are several approaches to defining personality, one commonly accepted formula for this is known as the "Big Five" personality traits, which you can remember using the acronym OCEAN. Personality psychologist Lewis Goldberg popularized the use of the following five traits in describing personality:

- **Openness:** how willing and eager an individual is to try new experiences and consider new ideas
- **Conscientiousness:** how concerned an individual is to be organized, punctual, reliable, and dependable
- **Extraversion:** how eager an individual is to be outgoing and have social interaction
- **Agreeableness:** how desirous an individual is to please others and be friendly, sensitive, and kind
- **Neuroticism:** how negative, moody, and emotionally unstable an individual is

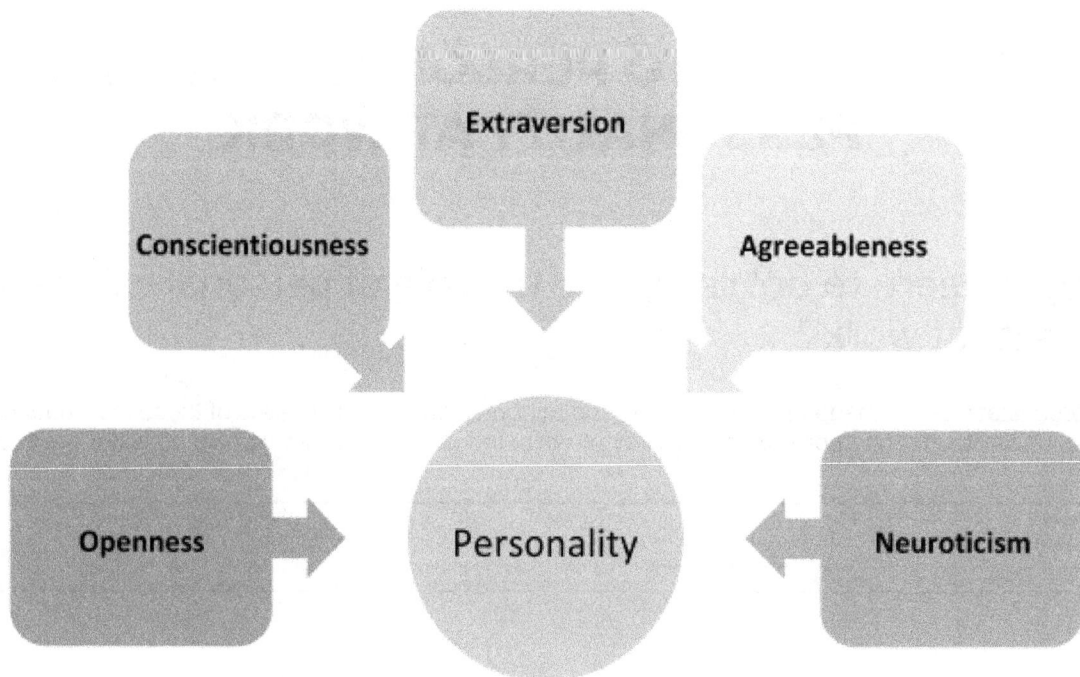

Goldberg's Big Five personality traits

Many studies have been undertaken in attempt to measure the relationship between personality traits and job performance. Though these studies are far from definitive, each trait seems to show connections with certain tendencies, as shown in the following table.

Personality Trait	Employee Tendencies
Openness	• excel when flexibility is required • do well in training • adapt well to unexpected changes • can become bored with routine jobs
Conscientiousness	• high levels of effort and motivation • low levels of absenteeism and turnover • only personality trait that is consistently linked to career success over time • can become consumed with details and miss the big picture
Extraversion	• can be successful managers who motivate employees • often successful in jobs involving sales • can be poor fits for jobs that do not provide sufficient social interaction
Agreeableness	• often display high willingness to help others at work and display good organizational citizenship behaviors • create fair environments when in management positions • work well in team settings

	• might be hesitant to engage in constructive criticism and encourage change, even when it is needed
Neuroticism	• excitable, often very dynamic • tendency to analyze self and world more realistically and critically (Note: Susan Krauss Whitbourne, "The Neuroticism Paradox," Psychology Today, October 19, 2010, https://www.psychologytoday.com/blog/fulfillment-any-age/201010/the-neuroticism-paradox.) • high tendencies towards job dissatisfaction and intention to leave their jobs • tend to create unfair environments when in leadership positions

Though the "Big Five" list is a commonly used summary of personality traits, other aspects of an individual's personality are often identified as significant in relation to job performance. These include self-esteem (how positive an individual feels about himself), self-efficacy (how confident an individual is in his own abilities), tendency to be proactive, and the ability to monitor oneself. These are obviously significant features of an individual's makeup and character, though it is questionable whether they should be classified as true personality traits.

Myers-Briggs Type Indicator

The Myers-Briggs Type Indicator (MBTI) relies on the psychological theories of Carl Jung and works on the basic assumption that individuals fall into fairly distinct classes, or types, of personalities. Those types are created by combining personality categorizations along four distinct axes. Individuals are classified as characterized by either:

- Extraversion (E) or Introversion (I)
- Sensing (S) or Intuition (N)
- Thinking (T) or Feeling (F)
- Judging (J) or Perceiving (P)

A person's classifications within each of these four categories are then combined to create 16 unique personality types identified by the MBTI. Four-letter acronyms are used to name these personality types, with the letters representing the corresponding trait within each category. For example, a person who exhibits characteristics of extraversion, intuition, thinking, and judging would be classified as ENTJ.

The MBTI has been popular with businesses for decades. Despite many studies, the MBTI lacks scientific evidence showing reliability in identifying personality types and, crucially, in predicting job performance.

Another potential weakness of the tool is that it divides individuals into completely distinct classes for each category, not indicating how strong an individual's preference is toward that end of the spectrum. What that means is that if someone is just slightly more introverted than extraverted, he or she receives the same classification as someone who is intensely introverted. The distinction between the two individuals is not represented.

Another significant factor in evaluating the MBTI is the question of stability and reliability. Critics point to data that shows that as much as 50 percent of an individual's MBTI classification will change from test to test with as little as only four or five weeks between tests. (Note: David J. Pittenger, "Measuring the MBTI... And Coming Up Short," Journal of Career Planning & Placement, Fall 1993, http://www.indiana.edu/~jobtalk/HRMWebsite/hrm/articles/develop/mbti.pdf.) However, proponents question the validity of this argument, pointing to data that shows between 75 and 90 percent of subjects receive the same classification in at least three of the four categories on repeat tests. (Note: "Reliability and Validity," The Meyers & Briggs Foundation, accessed August 14, 2017, from http://www.myersbriggs.org/my-mbti-personality-type/mbti-basics/reliability-and-validity.htm?bhcp=1.) They suggest that this is a very favorable level of consistency when compared to other personality testing tools.

In the end, proponents of the MBTI stress that the usefulness of the tool depends largely on how it is used. They warn strongly against its use for the purposes of hiring or promoting employees. For one thing, this only provides incentive for the test takers to falsify their answers to appear more favorable. The ease with which results can be manipulated by dishonest subjects is another potential weakness of the tool, according to detractors.

Instead, the MBTI is intended as a learning tool. It is meant to be taken for the sake of self-analysis with the goal of better understanding oneself and providing insight into how people can best use their personal traits and how they might be able to grow and improve on weaknesses. Administration of the MBTI is strictly controlled by the MBTI Foundation. It requires extensive training before anyone is allowed to administer it. In 2017, training cost $1,800. (Note: "Myers-Briggs Training Schedule & Registration," The Meyers & Briggs Foundation, accessed August 14, 2017, https://mbtitraininginstitute.myersbriggs.org/mbti-training/schedule/?clear.) The foundation and the trained administrators have strong incentives to defend it.

Values

Personality traits are one large aspect of an individual's makeup, but personal values introduce another vital area of interest and importance. Values are described as the stable, enduring goals that one has for life, the things that are counted as most important to the individual.

As with personality traits, many systems have been proposed for analyzing the values of individuals. One widely accepted system was developed by Shalom H. Schwartz and is known as the Schwartz theory of basic values. It identifies 10 such basic values:

- Power
- Achievement
- Hedonism
- Stimulation
- Self-direction
- Universalism
- Benevolence
- Tradition
- Conformity
- Security

Another important value analysis system, the Rokeach Value Survey, analyzes an individual's values within a framework of 18 "terminal values" and 18 "instrumental values." Terminal values are those end goals that people hope to reach in life, such as having a life that is comfortable and secure or reaching a place of self-respect. Instrumental values are the modes of conduct that are considered appropriate and right, such as honesty, integrity, and even ambition. Simply put, terminal values are the goals we want to reach, and instrumental values are the proper ways to act in order to reach those goals.

Most theories assert that the creation of personal value systems is strongly influenced by early life experiences. Those values tend to remain relatively stable, though they are certainly still influenced by the accumulation of further experiences throughout life.

When we recognize and consider an individual's personality and values, we can more clearly predict how that person will behave. Though a word of caution should be added to remind us that behavior is influenced by many factors and that every situation is unique, personality and values still remain helpful predictors.

Businesses (and individuals) use these attributes to identify the best fit for employees and potential future employees. Will a certain candidate for a job be a good fit for that position? Do the requirements and expectations of the position match both the person's personality preferences and his or her value system? If not, the likelihood for poor performance or poor attitude increase, as does the likelihood that the employee will eventually leave the company in search of a better fit.

A wise business practice is to try to match individuals with the optimum role in light of their personality and values. If a business identifies an employee to be high in openness, that person should try to find a role that involves new and diverse activities rather than unchanging routine. Likewise, some roles are more suited for introverts than extraverts. Placing individuals in the role where they are most likely to succeed will certainly benefit the business as a result. The following table shows how individuals with certain values might excel in particular roles.

Value	Example of Role Application
Universalism	An individual with a strong commitment to universalism might make a good fit for a role as a cultural analyst and advisor for a company expanding its activities into new and foreign markets.
Benevolence	An individual who places much emphasis on benevolence would potentially be effective in a role focused on organizing activities giving back to a company's local community.
Security	An individual who places high value on security might be considered for a role in risk analysis and contingency planning.

Beyond the consideration of job fitting, companies are increasingly aware of the importance of looking for employees whose individual values match those of the organization. This is particularly visible in organizations that are charitable in nature, whose existence revolves around a particular humanitarian cause. However, each business organization has its own particular set of values, and many businesses strongly promote those values. For example, if creative innovation is a large part of a company's focus, it will likely look for employees who also share that focus personally.

People and jobs are complex, so a simple test is not the final answer. Businesses recognize that flexibility in some environmental aspects may make room for more diversity. For example, more and more companies are allowing employees freedom to work flexible hours and in convenient locations. This may cater to an employee's value of family focus, autonomy, or freedom of expression. Employees whose values are met in their work environment are more likely to be satisfied and productive.

Working from a home office is becoming a more common part of business.

INTRODUCTION TO COMMON MANAGEMENT BIASES

What you'll learn to do: explain common biases that can affect a manager's perception of employees

Individuals are complex in their combinations of personality and values. It can be difficult to analyze and identify the many features in an individual's makeup. However, managers regularly attempt that task, and when they seek to categorize their employees, it can sometimes lead to difficulties. A number of biases often skew a manager's perception. We'll investigate them in this section.

COMMON MANAGEMENT BIASES

Learning Outcome

• Explain some of the biases that affect a manager's perception of employees.

Perception and Attribution

As we make observations, form opinions, and make judgments in the workplace—something every manager must do—we rely significantly on our perception. This is the process through which we take in and process information from our surroundings: what we see, hear, feel, etc.

Though you might think that you can trust information you take in with your own eyes and ears, you might be surprised sometimes to find out how that information can become distorted. Our feelings, emotions, desires, and values can lead us to perceive things in a less than objective way. For example, studies have found that people who are afraid of spiders tend to exaggerate their size. (Note: Laura Geggel, "Spiders Look Bigger If You're Afraid of Them." Live Science, February 18, 2016, https://www.livescience.com/53765-arachnophobes-perceive-spiders-as-bigger.html. Laura Geggel, "Spiders Look Bigger If You're Afraid of Them." Live Science, February 18, 2016, https://www.livescience.com/53765-arachnophobes-perceive-spiders-as-bigger.html.)

Further, even when we do process sense-based information in an objective way, we often tend to engage in a process called **attribution**, which means we look for the unseen cause behind what we see. For instance, if a coworker is late to a meeting (the observable information), we might make an assumption about why he is late. We might attribute it to the coworker's poor character and lack of responsibility. In that case, we are making a negative attribution to an internal cause. However, if we think well of the coworker, we might assume that something unexpected and unavoidable delayed him. In that case, we are making an external attribution that would reflect a positive view of the individual. In either case, the attribution is not based on an observable cause, and we are going beyond the information provided to us by our senses.

Biases

Though we should strive to be as fair in judgment as possible, the reality is that we all have biases that affect our judgments. Managers are certainly no exception to this rule, and a number of common biases affect how they evaluate their employees. Some of the most common are stereotypes, selective perception, confirmation bias, first impression bias, recency bias, spillover bias, ingroup bias, and similarity bias.

Stereotypes

A stereotype is a general opinion or assumption about a class of individuals who share a particular trait. We often have general feelings or ideas about people based on their gender, ethnic background, or age. When we form opinions or make judgments about people based on a preconceived image of people with that trait, we are not being fair and objective.

Many people have negative feelings about people of different ethnicities than themselves and treat them in a less positive manner than people like themselves. Women have also often been negatively affected by stereotypes. The workplace is not an exception to that tendency. When managers make hiring decisions or give performance reviews, for example, they are too often influenced by gender or ethnic considerations.

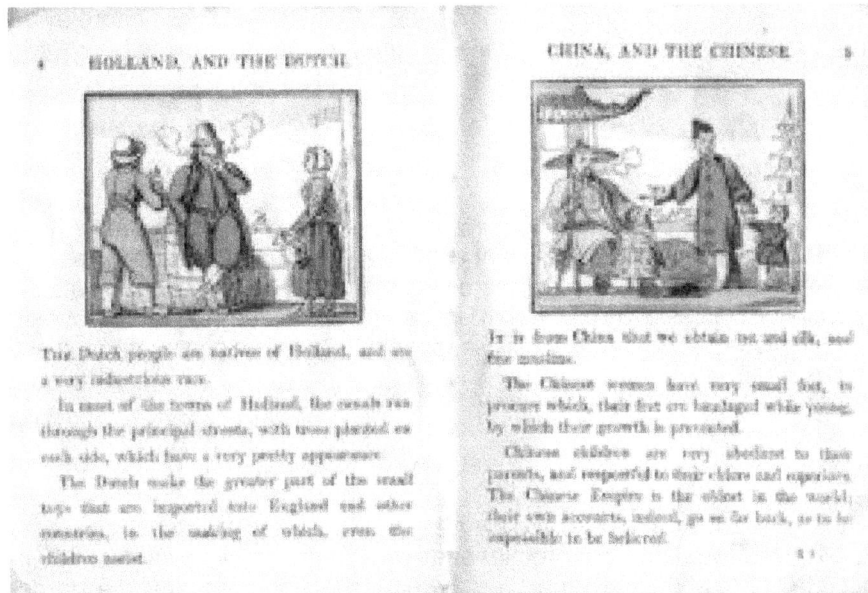

Ethnic stereotyping comes in many forms, some of which are more dangerous than others.

Age is another categorizing characteristic that is too often used in stereotypical ways. Suppose a manager is looking for a new employee for his team. He believes that company loyalty and respect for authority is very important in this new hiring decision. As he sorts through applications, the manager pays close attention to the age of each applicant. He decides not to consider any applicants who are a part of the "Generation X" age category because that generation has a reputation for not being loyal and not having high respect for authority. This type of decision-making process stereotypes people by age and does harm to applicants and the hiring organization both. Applicants of that generation are not given fair consideration for the position, and the organization may well miss out on the best applicant.

Stereotypes can also be made in such a way as to lead to favorable treatment of individuals. Though not all studies agree, many have suggested, for example, that more attractive people tend to receive better grades in school, have a higher likelihood of being hired for a job, and also earn more money on average. Also, some professionals receive more respect and better treatment simply because they are older, the assumption perhaps being that they are more experienced and thus better qualified.

Selective Perception and Confirmation Bias

Managers can also exhibit bias in their perception by unknowingly paying attention to only a portion of the information available to them, which is known as selective perception. For example, perhaps a manager has a keen interest in and enjoys talking about financial data. An employee owes the manager three reports, only one of which is about finances. The employee turns in two well-prepared and helpful reports, but the financial report is obviously rushed and incomplete. If the manager focuses his attention on the poor quality of the financial report (simply because it is of special interest to him), ignoring the high quality of the other two, he is exhibiting selective perception. Three examples of the employee's work are in front of him, and he pays attention to only a part of the evidence.

Selective perception often reinforces other types of biases. If a manager has a negative opinion of an individual, he or she might be prone to pay more attention to negative behaviors or actions from that individual and ignore the positive actions that would contradict the opinion. When selective perception is employed to confirm existing opinions, it is known as a confirmation bias.

First Impression Bias

Managers are also selective in many other ways, one of which involves giving too much prominence to their first impression of an employee. In this situation, the initial judgments the manager makes about the employee, often with very limited information, shape and control how he or she interprets and views future evidence. Even when the future information would seem to contradict the initial picture, the manager might be unwilling to change the perspective.

Recency Bias

The recency bias is somewhat of the opposite of the first impression bias. In this case, the manager's focus is unduly balanced in favor of an employee's most recent activities. This often happens in the cases of annual performance reviews. It can be difficult to keep an entire year's activities in full view, and often the employee's most recent activities are over-weighted. If recent activities are negative, they can easily overshadow many months' worth of strong previous performance. Likewise, poor past performance might be mostly forgotten if the employee has recently excelled.

Spillover Bias

Like the first impression bias, spillover bias can skew a manager's perspective by paying too much attention to past information. This bias usually relates to a prominent episode in the employee's past activities that comes to dominate the manager's thoughts about that employee. Perhaps the employee played a starring role in a wildly successful project, and the manager always thinks of the employee in terms of that success, even if the employee consistently underperforms after that. Inversely, if the employee is unfortunate enough to be guilty of a major failure or blunder, it might be difficult for him or her to change the manager's opinion in the future, even if the employee consistently provides excellent work thereafter.

Negativity Bias

The negativity bias is an unfortunately common characteristic of human nature. When we are presented with information about a situation, some of which is positive and some of which is negative, we are prone to give more attention to the negative information. Though it is not fair, the negative information predominates our thoughts and moves us to form imbalanced conclusions on the negative side.

Ingroup Bias

The ingroup bias is basically a way in which managers might tend to show favoritism in judgment. Those who have been fortunate enough to be accepted in the manager's "in" circle receive special positive judgments, while those not in that circle do not. The strength of this influence can vary dramatically, of course, and it may or may not be true that an actual negative perspective is displayed toward those not in the group.

Similarity Bias

The similarity bias reflects the human tendency to focus on ourselves and prefer those who are like we are. It leads managers to give special, positive attention and judgments to those who somehow remind the manager of himself or herself. Perhaps the employee shares an interest with the manager, such as a hobby they have in common, or maybe the manager and employee come from the same home area or attended the same college. The manager might recognize similar personality traits in the employee, or the employee somehow reminds the manager of a younger version of himself or herself. These identifications can lead to the manager giving preferential treatment to the employee.

Consequences

Within the organizational environment, biases such as these are most often negative influences. Openly discussing the dangers of these biases can be a helpful step in identifying and removing or preventing them.

If such biases are present, they generally have a negative impact on employee attitude and behavior. At the very least, employees can be forced to work extra hard to overcome the unfair biases. This can lead to resentment on the part of those employees. More often, however, the employees find that they do not overcome those biases and grow discouraged at the prospects of never being given a fair opportunity. Studies have shown that employees who labor under negative biases tend to underperform as a result. (Note: "Study Finds That Working under Biased Managers Can Impact Workplace Performance," Phys.org, February 13, 2017, https://phys.org/news/2017-02-biased-impact-workplace.html.)

Also, even biases that might seem positive can actually have a negative impact. If a manager is prone to think too positively about an employee, he might overlook significant faults and dangerous behaviors that need to be addressed. These behaviors can lead to serious mistakes and problems for the organization that could have been prevented with a more objective evaluation process. Also, if an employee realizes that he or she will be given special, positive evaluations, this can lead him or her to give slightly less effort and demonstrate lower levels of commitment to excellence. The employee might feel it unnecessary to provide the highest level of work possible, knowing that he or she will still be given positive feedback and evaluation regardless.

INTRODUCTION TO ATTITUDES THAT AFFECT JOB PERFORMANCE

What you'll learn to do: explain the major attitudes that affect job performance

One of the largest factors that most strongly affects an employee's performance is his or her individual attitude, both about the person's particular job and about the organization as a whole.

ATTITUDES THAT AFFECT JOB PERFORMANCE

Learning Outcomes

- Differentiate job satisfaction and organizational commitment.
- Explain the use of employee attitude surveys.
- Explain employees' perceptions of organizational justice.

Introduction

When you think of how effective an employee is for an organization, a number of factors might come to mind: intelligence, skill, training, and others. However, as important as these matters are, perhaps there is an even greater and more influential factor: attitude. Even the most skilled and talented employee might be prone to severe underperformance if his or her attitude in the workplace is lacking. On the other hand, employees whose positive attitude of dedication and commitment leads them to high levels of effort often excel even when they are not the most talented and skilled. Organizations have grown increasingly aware of the significance of this matter and are investing more time and effort than ever to create the best attitude possible among their employees.

Job Satisfaction and Organizational Commitment

Though the issue may be complex, it is widely recognized that employees who have a positive attitude are more productive and useful to the organization. One of the primary factors in employee attitude is **job satisfaction**. If employees enjoy their work, feel confident in their abilities to succeed in the tasks assigned, and appreciate the role they are assigned, they are far more likely to have a positive attitude in the workplace.

A focus on optimizing job satisfaction will influence an organization's priorities from the earliest stage in its interaction with employees—even before they become employees. Specifically, the organization will be attuned to the value of a good employee-to-job fit. When the organization is looking to hire someone to fill a role, it might be tempted simply to hire the most generally talented or experienced applicant regardless of whether that person's interests and preferences match the potential role. An applicant who has excellent knowledge of the industry but prefers to work in research and development should likely not be hired for a role in marketing. Similarly, many excellent technicians are not interested or comfortable in management roles, and placing them in those positions simply because they excel as a technician might be a disastrous choice. Even if they have the skills to succeed, asking them to accept a role that they are not comfortable with or that they do not enjoy does not provide the highest likelihood of success for the company or the employee himself.

The same principle of employee-to-job fit applies to existing employees as well. Careful management practices will keep an eye on the changing developments of employee interests. As team members grow in their skills, interests, and ambitions, it is good policy to provide avenues that enable those employees to pursue the course that most excites them. This will encourage their highest levels of effort and commitment, keep their attitudes positive, and thus make for greater productivity. Sometimes this means allowing employees to move departments, or it could simply mean adjusting their responsibilities and focus within their current role. Of course, it may not always be possible to cater to every preference of every employee—and trying to do so can become a self-defeating proposition—but making a sincere commitment to this principle is likely to result in positive outcomes for the organization.

The Society for Human Resource Management conducts an annual survey to gauge employee job satisfaction and engagement. While the factors that most influence job satisfaction can change from year to year, employees consistently cite some factors as important to their job satisfaction. These include the following:

- Respectful treatment of all employees at all levels
- Compensation/pay
- Trust between employees and senior management
- Job security
- Opportunities to use their skills and abilities at work (Note: 2017 Employee Job Satisfaction and Engagement: The Doors of Opportunity Are Open. (2017, April 24). Retrieved September 21, 2017, from https://www.shrm.org/hr-today/trends-and-forecasting/research-and-surveys/Documents/2017-Employee-Job-Satisfaction-and-Engagement-Executive-Summary.pdf)

Here is a video that explains some of the commonly identified factors that contribute to job satisfaction:

https://www.youtube.com/watch?v=8DOR3AnyLOQ

Job satisfaction is a primary factor in employee attitude, but it is also worth distinguishing it from the broader category of **organizational commitment**. While job satisfaction focuses on the employee's feelings about his particular role, organizational commitment looks at how the employee feels about the organization as a whole. Does he identify with and care deeply about the organization and its success? If so, he will be far more likely to offer maximum effort and strive for high performance.

When high job satisfaction is matched with a high organizational commitment, employees are very likely to have a positive work attitude. If both job satisfaction and organizational commitment are low, employees are not nearly as likely to work as diligently as possible. They are also far more likely to leave the organization in search of another work opportunity. Though having employees whose attitudes are poor is not a good situation, neither are the instability and disruption that result from high levels of employee turnover.

What happens when either job satisfaction or organizational commitment is high but the other is low? Employees who are very satisfied with their job but not committed to the organization are still likely to provide good effort, though perhaps not as high as possible, but they also remain more likely to depart the company in the future. If a new opportunity with another organization arises that offers better pay or a better match for their interests, they see little reason to stay with their current company.

On the other hand, what happens if an employee is committed to the organization but has low job satisfaction? In such situations, it is common that the employees are willing to struggle through the low job satisfaction on account of their general belief in and commitment to the organization. However, over time, their dissatisfaction with the job is likely to wear on their attitude. They will likely not be able to retain their positive view on the organization forever, and it will be far better if their role can be changed. Otherwise, they too will be more likely to seek another working situation, even if it means leaving the organization.

Managers can use two general approaches to create organizational commitment among employees. First, they can tie employee rewards directly to the success of the organization. This often happens in the form of monetary compensation of some sort. Annual bonuses could be determined in part by the success that the company enjoyed during the year, giving an obvious incentive for employees to seek the good of the company. Also, studies have shown that when employees have a vested financial interest in the organization, such as in the form of stock shares, they exhibit higher levels of commitment.

On a different level, many organizations also seek to develop organizational commitment by emphasizing and seeking to align employee perspectives with the vision and values of the organization. If the company mission resonates with the deep, personal values of employees, they are far more likely to commit to the organization. Efforts can be made to shape the values of employees to conform them to those of the company, and highly inspirational leaders are often successful in this. However, it can be difficult to change employees' values, so many organizations focus on the process of recruiting employees who already share company values.

Organizational Justice

In addition to job satisfaction and organizational commitment, another often-significant factor in employees' attitude is the sense of **organizational justice**. Naturally, employees want a workplace characterized by fairness, a place where everyone is treated with equal respect and given equal opportunities. If they feel otherwise, it is almost certainly going to have a negative impact on their attitude over time.

Employees tend to focus especially on pay equality and advancement opportunity when evaluating organizational justice. If they feel that their effort and production is not compensated appropriately, especially as compared to that of their coworkers, it generally leads to dissatisfaction and disgruntlement. Divisions between employees can arise, as well as between employees and their managers, creating an atmosphere of tension and making productive teamwork a more difficult proposition.

The same holds true if employees feel that they are not given a fair opportunity for advancement. If it is perceived that promotions are given to employees based on favoritism rather than as a fair reward for the highest performance, employee attitude is likely to suffer as a result.

It is highly important to provide a fair workplace and promote a sense of organizational justice. This can be rather difficult at times, however, because employees exhibit bias in their evaluations just as managers do. They can be prone to think too highly of their own abilities and performance, which leads to a sense that they are not receiving due appreciation and compensation. Still, a strong commitment to fairness can go a long way in limiting the negative effects of such biases.

Employee Attitude Surveys

The importance of employee attitude has led to an increased use of employee attitude surveys. These surveys are used to identify areas of concern that employees have. It is generally wise to keep the individual answers confidential, and the use of online technology has made that easier than ever to do. This gives employees an opportunity to share their concerns or criticisms with management without the fear of being punished for voicing negative thoughts.

The leaders in an organization should want to hear those criticisms and be aware of the concerns employees have. If there are problems, knowing about them provides an opportunity to address and fix them before they grow out of hand and lead to serious problems. The sooner action is taken, the better. For this reason, many organizations encourage regular communications about employee attitude.

Employee attitude surveys are generally only beneficial, however, if the results of those surveys actually lead to substantial action and change. For the short-term, employees may receive a sense of catharsis in being allowed to vent their frustrations, but if nothing ends up changing in the long run, employees will simply become jaded and disillusioned. They will not respect the attitude surveys, which may actually become an object of disdain.

On the positive side, however, if management shows a willingness to listen and adapt, that very attitude itself can provide hugely significant boosts to morale. This can be true even if the actual issues being dealt with are relatively minor. When employees believe that management listens to concerns, cares about them, and is willing to make changes, that goes a long way toward creating a positive atmosphere and positive attitudes among employees.

A great deal of research and discussion has taken place concerning the most effective ways to measure employee attitudes. Trying to gauge things such as job satisfaction can be difficult in light of the potential for emotional change on a day-to-day or week-to-week basis. If surveys are taken during a time of abnormally high stress on the job or after an unsuccessful project, the survey results might give

Employee attitude becomes significant when interacting with customers and clients

a worse picture of satisfaction than is fair. Also, companies have found that surveys can easily introduce biases that make objective measurement of attitudes difficult. Using professionally designed surveys and working with independent agencies who specialize in such surveys can help an organization measure and improve employee attitude more effectively.

Similar to employee attitude surveys, exit interviews with employees who are leaving the organization can also provide valuable insight into workplace issues. In fact, it is sometimes only in such exit interviews that employees are willing to be fully honest about their feelings. At the same time, there can be a tendency for such employees to be unduly negative in their assessment, especially if their departure is directly tied to workplace conflict or problems. Though this must be taken into account, conducting exit interviews remains a wise and helpful practice.

Though often these surveys are intended to discover potential problems, they also can be useful in identifying where a company is successful in encouraging positive attitudes and feelings. Identifying areas of strength can reinforce helpful policies and encourage organizations to continue the programs or initiatives that prove beneficial.

INTRODUCTION TO JOB FITNESS AND PERFORMANCE

What you'll learn to do: list and explain common factors that influence job fitness and performance

What other factors influence job performance? How can organizations provide an environment where employees are most likely to excel? Let's consider some key elements of organizational fitness that contribute to productivity.

JOB FITNESS AND PERFORMANCE

Learning Outcomes

- Explain the concept of "fitness" within an organization.
- Explain the influence of common factors (such as work-life balance, stress, interpersonal relationships, attitudes, work ethic) on job performance.

Hiring new people is expensive, so organizations look for any edge to improve performance and retention. They want new hires to "fit" into this new environment. According to Dr. Kerry L. Schofield of Good&Co, "Research shows that workers who have good cultural fit to their organization are a third more productive, three times more creative and almost 90% less likely to quit. Cultural fit accounts overall for around two-thirds of the differences between people in both job satisfaction and performance. Poor fit is estimated to cost US industry $15 billion a year; 86% of new hires that fail within a month do so because of this." (Note: Schofield, D. K. (2016, July 22). Gen Y and Workplace "Fit". Retrieved September 06, 2017, from http://www.huffingtonpost.com/dr-kerry-l-schofield/gen-y-and-workplace-fit_b_11118852.html)

Person-environment fit is the degree to which a person's personality, values, and other characteristics match those of the company's. A strong culture and shared values among coworkers can lead to a good fit. This can translate to increased levels of trust and a shared sense of corporate community. (Note: Boon, C., & Den Hartog,

229

D. N. (2011). Human Resource Management, Person–Environment Fit and Trust. Trust and Human Resource Management, 109-121. doi:10.4337/9780857932006.00013) For the organization, this means reduced turnover, increased citizenship behaviors, and organizational commitment. (Note: Andrews, M. C., Baker, T., & Hunt, T. G. (2011). Values and person–organization fit: Does moral intensity strengthen outcomes?Leadership & Organization Development Journal, 32(1), 5-19. doi:10.1108/01437731111099256)

Person-job fit measures how a person's knowledge, skills, abilities, and other characteristics match the job demands. This is sometimes abbreviated as KSAO within the HR field. Someone who is conscientious and prefers routine may be the right fit at a power plant, while someone who is innovative and proactive may do well at a technology startup.

Consider the varied ideas in this chapter and your own experience with work, and you'll see that this is a complex topic. Attempts to measure person-environment fit or person-job fit have had mixed results. More recent work suggests the relationships are not linear. For example, the performance of a misfit is not much different than that of an average person. But the performance of a person who is a strong fit is much better than an average person.

Organizations Have Their Own Culture

As you've learned in a previous module, every organization promotes and has a particular culture. That culture may be healthy or unhealthy, but either way it has a strong influence on the performance and productivity of its members. Organizations that actively embrace the concept of organizational culture have an opportunity to intentionally shape that culture into a productive force.

Healthy Environment, Productive Employees

The benefits of a generally healthy culture and atmosphere within an organization are manifold and significant. The basic idea is summarized in the concept that a healthy environment results in productive employees. An unhealthy organizational culture leads to lower job satisfaction, worse attitudes, less productivity, increased levels of absenteeism, higher rates of employee turnover, and many other undesirable results. An organization can follow some strategies to promote a healthy work environment.

Managing Employee Stress Levels

Many of the negative results of an unhealthy environment are closely tied to high levels of stress, so many of the specific considerations here have significant ties to stress levels. In many ways, stress levels can become a helpful overall indicator of how healthy the organizational environment is. At the very least, high stress levels should serve as a warning sign that things need to change.

The reality is that stress is a part of life. Attempting to remove all stress would not be realistic, and chances are that it would not be healthy, either. An appropriate level of stress may actually be an essential part of a healthy environment. Stress may be an inherent part of the opportunity to achieve difficult and worthwhile goals that bring fulfillment. If there is no challenge or difficulty, there may be little to no satisfaction or sense of achievement either.

One approach to dealing with stress in the workplace is to train employees to manage their stress. Programs and resources for stress management can be helpful, but if stress levels are unreasonably high, organizations need to do more than try to help employees manage stress. Instead, they need to focus on changing the basic system and the forces in their organization that are causing those unhealthy levels of stress.

Work-Life Balance

One of the major issues that organizations and employees face is the difficulty in finding balance between work and personal life. It is not possible to separate those two areas completely, as problems or stress in one area strongly affect the other. Further, the two areas often compete with one another for individuals' time, energy, and attention. This leads to conflict and stress, which in turn causes lower performance levels on the job.

Organizations realize that this is not a beneficial situation, and there are many things they can do to support the right balance between work and life. One of the most obvious is to limit expectations to reasonable levels of work commitment each week. Overloading employees and demanding an unreasonable portion of their time and energy inevitably leads to difficulties. Along these same lines, providing ample vacation time has also been identified as a wise policy that prevents employee burnout and increases productivity in the long run.

Many organizations are also increasingly open to the use of flexible hours for employees. Where possible, this allows employees the freedom to adapt their work schedules to the needs of their personal and family lives. Similarly, many organizations allow employees to do at least some of their work from home or other remote locations. Finding ways to accommodate family needs results in happier, more productive employees.

Some companies provide child care services to help employees manage their work and personal life balance.

Interpersonal Relationships

Another major area of concern for a healthy work environment is the nature of the interpersonal relationships employees have. Because members of an organization spend a lot of time together and must collaborate with each other, often closely, how these relationships function is important.

On the negative side, interpersonal conflict can become a major obstacle to productivity. Being aware of such situations and having plans for resolving tensions and disagreements are essential to the goal of maintaining a healthy environment.

Ideally, the goal for interpersonal relationships is deeper than merely avoiding major conflict. If employees develop strong relationships of friendship and respect, the organization is likely to reap the benefits. Employees will work together better, enjoy their time together better, and be much less likely to want to leave the organization. For this reason, some organizations invest in providing social opportunities to build those relationships.

Health, Relaxation, and Entertainment

When considering how to create a healthy environment for employees, the whole person should be considered in its various aspects. For example, one area of increasing focus for businesses is the physical health of their employees. Organizations have realized that physically healthy employees are more productive. They have more energy and miss fewer days for sickness and health care issues. Companies often offer health-related incentives and create programs that promote physical well-being among their employees.

Along these same lines, many companies find it beneficial to provide certain types of extracurricular facilities for their employees. These might include fitness rooms, entertainment rooms, sports facilities, nap rooms, and other areas that are not directly tied to work matters. Even the simple act of beautifying the workplace can aid in creating a happier, more positive atmosphere.

Company fitness centers are places for employees to relieve stress and improve physical health.

Personal and Professional Development

Another final area we will consider along these lines is that of personal and professional development. It makes sense for businesses to invest time and resources into building and developing employee skills and strengths. On a professional level, increasing employee skills and understanding strengthens the business. Many companies will help fund employees' education who want to pursue advanced degrees or certifications in their field. Training seminars and programs can also be useful tools for professional development.

Can you envision how providing a program such as chess training could be beneficial to an organization?

Though it might not seem to be as directly related to business goals, investing in the personal development of employees also benefits the organization. This type of development could still be related to professional functions, such as programs that help develop leadership skills or seminars that train employees in how to manage interpersonal communication skills. These would have obvious practical value in most organizational settings. Even if personal development programs do not have direct application to the workplace, helping employees become well-rounded individuals and reach stability and fulfillment in their personal lives will always provide a carryover benefit to the organization.

PUTTING IT TOGETHER: THE INDIVIDUAL AND THE ORGANIZATION

Let's return to William and Samantha, whom we met in the introduction to this module. Samantha was struggling to see the professional relevance of a personality test she recently took. William's last comment to her was that they would be crossing an OCEAN together. Next he explained what he meant.

"Samantha, you're about to pull together a team to design that new manufacturing tool. What would you say if I told you that the personality type training you just received would enable you to put together a better team?" Samantha looked skeptical, so William continued. "How will you select the members of your team?"

Build a strong team by understanding personality.

She considered his question and then responded, "Well, I tend to think about the various technical skills we need on the team, and I go find people who have them." William asked, "And what has your success rate been with that approach?"

After reflecting briefly, Samantha said, "It's been pretty good. At least it's as good as the other project managers I know. Some teams perform well, while others have been challenging."

William nodded his head knowingly and asked, "What makes the difference? Do the successful teams typically have greater technical abilities?"

"No, that hasn't been my experience. The teams that have done the best just 'clicked' as a group. They worked well together and produced amazing results."

She continued, "I see what you're getting at, William. Good technical skills are not enough to make a great team. They have to work well together, and understanding their personalities might help achieve that."

"You've got it," he said. "Do you remember the acronym OCEAN from your personality class? What did it stand for?" She reached for her course notebook and turned to a page with the following diagram:

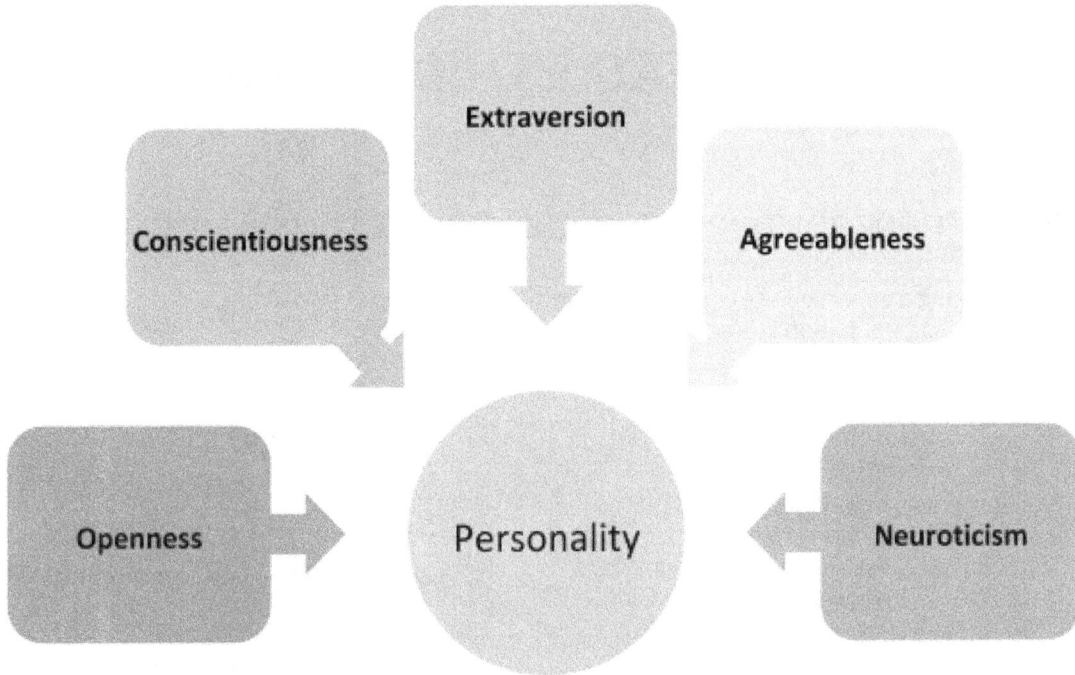

"Now think about how you might consider these traits when building your next team," William suggested.

Samantha began to see the potential uses. She realized that if everyone on the team has a high level of agreeableness, then it might be hard to be successful because everyone will be slow to challenge the prevailing opinion. Likewise, if everyone on the team has a high level of neuroticism, they will find it challenging to work together.

As Samantha went back and evaluated teams from her past that were successful, it confirmed her new understanding about a diversity of personalities and how they might shape a team.

You've now learned about various theories of personality types along with their uses and limitations. Being aware of how you perceive various personalities will make you more effective as a manager. Likewise, you are now able to see how these factors affect job performance and can help you shape a stronger culture within your organization.

MODULE 13: ETHICS IN BUSINESS

WHY IT MATTERS: ETHICS IN BUSINESS

Why does a manager need to understand ethics in business?

Why is the study of ethics important? Given all the things that a student of management needs to learn, why include ethics? In this module, you'll begin to understand just how much of an impact the decisions that businesses make can have on society. Let's start with a recent historical example.

The Great Recession was a period of significant economic stress that the United States faced during 2008 and 2009. The nation experienced massive job loss, a significant stock market swing, and the collapse of the housing market. But what does this have to do with ethics?

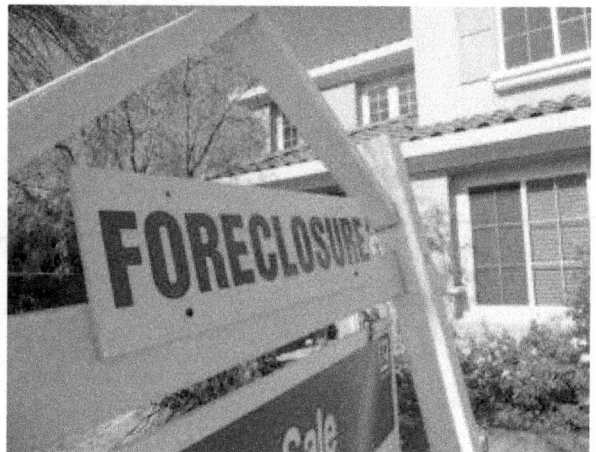

If you've read the book *The Big Short* by Michael Lewis or seen the movie of the same name, then you'll recall that one of the primary reasons for the collapse of the housing market was that many mortgages were extended to individuals who were terrible credit risks. These mortgages were known as "liar loans" because borrowers could put

The events leading to the Great Recession highlighted the importance of ethics in business.

almost anything on a mortgage application, and lenders were not confirming the information. The lenders adopted these practices because they could easily sell these loans, and they were making a lot of money. They were willing to put aside ethics and overlooked their responsibility to verify the accuracy of the information on the loan applications they were approving.

Another factor was that all of these loans were being packaged together to be sold as a financial product called a collateralized mortgage obligation, or CMO. These CMOs were reviewed by many of the large credit rating agencies and given the highest credit ratings. In truth, the rating agencies were not fulfilling their obligation to thoroughly analyze these products because they were being paid millions of dollars by the financial institutions that were selling them.

Your study of ethics in this module will help you understand how to evaluate situations like these. Why is it important to have ethical standards in business, and how can managers ensure that employees act ethically? These are important questions given that businesses are part of the social fabric that makes up our culture.

INTRODUCTION TO THE NEED FOR ETHICS IN THE WORKPLACE

What you'll learn to do: explain the need for ethics in the workplace

Corporate fraud can create negative consequences that not only harm individuals but also ultimately lead to the economic downfall of a nation. Managers must prevent harm by understanding what is considered ethical behavior, by being committed to making ethical decisions, and by encouraging stakeholders to take ethical actions. Exhibiting good ethics not only protects the external constituents of a company but also members of the organization.

THE NEED FOR ETHICS IN THE WORKPLACE

Learning Outcomes

- Explain the need for ethics in the workplace.
- Describe the costs to a company's health of unethical behavior.

The Association of Certified Fraud Examiners estimates that fraud costs US companies about 5 percent of their revenues. In 2016, this meant roughly $900 billion was lost to fraud. (Note: The Association of Certified Fraud Examiners, ACFE Report to the Nations on Occupational Fraud and Abuse, 2016, https://s3-us-west-2.amazonaws.com/acfepublic/2016-report-to-the-nations.pdf.) This includes the identity and credit card thefts that concern everyone and the massive corporate frauds that bring down companies. This estimate includes only *reported* fraud. We don't know the cost of unreported fraud and unethical behavior, but we can assume it's significant. This is a continuing battle that managers cannot delegate to HR or the legal department.

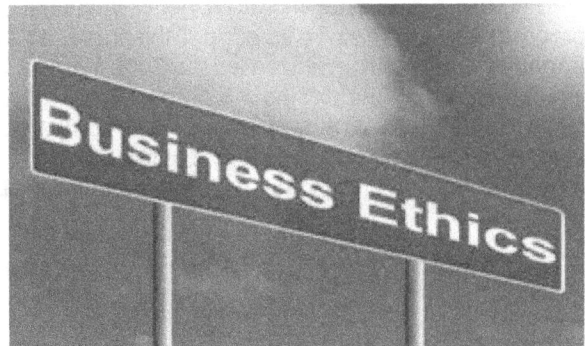

Just how much can unethical behavior cost a business? In some cases, billions. For example, in 2004 and 2005, General Motors engineers "misdiagnosed [an ignition switch problem] as a customer satisfaction issue and not a safety issue," according to GM CEO Mary Barra, and they hid information from regulatory agencies and the public. Their unethical decisions led to 124 deaths. "A series of mistakes were made over a period of time . . . . This had tragic consequences," said Barra. (Note: Margaret Cronin Fisk and Laurel Brubaker Calkins, "GM CEO Barra Tells Jury Company Flubbed Fatal Ignition Flaw," August 15, 2016, https://www.bloomberg.com/news/articles/2016-08-15/gm-ceo-barra-tells-texas-jury-company-flubbed-fatal-switch-flaw.) GM has paid settlements, penalties, and legal costs close to $2.5 billion, and it could face additional lawsuits. (Note: Melissa Burden, "Lost

Appeal Could Cost GM Billions," April 24, 2017, http://www.detroitnews.com/story/business/autos/general-motors/2017/04/24/gm-ignition-switch/100837116/.)

The improper actions of board members, corporate-suite (C-suite) executives, mid-level managers, and nonmanagerial employees can create negative consequences ranging in intensity from petty annoyances to global recessions. Those affected by the consequences can include stakeholders, customers, and the general public. When the stakes are so high, it's imperative that the leaders of an organization understand ethical behavior, be committed to making ethical decisions, and encourage and empower all stakeholders to take ethical actions.

Ethics is defined as principles of conduct or moral behavior. **Business ethics** is ethics as it relates to the conduct or behavior of the members of a business organization. The need for ethics in business is twofold. First, it prevents the external constituents of an organization (i.e., the public, other organizations, and the environment) from being harmed. Second, it benefits the organization internally by helping to ensure its success.

Good business ethics involves, but is not limited to, adhering to laws, regulations, and standards related to fair employment, product safety and quality, truthful advertisement, and environmental responsibility. Companies do suffer for bad ethical behavior and gain from good ethical behavior.

The reputation of a company reflects the ethical or unethical decisions of managers, and consumers often purchase the products or services of companies with a good reputation. If a business has a good reputation, consumers may prefer that company over similar businesses that offer the same products or services, even at higher prices. The companies Tom's Shoes and Patagonia both advertise their ethical practices. And wise executives go to great lengths to repair their company's reputation. For example, British Petroleum (BP) has extended cleanup and conservation efforts following oil spills, and Toyota has issued several major recalls to address potential problems associated with a faulty accelerator pedal.

A broad survey of consumers shows that many factors affect reputation but that ethics is the primary concern. (Note: Percy Marquina Feldman, Rolando Arellano Bahamonde, and Isabel Velasquez Bellido, "A New Approach for Measuring Corporate Reputation," Revista de Administração de Empresas 54, no. 1 (2014): 53–66, http://www.scielo.br/pdf/rae/v54n1/a06v54n1.pdf.) Customers will switch to other brands when a company appears in headlines reporting ethics violations. BP gas stations suffered a boycott for a year after the Gulf of Mexico spill. The volume of sales did not recover to pre-spill levels in that time. (Note: Zhongmin Wang, Alvin Lee, and Michael Polonsky, "Egregiousness and Boycott Intensity: Evidence from the BP Deepwater Horizon Oil Spill" (discussion paper, Resources for the Future, February 2015), http://www.rff.org/files/sharepoint/WorkImages/Download/RFF-DP-15-06.pdf.)

A good reputation creates a buffer, a "halo" effect, where customers, suppliers, and regulators are slower to judge a company. Employees' morale is better in ethical companies, and new employees are easier to hire. An ethics program also gives stock an edge. Ethisphere, an ethics consulting firm, found that share price of the publicly traded companies recognized as the 2016 World's Most Ethical Companies consistently outperform other major indices, including performing 3.3 percent higher than the S&P 500 last year. Exhibiting good business ethics is essential to the survival and success of a company. (Note: The Ethics Centre, "Investing in Ethics Pays Off Financially—Three Reasons to Care about Culture," May 10, 2016. http://www.ethics.org.au/on-ethics/blog/may-2016/investing-in-ethics-pays-off-financially-%E2%80%93-three-r.)

Costs of Unethical Behavior

The costs of unethical behavior are varied and numerous. In addition to a poor reputation, these costs can include reduced customer loyalty and subsequent revenue loss, heavy fines, probation, criminal or civil prosecution, and the loss of needed employee talent. For example, Wells Fargo has paid penalties totaling $170 million and faces civil lawsuits for defrauding customers.

To reach high sales goals, Wells Fargo employees opened unauthorized customer accounts, forged client signatures, charged unnecessary fees on unwanted accounts, and misstated customer phone numbers to hinder customer-satisfaction surveys. Employees resorted to issuing illegal credit cards and lines of credit to avoid pressure from managers. Some employees lost their jobs after reporting the illegal tactics. A civil lawsuit filed in California in 2015 called for reimbursement of the fraudulent fees charged to customers, a fine of $2,500 for each violation of California's Unfair Competition Law, and an injunction against unethical practices. (Note: Zacks Equity

Research, "Wells Fargo Faces LA Lawsuit for Unethical Conduct," May 5, 2015. https://www.zacks.com/stock/news/173783/wells-fargo-faces-la-lawsuit-for-unethical-conduct.)

As a result of the unethical behavior of executives and employees, there has been a strong drive to improve business ethics. Congress passed the **Sarbanes-Oxley Act** in 2002 to impose sanctions on executives who commit unethical acts in financial reporting and to protect employees who report fraud. In addition, business schools have increased their focus on informing students of ethical/unethical acts, and more individuals and organizations have filed lawsuits against companies involved in fraud, regardless of whether senior executives are aware of the unethical acts committed. (Note: Eugene Brigham and Joel Houston, Fundamentals of Financial Management, 12th ed. (Mason, OH: South-Western, Cengage Learning, 2009).)

INTRODUCTION TO US SENTENCING GUIDELINES FOR ORGANIZATIONS

What you'll learn to do: explain the US Sentencing Guidelines for Organizations and how the compliance steps encourage ethical behavior

An organization can be held criminally liable for the illegal actions of any of its employees even when the act goes against company policy. For example, a slot machine company, ETT, was ordered to pay $8.2 million in damages for the wrongful death of Roja Delgado. A temporary employee driving an ETT van hit Delgado's car, killing her. At the time of the accident, the ETT driver's blood-alcohol level was three times the legal limit. The court assigned 75 percent of the fault to ETT and 25 percent to the driver. (Note: Eglet Wall Christiansen, "Holding Employers Liable for Employee Wrongs," HG.org Legal Resources, accessed July 29, 2017, https://www.hg.org/article.asp?id=19044.) The Federal Sentencing Guidelines are rules that set out a uniform sentencing policy for individuals and organizations convicted of felonies and serious misdemeanors in the US federal courts system. Chapter eight of the guidelines explains how organizations can reduce their culpability and reduce fines. A company with a strong ethics program is judged less responsible for misbehaving employees. In this section, you'll learn about the guidelines and how they encourage ethical behavior.

US SENTENCING GUIDELINES FOR ORGANIZATIONS

Learning Outcomes

- Explain the US Sentencing Guidelines for Organizations.
- List the compliance steps from the U.S. Sentencing Commission Guidelines.

Purpose of Sentencing Guidelines

Even when an employee's actions go against company policy, the company can be held legally responsible, despite its best efforts to prevent unethical behavior. This applies only when the employee acts within the scope of employment. An employee who deals drugs while on the job is not operating within the scope of employment, so the company would not be held liable for the offense. However, if an employee uses the account information of bank customers to steal money from them, the bank would be held responsible. The most common offenses related to companies include fraud, hazardous waste discharge, tax evasion, antitrust offenses, and food and drug violations.

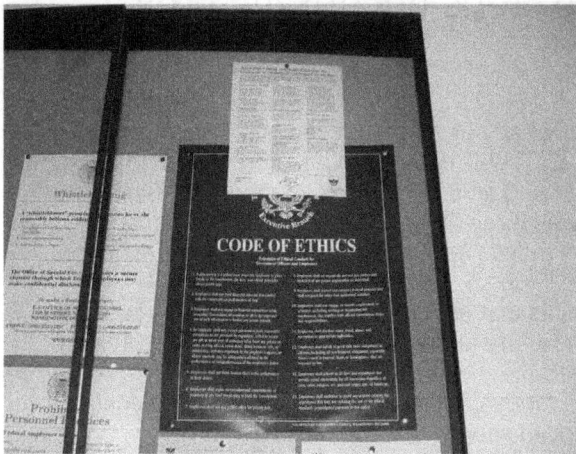

Compliance steps are posted in a workplace.

Punishment for corporate offenses is governed by chapter eight of the Federal Sentencing Guidelines for Organizations. These guidelines were designed to enhance two purposes of criminal sentencing: "just punishment" and "deterrence." The guidelines apply to corporations, partnerships, nonprofit entities, government bodies, trusts, labor unions, and pension funds. They govern only sentencing for felonies and serious misdemeanors.

Guideline Compliance Steps

The US Sentencing Commission has done the hard work of designing an ethics program, and this model has become the backbone of every corporate ethics program. Essentially, organizations are offered incentives for detecting and preventing crime, provided that any offense is reported to the authorities, and no high-level employee has committed the offense. Some incentives include reduced fines, the avoidance of incarceration, supervised release, and reductions in the time to be served.

The guidelines are only a model of "corporate good citizenship" and do not include details for implementation. The compliance steps from the Federal Sentencing Guidelines include the following:

- Establish standards and procedures to prevent and detect criminal conduct, which starts with a code of ethics or statement of values.

- Senior management must be knowledgeable about the compliance and ethics program as well as oversee its implementation and make reasonable efforts to ensure its effectiveness.

- Make reasonable efforts to exclude any individual who has committed an illegal act or engaged in other activities inconsistent with a compliance and ethics program from substantial authority in the organization.

- Periodically communicate the aspects of the compliance and ethics program to its members by conducting training programs and disseminating relevant information.

- Ensure that the program is followed by (1) monitoring and auditing activities to detect criminal conduct, (2) periodically evaluating its effectiveness, and (3) employing systems that allow for anonymity or confidentiality if employees want to report criminal conduct without fear of retaliation. A common practice is a whistleblower hotline.

- Promote and enforce the program by offering incentives for performance in accordance with the program and instituting disciplinary measures for engaging in or failing to take reasonable steps to prevent/detect criminal conduct.

- Respond to criminal conduct and take steps to prevent future and similar offenses when criminal conduct has been detected.

By establishing and enforcing a compliance and ethics program, a company can prevent fraud and shield itself, although not completely, from the repercussions of the unethical and illegal acts of its employees.

INTRODUCTION TO INFLUENCES ON ETHICAL CHOICES

What you'll learn to do: describe the influences on an employee's ethical choices

After the law is satisfied, issues of ethics become more difficult to judge. The first question is the importance or ethical intensity of the issue. People of good conscience will differ on the importance of an issue. Next, several principles may guide a decision. Again, people may disagree on which principle is key. A manager will need to consider the company's stakeholders, the company's values, and his or her own values to make a decision.

INFLUENCES ON ETHICAL CHOICES

How might ethics affect the decisions you make as an employee?

Ethical Intensity

The 2016 presidential election showed how much people can disagree on the relative importance of ethical issues. Opinions that were anathema in prior elections became common, because people saw that other issues, economic issues, were neglected in the push for political correctness. Similarly in business, a manager must prioritize issues. Each issue will be unique in some ways, but there are some general factors to guide a decision. Ethical intensity is the degree of importance of an issue for an individual or group. The factors that determine ethical intensity include the following:

- **Magnitude,** or significance of the consequences
- **Concentration of effect,** or the number of people affected
- **Proximity** of the decision maker to the victim or beneficiary of the decision
- **Probability** that the decision implemented will lead to the predicted consequence
- **Social consensus** that a proposed decision is negative or positive
- **Temporal immediacy,** or the elapsed length of time between when a decision is made and when the resulting consequences occur

The significance of the consequences refers to the total harm or benefit that follows from the decision. If a few customers were overcharged a small amount by mistake, it may not be worth correcting the mistake. If thousands were overcharged, then the ethical intensity is much higher. If the overcharged customers are friends or neighbors (proximity), it becomes more important to address the issue.

Drug companies often deal in probabilities of harm. A drug may help many people, but there is a chance that it will harm a small number. The measles, mumps, and rubella (MMR) vaccine can cause serious side effects. The company and the Food and Drug Administration (FDA) trade off the benefit to millions and risk of harm to a few in an ethical decision. After much debate, society has developed a consensus that this is the best course. Other behaviors blessed by social consensus in the United States are considered unfair or illegal in other countries. For example, some food dyes banned in the United Kingdom are widely used in the United States.

Some consequences are distant in time. People deal well with issues where they can see the consequences quickly. The fire retardant benefit of asbestos was easy to see. The lung cancers from exposure often did not appear for 30 to 40 years. It took 50 years for lawmakers to make the ethical choice after the dangers were recognized. The perspective taken based on the intensity factors can vary between individuals and groups. Reaching a decision in a group setting like a company can take a long time.

Principles of Ethical Decision Making

After ethical intensity, a thoughtful manager will consider the principles that might apply to an issue. There is no one set of principles to check off, but the seven listed here are common to most people.

- **Legal and regulatory requirements** set the minimum standard for behavior. Any company or individual can disagree with the law, but given the consequences, it must be done carefully. The Hobby Lobby stores refused, on religious grounds, to follow the Affordable Care Act requirements for certain health benefits. The US Supreme Court found in their favor in 2014.
- **Long-term self-interest** means the pursuit of outcomes that will benefit the self in the long run. For example, a company must make choices to ensure its continued existence. The costs and harm from failure are substantial.
- **Personal virtue** refers to conformity to a standard of righteousness. You should make choices that are honest and truthful individually. The good of the company does not justify lying.
- **Utilitarianism** seeks the greatest benefit for the maximum number of people. This is often difficult to judge over large groups of people.
- **Individual rights** are related to the freedom to act and think without punishment through regulatory, legal, or societal means. For example, we make individual health decisions to smoke or drink beverages loaded with sugar even though the health costs are borne by many through private and government insurance programs.
- **Distributive justice** is the fairness of the outcomes. That is, how are the benefits shared or distributed among the individuals in a group? The US market system can have winner-take-all outcomes. Our welfare system redistributes a little to the losers in the market game who are also part of our society.
- **Religious injunction** is the main moral and ethical guide for many people.

Watch the following video for an overview of the ethical decision making process:

https://www.youtube.com/watch?v=IwK-CshmH7M

Disagreements among Managers during the Decision-Making Process

Achieving an ethical outcome while being guided by these principles is not always simple. Each individual has a different combination of perceptions, moral codes, interests, religious beliefs, convictions, and motives. Furthermore, what may be morally sound to one individual may be depraved to another. What may harm one individual or group may benefit another. Therefore, managers often disagree about what is considered ethical.

For example, UTP, which is devoted to treating employees well, often runs into ethical issues. The company experienced a growth spurt about 10 years ago, and senior executives decided to have a larger building constructed to provide a more comfortable and spacious working environment for its employees. It also planned to continue growing, so a larger building was designed than was projected to be needed at the time.

Unfortunately, the company grew in a way that was unexpected. Customer demand and an evolving business model required that the company hire more mid-level managers that specialize in a certain skill. In the old building, these managers had midsize offices. They moved into midsize offices in the new building, and more midsize offices were left over. The company grew to the point that all of these offices were filled.

New hires were placed in smaller offices until these offices were also filled. After a couple of years, a midsize office became available when one midlevel manager, who had been with the company for more than 20 years, retired. However, the office sat vacant for about a year because senior executives did not want to offend any of the recently hired midlevel managers by offering one of them that office. The company needed to replace the retired employee, which meant the office had to be filled.

The ethical issue was whether to give the midsize office to an employee who started with the company 17 years prior as a nonmanagerial employee and then was promoted to midlevel manager or to the recently hired and ambitious midlevel manager with an advanced degree. Each decision could be considered fair to one individual and unfair to the other, depending on the views of those involved. For each individual involved, the principle of utilitarianism would influence the decision and be used to determine fairness. It would be in the best interest of the individual who does not get the office to focus on other benefits of being employed by the company rather than the perceived injustice of losing the office battle because the situation is not very ethically intense.

INTRODUCTION TO HOW MANAGERS CAN ENCOURAGE ETHICAL BEHAVIOR

What you'll learn to do: describe practical steps that managers should take to model ethical behavior and encourage ethical choices

Management cannot guarantee that employees will behave ethically. But there are processes that significantly improve average behaviors. For some companies, these processes are legally required.

In response to the Enron accounting scandal, the government passed the Sarbanes-Oxley Act, which requires that companies listed or applying to be listed on a public stock exchange establish and enforce a code of ethics. Even companies that are not required to have a code of ethics should take steps to encourage ethical choices. Although it is important to establish an effective code of ethics, it is crucial that ethical employees first be hired. An effective ethics program should also be set in place to deal with violations. Despite a company's best efforts to prevent any wrongdoing, offenses will happen, so action must be taken against the offender. And when employees report wrongdoings, they need to be offered whistleblower protection.

HOW MANAGERS CAN ENCOURAGE ETHICAL BEHAVIOR

Learning Outcomes

- Explain the purpose of a code of ethics (why US laws require one for companies listed on the largest stock exchanges).
- Explain the benefits of ethics training.
- Describe the methods of selecting and hiring ethical employees.
- Explain whistleblower protection.
- Explain senior management's role in fostering ethical decisions and behavior.

Codes of Ethics

A code of ethics, also known as a code of conduct or statement of values, is a policy statement of a company's values, responsibilities, and conduct expectations. The purpose of a code of ethics is to guide employees in handling ethical dilemmas. It is essentially a moral compass.

The ethical lapses of global companies, such as Enron, Arthur Andersen, and WorldCom, over the span of a few years caused much devastation. Enron and WorldCom executives used deceptive accounting and sold inflated stock while recommending it to employees and external investors. Arthur Andersen's accountants, who audited Enron and WorldCom, turned a blind eye to the fraud. As a result, in 2002, Congress passed the Sarbanes-Oxley Act, which requires that companies listed or applying to be listed on a public stock exchange establish and enforce a code of ethics. It also requires that any changes to an established code of ethics be disclosed to the public. A code of ethics that meets the requirements of the act comprises the standards necessary to promote "honest and ethical conduct; full, fair, accurate, timely and understandable disclosure in periodic reports" and "compliance with applicable governmental rules and regulations." (Note: In LaToya J. Murray's "Sarbanes-Oxley Code of Conduct Requirements," Chron.com, accessed July 29, 2017, http://smallbusiness.chron.com/sarbanes-oxley-code-conduct-requirements-4060.html)

Codes of ethics vary in content, length, and complexity. Johnson & Johnson has a relatively simple code of conduct, with just four paragraphs that can be summarized as: Our customers are our first priority, then our employees, then our communities. Stockholders come last. But if we take care of the others, then stockholders will do well. (Note: Johnson & Johnson, "Our Credo," accessed August 03, 2017, https://www.jnj.com/about-jnj/jnj-credo) Without being too detailed or lengthy, this credo expresses the company's values and gives employees the guidance they need to make ethical decisions.

Ethics Training

Having codes and policies in place that address ethics is not enough. Employees need to be taught how to respond in situations involving ethics. Therefore, many managers enroll their employees in an ethics training program. Ethics programs often involve activities that encourage ethical behavior and reinforce a company's ethics code/policies.

One ethics activity involves having employees match various scenarios on one set of cards with the possible responses on another set of cards. Every scenario will have appropriate and inappropriate answers. After the participants match scenarios with responses, the group discusses the decision. Discussing the responses gives managers the opportunity to explain why some policies are in place and demonstrate how employees should respond in ethical situations they will likely face on the job.

Selecting and Hiring Ethical Employees

Although it is important, or even required in some cases, to have an established and effective code of ethics, it is crucial to the stability of a company to first hire ethical employees. It is better to hire someone who is naturally inclined to behave in an ethical manner than to rely on a company code of ethics to encourage an unethical employee to make ethical choices.

One method of selecting and hiring ethical employees is the use of personality tests or situation-specific questionnaires. Personality tests can be used to determine temperament, outlook (i.e., whether positive or negative), and mood. Situation-specific questionnaires can be customized by a company and used to uncover how a candidate would react when faced with an ethical dilemma.

Calling personal references may also help hiring managers filter out less ethical candidates. Although this method is used often, it is important to be aware that references often withhold negative information about a candidate. Managers should supplement references with another method of weeding out dishonest candidates.

Best practices in the selection and hiring of ethical employees involve including the company's most ethical employees in the interview process. Interviewers already doing the job a candidate is applying for can ask relevant questions that can lead to answers that reveal a lot about the candidate, such as a propensity to make unethical decisions.

Whistleblower Protection

One of the best enforcement tools is a **whistleblower hotline**, which is a phone number or other method for employees or other stakeholders to report suspected acts of impropriety, such as fraud, waste, abuse, misconduct, or violations of policy, laws, or regulations. These reports are usually confidential and may be anonymous. Colleagues often see suspicious behavior and are well-positioned to report it or fix it. However, some employees are reluctant to speak up for fear of retaliation. (Note: Ethics Research Center, "National Business Ethics Survey (NBES) 2013," accessed August 3, 2017, https://www.ethics.org/ecihome/research/nbes/nbes-reports/nbes-2013)

A **whistleblower** is an individual such as an employee who reports the misconduct of someone in a position of authority in his or her own organization. In the past, whistleblowers had no protection from retaliation by those they reported—reporting a superior's wrongdoings often required risking one's livelihood. This discouraged employees from reporting offenses.

Under the whistleblower protection offered by the Sarbanes-Oxley Act, anyone who reports a corporate wrongdoing and believes he or she could be penalized for it can request that the Occupational Safety and Health Administration (OSHA) investigate the matter. If the whistleblower is an employee who was fired and the termination of employment was found to be improper, the company can be ordered to rehire the individual and give him or her back pay as well as a penalty award.

The US Securities and Exchange Commission has strengthened whistleblowing protections and rewards

In 2017, OSHA ordered Wells Fargo to pay $5.4 million to a former manager who said he was fired in 2010 after reporting to his supervisors and to a bank ethics hotline what he suspected was fraudulent behavior. OSHA also said the bank must rehire him.

The $5.4 million, intended to cover back pay, compensatory damages, and legal fees, was the largest individual award ever ordered through OSHA's whistleblower protection program at the time. (Note: Stacy Cowley, "Wells Fargo Whistle-Blower Wins $5.4 Million and His Job Back," April 3, 2017, https://www.nytimes.com/2017/04/03/business/04-wells-fargo-whistleblower-fired-osha.html?_r=0.)

Another agency, the Securities and Exchange Commission, also strengthened whistleblower protections and rewards. In 2011, the SEC issued new whistleblower rules, required by the Dodd-Frank Act. Under the new rules, a whistleblower is eligible for a bounty equal to 10 percent to 30 percent of monetary sanctions resulting from an enforcement action. Accordingly, companies will be faced with the prospect that their employees, suppliers, customers, consultants, advisors, and others may report possible violations directly to the SEC without providing the companies with an opportunity to first investigate the allegations and remediate any violations. Under the act, employers are prohibited from retaliating against whistleblowing employees.

The SEC announced the largest award ever in July 2017. Two whistleblowers are set to share a record $61 million award from the SEC for helping make the case that JPMorgan Chase & Co. failed to disclose to wealthy clients that it was steering them into investments that would be most profitable for the bank. (Note: Neil Weinberg, "JPMorgan Whistle-Blowers Set to Reap Record $61 Million Bounty," July 20, 2017, https://www.bloomberg.com/news/articles/2017-07-20/jpmorgan-whistle-blowers-seen-reaping-record-61-million-bounty.)

Whistleblowing pays, and so does an ethics program that prevents the need for whistleblowers.

Fostering Ethical Decisions

In addition to establishing a code of ethics, hiring ethical employees, and protecting whistleblowers, key aspects of senior management's role in fostering ethical decisions and behavior in any organization include planning, implementing, and communicating the specifics of an ethics program. Ethics programs disclose important corporate values, often through the use of policies and employee/manager training. After a program has been implemented, senior management should monitor and evaluate it and then modify the program as needed or desired to ensure its effectiveness.

It is also important for senior management to model ethical behavior. The responsibilities of senior management in modeling ethical behavior include the following:

- Act ethically and be seen to act ethically.
- Be active in the ethics program. For example, introduce the ethics training or be the person to speak.
- Encourage employees to raise issues.
- Address ethics issues.
- Enforce the ethics program, such as by punishing violators.

Ethics programs are like an insurance policy. They help mitigate the worst consequences when employees do stray, and they help prevent "accidents" by raising employee "safety" awareness.

INTRODUCTION TO CORPORATE SOCIAL RESPONSIBILITY

What you'll learn to do: explain corporate social responsibility (CSR) and its relationship to economic performance

In addition to profitability, consumers now expect companies to be socially responsible. The main categories of corporate social responsibility include environmental efforts, philanthropy, ethical labor practices, and volunteerism. Managers who wish to create shared value for stakeholders, and thus make their companies thrive, are socially responsible.

CORPORATE SOCIAL RESPONSIBILITY

Expectations of Corporate Social Responsibility

Consumers today expect a lot out of companies. According to a study by Cone Communications, 9 out of 10 consumers expect companies to operate responsibly and address social and environmental issues rather than simply make a profit. In addition, 84 percent of consumers seek out responsible products. (Note: Post, J. (2017, April 03). What is Corporate Social Responsibility? Retrieved September 19, 2017, from http://www.businessnewsdaily.com/4679-corporate-social-responsibility.html)

To please consumers, many companies now practice corporate social responsibility. **Corporate social responsibility (CSR)**, also known as corporate citizenship, is a business concept in which social and environmental concerns are integrated into a company's operations. Whole Foods Market CEO John Mackey refers to CSR as **conscious capitalism**, in which businesses "serve the interests of all major stakeholders—customers, employees, investors, communities, suppliers, and the environment." (Note: Mackey, J., & Sisodia, R. (2014). Conscious capitalism: liberating the heroic spirit of business. Boston, MA: Harvard Business Review Press.) Mackey witnessed the benefits of conscious capitalism when a Whole Foods Market store was terribly affected by a flood. Unexpectedly, customers and neighbors helped, employees worked for free, suppliers resupplied products on credit, and its bank loaned it money to restock. The Whole Foods store was able to reopen 28 days after the flood.

Although there are multiple versions of CSR, the general main categories of CSR include environmental efforts, philanthropy, ethical labor practices, and volunteerism. Let's take a closer look at each of these.

Environmental Efforts

The primary focus of many companies in their commitment to CSR is through environmental efforts. For example, companies can have a large carbon footprint on the environment, which is the amount of greenhouse gases, especially carbon dioxide, emitted by an individual, organization, process, event, structure, or product. The majority of scientists believe that greenhouse gases are causing changes in the global climate, sea level, ecosystems, and thus, agricultural patterns. The carbon footprints of companies vary greatly depending on business operations, their size, and their location.

Any action taken to reduce a carbon footprint is considered beneficial for the environment. These efforts have included minimizing the amount of land occupied or used, constructing/occupying energy-efficient buildings, planting trees in the rainforest, and using locally sourced products. For example, the Bingham Hotel outside of London sources as much food as possible from suppliers within a 10-mile radius and the rest of its food from the British Isles. (Note: Manson, E. (2011, September 29). The Benefits of Local Sourcing. Retrieved September 19, 2017, from https://www.thecaterer.com/articles/340407/the-benefits-of-local-sourcing) Purchasing locally sourced products supports local employment and reduces pollution by limiting the distances products must be transported.

Philanthropy

Many companies practice CSR by donating to various charities, starting charitable programs, and offering scholarships to underprivileged students wanting to attend college. Nu Skin, a personal-care company, developed a charity called Nourish the Children, which allows leaders, employees, and customers to donate nutrient-rich meals to children around the world. From 2002, when the program began, to 2017, people had donated more than 500 million meals through the program. (Note: "Why Nourish the Children?" Nu Skin, accessed July 29, 2017, https://www.nuskin.com/en_US/community/nourish_the_children.html)

Ethical Labor Practices

Labor practices are often controversial from an ethical perspective. For example, Apple's iPhones contain parts from companies in other countries. Specifically, the tin, which is used for a part, comes from mines in Indonesia. With labor laws that vary from one country to another, the company exercised due diligence in ensuring that its sourcing companies follow all applicable labor laws in their country of operation. But it was revealed to consumers in the United States that the tin was mined from companies in Indonesia that use child labor. Moreover, during the mining process, laborers as young as 12 years old were subject to the hazards of unstable soil. US consumers were appalled.

To address the issue, Apple instituted more robust labor practices, which were communicated to consumers. In a statement, Apple said, "the simplest course of action would be for Apple to unilaterally refuse any tin from Indonesian mines. That would be easy for us to do and would certainly shield us from criticism. But that would also be the lazy and cowardly path, since it would do nothing to improve the situation. We have chosen to stay engaged and attempt to drive changes on the ground." (Note: Atkinson, L. (n.d.). Apple Suppliers & Labor Practices. Retrieved September 19, 2017, from http://ethicsunwrapped.utexas.edu/case-study/apple-suppliers-labor-practices) For improved transparency, Apple has released annual reports that include details of its work with suppliers and their labor practices. Recent investigations have shown some improvements to the working conditions of the employees of Apple's suppliers. However, the company still faces some criticism.

Volunteerism

Many companies are encouraging volunteerism by incorporating it into their policies and establishing employee volunteer programs. For example, some companies make a donation to the charities their employees volunteer at, in the amount equivalent to the employees' regular pay for the same number of hours volunteered. Other companies offer gift cards to employees who volunteer. Companies are finding creative ways to encourage and reward the volunteerism of employees not only to help society and the environment but also so that consumers and stakeholders will perceive them as socially responsible.

Watch the following video to learn more about CSR and see examples of how companies practice it.

https://www.youtube.com/watch?v=xoE8XlcDUI8

The Stakeholder-CSR Relationship

The stakeholders of any company are interested in the well-being of that company and can include employees, board members, stockholders, suppliers, distributors, customers, and the community.

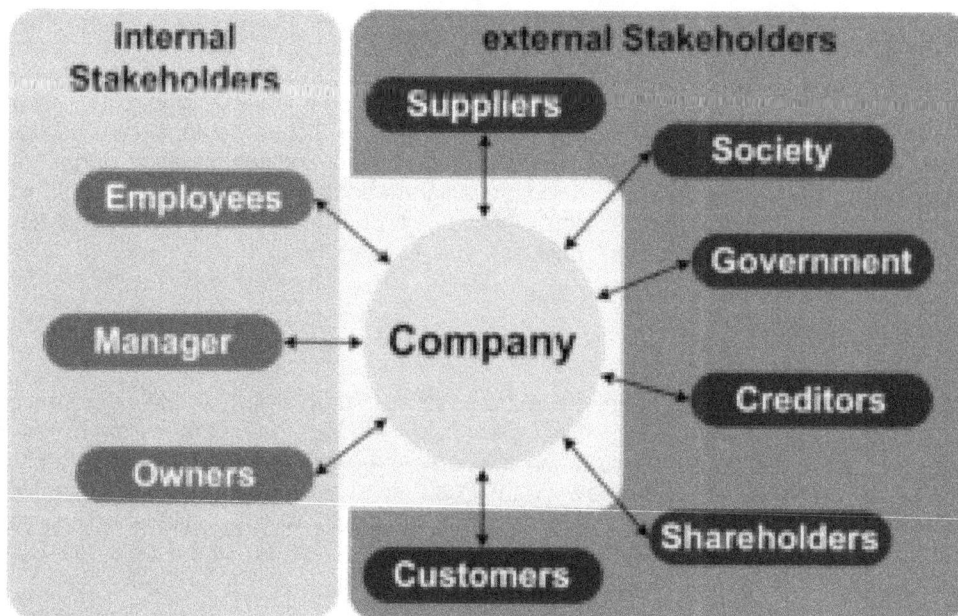

Companies have both internal and external stakeholders.

When a company is in a good state, the stakeholders are affected positively. Communities benefit when their citizens are employed and when local companies are good stewards of the environment. Suppliers benefit from having a steady, profitable outlet for their products. Consumers benefit from consistent sellers and more competition in the market. For example, an employee stakeholder may receive annual bonuses based on company profits. Stockholders may receive dividends or sell high when the price of the stock they hold rises. Managers who wish to create shared value for stakeholders, and thus make their companies thrive, embed CSR into their business operations.

While CSR is positive for companies, there's no guarantee that a company will see an increase in profits due to CSR. More important than profitability, consumers and stakeholders expect the triple bottom line—profit, people, planet—of companies to improve and be set high. Companies that meet these expectations can reap the benefits of a positive reputation. Their positive reputation cycles back to improve their triple bottom line. Engaging in socially responsible activities is a win-win-win situation for stakeholders, the environment, and companies.

Consulting companies offer ethical compliance systems for client organizations. The systems they create integrate governance, risk, and compliance (GRC). For example, OCEG, the nonprofit think tank that supports GRC, promotes **principled performance**, which is the "reliable achievement of objectives while addressing uncertainty and acting with integrity." (Note: O. (2017, September 13). About OCEG - How we invented GRC with standards and certification. Retrieved September 19, 2017, from http://www.oceg.org/about/what-is-oceg/)

CSR and Economic Performance

Research on the relationship between firm value and CSR presents strong evidence that CSR activities enhance a firm's value. Various studies have found benefits in operating efficiency, product market gains, attracting highly qualified personnel, employee productivity, capital market execution, risk management, and earnings quality. In aggregate, the studies recommend strategic CSR, not just doing good. **Strategic CSR** means activities that support company goals or enhance the company's reputation. (Note: Malik, Mahfuja. "Value-Enhancing Capabilities of CSR: A Brief Review of Contemporary Literature." Journal of Business Ethics (Jan. 2014) 127: 419-438) (Note: Hernández-Murillo, Rubén & J. Martinek, Christopher. "Corporate Social Responsibility Can Be Profitable." The Regional Economist (2009) 4-5. Retrieved August 28, 2017, from https://www.stlouisfed.org/publications/regional-economist/april-2009/corporate-social-responsibility-can-be-profitable)

PUTTING IT TOGETHER: ETHICS IN BUSINESS

Let's return to our opening scenario and apply what you've learned in this module. We started by considering the impact of ethical decisions related to the housing market leading up to the Great Recession. Mortgage brokers, ratings agencies, and financial institutions sacrificed good ethics for significant profits.

But how important were these ethical lapses, and how much focus should have been given to these errors in judgment?

In this module, you learned about the factors that determine the ethical intensity of an issue. Because ethical dilemmas can vary, this is a framework that helps us understand how important it is to address a particular topic. Let's use this framework to evaluate the ethical problems during the housing meltdown.

Magnitude of Consequences

The size of benefits that passed to the companies involved in creating these high-risk loans during the housing crisis was measured in the billions of dollars. Likewise, the magnitude of the impact on the economy when the tipping point was reached was even greater. Millions of people lost their jobs and homes. So the magnitude of this dimension shows an ethically intense decision.

Probability of Effect

Experts leading up to the housing crash were split on the probability dimension. Many believed that housing would not go down in value and that even if customers couldn't repay their loans, the financial institutions could simply foreclose and resell the assets. On the other hand, there were many investors who were very vocal in their certainty of a coming collapse. For a lender uncertain of the probability, this dimension would add little to the intensity.

Social Consensus

While industry insiders knew that "everyone was doing it" when it came to making bad loans, it wasn't openly discussed. Ultimately, those involved knew that the social consensus would be opposed to what was done—especially given that the motivation was almost exclusively profit. Therefore, the social consensus dimension would suggest a high-intensity issue.

Temporal Immediacy

Lenders knew that even if the loans they made went bad, it would be some time before the effects were realized. Most customers would make payments for several months in order to keep their home. When they started getting behind, the servicing companies would make concessions to keep the borrower in the home. Likewise, foreclosure tends to be a relatively slow process. All of these factors suggest a low temporal immediacy, lessening the intensity of the ethical issue.

Proximity

Did the decisions the lenders made impact those close to them or strangers? Though the lenders likely assumed that the impact would be only to strangers, the economic storm that followed affected most households to some extent. This misjudgment put less weight on proximity.

Concentration of Effect

The benefits of these lending decisions accrued to only a relatively small number of individuals. However, the negative consequences were felt by millions. Given the asymmetrical weight to the negative consequences, the effects were broadly felt. As such, that would add intensity to the ethical problem.

Using the framework that you learned, you can understand why the government stepped in with a massive overhaul of the regulatory framework of financial institutions. If the individuals involved had used a similar framework when making their personal decisions, perhaps the crisis would never have occurred. Those in positions of leadership and authority should be held to a high standard of integrity, which is why the study of ethics is foundational to the field of management.

In this module, we have covered creating a company ethics program both to avoid fines when someone breaks the law but also to encourage better behavior toward stakeholders. Research strongly suggests that stakeholders will reward good citizens. (Note: Webley, S., & More, E. (n.d.). Does Business Ethics Pay? Retrieved September 19, 2017, from http://www.ibe.org.uk/userfiles/doesbusethicpaysumm.pdf) Like Whole Foods' flooding experience, stakeholders will look out for firms that look out for them.

MODULE 14: COMMUNICATION

WHY IT MATTERS: COMMUNICATION

Why does a manager need to understand effective communication?

Tony is a manager with Precision Manufacturing. He's talking to a couple of other managers after the weekly departmental meeting. He is filling them in on an issue he's having with one of his team members, James.

"I'm completely fed up with James. I've been waiting on him to complete a new production schedule for two weeks, and we're going to miss our deadline."

"Really? That doesn't sound like James," replies Sandra, one of the managers. "Have you said anything to him about it?"

"Of course I have. I went up to him again two days ago and asked if the new schedule would be ready today. He told me it still wasn't finished. I can't believe he's ignoring my request!"

"Well, based on what you just told me, you didn't actually make a request. You just asked a question."

We learn to communicate early, but effective communication is a skill that we continue to develop throughout life.

Tony looks surprised and says, "What do you mean? He has to know that the only reason I'm asking is that I need it right now."

"Are you sure he knows? That's not what I heard you say."

Communication is easy, right? After all, we learned to communicate during our first years of life, and we've been doing it ever since. Unfortunately, it isn't that simple. Almost every aspect of management requires communication skills; however, time and time again, ineffective communication leads to business problems—and at times, disasters!

In this module, you'll take a look at principles of communication and learn about barriers to effective communication. By the end of this study, you'll see that good communication takes intentional focus, but it is a skill you can learn.

INTRODUCTION TO COMMUNICATION AND MANAGEMENT

What you'll learn to do: recognize the role of communication in the management function

Without communication there is no management. How exactly do managers use communication to meet the goals of the organization? Why are some people effective communicators and others can't seem to make themselves understood? How do formal and information networks both support organizational goals? These are some of the questions that we'll address in this section.

COMMUNICATION AND MANAGEMENT

Learning Outcomes

- Describe the components of the communication-process model.
- Recognize common missteps in communication.
- Differentiate between formal and informal communication networks.

Introduction

Mathias Mendez had recently been hired as the manager of the purchasing department of an online retailer. His appointment was announced through an e-mail to all company employees, and his department was expecting his arrival. His managers told him his first task was to try to cut costs in the department. Mathias hadn't determined exactly what to do, but he had determined that he could reach the target cuts through a combination of a freeze on new hiring, cutting all but critical travel, reducing training, and cutting back on the use of temporary and contract workers.

He was anxious to show his superiors that he was working on the problem, so he sent an e-mail to his managers and employees that said he would be announcing cost-cutting measures soon. Unfortunately, employees interpreted this to mean there would be layoffs. Rumors soon started flying about how "Matt the Knife" had been hired to outsource the department and that everyone was going to be laid off. Morale plunged and people started using their time to polish their resumes and apply for jobs. The employees distrusted Mathias and he was cut off from all but routine communication with them.

Communication and management are closely linked. **Communication** refers to the process by which information is exchanged between two or more people (increasingly, machines are also included in communication, but we limit the discussion here to communication between people). Each of the management roles—planning, organizing, leading, and controlling—depends on effective communication. Managers must be able to receive accurate

252

information to determine plans, and they must be able to send accurate information for the plans to be implemented. When information is accurately sent and received, everyone in an organization can be informed. As we see in the earlier example, however, when information is misinterpreted or when incorrect information spreads, communications can create significant problems in organizations.

The Role of Communication in Management

The role of management is to accomplish the goals of an organization. To do this, managers create a plan that defines what needs to be done, when it will be done, and how it will be done. To implement the plan, managers must convey this information to everyone in the organization. That is, they must communicate the plan to members of the organization. However, managers need to do much more than just inform people what they need to do to support the plan. They also must motivate people to support the plan, build commitment to the organization, establish rapport and collaboration, and keep everyone informed of events and actions that affect the organization. Good communication not only informs but also helps to create a culture that makes people feel like they belong to and want to support the organization. The opening example shows what can result from poor communication. Following are some of the benefits of effective communication.

- **Provides clarity.** Confusion, uncertainty, and ambiguity make people uncomfortable and uncooperative. Making roles, responsibilities, and relationships clear gives everyone the information they need to do their jobs and to understand their contributions to the organization. Effective communication reduces the cost associated with conflicts, misunderstandings, and mistakes.
- **Builds Relationships.** A culture that promotes open communication reduces tension between hierarchical levels of employees, both professionally and socially. In a trusting and collaborative culture, people are more likely to seek help with problems and to suggest solutions and improvements. Effective communication creates a collegial culture that fosters teamwork and encourages cooperation.
- **Creates commitment.** Effective communication involves not only sending information but also receiving it. By listening to employees' concerns, allowing them to have input on their work and their workplace, and giving consideration to their suggestions, managers can make everyone in the organization feel like they are valued contributors. When employees feel like they are valued in the organization, they will likely be more engaged and motivated. Effective communication creates support and commitment.
- **Defines expectations.** When people are uncertain about what is expected of them and how they will be evaluated, they can't do their jobs well. Performance reviews are difficult because the employee does not know the performance standards they are expected to meet. And if corrective measures are necessary, the employee may be resentful if he can't see how his behaviors reduced his effectiveness. When expectations and standards are clear, employees know what they need to do to get a positive review and the benefits that come with it.

These are just a few of the many benefits that come from effective communications. Managers can only reach organizational goals when the people in the organization are committed to the goals. People perform much better when they are informed and involved.

The Communication-Process Model

The communication process may seem simple: one person sends a message and others receive it. The process becomes more complex, however, because the information in the message must be sent and received accurately. The communication-process model describes how the *information* is sent and received.

The following diagram shows this model.

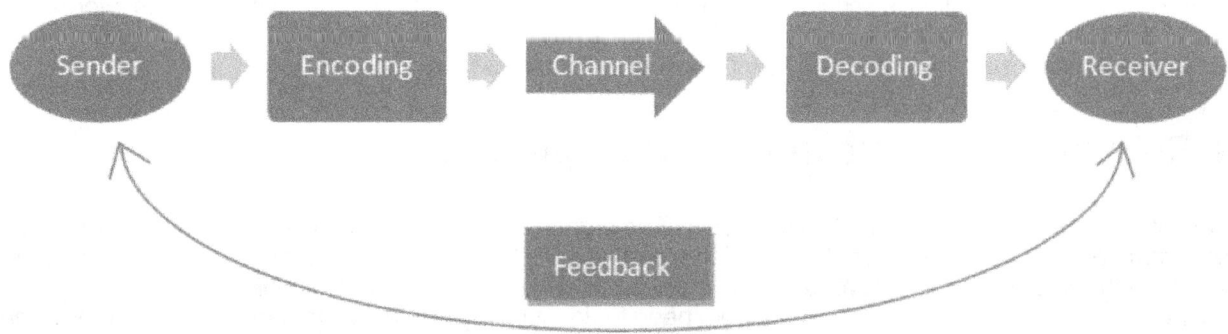

The communication-process model

It is easiest to understand the model when one person is communicating with another person. The person initiating the communication, the **sender**, has information he wants the other person, the **receiver**, to know. However, before it can be sent, the information has to be encoded into a form that can be transmitted. In a simple case, the information is put into words spoken to the receiver. Or the information may be converted into printed text, tables, charts, or graphs given to the receiver. In a more complicated case, the information is encoded into words or images that are then converted into electronic signals sent to the receiver. The **channel** is the medium through which the information is conveyed. It could be air conveying sound waves, paper conveying text and images, or wires or magnetic fields conveying electronic signals. (We will discuss channels in more detail later in this module.) In the opening example, the management had information that Mathias had been hired and when he would start. They wanted the employees in the company to have that information so they put it in a message and sent it to employees.

The receiver reverses the process. She receives the encoded message and then decodes it. That means she converts the message back into information that can be understood. In the opening example, an employee reads the message and knows who has been hired and when he will start. Information has been transferred from managers to employees. In an interactive communication process, the receiver can send **feedback** to the sender to indicate that the message has been received and how it has been interpreted. This can start an interactive back-and-forth exchange that can assure the sender that the message has been received and understood correctly.

The two-person model can be generalized to the case of one person communicating with many others. It could be a person making a presentation to a roomful of people, a manager sending an e-mail to employees, a Facebook post to friends, or a tweet to hundreds of followers.

The following video provides a helpful overview of the communication process and some of the barriers that can arise during communication:

https://www.youtube.com/watch?v=q6u0AVn-NUM

Common Missteps in Communication

Each step in the communication-process model introduces the potential for missteps to occur. In the opening scenario, two e-mail messages were described. They were both internal to the company, but they achieved much different results. What was different about the messages that caused the different outcomes?

The first misstep can occur when the information to be communicated is not encoded correctly. Consider the e-mail sent by management to announce Mathias's appointment. Management had clear information to convey, and a simple e-mail conveyed it.

Mathias's e-mail had a different purpose. He wanted to convey to his superiors that he was following their directions and was working on a plan to cut costs. But when he put the information into text, he didn't encode it well. He wanted to convey that he was working on the problem but had not made any decisions. What he actually conveyed was that he was going to cut costs by whatever means necessary and soon. Because the information was not encoded accurately, the wrong information was sent.

The first step in good communications is being able to clearly and concisely convey information, whether written, spoken, graphic, or numerical. If information is not encoded properly, nothing else matters. Later on we will look at specific suggestions for how to tailor messages to take the needs of the receivers into consideration

Missteps also occur during decoding when the receiver interprets the message differently than the sender intended. In Mathias's case, the message he sent was "I'm thinking about ways to cut costs and I will let you know when I have a plan." But employees interpreted the message as "I'm going to do whatever I have to in order to cut costs."

Because feedback is a message sent in the opposite direction, from the receiver to the sender, all of these problems can occur during feedback. In many cases feedback is not important and is not wanted. Much information that is communicated is intended to keep people informed, and acknowledgement or response is not expected. When management sent the notice about Mathias's appointment it did not expect every employee to respond. Sometimes, though, feedback is important to be certain that both the sender and receiver have the same information and interpret it the same way. The initial sender must be sure that she understands the feedback provided by the sender, asks questions to clarify any misinterpretation, and responds to any questions. The last step in good communication is to be a good listener. In the following sections we will look more closely at the issues of miscommunication and ways to collect feedback.

Formal and Informal Communication Systems

In most organizations there are both formal and informal information systems. **Formal communication systems** are the methods used to convey information necessary for conducting the business of the organization. Formal communications conform to rules and regulations prescribed by the profession or law (for example, formal reporting procedures for tracking injuries in the workplace). This is information that flows within the chain of command or within task responsibilities. The message may be procedures to provide regular progress reports to managers. It may be scheduled meetings to exchange information on the status of a project. Human resources may arrange seminars to convey new policies and procedures. The formal communication system makes sure necessary information flows through the organization and that dissemination of this information is controlled. Not everyone in an organization has access to progress reports or attends project meetings. Formal communication systems ensure that information is available to those who need it and not to others.

Not all communication in an organization is formal, and not all communication is controlled. **Informal communication systems** are outside of the formal system. Informal systems can connect almost anyone in an organization to anyone else. They skip over hierarchical levels and between departments and functions. In the opening scenario we saw how misinformation spread through the informal system can harm an organization. However, informal communication systems are not necessarily disruptive. In many organizations, the informal network is the primary way information is spread and work gets done. There are some organizations where getting a job done depends more on who you know than what you know.

There are two main types of informal communication systems: **social networks** and the **grapevine**.

A **social network** is a system of personal relationships that cross hierarchical, departmental, and organizational boundaries. A simple social network system is shown in the following diagram.

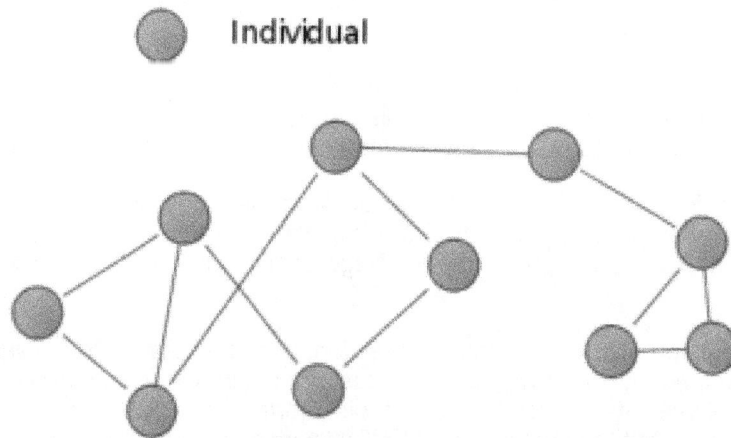

In this diagram of social networks, each circle represents an individual.

In a social network, an individual can reach out to anyone else in his network for information or assistance. Through the linking member, he can also seek help from another group. People with large social networks have access to much information, and linking individuals can spread information through an organization. Linking individuals can be very influential in an organization.

The **grapevine** is how gossip is spread through an organization. Another term for a grapevine is a rumor mill. Almost everyone engages in gossip in some manner, so it is a very effective way of spreading information. In fact, information often spreads faster through the grapevine than through formal information channels. Unfortunately, the information is not controlled, and it can be distorted or even totally fabricated. The grapevine is particularly important when formal communications are inadequate. People don't like to be uncertain about conditions that affect them. When information is not provided by the formal system, they seek and spread information through the grapevine.

Unlike a social network, a grapevine is unstructured and transitory, although the grapevine can follow social network links. Information flows in the grapevine through chance encounters, informal meetings, and overheard conversations. Electronic communication and social media has greatly increased the speed and spread of grapevines.

INTRODUCTION TO TYPICAL COMMUNICATION FLOWS

What you'll learn to do: differentiate between typical communication flows within an organization

How does communication move within an organization? Is there a pattern to the kinds of communication that come from senior management, from middle management and from workers? What do typical information flows tell us about the kind of information that is communicated within the organization? And what does it tell us about who controls the flow of information? This section describes how information in an organization follows established and predictable routes.

TYPICAL COMMUNICATION FLOWS

Learning Outcome

- Differentiate between downward, upward, horizontal, diagonal, and external communication flows.

Organizational Communication Flows

Information can flow in four directions in an organization: downward, upward, horizontally, and diagonally. The size, nature, and structure of the organization dictate which direction most of the information flows. In more established and traditional organizations, much of the communication flows in a vertical—downward and upward—direction. In informal firms, such as tech start-ups, information tends to flow horizontally and diagonally. This, of course, is a function of the almost flat organizational hierarchy and the need for collaboration. Unofficial communications, such as those carried in the company grapevine, appear in both types of organizations.

Downward Communication Flows

Downward communication is when company leaders and managers share information with lower-level employees. Unless requested as part of the message, the senders don't usually expect (or particularly want) to get a response. An example may be an announcement of a new CEO or notice of a merger with a former competitor. Other forms of high-level downward communications include speeches, blogs, podcasts, and videos. The most common types of downward communication are everyday directives of department managers or line managers to employees. These can even be in the form of instruction manuals or company handbooks.

Downward communication delivers information that helps to update the workforce about key organizational changes, new goals, or strategies; provide performance feedback at the organizational level; coordinate initiatives; present an official policy (public relations); or improve worker morale or consumer relations.

Upward Communication Flows

Information moving from lower-level employees to high-level employees is upward communication, as when workers report to a supervisor or team leaders report to a department manager. Items typically communicated upward include progress reports, proposals for projects, budget estimates, grievances and complaints, suggestions for improvements, and schedule concerns. Sometimes a downward communication prompts an upward response, such as when a manager asks for a recommendation for a replacement part or an estimate of when a project will be completed.

An important goal of many managers today is to encourage spontaneous or voluntary upward communication from employees without the need to ask first. Some companies go so far as to organize contests and provide prizes for the most innovative and creative solutions and suggestions. Before employees feel comfortable making these kinds of suggestions, however, they must trust that management will recognize their contributions and not unintentionally undermine or ignore their efforts. Some organizations have even installed "whistleblower" hotlines that will let employees report dangerous, unethical, or illegal activities anonymously to avoid possible retaliation by higher-ups in the company.

Horizontal and Diagonal Communication Flows

Horizontal communication involves the exchange of information across departments at the same level in an organization. The purpose of most horizontal communication is to request support or coordinate activities. People at the same level in the organization can work together to work on problems or issues in an informal and as-needed basis. The manager of the production department can work with the purchasing manager to accelerate or delay the shipment of materials. The finance manager and inventory managers can be looped in so that the organization can achieve the maximum benefit from the coordination. Communications between two employees who report to the same manager is also an example of horizontal communication. Some problems with horizontal communication can arise if one manager is unwilling or unmotivated to share information, or sees efforts to work communally as threatening his position (territorial behavior). In a case like that, the manager at the next level up will need to communicate downward to reinforce the company's values of cooperation.

Diagonal communication is cross-functional communication between employees at different levels of the organization. For example, if the vice president of sales sends an e-mail to the vice president of manufacturing asking when a product will be available for shipping, this is an example of horizontal communication. But if a sales representative e-mails the vice president of marketing, then diagonal communication has occurred. Whenever communication goes from one department to another department, the sender's manager should be made part of the loop. A manager may be put in an embarrassing position and appear incompetent if he isn't aware of everything happening in his department. Trust may be lost and careers damaged by not paying attention to key communication protocols.

Diagonal communication is becoming more common in organizations with a flattened, matrix, or product-based structure. Advantages include:

- Building relationships between senior-level and lower-level employees from different parts of the organization.
- Encouraging an informal flow of information in the organization.
- Reducing the chance of a message being distorted by going through additional filters.
- Reducing the workloads of senior-level managers.

External Communication Flows

Communications do not start and stop within the organization. External communication focuses on audiences outside of the organization. Senior management—with the help of specialized departments

Examples of channels that carry external communication include press briefings, fact sheets, press kits, newsletters, magazines, brochures, news releases, annual reports, invoices and purchase orders.

such as public relations or legal—almost always controls communications that relate to the public image or may affect its financial situation. First-level and middle-level management generally handle operational business communications such as purchasing, hiring, and marketing. When communicating outside the organization (regardless of the level), it is important for employees to behave professionally and not to make commitments outside of their scope of authority.

INTRODUCTION TO BARRIERS TO EFFECTIVE COMMUNICATION

What you'll learn to do: explain barriers to effective communication

Barriers to communication are things that get in the way of a message being received. They could be physical, such as loud music playing, or emotional, such as when a person is too angry or fearful to listen to what another individual is saying. Culture, language, and social status can also represent barriers to effective communication. Managers need to be aware of barriers and how to overcome them to improve the communication process.

BARRIERS TO EFFECTIVE COMMUNICATION

Learning outcomes

- Differentiate between filtering, selective perception, and information overload.
- Differentiate between emotional disconnects, lack of source credibility, and semantics.
- Explain active listening.

Introduction

"I already talked to him about the schedule. Wasn't he listening?" How often have you said words like these (or heard them said about a coworker)? Every time we talk or listen, there are things that get in the way of clear communication—things that interfere with the receiver getting the message from the sender. This interference is referred to as "noise," and there are various types of noise that can cause a message to be misinterpreted.

Barriers to Effective Communication

Common sources of noise are explained in this section. How many of these examples can you remember affecting your conversations with friends, classmates, or coworkers?

Physical Conditions

Sometimes "noise" is just exactly that—loud or distracting sounds that make it impossible to hear or concentrate. Or the general level of background noise can be so intense that it is hard to focus for long on one particular voice. A room may be so hot or so cold that people can't get comfortable and cannot pay attention. Outside activities may be a distraction to those with a view out windows. Finally, it may be lunchtime or too close to quitting time to keep people focused. Fortunately, with some awareness and advance planning, physical barriers to effective communication are some of the easiest to overcome.

Even though the setting is informal, can you identify some signs that indicate that good communication is taking place? Check your ideas with the author's list at the end of this section.

Filtering

Personal and particular experiences color how people view the world and how they communicate. A message sender sees the world through one set of filters (experiences and values) and the receiver sees it through a different set of filters. Each message has to pass, therefore, through at least two sets of filters. The more similar people are in lifestyle, experience, culture, and language, the more similar their mental filters are likely to be and the less distortion should occur. This is why people who come from very different social and economic situations than their audience must work extra hard to say exactly what they mean to avoid confusion. Also, the fewer people involved in the transmission of a message, the greater the chance that it will be received as the sender intended. In business, however, messages may be summarized by a manager and relayed through an administrative assistant who has clarified or edited the message. Messages exposed to many filters should be repeated in various ways to make sure they were understood as the sender intended.

Selective Perception

Selective perception is the tendency to either "under notice" or "over focus on" stimuli that cause emotional discomfort or contradict prior beliefs. For instance, some people live purposefully healthy lifestyles by frequently exercising and eating only nutritious food but still smoke cigarettes. Psychologists believe that they are selectively ignoring the evidence that smoking is dangerous to their health. They have chosen to disregard the information that would make them feel guilty or fearful about this habit. This is called *perceptual defense*. Selective perception can also be *vigilant*, meaning people are extra sensitive to things that are significant to them. If a manager doesn't like a particular employee, for example, she may be super critical of that person's behavior and notice every time he is a minute late to a meeting. On the other hand, a favorite employee coming late to work one morning might elicit concern that she had car trouble. Selective perception introduces bias into the communication process.

Information Overload

We have all been in situations when we felt that too much information was coming at us. When this happens, we feel overwhelmed and fear that we will not be able to retain any information at all. Sometimes it is not just the quantity of communication but the level that causes overload. If the message contains information that is new to the receiver, including processes or concepts that are not familiar, then the chances of overload increase greatly. The sender should break up the message into more palatable or digestible bits and reduce the amount of information that has to be absorbed at any one time. One technique is to make a high-level announcement and then follow it up later with more details. The sender has the primary responsibility to check that the receiver has understood the message. This means that a manager may have to adjust a message to reflect the various experiences of the employees. A new employee may need repeated explanations before beginning an operation, whereas an experienced employee may start rolling his eyes at the same old instructions.

Semantics

Semantics is the study of the meaning of words and phrases. You might hear one person say to another "Let's not argue semantics," meaning he doesn't want to get caught up in trivial and unimportant details or playing with words. But semantics is extremely important in effective communication. There are some semantic rules in English that may trip up non-native English speakers, such as the concept of subject-verb agreement and gender pronouns. These can cause confusion, as seen in the following examples:

- Six man is coming to the meeting on Tuesday. (How many men are coming?)
- Rachel is going to introduce the speaker at the conference. He may be asking you for information about her to make the job easier. (Who is asking for information, Rachel or the speaker?)

When your audience involves people whose native language is not English or individuals of different educational backgrounds, messages need to be direct and clearly stated to help ensure they are understood.

Denotation and Connotation

Confusion can also arise from the use of language by people from different educational levels, culture, and dialect. For instance, the terms *lift* and *braces* denote two entirely different meanings in the United States and in England. A Londoner might reasonably ask her partner if he was planning on wearing braces with his pants.

Some words have a connotation for one group of people that is not shared by another. "That's sick!" could be a compliment or an insult, depending upon the listener. (You probably already know that slang does not belong in written business communications.) Fortunately for all of us, paying attention to the context of the message often reduces confusion. The meaning of *homophones* (buy, by, bye; meet, meat, mete; pair, pare, pear) and *homographs* (read, read; lead, lead) are often easily understood by their context or pronunciation.

Emotional Disconnects

Almost the first thing parents learns is never to try to have a rational discussion with a screaming toddler or an angry teenager. If they wait until the young person is more receptive to what they have to say, the odds of a successful conversation improve dramatically. Adults also experience emotional disconnects that affect the chance of successful communication. For example, when a person is feeling stressed or anxious, an expressed concern is more likely to be interpreted as criticism. Constructive criticism made while an employee is emotionally fragile may be perceived as a personal attack. If possible, it is better to postpone a communication if there is a strong likelihood that the intended receiver will misinterpret it because of his emotional state.

Credibility

In communication, the validity of the message is tied to the reputation of the sender. If the receiver doesn't trust the sender, he will view the message itself with skepticism or suspicion. If the sender is trustworthy, the receiver will likely believe the message despite her personal opinions about that subject. In other words, the trustworthiness of a communication, regardless of format, is heavily influenced by the perceived credibility of the source of that communication. **Source credibility** describes the sender's positive characteristics that affect the receiver's acceptance of a message. A manager's source credibility is based on experience, knowledge, and interpersonal skills. Managers who deal openly and candidly with employees will find it easier to solicit the kind of feedback that tells them whether their message has been understood.

There are better ways to communicate your credibility than reminding everyone of your position.

Message Sent—But Was It Received?

After delivering a message, how does the sender know if the receiver got the message that was intended? Is it the job of the sender or receiver to make sure that the communication has been understood? The answer is that both ends of the communication chain have some responsibility to verify what was both said and heard. In the workplace, however, the manager has the primary responsibility because a main part of her role is to gather and disperse information so organizational goals can be achieved. Managers need to have strategic conversations by asking questions and collecting feedback. One technique to gather feedback is active listening.

Active listening is a communication technique that has been around for many years and that has been used successfully in all types of endeavor—not just business. Parenting classes, marital relationships, public schools, counseling, and tutoring are just some of the areas where active listening is a valued skill. As the name implies, the focus of active listening as a tool for improving communication is on listening rather than talking. (Think here of the expression "You have two ears and one mouth for a reason.") It is a process where the listener sets aside his own thoughts to concentrate more clearly what the speaker is actually saying instead of what the listener *thinks* the speaker is saying.

It takes practice to master the basic techniques of active listening, and you will probably feel awkward applying the technique in the beginning. But because the point is to increase effectiveness by decreasing the possibility of misunderstandings, it is worth a little discomfort. The basic method is briefly summarized in these steps:

- Look at the speaker and make eye contact to indicate that the speaker has your undivided attention.
- Note the body language of the speaker to help process the speaker's message. Is the speaker angry, frustrated, frightened, rebellious, or tentative? Classic signs of anger include arms folded tightly in front of the body or held rigidly at the side. Fright or guilt may be shown by the refusal to look at you directly in the eyes or continually shifting gaze away from the listener's face. The speaker may be feeling confrontational if his arms are on his hips and his legs are spread apart as if ready to move. If the speaker is constantly turning away from you, she may be hiding something and definitely wants to leave. If any of these signs are present, it is probably better to finish the conversation at a later time.
- Don't allow yourself to prepare a response before the speaker has finished his remarks. Keep your mind open and free of judgment until the end.
- Ask questions to verify or confirm what you heard the speaker say. You might even ask a question or make a statement using the very same words as the speaker. "I heard you say that you were unhappy with the way John is managing the team." Or "You said that you feel left out of the decision-making process for the project."
- Wait for the speaker to confirm or to correct your understanding of his message. He may respond with something like "Well, unhappy is too strong a word. I meant that there are times when I disagree with the decisions that John makes." Then you can respond, "OK. You are not completely unhappy. You don't always disagree with John." Here you are confirming your understanding of the speaker's corrected statement.

The other major advantage of active listening (besides preventing misunderstandings) is that you convey to the speakers that you care about them and their opinions. They become empowered to be more proactive because they believe they will get an unbiased hearing. For busy managers, actively listening can be time-consuming and require emotional investment. You really have to interrupt your work to stop and listen. The speaker may become emotional during the attempt to clarify the communication, especially while you are learning the approach. But in the end, you will have earned the trust and respect of an employee, and that is a worthwhile goal.

The answer to what signs in the photo above indicate good communication are as follows:

- well-lit room
- comfortable but upright seating
- listener making eye contact
- one man leaning forward to show interest
- noiseless background

Did you find others?

INTRODUCTION TO CHANNELS OF BUSINESS COMMUNICATION

What you'll learn to do: differentiate between typical channels of business communication

The previous section looked at common barriers to communication. This section will identify different methods, or channels, of communication and how to tailor a message to its audience. What is the best way to tell your boss that you are leaving to work for a competitor? How would you communicate your concerns about a disappointing customer reaction to a rollout of a new product? Would you send a business memo to invite a coworker to join you for lunch? Effective communicators have mastered the skill of choosing the channel and style that is most appropriate for the message.

CHANNELS OF BUSINESS COMMUNICATION

Learning Outcomes

- Differentiate between face-to-face, written, oral, web-based, and other typical channels of business communication.
- Explain the importance of tailoring the message to the audience.

Introduction

Business communication is held to a higher standard than everyday communication. The consequences of misunderstandings are usually higher and the chances to recognize and correct a mistake are lower. The barriers to communication and technique for improving communication are the same regardless of where the conversation takes place.

Business Communication Channels

A communication channel is the medium, mean, manner or method through which a message is sent to its intended receiver. The basic channels are written (hard copy print or digital formats), oral or spoken, and electronic and multimedia. Within those channels, business communications can be formal, informal, or unofficial. Finally, communications can be rich or lean.

There's a well-known expression that goes "It's not what you say, it's how you say it." It's really both.

Channel richness refers to the amount and immediacy of information that can be transmitted. Face-to-face communication is very high in richness because it allows information to be transmitted with immediate feedback. A tweet is very low in richness because it allows only 140 characters to be transmitted with no feedback. On the other hand, face-to-face communication is limited to one person communicating with a few other people in close proximity, whereas a tweet can go out to thousands of followers around the world. The following diagram shows the richness of different types of communication.

Different types of communication media have varying channel richness.

Oral Communications

Oral channels depend on the spoken word. They are the richest mediums and include face-to-face, in-person presentations, mobile phone conferences, group presentations, telephone, video meetings, conferences, speeches, and lectures. These channels deliver low-distortion messages because body language and voice intonation also provide meaning for the receiver. They allow for immediate feedback of the communication to the sender. They are also the most labor-intensive channels in terms of the number of people involved in the transaction. Oral channels are generally used in organizations when there is a high likelihood of the message creating anxiety, confusion, or an emotional response in the audience. For instance, a senior manager should address rumors about layoffs or downsizing in face-to-face meetings with management staff. This allows the receiver (audience) to get immediate clarification and explanations, even if the explanation is a simple but direct: "At this time, I just don't know."

Oral communications are also useful when the organization wants to introduce a key official or change a long-established policy, followed up with a written detailed explanation. Senior managers with high credibility usually deliver complex or disturbing messages. For example, a senior manager will usually announce plans to downsize in person so that everyone gets the same message at the same time. This will often include a schedule so people know when to expect more details.

Written Communications

Written communications include e-mails, texts, memos, letters, documents, reports, newsletters, spreadsheets, etc. (Even though e-mails are electronic, they are basically digital versions of written memos.) They are among the leaner business communications. With written communications, the writer must provide enough context that the words can be interpreted easily. The receiver should be alert for ambiguity and ask for clarification if needed. An e-mail sender cannot take receipt for granted. Most people receive too much e-mail and sort and filter it quickly, sometimes incorrectly.

Written messages are effective in transmitting large messages. Humans are limited in the amount of data they can absorb at one time. Written information can be studied over time. Reports can include supporting data and detailed explanations when it is important to persuade the receiver about a course of action. Written communications can be carefully crafted to say exactly what the sender means. Formal business communications, such as job offer letters, contracts and budgets, proposals and quotes, should always be written.

Electronic (Multimedia) Communications

Television broadcasts, web-based communications such as social media, interactive blogs, public and intranet company web pages, Facebook, and Twitter belong in this growing category of communication channels. Electronic communications allow messages to be sent instantaneously and globally. People can talk face-to-face across enormous distances. Marketing and advertising can be targeted to many different types of customers, and business units can easily communicate in real time. This is especially important when customers must be advised of product recalls or security issues.

Although extremely effective, the widespread utilization of electronic communications for business purposes can also be risky. In recent years, the private communications and customer files of many large corporations have been hacked and their data stolen. In 2016, New Jersey Horizon Blue Cross Blue Shield was fined $1.1 million for failing to safeguard the personal information of medical patients. The company stored unencrypted sensitive data including birth dates and Social Security numbers on laptops that were stolen out of their main offices.

MAJOR TYPES OF BUSINESS COMMUNICATION CHANNELS		
TYPE OF CHANNEL	ADVANTAGES	DISADVANTAGES

Oral communications	Build relationships and trust; accelerate decision making due to immediate feedback	Spontaneous nature may lead to unwise statements, people are unable to refer to the communication once it is said unless a record is made.
Written communications	Message can be revised for exactness; can be archived for reference; can be studied. Appropriate for legal and formal business functions.	Message is static; sender does not receive immediate feedback. Hard for the sender to gauge if the receiver has understood.
Multimedia	Instant, global, and adaptable to multiple targets.	Technical difficulties and hack attacks threaten the security of organizations and their customers/clients.

Which Channel Is Best?

Quite simply, the best channel is the one that most effectively delivers the message so that it is understood as the sender intended. Nuanced or emotionally charged messages require a rich medium; simple, routine messages don't need the personal touch. If you want to advise your department that at 2 p.m. you want to have a five-minute stand-up meeting in the hallway outside of your office to congratulate them on meeting a goal, then send a quick e-mail. You really don't want people to reply with questions. E-mail is a lean medium but works very well when the content of the message is neither complex nor emotionally charged. On the other hand, a telephone call is a more appropriate channel to apologize for having to cancel a lunch date. The speaker can hear the sincerity in your voice and can express their disappointment or offer to reschedule.

A good rule of thumb is the more emotional the context of the message, the richer the medium should be to deliver the message. But remember—even face-to-face business meetings can be followed up with a written note to ensure that both parties are truly on the same page. If a meeting results in assignments or agreements, then a written note will be useful documentation for future reference.

Tailoring a Message to an Audience

Have you ever had to converse with a young child and really needed him to listen to you? You probably knelt down so that you were at eye level. You may have even put your hand gently on his arm to focus his attention on you. Speaking clearly and slowly in words that you knew he understood, you made exaggerated facial gestures of fear or surprise or happiness to emphasize your points. In brief, you tailored your message to your audience so that it would be effective.

Although the channel of communication you select to transmit your message is important, so also is knowing the intended audience. Effective communicators seem to instinctively adjust their styles to their audience, but it is a skill that can also be learned. The way the information is conveyed should complement the audience, whether it is one person or a roomful of people. Three factors are involved in tailoring a message: the sender, the message itself, and the audience.

Steve Jobs, one of the founders of Apple, was a great communicator who used his passion, focus, and storytelling ability to make his presentations memorable.

The Sender

For the majority of everyday business communications, a manager needs only to focus on presenting a professional image. On different occasions, she may want to present herself as a serious and responsible leader, a technical expert, or informally casual. But when uncertain what a situation calls for, always err on the side of professionalism. Studies have shown that an audience reacts initially to the demeanor of the speaker and not to what is being said. If you appear nervous, your audience will pick up on that and become nervous as well.

The Message

The first step in tailoring a message, of course, is to choose the right communication channel. But even then, there are questions to ask about the message itself that will influence how it is presented. Some of these questions are listed below:

- **Which channel suits the content best?** A critical or urgent message may demand the fastest channel, whether that is in-person, text-message, or e-mail. A scripted presentation requires planning and preparation. Businesses can use journalists or Twitter for brief announcements. If you want to demonstrate how your organization does something, clarify values, or construct common meanings for people across an organization, you might tell a memorable story in either an oral or written presentation. Decide which channel best suits the content.
- **What do you want to achieve by sending the message?** Is it intended to persuade or to inform? Are you just reassuring your boss that everything is on track? A face-to-face communication is much more effective than an e-mail or report in trying to convince someone to change a belief or a behavior.
- **Does the message require interaction from the audience or is it more of an "information dump"?** Don't try to deliver a rationale for a $1 million investment in a phone call, especially if you need supporting evidence. Allow enough time to answer all questions.
- **Will visual aids help the message or will they just distract from it?** Arguments that a new computer software program will increase your department's productivity will need to be backed by solid evidence presented in charts or graphs. But excessive or unfocused visuals may irritate senior-level managers who want just the concise summation and the triple bottom line (economic, social and environmental impacts).
- **Do you have to establish your credibility?** Does the audience know you? Are you speaking to people who know more than you about the topic? The answers to these questions will influence how you design your message.
- **Most importantly, before deciding on a communication, ask yourself why the audience should care about it.** When you know, then tailor the communication so that it answers that question. The story of United Airlines Flight 4311 is example of a CEO who failed to identify his primary audience and ask himself what they cared about before he spoke. In June of 2017, a seated passenger was informed by the flight attendants that his seat was needed and that he would have to leave the plane. He refused to give up his seat and was eventually dragged, literally kicking and screaming, off the plane. The video immediately went viral. In an effort to prevent a public relations nightmare, the CEO initially blamed the passenger and defended the actions of the United Airlines employees and security guards. When public outrage grew and customers threatened a boycott, the CEO finally realized that the first communication should have focused not on the employees and the company but on the passenger, who was, after all, a paying customer.

The Audience

You can't tailor your communication to the sender if you don't know your audience. Here are some questions to consider when getting to know your audience.

- **How big is your audience?** Is it one person or a large group? One individual means getting "up close and personal" as opposed to a conference room. If a large group, is it diverse or fairly homogenous? Do you need language translators or signers for the hearing impaired?
- **What is the status of your audience?** Is the audience mostly senior-level managers, peers, or subordinates? Your body language, presentation, and formality will vary depending upon the status of the group. Although subordinates may be more easily put at ease with an informal, relaxed approach, high-level managers usually want to get straight to the point and move on to the next thing.
- **Can you establish empathy with the audience?** The more the audience trusts you, the easier it will be to retain their attention. Notice the audience—are people shifting around, avoiding eye contact, yawning, or are they nodding in agreement and focused? You may have to adapt your message to meet the mood of the audience.

PUTTING IT TOGETHER: COMMUNICATION

As you'll recall, we started this module with a conversation between Tony and Sandra. Tony was upset with James, his employee, because James was not completing a new production schedule. Let's fast forward about three weeks and catch up with Tony and Sandra after another departmental meeting.

Sandra catches Tony and asks, "Hey Tony, how are things going with James? I sure was surprised that you were having trouble with him."

Tony gets a sheepish grin on his face and says, "You know what Sandra? You were right! I finally brought James into my office and asked him why he was ignoring my requests. He got a really confused look on his face and said he had no idea what I was talking about. He knew that I had asked

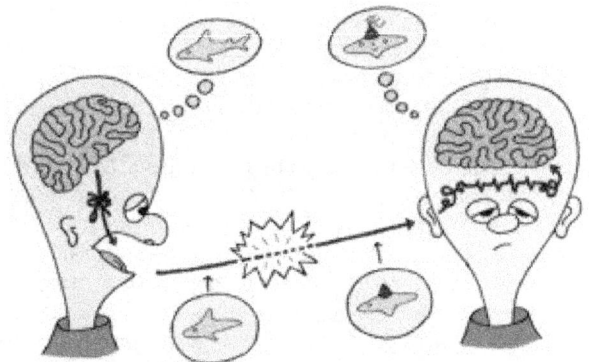

Good communication requires the speaker and the hearer to understand the message the same way.

about the production schedule a couple of times, but he didn't assume that meant I wanted him to prioritize that above other projects."

Tony can see that Sandra is relieved. He goes on to tell her that a couple days after he spoke with James, he came across an article on effective communication.

Tony remembered that effective communication means that the receiver understands the message as intended by the sender. If that doesn't happen, then real communication didn't occur. There are many barriers to effective communication, as you have learned in this module. A good communicator must be aware of the medium through which the message is being transmitted as well as the noise that exists in that environment.

The tools you have learned in this module will make you a better communicator in every aspect of your life. And being a better communicator will make you a better manager.

MODULE 15: CONTROL

WHY IT MATTERS: CONTROL

Why does a manager need to understand the methods and need for control within an organization?

Dana is a recent graduate who was selected to be part of ABC Corporation's management training program. She has her master's degree in engineering and wants to become a project manager in the company's research and development division. She receives her training schedule and syllabus and notices that a large portion of the program is devoted to understanding income statements, balance sheets, and cash flow statements. Given that she has no desire to ever work in finance, Dana questions the need to focus so much on financial management.

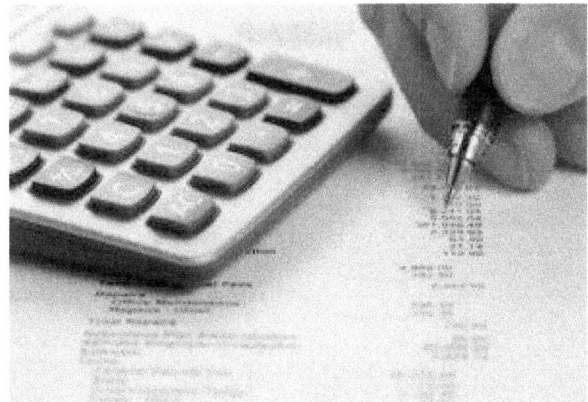

Why do you think that Dana's program contains such a high degree of focus on financial concepts? In fact, many of the most highly regarded corporate training programs have a similar focus.

Thinking back to the P-O-L-C framework that we've used throughout this course, you'll remember that the C stands for control. One of the key functions of a manager is to ensure that all parts of the organization are working to achieve the overall strategic objectives of the company. Properly designed and implemented controls are the method by which managers carry out this responsibility.

In this module you will learn about business control processes and other tools that are extremely important for managerial success. Become familiar with these various tools—they will serve you well in the future.

INTRODUCTION TO CONTROL IN THE BUSINESS SETTING

What you'll learn to do: explain what control means in a business setting and why it is needed

Control can mean a lot of things to different people. In a business setting, it means guiding the activities, employees, and processes of an organization to reach goals, prevent errors, and abide by the law. There are various styles, types, and levels of organizational control. A good manager applies the best combination of these elements, based on the needs and culture of the company, to successfully run the organization.

WHAT DOES CONTROL MEAN IN THE BUSINESS SETTING?

Learning Outcomes

- Explain what control means in a business setting.
- Describe the benefits and costs of organizational control.

Control in general is a device or mechanism used to regulate or guide the operation of a machine, apparatus, or system. Control in a business setting, or **organizational control**, involves the processes and procedures that regulate, guide, and protect an organization. It is one of the four primary managerial functions, along with planning, organizing, and leading.

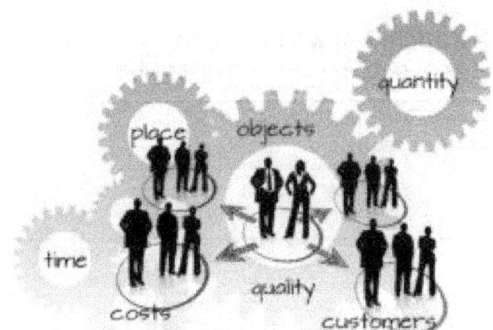

One common type of control companies use is a set of financial policies. These policies may not be communicated to all employees, but they exist for all but the smallest firms. Controls start with managing cash. For example, controls limit check-writing authority and the use of company credit cards. For example, a firm may require two signatures on checks more than $10,000 or have one person to log journal entries and another person to review the entries. These policies help prevent fraud and errors as well as monitor whether company goals are being met. In larger companies, each department manager submits an annual budget and profit-and-loss statements.

The most common style, or approach, of organizational control is **top-down** control. With top-down control, decisions are made by high-level executives, and information flows down to the lower-level employees of the organization.

The three types of organizational control include the familiar feedback, proactive, and concurrent controls. We'll talk about these more later, but first, let's explore some of the benefits and disadvantages of organizational control.

Implementing Organizational Control

Organizational control involves developing rules, procedures, or other protocols for directing the work of employees and processes as well as monitoring the work. Organizational control is an important function because it helps identify errors and deviation from standards so that corrective actions can be taken to achieve goals. The purpose of organizational control is to ensure that a specific function is performed according to established standards.

Benefits

Organizational control has many varied benefits, including improved communication, financial stability, increased productivity and efficiency, help in meeting annual goals, improved morale, legal compliance, improved quality control, and fraud and error prevention.

Controls help to better define an organization's objectives so that employees and resources are focused on them. They safeguard against misuse of resources and facilitate corrective measures. Having good records means management will better understand what happened in the past and where change can be effective.

All businesses need controls. Even sole proprietor businesses must keep records for tax reporting. Public companies are legally required to have extensive controls to protect stockholders, and good controls help a company to raise funds through stock and debt issuance.

Employee morale may be higher when workers see that management is paying attention and knows what it is doing. As an earlier module discussed, better morale means better productivity. Better controls can mean more freedom and responsibility for employees. Management is able to step back a little, knowing that the controls will flag any exceptions.

Toyota has made control a competitive advantage. As an article in the Harvard Business Review says, "Toyota's way is to measure everything—even the noise that car doors make when they open and close as workers perform their final inspections on newly manufactured automobiles." (Note: Thomas A. Stewart and Anand P. Raman, "Lessons from Toyota's Long Drive," Harvard Business Review, July–August 2007, https://hbr.org/2007/07/lessons-from-toyotas-long-drive.) After bad publicity over unusual brake issues, Toyota was again at the top of Consumer Reports' 2016 reliability report. (Note: Michelle Naranjo, "CR's Car Reliability Survey Reveals Shuffles in Brand and Model Rankings," Consumer Reports, October 24, 2016, https://www.consumerreports.org/car-reliability/car-reliability-survey-2016/.)

Disadvantages

Even the simplest control is an added expense. Some systems can be very expensive, so management must weigh the cost versus the benefit for each control. Banks spend billions on controls, but it is worthwhile for the large banks, because they handle trillions and their profits are still in the billions.

A control mentality can lead to overstaffing and unsustainable costs for some businesses. Community banks, for example, feel the burden of new regulations on the banking industry more heavily than the largest nationwide banks. Research from the Federal Reserve Bank of Minneapolis, Minnesota, and quoted in the New York Times "suggests that adding just two members to the compliance department would make a third of the smallest banks unprofitable." (Note: Marshall Lux and Robert Greene, "Dodd-Frank Is Hurting Community Banks," New York Times, last updated April 14, 2016, https://www.nytimes.com/roomfordebate/2016/04/14/has-dodd-frank-eliminated-the-dangers-in-the-banking-system/dodd-frank-is-hurting-community-banks.)

A less obvious expense is maintaining the controls. Systems need continuous updating as the organization changes. If they are not maintained, the controls may become ineffective.

Controls can become a blind spot for management. Overreliance on controls may lead to relaxation in supervision and allow manipulation of accounts and assets. Employees tend to follow the letter of rules, not the intent, so management needs to check in regularly on how controls are actually operating.

A rigid implementation may lead to a slowdown in the operation of the business. At Freddie Mac, a financial services company, the new product approval process required 25 signatures and took more than a year. The new opportunities in the market disappeared before products could be approved.

The wrong controls may expose the firm to more errors and fraud. And employees will be frustrated if the controls are cumbersome.

INTRODUCTION TO THE CONTROL PROCESS

What you'll learn to do: explain the basic control process and monitoring points

Controlling activities and behaviors is a dynamic process, a cycle of repeated corrections. The steps in the control process will be repeated in the course of production activities. The categories of control, based on the perspective of time, include feedback, concurrent, and proactive controls. These use past and present information or future projections to improve an activity. Managers use all of these controls to manage their business.

THE CONTROL PROCESS

Learning Outcomes

- Explain the basic control process.
- Differentiate between feedback, proactive, and concurrent controls.

The proper performance of the management control function is critical to the success of an organization. After plans are set in place, management must execute a series of steps to ensure that the plans are carried out. The steps in the basic control process can be followed for almost any application, such as improving product quality, reducing waste, and increasing sales. The basic control process includes the following steps:

1. **Setting performance standards:** Managers must translate plans into performance standards. These performance standards can be in the form of goals, such as revenue from sales over a period of time. The standards should be attainable, measurable, and clear.
2. **Measuring actual performance:** If performance is not measured, it cannot be ascertained whether standards have been met.
3. **Comparing actual performance with standards or goals:** Accept or reject the product or outcome.
4. **Analyzing deviations:** Managers must determine why standards were not met. This step also involves determining whether more control is necessary or if the standard should be changed.
5. **Taking corrective action:** After the reasons for deviations have been determined, managers can then develop solutions for issues with meeting the standards and make changes to processes or behaviors.

Consider a situation in which a fictional company, The XYZ Group, has suffered a decrease in the profits from its high-end sunglasses due to employee theft. Senior executives establish a plan to eliminate the occurrence of employee theft. It has been determined that the items are being stolen from the company warehouse. The executives establish a goal of zero thefts ($0) within a three-month period (Step 1). The company currently loses an average of $1,000 per month due to employee theft.

To discourage the undesired behavior, XYZ installed cameras in the warehouse and placed locks on the cabinets where the most expensive sunglasses are stored. Only the warehouse managers have keys to these cabinets.

After three months, XYZ managers contact the bookkeeper to get the sales and inventory figures for the past three-month period (Step 2). The managers then compare the figures with the previous period, taking into account orders for deliveries, returns, and defective merchandise (Step 3). It has been determined that the company lost $200 the first month, $300 the second month, and $200 the third month due to theft, which is an improvement but short of the goal. Managers then come up with suggestions for making adjustments to the control system (Step 4).

XYZ senior executives approve of the suggestion to institute a zero-tolerance policy for employee theft. Now, if there is evidence that an employee has stolen a pair of sunglasses, that employee's job will be terminated. The employee handbook is updated to include the change, and XYZ executives hold a meeting with all warehouse employees to communicate the policy change (Step 5).

Timing of Controls

Controls can be categorized according to the time in which a process or activity occurs. The controls related to time include feedback, proactive, and concurrent controls. Feedback control concerns the past. Proactive control anticipates future implications. Concurrent control concerns the present.

Feedback

Feedback occurs after an activity or process is completed. It is reactive. For example, feedback control would involve evaluating a team's progress by comparing the production standard to the actual production output. If the standard or goal is met, production continues. If not, adjustments can be made to the process or to the standard.

An example of feedback control is when a sales goal is set, the sales team works to reach that goal for three months, and at the end of the three-month period, managers review the results and determine whether the sales goal was achieved. As part of the process, managers may also implement changes if the goal is not achieved. Three months after the changes are implemented, managers will review the new results to see whether the goal was achieved.

The disadvantage of feedback control is that modifications can be made only after a process has already been completed or an action has taken place. A situation may have ended before managers are aware of any issues. Therefore, feedback control is more suited for processes, behaviors, or events that are repeated over time, rather than those that are not repeated.

Proactive control

Proactive control, also known as preliminary, preventive, or feed-forward control, involves anticipating trouble, rather than waiting for a poor outcome and reacting afterward. It is about prevention or intervention. An example of proactive control is when an engineer performs tests on the braking system of a prototype vehicle before the vehicle design is moved on to be mass produced.

Proactive control looks forward to problems that could reasonably occur and devises methods to prevent the problems. It cannot control unforeseen and unlikely incidents, such as "acts of God."

Concurrent control

With concurrent control, monitoring takes place during the process or activity. Concurrent control may be based on standards, rules, codes, and policies.

One example of concurrent control is fleet tracking. Fleet tracking by GPS allows managers to monitor company vehicles. Managers can determine when vehicles reach their destinations and the speed in which they move between destinations. Managers are able to plan more efficient routes and alert drivers to change routes to avoid heavy traffic. It also discourages employees from running personal errands during work hours.

In another example, Keen Media tries to reduce employee inefficiency by monitoring Internet activity. In accordance with company policy, employees keep a digital record of their activities during the workday. IT staff can also access employee computers to determine how much time is being spent on the Internet to conduct personal business and "surf the Web."

The following diagram shows the control process. Note that the production process is central, and the control process surrounds it.

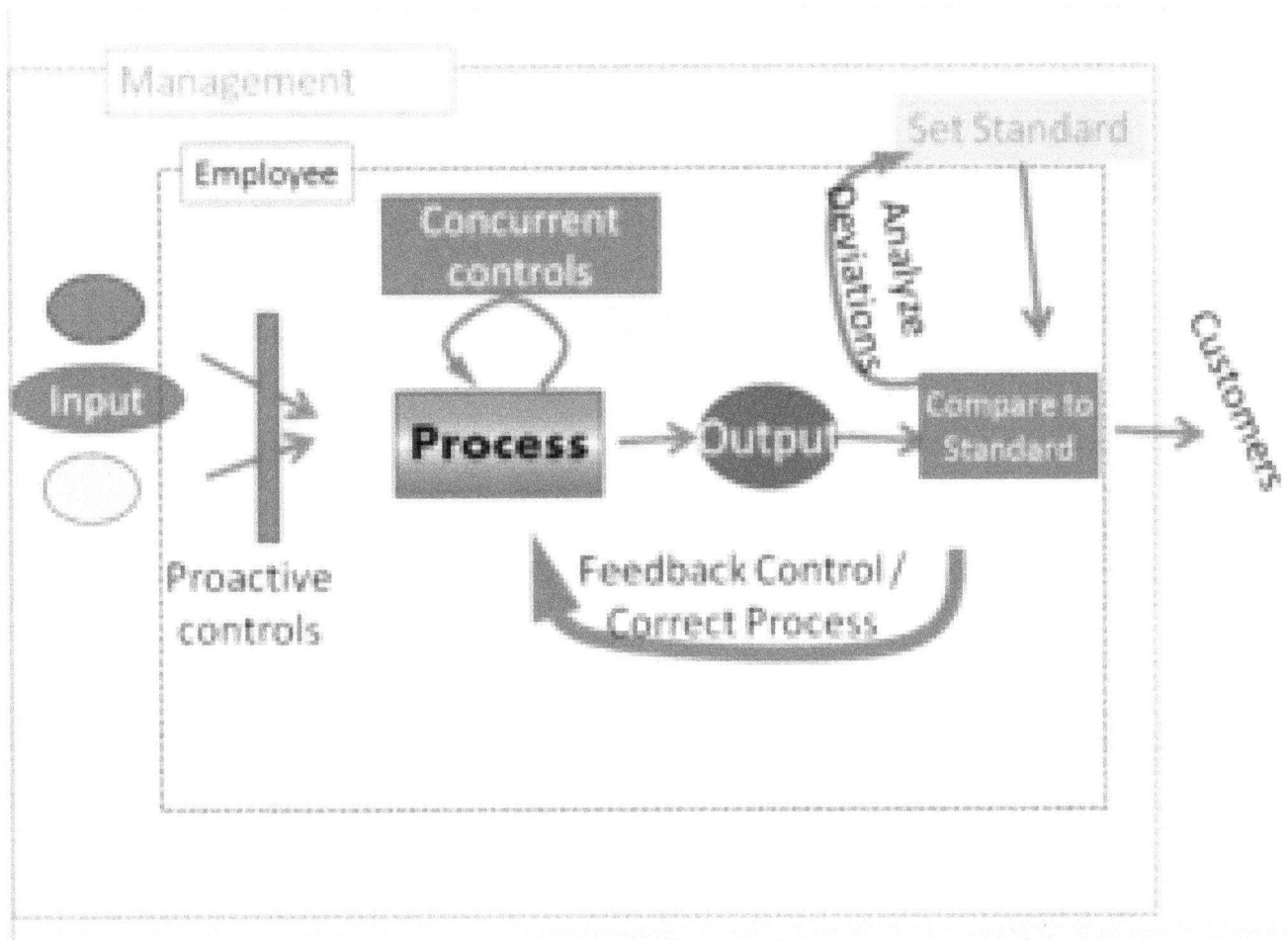

The control process

INTRODUCTION TO LEVELS AND TYPES OF CONTROL

What you'll learn to do: describe the different levels and types of control

In management, there are varying levels of control: strategic (highest level), operational (mid-level), and tactical (low level). Imagine the president of a company decides to build a new company headquarters. He enlists the help of the company's officers to decide on the location, style of architecture, size, etc. (strategic control). The project manager helps develop the project schedule and budget (operational control). The general contractor directs workers, orders materials and equipment for delivery, and establishes rules to ensure site safety (tactical control).

Control can be objective or normative. Objective control involves elements of the company that can be objectively measured, such as call volume, profitability, and inventory efficiency. Normative control means employees learn the values and beliefs of a company and know what's right from observing other employees.

LEVELS AND TYPES OF CONTROL

Learning Outcomes

- Differentiate between strategic, operational, and tactical controls.
- Differentiate between top-down, objective, and normative control.

Strategic Control

Managers want to know if the company is headed in the right direction and if current company trends and changes are keeping them on that right path. To answer this question requires the implementation of strategic control. Strategic control involves monitoring a strategy as it is being implemented, evaluating deviations, and making necessary adjustments.

Strategic control may involve the reassessment of a strategy due to an immediate, unforeseen event. For example, if a company's main product is becoming obsolete, the company must immediately reassess its strategy.

Implementing a strategy often involves a series of activities that occur over a period. Managers can effectively monitor the progress of a strategy at various milestones, or intervals, during the period. During this time, managers may be provided information that helps them determine whether the overall strategy is unfolding as planned.

Strategic control also involves monitoring internal and external events. Multiple sources of information are needed to monitor events. These sources include conversations with customers, articles in trade magazines and journals, activity at trade conferences, and observations of your own or another company's operations. For example, Toyota gives tours of its plants and shares the "Toyota Way" even with competitors.

The errors associated with strategic control are usually major, such as failing to anticipate customers' reaction to a competitor's new product. BlackBerry had a strong position in the business cell phone market and did not quickly see that its business customers were switching to the iPhone. BlackBerry could not recover.

Operational Control

Operational control involves control over intermediate-term operations and processes but not business strategies. Operational control systems ensure that activities are consistent with established plans. Mid-level management uses operational controls for intermediate-term decisions, typically over one to two years. When performance does not meet standards, managers enforce corrective actions, which may include training, discipline, motivation, or termination.

Unlike strategic control, operational control focuses more on internal sources of information and affects smaller units or aspects of the organization, such as production levels or the choice of equipment. Errors in operational control might mean failing to complete projects on time. For example, if salespeople are not trained on time, sales revenue may fall.

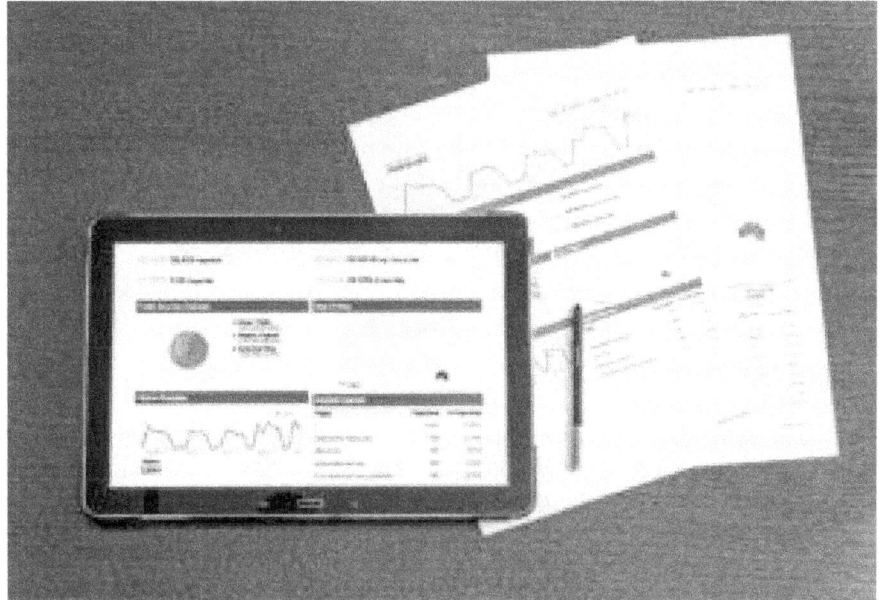

Tactical Control

A tactic is a method that meets a specific objective of an overall plan. Tactical control emphasizes the current operations of an organization. Managers determine what the various parts of the organization must do for the organization to be successful in the near future (one year or less).

For example, a marketing strategy for a wholesale bakery might be an e-commerce solution for targeted customers, such as restaurants. Tactical control may involve regularly meeting with the marketing team to review results and would involve creating the steps needed to complete agreed-upon processes. Tactics for the bakery strategy may include the following:

- building a list of local restaurants, hotels, and grocery stores
- outlining how the bakery website can be used to receive orders
- personally visiting local executive chefs for follow-up
- monitoring the response to determine whether the sales target is met

Strategic control always comes first, followed by operations, and then tactics. For example, a strategy to be environmentally responsible could lead to an operations decision to seek Leadership in Energy and Environmental Design (LEED) certification. This is a program that awards points toward certification for initiatives in energy efficiency, such as installing timed thermostats, using occupant sensors to control lighting use, and using green cleaning products. The tactical decision is deciding which energy-efficient equipment to purchase. At each level, controls ask if the decisions serve the purpose: actual energy savings, the LEED certification, and acting responsibly for the environment.

Top-Down Controls

Top-down controls are also known as bureaucratic controls. Top-down control means the use of rules, regulations, and formal authority to guide performance. It includes things such as budgets, statistical reports, and performance appraisals to regulate behavior and results. Top-down control is the most common process, where

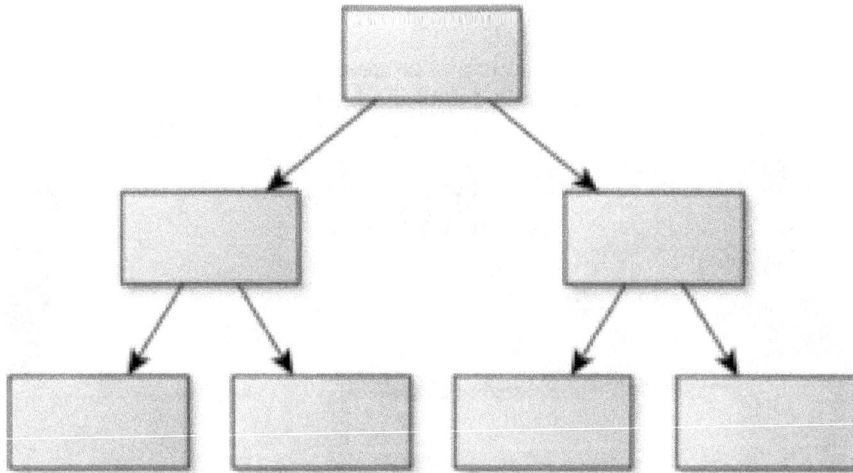

senior executives make decisions and establish policies and procedures that implement the decisions. Lower-level managers may make recommendations for their departments, but they follow the lead of senior managers.

Advantages: With top-down control, employees can spend their time performing their job duties instead of discussing the direction of the company and offering input into the development of new policies. Senior executives save time by not explaining why some ideas are used and not others. Heavily regulated businesses may find this approach to be most beneficial.

Disadvantages: The top-down approach has its drawbacks. The lower levels of a company are in touch with customers and recognize new trends or new competition earlier than senior management. A heavy-handed top-down approach may discourage employees from sharing information or ideas up the chain of command.

Objective and Normative Control

Objective control is based on facts that can be measured and tested. Rather than create a rule that may be ambiguous, objective controls measure observable behavior or output. As an example of a behavioral control, let's say that a store wants employees to be friendly to customers. It could make that a rule as stated, but it may not be clear what that means and is not measurable. To make that goal into an objective control, it might specify, "Smile and greet anyone within 10 feet. Answer customer questions."

Output control is another form of objective control. Some companies, such as Yahoo, have relaxed rules about work hours and focus on output. Because programmers' output can be measured, this has worked well, whether an employee works the traditional 9 a.m. to 5 p.m. or starts at noon and works until 8 p.m.

Normative controls govern behavior through accepted patterns of action rather than written policies and procedures. Normative control uses values and beliefs called norms, which are established standards. For example, within a team, informal rules make team members aware of their responsibilities. The ways in which team members interact are developed over time. Team members come to an informal agreement as to how responsibilities will be divided, often based on the perceived strengths of each team member. These unwritten rules are normative controls and can powerfully influence behavior.

Normative control reflects the organization's culture, the shared values among the members of the organization. Every organization has norms of behavior that workers need to learn. One company may expect employees to take the initiative to solve problems. Another may require a manager's approval before employees discuss changes outside the department. Some topics may be off-base, while others are freely discussed. Companies will have a mix of controls—top-down, objective, and normative.

INTRODUCTION TO THE NEED FOR A BALANCED SCORECARD

What you'll learn to do: explain the need for a balanced scorecard

Just as humans have different systems that interact to make up a person's overall health, organizations have many different components that contribute to organizational health. Though we tend to focus on symptoms to know whether we're healthy or not, it's a good idea to have regular physical exams to make sure we're not missing any health red flags. In the case of an organization, this is where a balanced scorecard comes in. A balanced scorecard is the health checklist, monitoring and measuring the health of the company.

THE NEED FOR A BALANCED SCORECARD

Learning Outcomes

- Identify the four typical components of the balanced scorecard.
- Explain the need for a balanced scorecard.

The Gartner Group has found that more than 50 percent of large US firms use a balanced scorecard (BSC). Moreover, many large firms all over the world use the balanced scorecard in business operations. (Note: What is the Balanced Scorecard? (n.d.). Retrieved September 19, 2017, from http://www.balancedscorecard.org/BSC-Basics/About-the-Balanced-Scorecard) The scorecard system is a reaction to earlier mistakes driven by a narrow focus on financial results. The balanced scorecard adds goals for a company's customers, internal quality, and learning and growth.

The following video helps explain the purpose of the balanced scorecard:

https://www.youtube.com/watch?v=H_6rSK0S8lc

Balanced Scorecard Components

Bain & Company, a global consulting firm, ranks the balanced scorecard fifth of the top 10 management tools used around the world. The balanced scorecard is a system used by organizations to do the following:

- communicate goals
- align daily tasks with strategies
- prioritize projects
- measure performance
- monitor progress

Traditionally, companies have used financial measures to determine their health. The term "balanced scorecard" comes from looking at strategic measures in addition to financial measures for a balanced view of performance. The BSC typically looks at the company from four different perspectives to measure learning and growth, internal business processes, customers' perspective, and financials.

Learning and growth

The learning and growth perspective involves the culture of a company. When managers look at their company from this perspective, they ask themselves questions such as: Are the employees learning? Is the company growing in its capacities? Are we using the latest and best technology and software? Do employees have access to continuing education, and if so, are they taking advantage of the opportunities? Is the company staying ahead of the competition regarding employee talent?

If a company is not learning and growing, it is dying. Learning and growth are necessary to ensure a company maintains or gains a competitive edge. Without it, a company is not sustainable.

Internal business processes

This perspective focuses on how well the company is running. Managers measure quality and efficiency and how to adapt to changing conditions.

Customer's perspective

The customer's view is often measured by surveying existing customers directly. Less obvious is talking to customers who defected, or switched to another brand or product. Harvard Business Review says, "acquiring a new customer is anywhere from five to 25 times more expensive than retaining an existing one." (Note: Amy Gallo, "The Value of Keeping the Right Customers," Harvard Business Review, October 29, 2014, https://hbr.org/2014/10/the-value-of-keeping-the-right-customers) The company must determine whether it is competitive in meeting customers' needs. Without the customer, there is no business.

Financial

Companies need to succeed financially to continue operating. Focusing on other aspects of a company while ignoring its financial state leads to disaster. Measures such as revenue, profit, and ratios such as return-on-equity (ROE) show performance. Other measures are asset turnover, liquidity, gross profit margin, and the current ratio.

Why a BSC Is Needed

Fannie Mae is a financial services company. Before 1992, Fannie Mae's compensation structure was linked to a wide range of performance measures. Beginning in 1992, earnings-per-share growth and growth were the only measures used to set incentive pay for Fannie executives. The incentive pay handed to Fannie executives more than quadrupled after this change, rising from $8.5 million to $35.2 million (1993 to 2000). In 2003, the regulator overseeing Fannie Mae found accounting fraud.

Without a balanced scorecard, executives focus on only one or a few aspects of the organization. A company may be doing well financially but performing poorly in another area. Even if a company is doing extremely well in one area and outperforming the competition, the area that needs the most improvement may destroy the company. For example, a company may exceed customer expectations related to product quality, corporate social responsibility, and customer service; however, its gross profit margin could be low. With a low gross profit margin, the company may not be able to grow, compete, or overcome obstacles.

A BSC forces managers to look at the company as a whole to measure performance and thus more accurately determine the company's overall state. Managers can then work to improve in areas in which it is lacking.

INTRODUCTION TO FINANCIAL AND NONFINANCIAL CONTROLS

What you'll learn to do: explain the use of financial and nonfinancial controls in business

Companies need both financial and nonfinancial controls to achieve goals, remain competitive in industry, and be successful. Financial controls include budgets and various financial ratios. These evaluate the performance of an organization. One important nonfinancial control is quality management.

FINANCIAL AND NONFINANCIAL CONTROLS

Learning Outcomes

- Explain the use of budgets to both control and delegate authority.
- Explain the use of financial ratios (comparisons) as a control method.
- Explain the benefits of quality management.
- Explain the costs of quality management.

Budgetary Control

	Actuals	Budget	Variance
Revenue	12,000	11,000	1,000
Cost of Goods Sold	7,400	7,000	400
Gross Profit	4,600	4,000	600
Admin. Expenses	950	1,000	-50
Selling Expenses	1,050	1,000	50
Financing Costs	900	1,000	-100
Total Expenses	2,900	3,000	-100
Profit Before Tax	1,700	1,000	700
Tax	510	300	210
Profit After Tax	1,190	700	490

A budget is a common type of financial control.

The standard financial reports are the statement of cash flows, the balance sheet, the income statement, financial ratios, and budgets. For most large companies, the first three are required by law. Stockholders need to know how their company is doing. Financial ratios help in investing decisions and in managing the company. They are common but not legally required. Budgets are internal plans, which the company does not typically disclose.

A budget sets a limit on spending and thus is a method of control used to help organizations achieve goals. The budget may be single number setting a manager's spending limit or a plan with limits for detailed items. Departments and the whole organization will develop budgets both for planning and control.

To follow a budget requires discipline. When an expense or desirable pops up, managers must prioritize purchases to stay within budget. In this sense, budgets help control spending and ensure that goals are reached by allocating money to the places where it is needed. Without this planned allocation of resources, there is the risk of spending too much money in one or a few areas, thereby not having enough for other areas.

Budgets can also be used to delegate authority. When an executive assigns a task to a subordinate, the executive needs to release the funds in order for the employee to complete the task. In releasing the funds with an assigned budget, the executive delegates the authority to make decisions regarding the proper use of the funds. The executive can use the budget as a means of monitoring and measuring the performance of the subordinate. With this means of control, the executive may feel comfortable with delegating authority.

Financial Ratios

When people think of management, they often visualize a person giving orders, hiring employees, checking the work of employees, establishing policies, and administering discipline. However, watching the numbers is also an important activity in management. The numbers can be converted to financial ratios, which allow easy comparisons.

Managers use ratios to analyze elements such as debt, equity, efficiency, and activity. For example, a debt ratio compares an organization's debt to its assets. It is calculated as total liabilities divided by total assets. The higher the ratio, the more leveraged the company is. If a company has a high debt ratio (relative to its industry), the company has to spend a significant portion of its cash flow on bills.

The key to understanding ratios is comparing them to relevant benchmarks. The debt ratio for a manufacturing company might typically be 50 percent, meaning debt funds half of the assets. In a bank the typical debt ratio is around 92 percent. The relevant benchmark for a bank is the banking industry average or another bank, not a manufacturer.

Analyzing financial ratios can help managers determine the financial health of the company. Knowing the state of the company in various areas (e.g., inventory, equity, and debt) allows managers to make the changes needed to course-correct and to reach goals.

Quality Management

Have you ever bought a product that was defective? Have you ever been served by a company representative in such a way that it made you want to tell people what a great company it is or give the company five-star ratings on social media? In both cases, quality management was behind the scenes of your customer experience.

Quality management involves controlling, monitoring, and modifying tasks to maintain a desired level of quality or excellence. At the core of quality management is customer satisfaction. Companies pursue the level of quality for their products and services that customers expect and desire. Managers strive to know what customers want, and they manage operations in such a way as to fulfill those desires. Total Quality Management (TQM) and Six Sigma are well-known programs for managing quality.

Benefits: Quality management helps companies please their customers. When customers are pleased, a company can thrive. A simple example of quality management is part inspection. When a part comes down the production line and is complete, an inspector, or quality-assurance technician, checks and tests the part to ensure that it meets quality standards. If it does not, the part is discarded. Thus, quality management helps to ensure that customers are not disappointed so that a company can maintain a good reputation, gain a competitive edge, and ultimately make a profit.

By reducing defects, companies save both time and money. There are fewer returns from customers, and customers are more loyal, reducing the need and cost of acquiring new customers. By catching mistakes early, the production process is not tied up with damaged materials. The final output of acceptable goods increases.

The Systems Sciences Institute at IBM has reported that the cost to fix an error found during beta testing was 15 times as much as one uncovered during design. If the same error was released, the cost to fix the error was up to 100 times more during the maintenance period. (Note: Maurice Dawson, Darrell Burrell, Emad Rahim, and Stephen Brewster, "Integrating Software Assurance in the Software Development Life Cycle (SDLC)," Journal of Information Systems Technology & Planning, 3, no. 6 (2010): 49–53. https://www.researchgate.net/publication/255965523_Integrating_Software_Assurance_into_the_Software_Development_Life_Cycle_SDLC.)

Costs: Regulations are a type of control that society puts on companies. For some large banks, the cost of complying with regulations averages about $12 billion per year. (Note: Saabira Chaudhuri, "The Cost of New Banking Regulation: $70.2 Billion," Moneybeat (blog), Wall Street Journal, July 30, 2014, https://blogs.wsj.com/moneybeat/2014/07/30/the-cost-of-new-banking-regulation-70-2-billion/) That is a hefty control cost until you consider the cost of control failure. Financial losses in the Great Recession were $10 trillion to $12 trillion! (Note: Eduardo Porter, "Recession's True Cost Is Still Being Tallied," Economic Scene, New York Times, January 21, 2014, https://www.nytimes.com/2014/01/22/business/economy/the-cost-of-the-financial-crisis-is-still-being-tallied.html)

A focus on customers often drives managers to great lengths to please customers. In doing so, quality management can become expensive. Typically, companies need to purchase new software and equipment, hire and train employees, conduct studies, and consult with experts to improve the quality of its products and services. These activities add to the cost of doing business. Management must weigh the costs and benefits.

The following video explains the role TQM plays in an organization as a whole:

https://www.youtube.com/watch?v=85Y8iBhzqwk

PUTTING IT TOGETHER: CONTROL

Do you remember Dana from the opening of the module? She is being trained in management with the ultimate goal of becoming a project manager in her company's research and development program. A significant portion of her training is going to be in the area of financial control, and she was questioning the need for it. Having completed this module, how would you answer her concerns? Why will she need financial training as a manager of a nonfinancial area?

It is important to have controls in place to track financial performance versus the plan.

Financial controls are usually the first and most important controls in any business. Using these is a fundamental skill that every manager needs. Thinking back to the P-O-L-C framework, a management team can plan, organize, and lead, but if there aren't adequate controls in place, the organization can still fail to achieve its mission.

This is why every successful organization implements controls. Let's reflect how this might look for Dana at ABC Corporation. The company's senior leadership will come together to plan the overall strategic goals to be achieved. These will be communicated to the various business groups who will plan their objectives to align with the overarching goals.

As part of this business planning process, each group will begin to develop budgets that will support and fund these goals. These financial plans, when developed and approved, are a tool for measuring performance. If individual projects begin to exceed their revenue or cost targets, management can begin to assess what needs to happen. The financial projections become a powerful benchmark to ensure that things are moving along as planned—to control the business.

One would be hard-pressed to overstate the importance of the control function. If a manager is to be successful, he/she must spend time becoming comfortable with the concepts covered in this module.

MODULE 16: GLOBALIZATION AND BUSINESS

WHY IT MATTERS: GLOBALIZATION AND BUSINESS

Why does a manager need to understand the current trends and challenges in the global business environment?

Why do you need to study globalization and business? After all, most people spend their lives working in the country where they were born. If you're not going to travel all over the world for your career, why is this an important topic?

The answer is simple: we live in a world that is growing ever more interconnected. Almost every business, regardless of size or industry, has connections that are global in nature. If you are going to be successful in business, you need to understand how this dynamic will affect you. According to the most recent data (2014), a total of 41 million US jobs—more than 20 percent of all jobs nationwide—are linked to exports and imports of goods and services. (Note: Trade & American Jobs: 2016 Update. (2016, January 8). Retrieved September 19, 2017, from http://businessroundtable.org/resources/trade-and-american-jobs-2016-update)

Apple is a global organization in every aspect of its operations.

For example, you need to think about the differences in culture and how they affect the way business transactions are completed and the nature of professional relationships. Likewise, you need to be aware of both the opportunities and risks associated with global trade.

For example, consider the Apple iPhone. In the company's 2016 fiscal year, it sold more than 211 million devices globally. (Note: "Unit sales of the Apple iPhone worldwide from 2007 to 2016 (in millions)," Statista, 2017, accessed July 30, 2017, https://www.statista.com/statistics/276306/global-apple-iphone-sales-since-fiscal-year-2007/) Compare that with the population of the United States: approximately 330 million people. If Apple were to only sell its products in the United States, the company's opportunities would be severely limited. However, Apple is a global company.

In fact, Apple not only sells its products globally, it manufactures them globally as well. One of the topics you will learn about in this module is the trend toward global supply chains. Apple's supply chain is generally considered to be one of the best in the world. (Note: Lu, C. (2017, April 3). Apple Supply Chain - The Best Supply Chain in the World. Retrieved September 19, 2017, from https://www.tradegecko.com/blog/apple-had-the-best-supply-chain-in-the-world-for-the-last-four-years-here-is-what-you-can-learn-from-it) Keep that in mind as you review this module, and we'll consider their supply chain in more detail at the conclusion of these lessons.

INTRODUCTION TO CURRENT TRENDS IN GLOBAL BUSINESS

What you'll learn to do: describe current trends in global business

Many people don't understand the extent to which globalization influences their daily lives. Do you want an ice cream cone to cool off? Ben & Jerry's is now owned by a Dutch and British firm. Brewing a nice cup of tea for an afternoon pick-me-up? Tata Group of India owns the Tetley Tea Company. Putting on your Nike running shoes for an early morning jog? Most Nike products are produced in China. There are very few large businesses today who can say they are "100 percent American owned and operated."

This section looks at how politics and economics affect business globalization and the factors that influence global competition. It will also examine the role of global supply chains in reducing costs and the need for innovation in the rapidly changing world of business.

CURRENT TRENDS IN GLOBAL BUSINESS

Learning Outcomes

- Describe key characteristics of business globalization.
- Explain global competition.
- Explain global supply chains.
- Give examples of the global nature of innovation.

Many businesses now urge their employees to "Think globally."

What Is Globalization?

Globalization is the process by which the exchange of goods, services, capital, technology, and knowledge across international borders becomes increasingly interconnected. Globalization creates new opportunities for businesses to increase profits by expanding markets and by allowing wider access to resources. On the other hand, globalization also opens domestic markets to new competitors, decreasing demand for local products. Arguing the advantages or disadvantages of globalization is a little like arguing about the weather: it's best just to admit it's here to stay and then figure out how it's going to affect you.

Important Global Trade Agreements and Organizations

After World War II (US involvement spanned from 1941–1945), many countries wanted to expand global cooperation—politically, economically, and socially. Nations agreed to work together to promote free trade and increase global cooperation. They also created regional custom and trade agreements and unions to facilitate economic interdependence. The most important of these organizations, treaties, and trade agreements are briefly summarized below.

The World Trade Organization

The **World Trade Organization (WTO)**, officially formed in 1995, grew out of the **General Agreement on Tariffs and Trade (GATT)**. The WTO oversees the implementation and administration of agreements between member nations. It provides a forum for negotiations and for settling disputes among nations. It also helps developing nations get experience and technical expertise needed to deal with large and very comprehensive trade agreements. Although there are ongoing controversies, its member states account for 97 percent of global trade and 98 percent of the global gross domestic product. The WTO is a truly global organization that deals with agriculture, labor standards, environmental issues, competition, and intellectual property rights.

The World Bank

The **World Bank** is an international financial institution that provides loans for capital programs to developing countries. It is a component of the World Bank Group, which is part of the United Nations system. The World Bank is comprised of 189 member countries represented by a board of governors. Although headquartered in Washington, DC, the World Bank has offices in almost every nation in the world. The organization has two goals to achieve by 2030:

1. End extreme poverty by decreasing the percentage of the world's population that live on less than US $1.90 per day to no more than 3 percent.
2. Promote shared prosperity by fostering the income growth of the bottom 40 percent in every country.

Some recent projects have been aimed at improving primary and secondary school education systems and basic infrastructure, such as building and maintaining safe water supplies and sanitary sewer systems in Africa and parts of Asia. Although the World Bank has come under fire in the past for budget overruns and poor project oversight, its role in promoting economic development has been undeniable.

The International Monetary Fund

The **International Monetary Fund (IMF)**, headquartered in Washington, DC, is comprised of 189 member countries. The IMF works to foster global growth and economic stability by providing policy, advice, and financing to its members. It also works with developing nations to help them reduce poverty and achieve macroeconomic stability. It now plays a central role in the management of balance-of-payments difficulties and international financial crises.

When the IMF was founded, its primary functions were to provide short-term capital to aid the balance of payments and to oversee fixed-exchange-rate arrangements between countries, thus helping national governments manage their exchange rates and prioritize economic growth. This assistance was meant to prevent the spread of international economic crises. The IMF mission changed slightly after 1971, and floating currency exchange rates made it harder to predict the economic stability of a region. Today the IMF plays an active role in shaping and managing economic policy around the world.

Watch the short video that follows for an overview of how the IMF and the World Bank are similar and how they differ.

https://www.youtube.com/watch?v=WG72yk60tbA

Global Trade Policies

In addition to international organizations, countries make agreements among themselves to reach trade advantages. There are four common types of **trade agreements** (also known as **trade blocs**) with different levels of trade dependencies: regional trade agreements (RTAs), custom unions, common markets, and economic unions.

- **Regional trade agreements** establish reciprocal (equally binding) treaties addressing tariffs and trade barriers with member countries. For example, the **North American Free Trade Agreement (NAFTA)** between Canada, the United States, and Mexico allows for tariff reductions or eliminations (free trade). The Association of Southeast Asian Nations (ASEAN) provides for the free exchange of trade, service, labor, and capital across ten independent member nations to provide a balance of power to the economic powerhouses of China and Japan.
- **Customs unions** are arrangements in which countries agree to allow free trade on products *within* the customs union. They may also agree to a **common external tariff (CET)** on imports from the rest of the world. It is the CET that distinguishes a customs union from a regional trade agreement. It is important to note that although *trade* is unrestricted within the union, customs unions do not allow free movement of capital and labor among member countries. An example is the customs union of Russia, Belarus, and Kazakhstan, which was formed in 2010. These countries eliminated trade barriers among themselves but have also agreed to some common policies for dealing with nonmember countries.
- **Common markets** are similar to customs unions in that they eliminate internal barriers between members and adopt common external barriers against nonmembers. The difference is that common markets also allow free movement of resources (e.g., labor) among member countries. An example of a common market is the Economic Community of West African States (ECOWAS), comprised of Benin, Burkina Faso, Cape Verde, Gambia, Ghana, Guinea, Guinea-Bissau, Ivory Coast, Liberia, Mali, Niger, Nigeria, Senegal, Sierra Leone, and Togo.
- **Economic unions** eliminate internal barriers, adopt common external barriers, and permit free movement of resources (e.g., labor). They also adopt a common set of economic policies. The best-known example of an economic union is the European Union (EU). EU members all use the same currency, follow one monetary policy, and trade with one another without paying tariffs.

Watch the video that follows for a brief look at the advantages and disadvantages of free trade among countries.

https://www.youtube.com/watch?v=FYRcfX_tp2U

Key Characteristics of Globalization

Debates about the characteristics and consequences of globalization generally focus on three areas: political, economic, and cultural. Globalization produces both positive and negative outcomes in all these areas.

Political

For thousands of years, treaties have shaped international relations and led to complex alliances. International cooperative bodies such as the United Nations and the World Trade Organization exist today because of the increasing need for political cooperation at the global level. It is impossible for a country to remain isolated from events around the world. People's ideas and expectations are shaped by what they see happening around them. Because of the rapid flow of information to most areas of the world, people are very aware of events taking place around the globe virtually as they happen. However, some nations, such as North Korea, choose to try to isolate themselves from the rest of the world. Others try to control the flow of information within their borders. But technology makes it very difficult to control access to information. Depending on how it is used, technology can both reduce and increase political tensions and military conflicts.

Labor and environmental abuses, traced to corporations taking advantage of weak protectionist laws in some countries, are uniting people who would otherwise not find political common ground. The fear of domestic job losses and concerns about manufacturing safety records in developing countries are becoming popular planks in many political campaigns.

Economic

As a result of globalization, nations with limited resources can access goods and knowledge that help to raise their standards of living. Trade treaties, such as NAFTA and the European Union (EU), lower or abolish tariffs that restrict the flow of products across borders. Nations with rare resources or specific skills are able to focus on their particular business or commercial strengths and sell their goods to a global market. *The Economist* magazine has reported that one billion people have been lifted out of poverty thanks to freer trade policies. (Note: "Towards the end of poverty," The Economist, June 1, 2013, accessed Aug. 5, 2017, https://www.economist.com/news/leaders/ 21578665-nearly-1-billion-people-have-been-taken-out-extreme-poverty-20-years-world-should-aim) On the downside, outsourcing allows businesses to exploit people as sources of cheap labor required to work under substandard conditions. There is also a trend toward the consolidation of businesses in many industries, hurting locally owned businesses and damaging local economies.

Cultural

Globalization has heightened the awareness of the many, many languages, religions, cuisines, arts, literature, and dress that constitute cultures around the world. Some people are worried, however, that cultures around the world are merging into a "world culture" in the process of globalization. As people emigrate to economic powerhouses in the search for higher standards of living, many local traditions and even languages are threatened with extinction. You will read more about this topic later in this module.

Global Competition

Global competition means the competing organizations that serve international customers through enhanced communications, improved shipping channels and supply chains, reduction of trade barriers, and centralized financial institutions. There are small players, such as a local entrepreneur who advertises handmade baby carriers on her website and ships products to other countries through Amazon or directly to the customer. At the other extreme are the giant multinationals such as Exxon Mobil, Apple, McDonald's, and Google.

Why do so many businesses make the financial investments and take the high risks involved with global business ventures? The chief reasons include the following:

- **Increased profits.** A wider market and customer base means the opportunity to sell more goods and services. Some countries have lower taxes, adding to the advantages of moving production there.

- **Greater access to suppliers for materials and at lower costs.** If a cold snap in southern Florida damages the crop of oranges for a season, juice manufacturers can import fruit from another country.
- **Reduced manufacturing costs through access to cheaper labor.** Even Levi's, which still makes its blue jeans in the United States, will pay Wipro $143 million over five years to handle information technology, human resources, finance, and customer service. (Note: McDougall, P. "Bored of the USA?: 'Made In America' Jeans Maker Levi Strauss to Move 500 Jobs Offshore," International Business Times, Nov. 13, 2014, accessed Aug. 5, 2017, http://www.ibtimes.com/bored-usa-made-america-jeans-maker-levi-strauss-move-500-jobs-offshore-1723477) Motorcycle maker Harley-Davidson moved 125 jobs overseas. It is also well-known that Apple has the iPad and iPhone assembled in China by contractor Foxconn, while parts for the devices are made in more than 20 different countries.
- **Social and environmental concerns.** Many US businesspeople are committed to improving the lives of people around the world and working with international organizations to address environmental concerns such as air pollution, clean water, and climate change.

The World Economic Forum has developed the *Global Competitiveness Report* that ranks countries on global competitiveness. It averages the different data points that encourage competitiveness, including such things as a stable government, good educational systems, a developed infrastructure, a strong market for goods and services, efficient labor pools, stable financial institutions, and the ability to innovate and use technology. The top ten most globally competitive countries in 2016 were as follows:

1. Switzerland
2. Singapore
3. United States
4. Netherlands
5. Germany
6. Sweden
7. United Kingdom
8. Japan
9. Hong Kong
10. Finland (Note: Klaus Schwab, ed., "The Global Competitiveness Report, 2016–2017," World Economic Forum, http://www3.weforum.org/docs/GCR2016-2017/05FullReport/TheGlobalCompetitivenessReport2016-2017_FINAL.pdf)

Another ranking that measures global competitiveness is the Ease of Doing Business Index created by the World Bank Group. This index lists the "friendliest" countries for starting commercial ventures. The ranking considers such factors as dealing with construction permits, getting electricity, legal procedures, getting credit, providing investor protections, paying taxes, enforcing contracts, trading across borders, regulatory issues, and transparency in government. (Note: "Ease of doing business index (1=most business-friendly regulations)," The World Bank, accessed Aug. 5, 2017, http://data.worldbank.org/indicator/IC.BUS.EASE.XQ)

Only Singapore, the United States, and the United Kingdom appear in the top ten of both lists.

Two key reasons that these countries are so globally competitive is that businesses operating within their borders have developed the most efficient supply chains and continually innovate to improve operations, products, and services.

Global Supply Chains

A **supply chain** is the network of suppliers and contractors that provide needed materials and services to a business. It includes all of the businesses involved with taking a product from raw material to manufacturing to the transporting and storage of the finished merchandise. Some supply chains include delivery to the consumer and even account for recycling of the used product. **Logistics** means getting materials from one place to another when they are needed and storing them if necessary. It is a popular field of study in many business schools. Logisticians study the latest innovations in shipping, warehousing, rail/road transportation, and airfreight.

For example, let's look briefly at what it takes to produce a typical T-shirt bought off Amazon. The cotton is grown in Texas or Mississippi with the help of agricultural subsidies to the farmers. The raw cotton is shipped to Indonesia (for example), where it is combed and spun into yarn. The yarn is sent to Bangladesh or another country where it's made into whole cloth, washed, and dyed. The cloth is then sent to Colombia (or whichever country has the lowest labor rates) to be sewn into T-shirts. The T-shirts are then shipped back to the United States, where they are printed and distributed to retail stores or Amazon warehouses. Getting the goods to the consumer is the most expensive part of the whole process. Finally, some T-shirts are recycled to East Africa. International agreements to keep tariffs low and improved shipping methods all contribute to making this global supply chain cost-effective. (Note: Aumann, T. "Supply Chain 101 The Journey of a T-Shirt (Updated," July 9, 2014, accessed Aug. 5, 2017, https://www.slideshare.net/TimAumann/supply-chain-101-journey-of-a-tshirt)

A global supply chain exists behind that Amazon package on your doorstep.

In the global economy, managing a supply chain requires dealing with trade and tariff controls, quality regulations, and international relationships. Global supply chain management is highly specialized and complicated. Some firms even do nothing but manage supply chains for other companies, whereas some other companies offer the service in addition to their core activity. For example, the following promotion appears on the FedEx website:

> FedEx Supply Chain is a third-party logistics provider that can support supply chain requirements throughout the product lifecycle, from kitting and product packaging through end-of-life services such as liquidation and recycling. (Note: "Supply Chain Fact Sheet," FedEx, accessed Aug. 5, 2017, http://about.van.fedex.com/our-story/company-structure/supply-chain-fact-sheet/)

The World Bank estimates that 13 percent of the world's gross domestic product (GDP) was earned from moving and storing goods around the planet in 2016.

Today's globally integrated economy makes it necessary for businesses to look as far as possible for both the cheapest and the best resources. The benefit of global supply chains is that businesses can take advantage of low-cost goods and services in foreign locations to bring down operating costs. However, when a business depends on outsourcing, it increases the number of risk factors outside of its control. Tsunamis in Japan shut down an auto assembly plant in Ohio when essential parts couldn't be shipped; severe flooding in Thailand delayed the manufacture of computers for the US market when hard drives failed to appear. Ethical considerations can also be a factor. Even when a firm tries to ensure that the factory owners it contracts with provide fair wages and safe working conditions, abuses still occur, and responsibility is hard to assess. A series of factory fires and disasters killed hundreds of workers in Bangladesh in 2013 and led to the Disney Company canceling the production of its licensed products in that country. (Note: Foroohar, R. "Bangladesh Factory Collapse Will Force Companies to Rethink Outsourced Manufacturing." Time, April 30, 2013, accessed July 30, 2017, http://business.time.com/2013/04/30/bangladesh-factory-collapse-will-force-companies-to-rethink-outsourced-manufacturing/)

Many companies have developed alternate supply chains that take over when the primary sources are unavailable. Managers must always be aware of changes in the economy and in politics that make one source a better choice than another. As energy prices increase in one location and go down in another, for example, shifts can be made to capture these savings. These kinds of efficiencies can occur when companies use technology to innovate their supply chain management systems.

The Global Nature of Innovation

Innovation in business is developing an idea or invention that increases efficiency, raises productivity, or creates value for which customers will pay. An innovation applies information, imagination, and initiative in ways that further the goals of the organization to satisfy customer expectations. Today, virtually every business believes that innovation is necessary for its sustainability and growth.

One of the most powerful drivers of innovation is technology. Not only is technology **scalable** (able to handle increasing amounts of work) but it can also be used to leverage and produce new innovations. Economists traditionally viewed competition as a function of investment, labor and other costs, and the general business climate. Today, competitiveness is based more on the ability to keep up with rapid technological and organizational changes. In a dynamic world, many people use the catchphrase "innovation-led economy."

When your business competes on a global scale, it is more important than ever to adapt and innovate to find ways to sustain a competitive advantage. Doing the same thing forever is not a viable option because the next company is committed to finding the key to take your market share. Blockbuster Video, for instance, failed to recognize customer demand for the new live-streaming innovation for computers, whereas Netflix jumped on the innovative technology and created a user-friendly interface. To succeed, organizations must continually adapt and apply new strategies.

A final example: Nestlé is the largest food and beverage company in the world. In 2016, it launched a crowdsourcing initiative to ease communication among the 36,000 people involved in its supply chain. The initiative, called InGenious, asks employees to communicate with each other about supply chain challenges, problems, and solutions. The company has also developed more than seventy massive open online courses (MOOCs) in multiple languages to educate its supply chain teams worldwide. Nestlé leaders believe that there is no one system that can track all of the agricultural suppliers in the world and how their products are distributed. They are developing "sharing economy" technologies that rely on crowdsourcing to alert the company to potential problems and help them develop solutions.

INTRODUCTION TO TRADEOFFS IN GLOBAL BUSINESS

What you'll learn to do: explain the risk tradeoffs in typical forms of global business

If you wanted to expand your business into the global marketplace, how would you go about it? Would you try to buy a competing company and take it over? Would you start a new business from scratch? Would you try to partner with a competing firm on equal terms? What is the most economical way to penetrate a new market that will provide the greatest profits? These are the very questions that business people all over the world today ask themselves (and their managers). And these are the questions that will be answered in the next section.

RISK TRADEOFFS IN GLOBAL BUSINESS

Learning Outcomes

• Differentiate among the risk tradeoffs for exporting, licensing, alliances, wholly owned affiliates, and global ventures.

Introduction

Improved transportation, low-cost communication technologies, and a growing mass of educated people in countries around the world are contributing to business globalization. This section will focus on some different ways businesses can enter these new global markets. We will look at the benefits and examine the risks of these enterprises.

Franchising, Licensing, and Export/Import Businesses

Export/Import Business

Exporting is the shipping of goods from the domestic country to a foreign country. Importing, the flip side, is bringing in goods from another country. Both types of businesses create local jobs and so are generally favored by governments. Both types of businesses are scrutinized by custom authorities and reported in various categories as part of a country's gross domestic product. The main advantage of an export business is a wider market for the products, as importers can frequently sell goods below the price charged for domestic items. You also retain control over how the product is designed and produced. But as with any international business, there are risks involved with interruptions in the supply chain and fluctuating foreign currencies. There are also increased transportation and tariff costs.

Licensing

Licensing is a strategic alliance made by a **licensor** that allows a **licensee** to provide products or services under the licensor's brand name. Let's say that a food snack manufacturer is prevented by a foreign government from competing against local sellers of food snacks. The company can license its formula to a local producer, thus avoiding the regulations. The licensee makes the product

293

This McDonald's restaurant in Bydgoszcz, Poland, is one of nearly 30,000 McDonald's locations worldwide owned and operated by franchisees.

and returns a percentage of the overall revenues to the outside company, usually in the form of royalties. There are subtle but key differences between franchising and licensing. An important one is that the owner of the license retains complete control over the product. For example, Microsoft licenses its software to users; it does not "sell" the product outright. The software is licensed to customers subject to strict terms and conditions. Licensing has many of the same advantages and disadvantages of franchising. Advantages include avoiding barriers to entering a foreign market, such as tariff and production costs. The major risk is that the licensor trusts their brand to an outside partner, and that partner may eventually become a competitor.

Franchising

Franchising lets businesses enter into foreign markets at a low cost while at the same time offering local entrepreneurs the chance to operate an established business. When McDonald's or Subway wants to expand into a new foreign market, it often arranges for a company or individual to pay for the use of its trademarked or protected resources, such as the plans for buildings, product ingredients, recipes, and management systems. The buyer, or franchisee, agrees to follow product and operating procedures to safeguard the franchiser's brand name and reputation. The franchiser receives a percentage of the revenue from the local operator. The benefits include relative low risk and easy market penetration for the franchiser. Franchising requires very little capital investment or effort on the corporation's side. A locally run franchise can avoid many of the cultural pitfalls facing a foreign-run investment. Risks, or downsides, include a loss of quality control and a lower rate of return than a wholly owned and operated business. The franchiser must also make sure the local manager can implement the required training and quality control measures to safeguard the corporate brand.

Strategic Alliances

Some types of businesses are strategic alliances in which international partners cooperate for mutual gains. Companies agree to combine key resources, costs, risks, technology, and personnel. Each organization sees an opportunity to get something they couldn't get on its own. Examples include joint ventures, affiliates, and subsidiaries. There are two types of strategic alliances: joint ventures and wholly owned affiliates.

Joint Venture

In an international joint venture, two or more companies (usually one foreign and one local) agree to work together on a new project. Each company contributes to the partnership in time, equity, or effort for the development of the project. Sometimes one company buys into an already established firm. Each partner benefits from the arrangement. One partner may hope to widen their market with the help of local experts; the other partner may want access to technology and training in advanced skills. The advantage is that each partner carries part of the burden of costs to start and run the joint company. The disadvantages may include leadership/management power struggles and the fact that profits must be shared. In 2014, Sony of Japan set up joint ventures in China to produce its popular PlayStation. One company produced the software; the other company produced the hardware.

Wholly Owned Foreign Affiliates

A business may decide that instead of partnering with a company in a foreign country to expand its market, it is more efficient to acquire an existing firm. The acquiring company takes full ownership of the acquired company. The advantage is that the company saves on transportation, distribution, and storage costs while gaining local business knowledge through the affiliate's (or subsidiary's) employees. For example, Kraft Foods bought Cadbury, an English confectionary (candy) company. Home Depot bought Home Mart, a popular home-improvement retailer in Mexico. Finally, in 2010 Wal-Mart Stores Inc. spent $2.4 billion to acquire Massmart, a South African retail store much like Wal-Mart with stores throughout Africa.

Greenfield Venture

A different type of foreign investment is called a **greenfield venture**, where a company builds a subsidiary from scratch in a foreign country instead of acquiring an established firm. This is the riskiest type of direct investment but also, if successful, can be extremely profitable because the profits do not have to be shared. The parent company can dictate from the beginning how the company should be managed and developed. But the company must be committed to a long-term association with the market and country it is entering. Large, multinational companies are most likely to use a greenfield strategy to enter a market because of the high start-up costs and the long-term commitment, as well as their experience in negotiating trade barriers. In July 2017, Foxconn, a large electronics manufacturer in Taiwan, announced plans to invest more than $10 billion in a greenfield venture in Wisconsin. The obvious risk with this business structure is that a great difference in the laws between the parent and subsidiary countries can lead to misunderstandings and false assumptions. This is especially true in the handling of intellectual property such as patents, trademarks, and copyrights.

Watch the following video to see some other recent greenfield ventures taking place in the United States.

https://www.youtube.com/watch?v=JhrBrvC35gA

INTRODUCTION TO DIMENSIONS OF CULTURAL DIFFERENCE

What you'll learn to do: explain the dimensions of cultural difference and their effect on global business

Very few managers assume today that because something works in one country, it should work all over the world. Managers are becoming very aware of the effect that culture has on the workforce and on consumer buying patterns. This section examines the work of Geert Hofstede, a Dutch management researcher, who conducted a multiyear, multicountry study to identify ways to describe differences in national cultures and how they affect business.

DIMENSIONS OF CULTURAL DIFFERENCE AND THEIR EFFECT

Learning Outcomes

- Explain the dimensions of cultural difference.
- Identify effects of cultural differences on global business.

Cultural Differences and Global Business

When considering going into international business, managers need to realize that conditions they take for granted may be different in other countries. For example, Wal-Mart's first international expansion was into Mexico. It modeled the Wal-Mart stores in Mexico after its stores in the United States, with a stand-alone store surrounded by large parking lots. But it soon realized this was a problem. Many of the customers rode on buses to the store. This meant customers had to walk through the parking lot to get to the store and could only buy what they could carry back to the bus. To address this, Wal-Mart added shuttle buses that took customers to and from the store.

Difficulties like those faced by Wal-Mart are easy to identify and often are easy to fix. **Cultural differences**, however, also concern deeply held beliefs, values, and customs that are more difficult to identify. Understanding cultural differences is particularly important for managers, because managers must understand their employees to motivate and lead them. Geert Hofstede, a Dutch management researcher, conducted a multiyear, multicountry study to identify ways to describe differences in national cultures. His research included more than 100,000 employees of a global corporation in 40 countries. A later study, called the GLOBE project, included 170,000 managers in 162 countries. These studies identified nine dimensions that describe differences in national cultures.

These dimensions are power distance, uncertainty avoidance, performance orientation, assertiveness, future orientation, humane orientation, institutional collectivism, in-group collectivism, and gender egalitarianism. Let's look at each in more detail.

1. **Power Distance.** Power distance is the degree to which people accept an unequal distribution of power and status privileges. In high power distance countries, there is respect for age and titles, people are expected to follow rules, and there is more tolerance for concentrated power. India, Mexico, and the Philippines have high power distance. The United States, Australia, and Israel have low power distance.
2. **Uncertainty Avoidance.** The degree to which people are uncomfortable with risk, change, and ambiguity is called uncertainty avoidance. In high uncertainty avoidance countries, there is a greater emphasis on rules, structure, order, and predictability. France, Japan, and Costa Rica, for example, are countries with high uncertainty avoidance. The United States, India, and Sweden have low uncertainty avoidance.
3. **Performance Orientation.** Performance orientation is the degree to which innovation, high standards, and excellent performance are encouraged and rewarded. Countries with high performance orientation value materialism and competitiveness, and they expect to invest in training to promote performance improvements. The United States and European countries have high performance orientations; Argentina, Russia, and Greece have low performance orientations.
4. **Assertiveness.** Assertiveness is the degree to which individuals are forceful, confrontational, and aggressive, as opposed to cooperative and compassionate. In high assertiveness countries such as the United States, Germany, and Mexico, communication is direct and unambiguous. Individual initiative is encouraged, and relationships are likely to be competitive. Countries with low assertiveness rankings are Switzerland and New Zealand. Managers in these countries are more likely to look for consensus and cooperative decision making.

5. Future Orientation. The degree to which delayed gratification and planning for the future are valued over short-term gains is called future orientation. Countries with high future orientation encourage investments for future payoffs over immediate consumption. It is similar to the ability of individuals to delay gratification. Canada, Switzerland, and Malaysia have high future orientation; Poland, Argentina, and Russia have low future orientation.

6. Humane Orientation. The degree to which fairness, altruism, generosity, and kindness are encouraged and valued is a measure of a country's humane orientation. In nations with high humane orientation, individuals are responsible for promoting the well-being of others as opposed to the state providing social and economic support. The Philippines, Ireland, and Egypt have high humane orientation; France, Germany, and Singapore have low humane orientation.

7. Institutional Collectivism. Institutional collectivism is the degree to which organizational and societal institutions encourage individuals to be integrated into groups and organizations. In high institutional collectivism countries, collective distribution of resources and collective action are encouraged. Group loyalty is encouraged, even if it undermines the pursuit of individual goals. Sweden, Japan, and Singapore are examples of countries that have high institutional collectivism; Germany, Argentina, and Italy have low institutional collectivism. In the United States, low institutional collectivism has resulted in debates on appropriate work-life balance.

8. In-Group Collectivism. In-group collectivism is the degree to which individuals express pride, loyalty, and cohesiveness in their organizations or families. In countries with high institutional collectivism, individuals identify with their families or organizations and duties and obligations determine behaviors. A strong distinction is made between individuals who are in a group and those who are not. India, Egypt, and China are examples of countries that have high institutional collectivism; Sweden, New Zealand, and Finland have low institutional collectivism.

9. Gender Egalitarianism. The degree to which male and female equality is actualized is called gender egalitarianism. Countries with high gender egalitarianism provide more opportunities for women and have more women in positions of power. Sweden, Poland, and Costa Rica have high gender egalitarianism. Japan, Italy, and Egypt have low gender egalitarianism. In these countries, women generally have lower status at work and in the culture.

In the chart that follows, Germany and Poland are similar in their cultural characteristics.

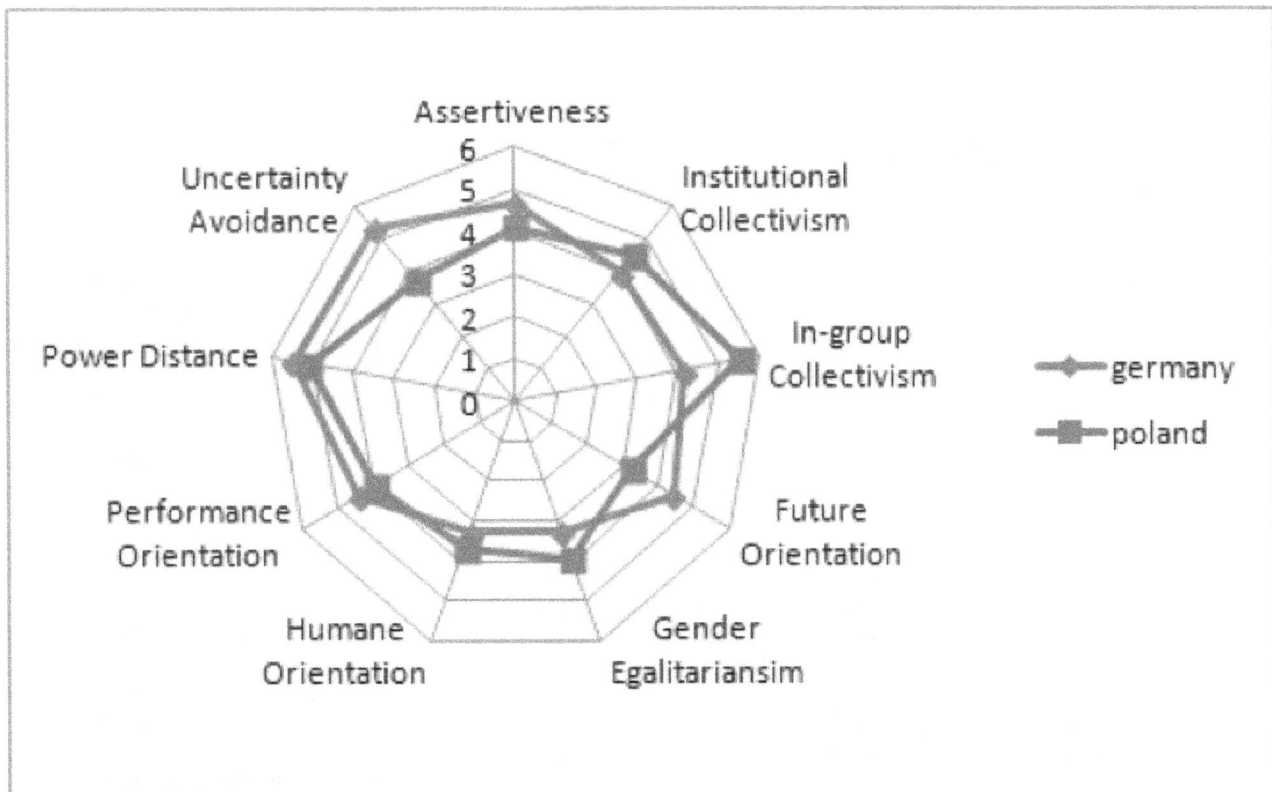

Comparison of cultural characteristics of Germany and Poland using data from GLOBE 2004 study

Effects of Cultural Differences on Global Business

When companies decide to expand internationally, they have to be aware of cultural differences. To be effective, managers need to be attuned to their cultural surroundings. There have been many examples of advertising that included images or phrases that were culturally offensive. For example, Pepsi lost its dominant market share to Coke in Southeast Asia when Pepsi changed the color of its vending machines to light "Ice" blue. The company failed to understand that light blue is associated with death and mourning in that region.

Managers must also consider different communication practices. In some countries, direct feedback is considered impolite, and managers must be able to read subtle body language to determine if the receiver has understood and accepted the message. For example, in many cultures, telling a superior that he has made a mistake is considered disrespectful.

Different cultures also have different ideas about time. In the United States, an appointment is the time someone is expected to arrive. In some countries, an appointment is the earliest someone is expected to arrive, but he could arrive much later. Global managers must appreciate and accommodate these cultural differences.

Management expert Peter Drucker

But what about the effect of cultural differences on the basic functions of management? Are there universal theories that will hold in any culture? The answer is yes and no. Peter Drucker, the famed management expert, observed:

"Management is deeply embedded in culture. What managers do in Germany, in the United Kingdom, in the United States, in Japan, or in Brazil is exactly the same. How they do it may be quite different." (Note: Peter Drucker, The Essential Drucker, New York: HarperCollins, 2001.)

In other words, the functions of management are the same everywhere, but the functions are performed differently in different countries.

We have defined the four basic management functions as planning, organizing, leading, and controlling. Consider how the GLOBE cultural dimensions could affect these basic management functions.

- **Planning.** Future orientation and uncertainty avoidance have a significant impact on how businesses plan. In cultures with high future orientation, the current conditions of the organization are assessed and planning is based on changes needed to reach future goals. In a low future orientation culture, the history of the organization is considered and planning is based on preserving traditions while moving forward. In high uncertainty avoidance countries, planning will be very deliberate, and only plans with a low risk of failure and high certainty of outcomes will be considered. In low uncertainty avoidance countries, planning will be much more flexible. Plans will accept that the future is unpredictable and will assume that problems will be addressed as they occur.
- **Organizing.** Performance orientation and institutional collectivism both affect how firms are organized. In countries with high institutional collectivism, organizations based on teams and group efforts would likely be most effective. In countries with low institutional collectivism, more hierarchical structures with clear lines of authority and well-defined responsibilities would likely work best. In high performance orientation cultures, organizations would be based on individual achievements. Individual goals would be set and performance would not be based on meeting fixed targets but on ranking compared to others. In low performance orientation countries, cooperation and collaboration would be emphasized. Goals based on organizational outcomes would be more effective.
- **Leading.** Power distance and humane orientation are important considerations for leaders. In high power distance countries, people would expect leaders to be more directive, and they would expect rules and procedures to be well-defined. In low power distance countries, leadership would have to be more collaborative and people would question rules and procedures they did not agree with. Humane orientation would have an effect on motivation. In high humane orientation cultures, leaders would be expected to be nurturing and empowering. People would be motivated by the contribution they are making to the organization and others in the organization. In low humane orientation cultures, leaders

would be expected to be clear in their expectations. People would be motivated by their wages and benefits and would challenge anything that threatened their well-being. Gender egalitarianism could also be a factor. In low gender egalitarianism countries, women's leadership would not be automatically accepted and women would have to assert their authority.

- **Controlling.** Assertiveness and power distance affect how organizations can be controlled effectively. In high assertiveness countries, managers would be directive and authoritarian. They would exert control through close observation and punishment. In a low assertiveness country, managers would be expected to be more tolerant and to exert control through encouragement and corrections. In high power distance countries, authoritarian and directive managers would likely be more effective than participative managers.

Key Points

Deciding to engage in global business exposes companies to risks and hazards. However, when companies research conditions and plan and prepare for cultural differences, they can benefit from the advantages of globalization. In the next section we consider strategies managers can use to respond to cultural differences.

INTRODUCTION TO RESPONDING TO CULTURAL DIFFERENCES

What you'll learn to do: explain the strategies managers can use to respond to cultural differences

When businesses decide to engage in international activities, they must carefully consider the strategy they will use to expand. Using the wrong strategy can have disastrous results. For example, Lincoln Electric was a successful manufacturer of welding equipment and supplies. It was famous for its human resources policies, particularly its compensation system. When it was faced with foreign competitors, it decided to expand its production overseas. When it opened new factories, it used the same compensation system that was so successful in the United States. However, it soon found that its labor practices created all kinds of unexpected problems, both legal and cultural. It was forced to close its factories, and the fallout essentially destroyed the company. Lincoln Electric learned the hard way that replicating methods around the world is not always a good idea.

This section will examine different strategies businesses use to respond to cultural differences that can affect their success in the global marketplace

GLOBAL BUSINESS STRATEGIES FOR RESPONDING TO CULTURAL DIFFERENCES

Learning Outcomes

- Explain export strategies for global management.
- Explain standardization strategies for global management.
- Explain multidomestic strategies for global management.
- Explain transnational strategies for global management.

Global Business Strategies

A major concern for managers deciding on a global business strategy is the tradeoff between global integration and local responsiveness. **Global integration** is the degree to which the company is able to use the same products and methods in other countries. **Local responsiveness** is the degree to which the company must customize their products and methods to meet conditions in other countries. The two dimensions result in four basic global business strategies: export, standardization, multidomestic, and transnational. These are shown in the figure below.

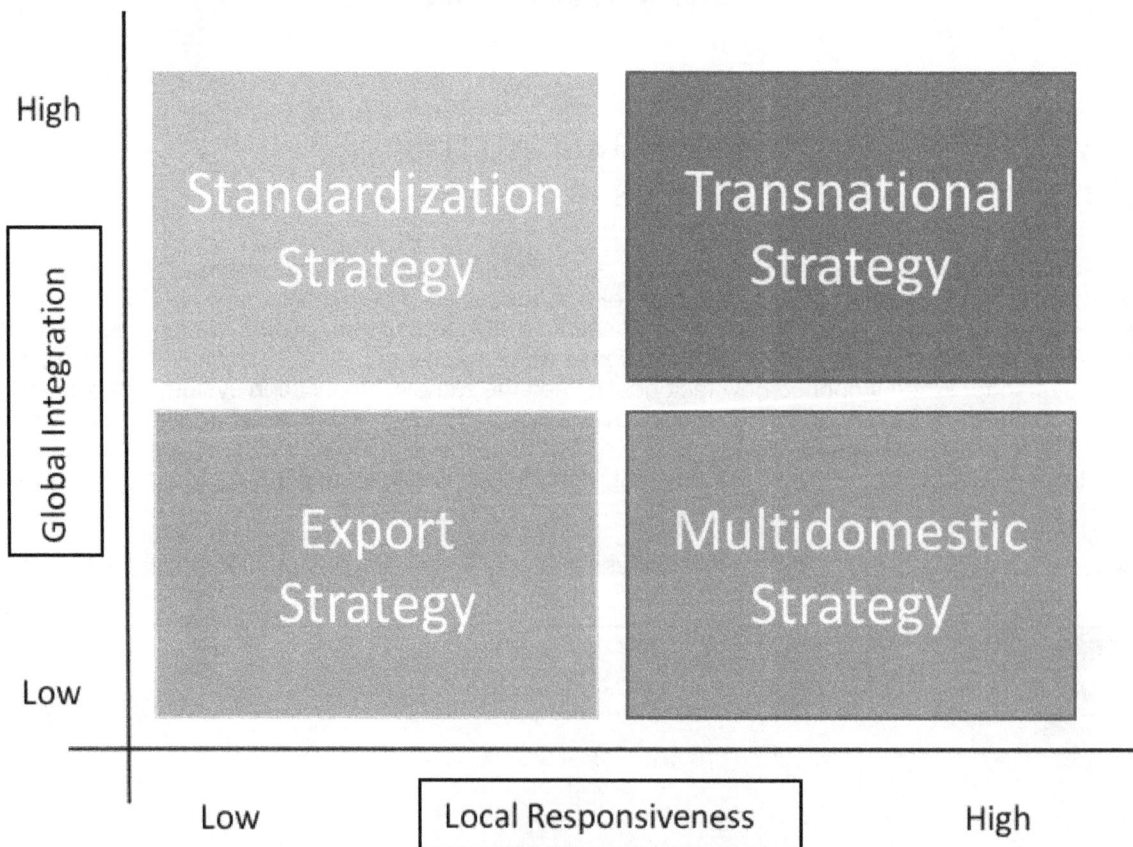

International business strategies must balance local responsiveness and global integration

Export Strategy

An **export strategy** is used when a company is primarily focused on its domestic operations. It does not intend to expand globally but does export some products to take advantage of international opportunities. It does not attempt to customize its products for international markets. It is not interested in either responding to unique conditions in other countries or in creating an integrated global strategy.

Standardization Strategy

A **standardization strategy** is used when a company treats the whole world as one market with little meaningful variation. The assumption is that one product can meet the needs of people everywhere. Many business-to-business companies can use a standardization strategy. Machines tools and equipment or information technologies are universal and need little customization for local conditions. CEMEX, the Mexico-based cement and building materials company, was able to expand globally using a standardization strategy. Apple uses a standardization strategy because its products do not have to be customized for local users. An iPod will look the same wherever you buy it. Domino's Pizza also uses a standardization strategy. Although toppings may vary to meet local tastes, the basic recipes are the same and the store model of carryout or delivered pizza is the same everywhere. A standardization strategy produces efficiencies by centralizing many common activities, such as product design, gaining scale economies in manufacturing, simplifying the supply chain, and reducing marketing costs.

Multidomestic Strategy

A **multidomestic strategy** customizes products or processes to the specific conditions in each country. In the opening example, Lincoln Electric should have used a multidomestic strategy to customize its manufacturing methods to the conditions in each country where it built factories. Retailers often use multidomestic strategies because they must meet local customer tastes. 7-Eleven is an example of a company using a multidomestic strategy. It tailors the product selection, payment methods, and marketing to the values and regulations in each country where it operates. For example, in Japan, 7-Eleven allows customers to pay their utility bills at the store. In a company with a multidomestic strategy, overall management is centralized in the home country but country managers are given latitude to make adaptations. Companies sacrifice scale efficiencies for responsiveness to local conditions. Companies benefit from a multidomestic strategy because country managers understand local laws, customs, and tastes and can decide how to best meet them.

Transnational Strategy

A **transnational strategy** combines a standardization strategy and a multidomestic strategy. It is used when a company faces significant cost pressure from international competitors but must also offer products that meet local customer needs. A transnational strategy is very difficult to maintain because the company needs to achieve economies of scale through standardization but also be flexible to respond to local conditions. Ford Motor Company is adopting a transnational strategy. Ford is producing a "world car" that has many common platform elements that accommodate a range of add-ons. That way Ford benefits from the standardization of costly elements that the consumer does not see but can add custom elements to meet country laws, can customize marketing to local standards, and can provide unique products to meet local tastes.

Key Points

In today's economy almost all companies must consider the opportunities presented by globalization, but global operations also present significant risks. Companies must research and plan thoroughly before engaging in international operations. And they must choose a strategy that matches their capabilities and objectives. The economies of standardization and the responsiveness of customization are competing pressures companies must resolve. The appropriate strategic choice is essential for a company to make the right choices.

INTRODUCTION TO EFFECTIVE TRAINING FOR INTERNATIONAL ASSIGNMENTS

What you'll learn to do: explain how managers can effectively train employees for international assignments

The United States does not keep records on **expatriates** (citizens living and working outside of the country), so researchers have to rely on estimates for numbers. The Migration Policy Institute published a report in 2014 called "Counting the Uncountable: Overseas Americans." The best estimates place the number of Americans living in another country, either on a temporary or permanent basis, between 2.2 million to 6.8 million. (This estimate does not include US military personnel.) Estimates of how many Americans become expatriates each year varies widely, ranging from eighteen thousand to forty-five thousand. What we can tell from these figures is that U.S. businesses spend significant amounts of money sending employees and their families around the world to work for international companies. This money is wasted if the employee is not given the tools needed to ensure a relatively smooth transition to life in another country.

EFFECTIVE TRAINING FOR INTERNATIONAL ASSIGNMENTS

Learning Outcomes

· Differentiate between documentary training, cultural simulations, and field simulation training.

Types of Training for Global Workers

Global companies often send managers from the home country office to work in foreign subsidiaries. Sometimes this is done for the development of the manager, so she can gain experience in the global operations of the company. It may also be so the company can exert more control over the subsidiary. When the assignment is for a long period, the manager's family may also be sent. This represents a significant investment for the company, and it does not want to see the manager fail and return home early. The cost of a three-year assignment averages $1 million. (Note: J. Stewart Black and Hal Gregerson, "The Right Way to Manage Expats," April 1999, accessed July 31, 2017, https://hbr.org/1999/03/the-right-way-to-manage-expats) One way the company can help the manager succeed is to provide training before she leaves so she knows what to expect.

Living and working in an international community, such as Hong Kong, can be rewarding and challenging—if you are adaptable and prepared for what to expect.

What constitutes an effective training program depends a lot on its "rigor," or how thorough and challenging the program is. If the employee is going for a relatively short time, say less than a month, then a **low-rigor program** may suffice. If the employee and his family are moving for a year or more with the intent of living in the host country, then **high-rigor training** is required. With a brief assignment, adequate training may involve watching some videos on local culture, going to lectures, and attending briefings on company operations in the host (destination) country. For longer assignments, extensive experiential learning, interactions with host country nationals, and language training may be offered not just for the employee but for the whole family. Studies have shown that international assignments are more effective when the employee's family is included and consulted in the relocation and training processes.

Documentary Training

Documentary training is textbook and classroom learning, which focuses on looking at differences between cultures and is a key part of both low-rigor and high-rigor training approaches. Differences are examined because they are potential friction points that create misunderstandings and hurt feelings. You have probably heard many examples of cultural differences involving common human interactions, such as greetings, gender relations, and the giving of gifts. For example, Asian business people defer to authority very differently from Westerners. They will not correct their managers nor will they make suggestions in public that would cause their managers embarrassment. Food in China is served hot, and to be offered cold food may be offensive or off-putting.

The perception of sickness and disease differs greatly in different cultures even among closely related ethnicities. A British worker would probably not take kindly to what you consider to be sympathetic inquiries about his latest illness and treatment. Americans, on the other hand, tend to "over share" and be more frank about personal health issues. Americans also tend to be casual about invitations and don't like to pressure people on the spot. An expatriate in India may invite a coworker to a party he is having on the weekend and then follow up with "Come over if you want to." To many cultures this is heard as "We don't really care if you come or not." There are many excellent sources of information on specific cultural traditions and norms of various countries, but multinational businesses often arrange for professional cross-cultural trainers to provide onsite lectures, videos, or workshops on cultural differences.

Cultural Simulation Training

After learning the cultural "do's and don'ts" of a host country, many companies will ask their employees to participate in **cultural simulations** in which they will role play various situations and practice responding in culturally sensitive ways. This process is most effective when the training takes place in the host country or when the trainer can include people from the actual host country to help. The goal is to duplicate as closely as possible scenarios that the employees may face, such as having to question or to reprimand a local employee, making a presentation to host country upper-level managers, or how to approach a person of the opposite gender in countries where the sexes do not mix as freely as in the United States.

Field Simulation Training

When the company believes that the employees have successfully passed the "survival training" stage, it is time for **field simulation training**. The employee (and family) visits a neighborhood of the same ethnic background as the destination or, if the trainees are already in-country, then they move out to the "real world." Depending upon the conditions, an individual may be dropped into a rural area with limited resources and told to get back to the office. Or a family may be moved into temporary housing so that they can meet their neighbors, shop for food, locate transportation, and just explore the area. When the simulation is over, the trainees come back to the center to compare notes and share experiences.

Benefits of Rigorous Training Programs

For extended assignments, a rigorous training program benefits both the employee and the employer. It prepares an employee (and family) for success by the following:

- Providing practical assistance for relocation efforts. Some questions the employee might have about the new location include: How long will it take to get there? What kind of money will I be using? How far is the office from my home? Do I need a car? What medicines can I get and what must I bring with me? What should I bring in the way of technology, and will I have to pay duties on imported goods?
- Giving the employee information that will allow her to make an informed decision about the assignment.
- Providing emotional security about the change. A rigorous training program greatly reduces the chance that the employee will leave the assignment early because of a misunderstanding.
- Increasing the cultural sensitivity of the employee. By training employees on cultural matters, the company lessens the likelihood that its reputation will suffer among the host country employees.

The disadvantage to the company involves the cost of the training and the out-of-office time of the employee to undergo the training, but this is a small price to pay considering the potential benefits.

Finally, companies preparing their employees for an expatriate experience should also offer readjustment counseling when the employee is due to return. Re-entering the home country can produce a reaction called **reverse culture shock** that describes the bewilderment and distress experienced by individuals suddenly exposed to a new, strange, or foreign social and cultural environment—in this case, their own.

PUTTING IT TOGETHER: GLOBALIZATION AND BUSINESS

Apple's Global Supply Chain

Let's return to our case study regarding Apple's global supply chain. It is interesting to see how many different countries are represented in Apple's supply chain related to the production of the iPhone. Although the company releases little data about its suppliers, it is estimated that iPhone production involves hundreds of suppliers in more than twenty countries.

For example, the gyroscope that allows you to move your phone around and change a picture from vertical to horizontal is made in France and Italy. A division of Sharp in Japan makes the retina displays for a couple of models. Other corporations in Taiwan, Singapore, and Korea produce additional key components. Finally, all the parts are shipped to China and assembled by Foxconn into a saleable unit.

Apple CEO Tim Cook is regarded as an expert in global supply chain management.

As you learned in this module, there are both opportunities and risks associated with globalization. Apple's CEO, Tim Cook, was the head of operations and supply chain before assuming the top role at the company. He has determined that the benefits of a globally diversified supplier network outweigh the potential risks. It's hard to argue with him given the company's amazing success.

Many people assume that Apple builds iPhones outside the United States to save on costs. Actually, it has been estimated that the added cost to produce an iPhone in the United States would only be about $4 per unit. So why would the company choose to produce phones outside the country where they will ultimately be sold?

One of the answers to that question is taxes. Another interesting facet of global business management is the implication of international tax structures. Apple currently pays approximately 2 percent on its overseas profits, but that would increase to about 35 percent for U.S.-made phones. So globalization applies to financial management as well. (Note: "How and Where iPhone Is Made: A Surprising Report on How Much of Apple's Top Product is US-manufactured," Finances Online, https://financesonline.com/how-iphone-is-made/)

In summary, if you're going to learn about management, your studies must be global in nature. The concepts that you have reviewed in this module will apply in practically every imaginable business, no matter its size. Having a good understanding of these trends will only become more important with time.

www.ingramcontent.com/pod-product-compliance
Lightning Source LLC
Chambersburg PA
CBHW081458200326
41518CB00015B/2306